ENDLESS CRUSADE

Endless Crusade

Women Social Scientists
and Progressive Reform

ELLEN FITZPATRICK

New York   Oxford
OXFORD UNIVERSITY PRESS
1990

Oxford University Press

Oxford   New York   Toronto
Delhi   Bombay   Calcutta   Madras   Karachi
Petaling Jaya   Singapore   Hong Kong   Tokyo
Nairobi   Dar es Salaam   Cape Town
Melbourne   Auckland

and associated companies in
Berlin   Ibadan

Copyright © 1990 by Ellen Fitzpatrick

Published by Oxford University Press, Inc.,
200 Madison Avenue, New York, New York 10016

Oxford is a registered trademark of Oxford University Press

Library of Congress Cataloging-in-Publication Data
Fitzpatrick, Ellen F. (Ellen Frances)
Endless Crusade: women social scientists and progressive reform /
Ellen Fitzpatrick.
p.   cm.
ISBN 0-19-506121-7
1. Women social reformers—United States—Biography.
2. Women social scientists—United States—Biography.
Progressivism (United States politics)   I. Title.
HQ1412.F56   1990
300'.92'2—dc20   89-16179   CIP

2 4 6 8 9 7 5 3 1

Printed in the United States of America
on acid-free paper

For my mother, the memory of my father,
and for Revan F. Miles

Acknowledgments

This book has been a long time in the making; with each passing year the list of those I hoped to remember here grew longer. It is a pleasure to acknowledge now the individuals and institutions who helped me in so many ways.

I am very grateful for the support provided by an Irving and Rose Crown Fellowship (Brandeis University), a Woodrow Wilson Dissertation Research Grant, a National Endowment for the Humanities Summer Stipend, an Andrew W. Mellon Faculty Fellowship in the Humanities (Harvard University), a Rockefeller Archive Center research grant, and a Wellesley College Faculty Award. Final revisions were made while I was a Fellow at the Charles Warren Center for Studies in American History, Harvard University.

I benefited greatly from the expert assistance of archivists and librarians at the University of Chicago Library, the Rockefeller Archive Center, the Library of Congress, the Arthur and Elizabeth Schlesinger Library, the Newberry Library, the Smith College Library, the Sophia Smith Collection, the Wellesley College Library, the Boston Public Library, the Brandeis University Library, Harvard University's Houghton and Widener Libraries, and the Cornell University Library. The University Registrar at Chicago graciously provided several important documents. Wallace Dailey, curator of the Theodore Roosevelt Collection at Harvard, went far beyond the call of duty in aiding my work. Anthony Goldner provided skillful assistance in Chicago during the final few weeks of manuscript preparation.

Jean Proctor, Jill Fink, and Dorlis French patiently typed and word-processed various drafts of the manuscript. Bette A. White brought me into the computer age with the same friendship and good humor she demonstrated when teaching me how to drive a car.

For sharing their research with me and suggesting additional sources, a special thanks to Pat Palmieri, Lynn Gordon, Raymann Solomon, Barbara

Brand, John Gable, and Estelle Freedman. Phyllis Holbrook is responsible for preserving the few traces of Frances Kellor's early life. Her archival work and her reminiscences of Coldwater, Michigan, left an indelible impression on this book and its author. I also learned a great deal from the friends and colleagues who read chapters and commented on earlier versions of this manuscript. They include: Catherine Clinton, Jill Ker Conway, Vanessa Gamble, Charles Grench, Alice Kelikian, Elizabeth Lunbeck, James T. Kloppenberg, Michael McGerr, Rosalind Rosenberg, Dorothy Ross, Barbara Sicherman, Theda Skocpol, Barbara Miller Solomon, and Mary C. Wilson. Catherine, Vanessa, and Alice also provided the best kind of encouragement and moral support, as did Jama Lazerow and Frances Gouda. Ellen Rothman applied her gift for language to my prose—I thank her and apologize for infelicities she will recognize as my own. Only Jacqueline Jones could manage to be a reader, colleague, department chairperson, and the best of friends. I am very grateful for her kindness to me.

Through their critical and perceptive readings of the entire manuscript, three friends helped shape this book, though not always in ways they will recognize. For their searching comments, penetrating criticism, and gentle reassurance, I thank Alan Brinkley, Elizabeth Pleck, and Susan Ware. My knowledge of American history has been improved, and my interest in the Progressive era inspired, by my teacher, Morton Keller. He has challenged, prodded, and encouraged me for many years. Mary Kelley's careful and perceptive reading of the entire manuscript meant a great deal to me. Sheldon Meyer's interest in this project and Rachel Toor's enthusiasm and expert editorial advice have made it a pleasure to work with Oxford University Press. Gail Cooper has been an efficient and attentive copyeditor.

This book could not have been written without the intellectual contributions of several historians who have studied women's higher education. In countless conversations, Lynn Gordon, Pat Palmieri, Linda Perkins, Sally Schwager, Margaret Rossiter, and Barbara Solomon shared their impressive knowledge and unique historical understanding with me. Pat Palmieri has been exceptionally generous as a colleague and a friend.

My family never wavered in their support throughout this project, and I thank my siblings especially—Bobby, Betsy, Mary, and Jean—for helping me keep everything in perspective. My older sister Maureen read every word I wrote, changed many of them, and (I am thankful) excised others. Most of all, from an early age she shared her love of books with me, reinforcing a tendency encouraged by my mother and father. She has always been a great friend to me.

As I look back over my years of work on this book, I remember most of all the hope Revan F. Miles gave to me. I'll always be grateful to her for helping me to learn the most important lessons, as James Joyce once wrote, "in my own life and away from home and friends." A final memory seems especially vivid: the warm summer nights I sat writing accompanied only by my silent friend Chuck. A final thanks to him.

Contents

Introduction *xi*

1 / Pathways to Chicago *3*

2 / White City, Gray City *28*

3 / Scientists of Society *39*

4 / "The Thing for Which You Are Well Fitted" *71*

5 / "A Most Scientific Institution" *92*

6 / "If Sex Could Be Eliminated" *130*

7 / "The School Is Yours" *166*

Epilogue *201*

Notes *218*

Index *259*

Introduction

On a sweltering Chicago afternoon in August of 1912, Theodore Roosevelt stood before an enthusiastic audience of over 12,000 gathered for the new Progressive party's first national political convention. In a thundering voice, Roosevelt called out "to you men who, in your turn, have come together to spend and be spent in the endless crusade against wrong." It was an exhortation tinged with irony. For amid the wildly cheering crowd and swirling scarlet banners, a remarkable number of women could be seen. American women had yet to win the vote, but their disfranchisement did little to dampen the spirits of these Progressive party loyalists. The cause they held dear had finally penetrated the dense rhetoric of national politics. The hour of women social reformers, and their male compatriots, seemed finally at hand.

This moment of high political drama brought deep personal satisfaction to four women reformers who championed the Progressive cause. For nearly a decade, Sophonisba Breckinridge, Edith Abbott, Katharine Bement Davis, and Frances Kellor had struggled to advance public recognition of modern social problems. Their enthusiasm for the Progressive party was only the most recent manifestation of a long-standing preoccupation with social reform. For them, the Bull Moose convention represented not simply the dawn of a new political party, but the triumph of principled social ideals.[1]

Their perspective reflected, at least in part, the women reformers' unusual life experiences. Breckinridge, Abbott, Davis, and Kellor were among the first American women to be trained as social scientists in the new research universities of late-nineteenth-century America. They derived understanding from their studies at the University of Chicago, and their experience as professional women, that profoundly influenced their approach to social problems and to social change. This book explores how the intellectual views they acquired and the professional struggles they endured came to have an impact on early-twentieth-century movements for social reform.[2]

All four women were prominent figures in Progressive reform crusades. Their effort to graft social analysis onto social policy reveals several important dimensions of the reform community to which they belonged. As influential contributors to an early-twentieth-century discourse about social problems, Abbott, Breckinridge, Kellor, and Davis helped lay the intellectual foundations for a modern social welfare policy. As administrators, the four women institutionalized key facets of their knowledge-driven program of reform. As social activists, they strove to harness the power of philanthropists and politicians to the interests of the reform community of which they were a part. Finally, as women, they insisted that the special burdens of their sex be given a prominent place on the reform agenda. In so doing, they advanced their own professional careers.

From their common experience as graduate students at Chicago during the university's founding decade (1892–1902), each woman pursued diverse, though sometimes overlapping, interests in reform. In every case, their endeavors brought them face to face with some of the most vital issues of their generation.

Katharine Davis left Chicago in 1900 with a Ph.D. in political economy, earned under the supervision of Thorstein Veblen. She became the first superintendent of the New York State Reformatory for Women at Bedford Hills, New York, and a leading figure in prison reform. Frances Kellor's sociological training gained her admittance to the smoke-filled rooms of national party politics. From her high-ranking position in the Progressive party, she helped direct Theodore Roosevelt's 1912 Bull Moose campaign. It was a remarkable achievement for a woman of her era. Sophonisba Breckinridge and Edith Abbott used their education in political science and political economy to expose the tragic conditions endured by the urban poor. Their efforts to institutionalize their compelling approach to social analysis and investigation resulted in the first graduate school of social work to be affiliated with a major research university—the University of Chicago's School of Social Service Administration.

Although these four women knew each other, only two (Abbott and Breckinridge) could be considered very close associates or intimate friends. They did not always have the same views of the social issues they collectively engaged. In fact, their varying interests and styles reflect a measure of the heterogeneity that has discouraged historians who have sought to define a singular Progressive movement.[3]

Yet, despite their differences, Abbott, Breckinridge, Davis, and Kellor had in common a set of decisive experiences. First, they were members of a generation of women who faced unparalleled opportunities in American higher education and persistent constraints in realizing professional goals. They confronted these tensions in similar ways, forsaking marriage and finding in the extraordinary social and political climate they lived in such important work that they helped shape the history of their times.

Second, the four women shared a critical intellectual experience. They undertook advanced study in political economy, political science, and sociology at a moment when academic social science was in the process of being professionalized and defined. This was a pivotal moment in American intellectual life, as social scientists sought to determine the purpose, parameters, and proper methods of their disciplines in a context of rapid social and economic change. Professors at Chicago and elsewhere struggled to distinguish academic social science from popular inquiry designed to ameliorate social problems. Yet they were equally dedicated to demonstrating the social value of their special scientific skills. These preoccupations created a lively intellectual environment that had a decisive impact on the four women students. They learned a distinctive approach to contemporary social problems, which they soon carried far beyond the university.

Their collective tie to the University of Chicago was, of course, a third factor linking Abbott, Breckinridge, Davis, and Kellor. Chicago offered not only similar intellectual influences but a chance to participate in an unusually well defined and self-conscious community of academic women. The city of Chicago, with its appalling urban problems and inspiring reform community, also provided the four women with a dramatic setting for their social scientific work.

Finally, and most important, were the similar uses these four women made of their academic skills. None of them ultimately became professors in the fields in which they had been so extensively trained. Rather, they applied their education as social scientists to new areas of social activism. They exercised leadership in early-twentieth-century reform circles, not only by actively participating in public life, but by writing extensively about social problems. They shared a commitment to advancing social knowledge and social reform.

In this they resembled many other reformers of the Progressive generation. Early-twentieth-century reform had an important intellectual dimension. Changes in social policy were often derived from, or at least justified by, shifting ideas about poverty, social unrest, labor, immigration, crime, and the myriad social problems endemic to the modern industrial age. Intellectuals and "fact-finders" helped give Progressive reform a special cast. Impatient with traditional modes of analysis and enamored of scientific fact, these men and women mounted social investigations at every turn, convinced that knowledge in itself was the key to intelligent reform. Research often served as an engine for reform—powering legislative change and political alliances, drawing in philanthropists, and justifying more sweeping intervention by the state.

Historians have long appreciated these intellectual dimensions of Progressive reform, as well as women's decisive contributions to social change. Suffragists and settlement workers hold an enduring place in the drama of that age. But very little attention has been given to the university-trained women who helped construct and carry out the Progressive agenda. This book seeks to link two major strands of Progressivism by examining a group of important women reformers who were formally trained as intellectuals.

Their higher education at the University of Chicago was not a *sine qua non* for Abbott's, Breckinridge's, Davis's, and Kellor's careers as reformers or their ideas about social problems. Progressives from all walks of life shared this generation's enthusiasm for scientific knowledge. Male and female social activists without doctoral degrees advanced a similar agenda for social change and embraced parallel views about social questions. The new ideas that inspired and sustained Progressive reform were rooted in the culture of late-nineteenth- and early-twentieth-century America.

Still, the universities played a critical role in shaping intellectual trends. Academic social scientists helped generate new theories of social problems and systematize existing fields of knowledge. They elevated modern explanations of social and economic unrest to the realm of science; they added the weight of intellectual authority to contemporary views of social change. Most of all, they educated young men and women, influencing their intellectual development and, at times, their careers.

The four women trained at Chicago offer an opportunity to explore how academic social science helped influence Progressive social reform. The confluence of the women's distinctive intellectual training, their marginal position in academia, and their subsequent careers as social activists makes such an endeavor possible. My aim has been to trace how one group of reformers arrived at their conception of social problems and then went about advancing their ideas. The transmission of social thought has thus been central to my interests.

My decision to focus on women deserves some explanation, for male academics also played a central part in molding the character of early-twentieth-century reform. Their contributions, however, have been much more widely recognized, even if not always fully explained or adequately explored. In addition, women figured prominently in early-twentieth-century social welfare reform. To ignore the genesis of some of their ideas and the import of their actions is to fail to see a critical dimension of Progressive reform. Finally, an intellectual history of women reformers underscores the rich, varied, and complex nature of the Progressive appeal.[4]

I have selected four women from the University of Chicago as the focus of this study for both pragmatic and intellectual reasons. There were women social scientists trained elsewhere who played equally compelling roles in Progressive reform. But Chicago was unusual in being home to four such women. Very few graduate research universities replicated Chicago's rare encouragement of women social scientists in the late nineteenth century. Before 1900 no university equalled, let alone exceeded, its record in conferring doctoral degrees upon women social scientists.[5]

The University of Chicago also helped lead the way in developing American social science. It boasted the first department of sociology in the United States. Even at the turn of the century, there were hints of the intellectual vigor that would lead to the dominance of "the Chicago school." The professors who trained Abbott, Breckinridge, Davis, and Kellor helped to put American social science on the intellectual map. All of these factors, and my desire to reconstruct this phenomenon in detail, suggested that Chicago would provide an appropriate setting for an examination of women social scientists and social reform.

There were, of course, many other women trained in the social sciences at Chicago alongside Edith Abbott, Sophonisba Breckinridge, Katharine Bement Davis, and Frances Kellor. Nearly a quarter of the social scientists enrolled at the university during its first decade were women. None of those who earned doctoral degrees or completed several years of graduate study, however, rose to such great prominence as social activists *and* social scientists. Only Edith Abbot's sister Grace came close to this distinction, though she began her studies later, and was as much influenced by her sister and Sophonisba Breckinridge as by the men with whom she studied. (Grace Abbott terminated her graduate studies after earning a master's degree.)

In short, nothing inherent in the training offered at Chicago prompted women social scientists to pursue careers as reformers. The women who placed their skills as social experts in the service of reform, however, made ample use of their university experience.

This book begins with a description of the various paths Abbott, Breckinridge, Davis, and Kellor traveled to Chicago. Their education at the university and the special dilemmas they faced in academia are then explored. The second half of the book consists of three case studies exploring their efforts to fuse social science and social reform. Abbott and Breckinridge are treated in one chapter because their careers and interests were strongly intertwined.

The revolution in American higher education, the turmoil of late-nineteenth-century intellectual life, and the Progressive-era context of social upheaval and reform converged in the lives of Edith Abbott, Sophonisba Breckinridge, Katharine Bement Davis, and Frances Kellor. Theirs is a story of oppression and opportunity, of stasis and of change. I have tried to look at the historical realities this group of women faced, and the choices they both discovered and made. Abbott, Breckinridge, Davis, and Kellor had a dynamic relationship with the times in which they lived. In seeking solutions to the restrictions placed on their sex, they helped write the history of a remarkable age.

ENDLESS CRUSADE

1

Pathways to Chicago

When the University of Chicago opened its doors in 1892, a lively assortment of students enrolled for graduate study. It was an exciting moment. The promise of the research university stirred members of a new generation. Perhaps no one among the early group felt the drama more than the young women in attendance. Recent beneficiaries of one revolution in women's higher education, Chicago's female students quickly took part in another. Leaving behind the women's colleges and state universities that had fostered their intellectual growth, they set out for Chicago to pursue advanced study. Among the pioneers were four remarkable women whose lives were formed in the crucible of late-nineteenth-century America.

From the bluegrass land of Lexington, Kentucky, came the first arrival, Sophonisba Preston Breckinridge. She was twenty-nine years old when she began her graduate education in 1895. For the rest of Breckinridge's life, the city and University of Chicago would figure prominently in her experience. After 1898 she "never left without either a round trip ticket or an arrangement that insured . . . [her] return." Yet her introduction to the university occurred by "pure accident." She made her way to Chicago along a circuitous path full of challenges posed, and opportunities afforded, by personal circumstance and the times in which she lived.[1]

The richness of Breckinridge's story throws into relief the conflicts privileged women of her generation faced. The women who studied at Chicago were daughters of post-Civil War America. As Breckinridge's childhood makes clear, this historical fact meant that they were simultaneously victims of Victorian values and heirs to a much more modern and inviting world.

From birth, Breckinridge enjoyed advantages unavailable to many other women of her day. Her family was well known throughout the Commonwealth of Kentucky; a rich heritage of Southern political achievement con-

3

tributed to their fame. Sophonisba's great-grandfather, John Breckinridge, served as Thomas Jefferson's attorney general. Her father's cousin, John C. Breckinridge, was a U.S. senator who held high office in the Confederacy and ran against Abraham Lincoln on a proslavery platform in the election of 1860. Sophonisba's father, William C. P. Breckinridge, fought as a colonel for the Confederacy against two of his own brothers who joined the Union Army. His quick acceptance of the Confederacy's defeat may have been spurred by the profound divisions secession created in the Breckinridge family. Robert Jefferson Breckinridge, Colonel Breckinridge's father, had been perhaps the most outspoken Unionist in Kentucky. Little wonder that William Breckinridge welcomed Sophonisba as his "peace baby" when she was born on Easter Sunday in April of 1866, just a year after the bloody war ended.[2]

Her father carried on the family legacy of public service during Sophonisba's youth. Amid frequent reminders of her distinguished inheritance, she glimpsed the many exciting aspects of her father's active life. After the war, William Breckinridge established a busy law practice riding circuit to outlying courts. He fast earned a reputation as a "liberal" Southern Democrat. Breckinridge lost his first bid for public office in 1868 after expressing his willingness to admit the testimony of black Americans in a court of law. He vocally supported the cause of black education. According to Sophonisba, Frederick Douglass considered her father to be "the white man with whom he could most freely and without consciousness of racial differences discuss problems of public concern."[3]

But to Sophonisba, Breckinridge's intense devotion as a father was a far greater gift. Having missed the infancy of his first child, Ella, because of the war, William Breckinridge dedicated himself to "training" his second girl. "You were my baby from the hour of your birth," he reminisced to Sophonisba on her nineteenth birthday. "I put you to sleep; I walked you when you were sick; and in spite of much you will never know I persisted in my purpose to give your brain a fair chance to show its power." Although two sons and another daughter followed, they never dislodged Sophonisba from her position as her father's favored child.[4]

Enthusiasm for women's education shaped Breckinridge's aspirations for Sophonisba. At Centre College in Danville, Kentucky, he had witnessed three classmates, his cousins, forfeit degrees in spite of excellent grades because they were female. Wanting no such obstacles to stand in the way of his own children, Breckinridge actively campaigned for advances in women's education. He used his position as lawyer for the Agricultural and Mechanical College in Lexington to obtain a new charter permitting coeducation in the 1880s. Sophonisba recalled her father offering "$1.00 or a little party" for "perfect" report cards. "I generally took the dollar while Ella took the party," she noted.[5]

The ill health of Sophonisba's mother, Issa, further enlarged the role and influence of William Breckinridge in their children's lives. Mrs. Breckinridge belonged to the respected Desha family. Her grandfather had been governor of Kentucky early in the nineteenth century. And thus she brought her own family's distinguished history to her early marriage. She also brought a frail constitution that dated from her youth. The third of five children, Mrs. Breckinridge lost three siblings to diphtheria when she was very small. She herself never seemed entirely well, although she bore seven children of her own. Devastated when two of them died in infancy, she never wavered in her dedication to the five who survived.[6]

As a result of her many bouts with sickness, and the persistence of a general malaise, Mrs. Breckinridge relied on her husband to shoulder duties usually considered a wife's exclusive province. Noting that "papa helped in many ways," Sophonisba remembered her father as being "wonderfully skillful in caring for us."[7]

No surer path to her father's affections could be found than the diligent pursuit of an education. Sophonisba's older sister Ella and her younger sister Curry displayed little interest in fulfilling their father's wishes in this regard. Their inattention to their studies led Mrs. Breckinridge to confide to Sophonisba, "I fear you [are] Papa's sole [and] only hope for an educated daughter." William Breckinridge had placed his hopes well. While still an adolescent, Sophonisba dutifully attempted to enroll at the Agricultural and Mechanical College in Lexington. The president of the school sent her right home. But her family directed her to return and remind President Patterson of a recently inserted provision in the college charter that permitted women to attend. Patterson yielded, and Sophonisba began her higher education.[8]

Although her experience at the Agricultural and Mechanical College ultimately proved dissatisfying, Sophonisba had her first chance there to study a variety of subjects, ranging from German to physical geography. Her classmates included close friends she had known all her life in Lexington. No one seemed dearer to her than Tom Morgan, an admirer who grew up to win a Nobel Prize for his achievements in genetics.[9]

But the attractions of the local college in Lexington soon paled when compared to those of Wellesley College, a new school already attended by several young Kentucky women. The more she learned about Wellesley, the more convinced Sophonisba became that the college "was made or established for me or the likes of me." The growing reputation of that Northern school and her family's acquaintance with the family of Wellesley's founder, Henry Fowle Durant, persuaded the Breckinridges to send Sophonisba there. In the fall of 1884, they accompanied their daughter to Massachusetts and enrolled her in the women's school.[10]

Sophonisba was fortunate that her growing intellectual aspirations coincided with increasing educational opportunities for women. Prior to the Civil War, few institutions offered women a college education equal to that available to men. Sophonisba came of college age at a moment when time-worn barriers to women's higher education were beginning to give way. Her social class and her family's progressive views enabled her to take advantage of a reformation that would reach large numbers of American women only many years later. When Sophonisba began her studies at the Agricultural and Mechanical College and went on to join the class of 1888 at Wellesley, she took her place among a group who would be remembered as pioneers: the first generation of college-educated women. It was an experience enjoyed by only two percent of American women in Breckinridge's age group.[11]

With unusual prescience, the Breckinridges sensed that women of their daughter's generation faced unparalleled opportunities. Each of Sophonisba's parents viewed this historical fact from different perspectives formed by their individual life experiences, but both welcomed it.

William Breckinridge was outspoken in urging Sophonisba to include useful work among her future plans. This insistence grew out of several concerns. In part, Breckinridge feared that his resources might prove inadequate to support his daughter. Shortly after Sophonisba began her studies at Wellesley, her father was elected to the United States Congress. The pressure of maintaining two homes, a large family, and later, two college students seemed to weigh heavily on him. Breckinridge may also have suspected, or hoped, that his daughter would never marry. In that case, no husband could be relied upon to ease parental financial responsibilities. But less pragmatic considerations also figured in Breckinridge's frequent musing about Sophonisba's fate. He doubted that traditional womanly pursuits could hold his daughter's interest, and he openly dreaded the possibility that they would.[12]

During her freshman year at Wellesley, Sophonisba's father expressed these views in his lengthy letters from home. "I trust you will like Chemistry + the sciences," he wrote early in the fall of 1884. "I have a notion that in Chemistry . . . botany + such sciences there is a great field of profitable + honorable work for women;—less onerous + more attractive than the [needles], the school-room + the store." As her first year at Wellesley came to a close, Breckinridge asked Sophonisba whether she wanted to return to the college. While making plain his deference to his daughter's wishes, he urged her to continue her schooling. Reflecting on the alternatives, he noted:

> And in deciding this question, you ought to look squarely in the face that if I die, you will have to make your own living; and if I live, you may have to do so anyhow. God preserve you . . . from the aimless, worse than aimless life of the young girls you would associate with here. Any honest toil, by which the day is made honorable, is far preferable to this; and as much as I love you + I do love you with an unutterable love, I would rather see you a drudge than living thus.[13]

Far more familiar than her husband with the female social circle of Lexington, Mrs. Breckinridge shared his disdain. When Sophonisba nearly succumbed to terrible homesickness during her first weeks at school, her mother begged her to put the situation in perspective. "I am grieved beyond expression that you are so homesick," she wrote.

> You know if you really want to come home your father will let you do so + you know I never wanted you to go to Wellesley—or any where from home— but you forget how much you wanted to go—how long you have wanted to go + how you felt when you thought may be you could not go. . . . —You forget how dull it is here—how one day is like another + how you were sort

of a school girl + sort of a young lady— + also how little there is among your companions to edify—or improve on. You know full well that . . . you have intellect and culture beyond girls of your age that you have everything to look forward to in life—if you keep well.

With frequent reminders of her love, Mrs. Breckinridge urged her daughter to persevere with her new life at Wellesley.[14]

The experience of attending college was a transforming one in important ways. In a society that provided few settings for middle-class women to live outside the home, attendance at college sometimes required a break with familiar surroundings. Schools that admitted women students went a long way toward reproducing the structure of family life in dormitories and making a community of the college campus. Nevertheless, going away to college provided privileged nineteenth-century women with an unusual taste of independence.[15]

Sophonisba flourished in this environment. She displayed a talent for leadership that immensely pleased her family. As head of the class of 1888, she developed a close relationship with Alice Freeman [Palmer], president of Wellesley from 1881 to 1887. An inspiring figure, Palmer had attended graduate school and received an honorary Ph.D. degree from the University of Michigan. Her considerable professional achievements were matched by an equally appealing charm that made her an especially attractive example to her young charges. Palmer returned the Wellesley students' affection; she considered Sophonisba her own "dear child" and often signed her letters with love from "your other mother." Their friendship gave Sophonisba the opportunity to observe first hand a perfectly "refined" woman shouldering important responsibilities and wielding influence and power.[16]

Wellesley also exposed Sophonisba to experiences that challenged the values revered by her family. When her family brought her to the campus they observed "a handsome, handsomely dressed couple of the negro race with an attractive daughter" headed for the college doors. A traveling companion of the Breckinridges asked, "Will you let Nisba go to school with a Negro?" "She got on all right with the boys; I think she will get on all right with the colored," her father answered.[17]

But the issue was not laid to rest. Mrs. Breckinridge was unenthusiastic about her daughter's exposure to black students. Still, she preached forbearance. "I hope there will be no necessity for you to come in contact with them but I have no fear of your contamination or of your not doing what is becoming a lady." Her mother asked Sophonisba to remember her principles and her breeding. "It is hard for people raised with our prejudices to ever treat them as equals," she said, "but they can do you no harm + I can trust you to treat them properly."[18]

Sophonisba found it difficult to follow her mother's advice when the Negro Jubilee Singers from Fisk University came to the campus and dined at Alice Freeman Palmer's table. "I found no difficulty in serving them but my own food I could not swallow," she remembered.[19]

Yet by the time she was a junior, Sophonisba had become more sensitive to racial injustice. When Ella Smith, a black student, attempted to invite as many guests to the Junior Promenade as her white counterparts, a group of Wellesley women sought to exclude Smith's invitees. With Alice Freeman Palmer's help, Breckinridge's view that "every experience at Wellesley was educational" prevailed, and Smith's guests attended the prom.[20]

Later, Breckinridge remembered that Ella Smith "had been the occasion of my working through the problem of racial relationships." Race appeared to be the first public issue to engage the young Kentuckian. But there was little else in her Wellesley years to suggest that she would one day become a founding member of the Chicago chapter of the NAACP.[21]

Her family's religious beliefs also fell under scrutiny during Sophonisba's college years. Although the Breckinridges were not zealous in their beliefs, they encouraged piety in their children. But as Sophonisba devoted increasing attention to intellectual endeavors, her interest in spiritual matters wavered somewhat. Admonitions from her father to study the Bible competed with a forceful tendency that eventually affected Sophonisba and other college students of her generation. Exposure to new ideas, including those of Darwin, posed a challenge to the traditional religious convictions of both men and women. Although few college students completely abandoned their faith, many redefined their interests in a way that embraced general humanitarian aims. For some, a focus on social issues gradually took the place of a preoccupation with exclusively spiritual concerns. Whatever the outcome, an examination of one's religious faith constituted another important stage in the achievement of intellectual independence. For Sophonisba, true independence proved far more difficult to acquire.[22]

The great contradiction of the revolution in women's higher education was that it prepared the first college graduates for a world of opportunities that did not really exist. Although frequently reminded of the special duties of their sex, women students were exposed to a variety of new experiences many were reluctant to leave behind. An independent existence away from home and the chance to devote oneself to interesting fields of study were only two of the many attractions that college life provided. Yet the education women acquired in school seemed of little use in the vast society outside collegiate walls. Although college-educated women became increasingly valued as teachers, the absence of a diploma was no obstacle for success in this profession in the nineteenth century. Women without college educations also led voluntary associations devoted to social betterment. And certainly, the human race had endured when mothers raised children without the benefit of Latin and Greek. For early college women, acquiring knowledge without a life mission was, in Jane Addams' words, "like eating a sweet dessert first thing in the morning."[23]

Thus the problem of what to do after graduation was a troubling one for the first generation of college women. In spite of prevailing societal expectations, many young girls had dreamed of having active and even nontraditional careers well before they went off to school. Sophonisba Breckinridge recalled, "I had promised myself to be a lawyer and had never thought of teaching." But it was often difficult to know how to prepare oneself to meet these self-appointed goals. Even when the road seemed clear, conflicting choices beckoned. Breckinridge knew of the University of Michigan's willingness to train women lawyers, yet she selected Wellesley. Later she remembered: "I had always pretended that I expected to follow my father's [footsteps] and go into the law but I reasoned in such a stupid way and instead of going to Ann Arbor, where progressive women like Miss Laura Clay went, I went to Wellesley and devoted myself to Latin and Mathematics." In spite of her affection for Wellesley, she realized, "I was no nearer earning my living when I came back from college than when I had left home four years before." Indeed, even at the age of eighty, she still found it "pitiful to recall how my college work had failed in every way to help me toward a profession."[24]

In a pattern that was typical of the first women graduates, Sophonisba returned home to her family after her Wellesley commencement in 1888. During the congressional term, the Breckinridges set up housekeeping in Washington, D.C. Sophonisba joined her family there, and through her father's intervention, acquired a position teaching mathematics at the local Washington High School. She had wanted to begin studying law, but practical considerations dictated otherwise. As she explained, "At that time there were not many law schools open to women. My mother's health was frail and the family expenses high. The only law school in Washington open to women had classes in the evening and that was when I could be of service at home." Even though she had never envisaged herself as a teacher, she drew great satisfaction from "contributing to the family income." In her spare time, Breckinridge participated in the activities of the Washington branch of the Association of Collegiate Alumnae (A.C.A.), an organization of recent women college graduates. She also expressed her interest in current affairs by joining Richard Ely's American Economic Association, a group dedicated to advancing social knowledge and reform.[25]

During one winter in Washington, the Breckinridges lived in a boardinghouse where, coincidentally, Susan B. Anthony also lodged. A warm relationship developed between Anthony and the Breckinridge family. The militant suffragist was delighted when Sophonisba confided her hopes of one day becoming a lawyer. Colonel Breckinridge did not endorse Anthony's demand for female voting rights, but he used his position in the House of Representatives to help Anthony gain access to other members. Nor did Mrs. Breckinridge's lack of interest in women's suffrage dampen her sociability with Anthony. Sophonisba explained, "Knowing that my mother was a woman who had 'all the rights she wanted,' Miss Anthony would share her knowledge and skill in the area of fancy work and sewing." For Sophonisba, Miss Anthony had encouraging words about the young woman's "penchant for a professional career."[26]

Those dreams seemed a long way off in the winter of 1890 when Sophonisba fell victim to an influenza epidemic that swept through Washington. Already "worked . . . into a state of panic" by an outbreak of typhoid fever contracted by several other teachers and pupils in her school, Breckinridge recovered very slowly from her illness. Indeed, by the late spring of 1890 she had become "a semi-invalid." Alarmed at her condition, Colonel Breckinridge suggested travel as an antidote, and in the late spring Sophonisba left for an extended trip to Europe with her younger sister Curry.[27]

Breckinridge's travels did little to ease her anxious worries about the direction of her life. Preoccupied with religion, Breckinridge would decide at one moment that "the Lord has planned a woman's work for me," but in the next, she would be poring over law books. Throughout her two years abroad, Breckinridge kept up her legal studies with the continued encouragement of her mother. Troubled by the recklessness of a son, Mrs. Breckinridge wrote to Sophonisba in May of 1891, "I am so glad you love law + are going to study + make it your profession—if God gave our girls more purpose than our boys, He intended they should do more." Two months later Mrs. Breckinridge was dead at the age of forty-eight. Little seemed clear in Sophonisba's life as she made her "sad journey home."[28]

Her mother's death deepened Sophonisba's depression and enlarged her responsibilities to her family. Returning to Lexington, she took her mother's place as head of a large and busy household in the summer of 1892. With fall came a letter from Vida Scudder, a professor at Wellesley College, asking Breckinridge to apply for a special fellowship the College Settlement Association was introducing for the coming year. The grant would sponsor a year's residence in a New York settlement house for a recent woman graduate interested in social work.

The College Settlement award had much to recommend it to Breckinridge. Social settlements provided an ideal solution to the plight of many late-nineteenth-century college women. Situated in poor neighborhoods desperately in need of social services, settlements offered residents a chance to use their educations to achieve social good. The houses also enabled single women and men to live respectable and independent lives away from home. In many ways, the social settlements extended the sense of community that women had discovered in college into the years that followed their graduation.[29]

Thus it was predictable that Sophonisba Breckinridge would be tempted by the possibility Vida Scudder raised, though she would rely on her father's counsel in making a decision. When Sophonisba broached her professors' suggestion to her father, William Breckinridge expressed disfavor. "You know, dear daughter," he replied, "Bowery boys can be found everywhere." Perhaps captive of the "family claim" whose hold Jane Addams so eloquently described, Sophonisba decided not to pursue the fellowship.[30]

Remaining in Lexington enabled Sophonisba to continue reading law in her father's office. When he returned to Congress, she had his library to herself. By November of 1892, she had read enough to feel confident about taking the Kentucky bar examination and on a day when her brother Desha had business in Frankfort, Sophonisba traveled with him. The chief justice of the court of appeals, a "mess mate" of her father's during the Civil War, and two colleagues questioned her for "three or four hours," Sophonisba remembered. "They agreed I was qualified to practice, and right there administered the oath required of members of the bar including the pledge that I had never fought a duel with deadly weapons." The following Monday brought Breckinridge's formal introduction to the Court of Lexington. She was the first woman to be admitted to the Kentucky bar.[31]

Her accomplishment became front page news in the *New York Times*. But her legal practice developed at a disappointingly slow pace. Sophonisba's first case—involving a "homestead" issue—came to her through a lawyer who had been in Colonel Breckinridge's regiment during the Civil War. Other business followed. "During the first weeks, three cases involving special women's interests were brought to me," Sophonisba noted. But soon it became apparent that few citizens already in trouble with the law were eager to take the further risk of being represented by a female attorney. Discouraged, Sophonisba faced the unhappy fact that all her hard work had still failed to provide her with a rewarding career.[32]

Ironically, a family disaster finally freed Breckinridge from her unfulfilling attachment to life in Lexington. In July of 1893, almost exactly a year after Mrs. Breckinridge's death, Sophonisba's father remarried. In fact, this wedding was his third. Prior to his marriage to Sophonisba's mother, William Breckinridge had been married to Lucretia Clay, the granddaughter of Henry Clay. She had died in childbirth in 1860; the young widower had waited a year and then married Issa Desha, a relationship that had endured thirty-one years. Within a month of William Breckinridge's third marriage to his cousin Louise Wing, a twenty-seven year old Washington D.C. woman sued him for breach of promise. Claiming an affair that lasted nine years, Madeline Pollard alleged that Breckinridge agreed to marry *her* once a decent interval had passed after his second wife's death. Pollard included in her charges assertions that over the course of the affair Breckinridge had fathered two children, delivered stillborn, and a third who died when born prematurely.[33]

The impact of a scandal over sexual misconduct by a public figure, damaging enough in the twentieth century, was devastating in 1893. The case received enormous publicity. The *New York Times* closely followed, in gossipy fashion, the sordid details of the trial that took place in Washington during March and April of 1894. Events were greatly complicated by William Breckinridge's reelection campaign, which, to his great misfortune, coincided with the injurious court action. When a jury found for Pollard, Breckinridge was ordered to pay the woman $15,000. Subsequent attempts to reverse the ruling were denied on appeal.[34]

Had the drama been confined to the courtroom, the suit against Congressman Breckinridge would surely have destroyed his reputation and political career. But it might not have leveled his family as well. When the case moved into the public arena, the effects were devastating. Social purity groups, religious associations, and women's rights activists joined with Breckinridge's partisan political enemies to drive him out of office.[35]

Opponents in Breckinridge's district sank to unbelievable depths in their campaign against him. One local newspaper published photographs of his dead relatives' tombstones "together with the inscriptions thereon," apparently as evidence of Breckinridge's hypocrisy. Rallies drawing 5,000 and 6,000 people were held where speakers reviled the congressman and his possible reelection as "a disgrace to Kentucky, a shame upon manhood, an insult to womanhood, a sinful example to youth, a menace to society and the home." The hostility of those within the Breckinridge's social circle must have been especially embarrassing for the family. At one "anti-Breckinridge" assembly, the *Times* reported, the platform held "members of the most prominent families . . . and some of the best known educators in Kentucky."[36]

Although his defeat was inevitable, William Breckinridge was a "crushed and disappointed man" after his humiliating political loss. Sophonisba remained deeply loyal to her father throughout his ordeal. But coming to terms with his affair and subsequent disgrace could not have been easy. Having only recently endured the loss of one parent, she faced the difficult task of accepting the weakness of another. It was a wrenching experience, complicated by the emotional instability of Sophonisba's new stepmother, Colonel Breckinridge's third wife.[37]

By the spring of 1894, Sophonisba's health and future had become an "acute" concern. To speed her recovery from the stress that she had been under, arrangements were made for a visit to the Oak Park, Illinois, home of a Wellesley classmate, May Estelle Cook. Cook had been attending classes at the University of Chicago, and she spoke excitedly to Breckinridge about the graduate school. Her curiosity aroused, Sophonisba accompanied her friend to the campus, where they planned a visit to Marion Talbot.[38]

It was natural that May Cook thought of Talbot when she considered how best to help her troubled Kentucky friend. Alice Freeman Palmer had come to Chicago in 1892, and Marion Talbot had followed as assistant dean of women and teacher of "sanitary science." President William Rainey Harper had hired Alice Freeman Palmer with difficulty. Although she had resigned the Wellesley presidency upon her marriage in 1887, Palmer was not anxious to leave the East, where her husband was a professor at Harvard. She agreed to assume the duties of dean of women under a special arrangement whereby she resided at the University of Chicago for only twelve weeks out of the year. As her assistant, Talbot played a central role in overseeing the university's women students.[39]

In 1894 Talbot resided in Kelly House, a women's dormitory, and as Breckinridge and Cook appeared there for their visit with the dean, they ran into two friends from Wellesley. Susan Wade Peabody and Ethel Glover were enrolled as graduate students at the university. Chicago was a popular place for Wellesley women, and several other graduates were attending the university as well.

The "Wellesley presence" at Chicago reflected the university's importance as an educator of women scholars in the late nineteenth century. It also revealed how attractive further study was for many of the first female college graduates. Eager to explore disciplines that captured their attention in college and unable to discover satisfying opportunities for professional work elsewhere, these women found graduate school an ideal, if temporary, solution to their unrest. By one informed estimate, nearly a third of the first generation of women to graduate from college between 1868 and 1898 went on to undertake formal postgraduate study. Sixty percent of Bryn Mawr's alumnae did so.[40]

The University of Chicago drew many women students because it made good its promises to welcome them. Propriety demanded the appointment of an older woman to look after female students. But a quest for excellence prompted Harper to seek out a leader in women's education—Alice Freeman Palmer—for the job of dean. The presence of Palmer and Talbot, powerful symbols of female intelligence and independence, inspired students. As one woman graduate student proudly described Alice Freeman Palmer, "hers is a charming personality, and all things gracious and womanly bloom naturally in her presence."[41]

The availability of financial support for graduate study increased Chicago's attractiveness to women. Although male graduate students far outnumbered females in the Department of Political Science from 1894 to 1898, women received six fellowships, almost half the number given to men. Between 1893 and 1899, the departments of political economy, political science, and sociology offered ten fellowships to female graduate students. Even though few in number, these awards enabled highly regarded women students to partially finance their graduate education.[42]

These details of academic life at Chicago were largely unknown to Sophonisba Breckinridge when she and May Cook sat down that day with Marion Talbot. But Talbot took an immediate liking to the young Kentuckian. Why not stay in Chicago and take up graduate studies? Talbot asked. Noting Breckinridge's interest in law, the dean of women suggested political science as a possible field of study. Taken with the dramatic city and the warm companionship of her Wellesley friends, Breckinridge required little persuasion. With a small sum of money, and an even smaller wardrobe, she moved into Kelly Hall and began her studies with Ernst Freund.[43]

Finally Sophonisba Breckinridge felt she had found her place. Although there would be further interruptions in her graduate education, she settled into life at the university and "began happily working" for her master's degree. In retrospect, the several years that followed Wellesley seemed a blur. "My own life during the years after Wellesley was a confused life," she recalled.

> There was first the attempt to help with the family income by teaching in the Washington High School, there was the severe attack of influenza which laid Papa low for several weeks and then struck me, there was the trip abroad with Curry for which I was so ill prepared, there was the sad journey home to find Mama already gone, there was the scandal that overshadowed my father's life, and then the wonderful experience of the University of Chicago.

For Breckinridge, the university meant freedom. In that new place, she set about the task of living her own life.[44]

II

As Sophonisba Breckinridge's difficult path to Chicago makes clear, only the exceptional woman embarked on a program of professional training. In spite of the interest in graduate school among college women, that population remained relatively small at the turn of the century. Smaller still was the group who went on for graduate study. Yet each year brought new arrivals to the University of Chicago. In 1897, Katharine Bement Davis made her way to the campus to study political economy. Davis's life until that point had been a mixture of advantages and some hardships. She shared with the Kentuckian a wish to find rewarding work.[45]

Her family boasted no politicians of the stature of the Breckinridges, but Katharine Davis also came from an old and respected American family. Born in Buffalo, New York, in January of 1860, Davis traced her family's American roots back to the 1630s. She counted Ethan Allen among her ancestors. The Davis family settled in Dunkirk, New York, when Katharine was three years old. There her father established a reputation as a man dedicated to education and committed to shouldering civic responsibilities. In 1877, he moved his family again—this time to Rochester, where he took a position as manager of the local office of the Bradstreet Company.[46]

Although they were not rich, the Davises provided "generously" for their children. Katharine was the oldest of three girls and two boys, all of whom enjoyed the benefits of "music, dancing, and art" lessons, in addition to regular schooling and "neighborhood good times." Proud of her middle-class upbringing, Davis liked to boast that for three hundred years there had been "neither poverty nor affluence" among her family. She never had to "drag" herself "up from the depths of poverty" or suffer from "the dangers that come from having a superabundance of money."[47]

While members of the Breckinridge clan rallied around the decaying Confederacy, Katharine Davis's grandmother agitated for the abolition of slavery. Like many active female reformers, Rhoda Denison Bement also embraced the causes of temperance and women's rights. She participated in the Seneca Falls, New York, woman's rights convention organized by Lucretia Mott and Elizabeth Cady Stanton in 1848. Her grandmother spoke enthusiastically about the early days of feminism and the impassioned quest for social change to the young Katharine. Long afterwards, Davis remembered those stories with affection.[48]

Davis also benefited from formal schooling at the Rochester Free Academy. Like Breckinridge, who favored mathematics, Davis found the sciences most fascinating. She devoted her time to studying chemistry. Her teachers recognized Davis's unusual intellectual skills, and encouraged her to seek a higher education. But when she graduated from the academy in 1879, Davis's family could not afford to send her off to college. Instead, she secured a position teaching science at the local high school in Dunkirk. She worked there for ten years, contributing a portion of her earnings to her family, and putting aside the rest in the hope that one day she could finance her own college education. After teaching all day, Davis studied at night. Her hard work was rewarded in 1890 when she was admitted to the junior class at Vassar College; she was thirty years old.[49]

Vassar gave Davis the opportunity to expand her knowledge of the sciences. Older than most of her classmates, she took her studies seriously and applied herself with diligence. Although the college itself was only twenty-five years old when Davis attended, Vassar had already gained a reputation for offering women students a respectable science education. Among the college's earliest faculty members was Maria Mitchell, a famous astronomer deeply committed to helping her students advance in scientific work. Several of Mitchell's students carried on her legacy elsewhere, including Ellen Swallow Richards, who pioneered in establishing the field of sanitary science at the Massachusetts Institute of Technology.[50]

Davis was drawn to the combined sciences of nutrition and food chemistry, two subjects under the rubric of sanitary or "domestic" science. As developed by Richards at M.I.T., sanitary science drew on aspects of public health, chemistry, nutrition, and home economics, and it included a strong sociological dimension. Public health problems of great magnitude had accompanied the urbanization and industrialization of late-nineteenth-century America. Richards reasoned that, as homemakers, women had a special role to play in the science of sanitation and in upgrading the human environment by applying what they learned in the laboratory to the home.[51]

Sanitary science defined a special area of expertise for women within the larger field of chemistry. As such, it enabled women scientists to create a place for themselves in the male worlds of research and college teaching. When Davis studied at Vassar, sanitary science was not included in the curriculum: food chemistry was taught as part of the general offerings in chemistry. Davis found in that field the chance to apply science to basic problems in "human welfare." When she graduated from Vassar with honors in 1892, at the age of thirty-two, Davis gave a commencement speech, "The Missing Term in the Food Problem," which grew out of her college work.[52]

Having secured the college education she held so dear, Davis returned to her job as a schoolteacher, this time at the Brooklyn Heights Seminary for Girls. Repeating the pattern that characterized her first working years, Davis pursued her own education while teaching science to her young students. She began taking graduate courses in food chemistry at Columbia University. By the spring of 1893, Davis's studies at Columbia had led to her appointment as director of an exhibit planned by New York State for the Chicago World's Fair.[53]

The model workingman's home Davis oversaw reflected the increasingly close alignment of her interests in science and social reform. Drawing on an idea first presented by Vassar professor Lucy Salmon, the exhibit used aspects of food chemistry and nutrition to show how laborers could live healthier lives within a meager budget. The low wages of American workers were taken as a given: the model home offered tips on how to prepare healthy and inexpensive meals. The Fair gave Davis a chance to see Chicago, a growing reputation for her work, and a one-way ticket home. After viewing the workingman's model home, one well-connected enthusiast offered her a position as head resident of the College Settlement in Philadelphia. Davis quickly seized the opportunity to continue with her work.[54]

The settlement offered Davis the occasion to try out her developing ideas about community life and reform. Philadelphia's College Settlement was located in a neighborhood populated chiefly by poor blacks and Russian Jewish immigrants. Although her own background could not have differed more from the people she hoped to serve, Davis felt fully in her element in the Philadelphia slum. She found herself especially drawn to a group of Russian immigrants whose political savvy and personal flair she admired. Much of her work as head resident consisted of such usual settlement activities as starting neighborhood clubs, organizing reading classes, and teaching English, but Davis went beyond the orthodox activities. She created in four tenements "model apartments" of the kind she had exhibited in Chicago. And she acted forcefully to combat the neglect of city government. When one dangerous and dilapidated boarding house was left standing after being condemned, Davis went through the place and smashed all the windows herself. Never considered shy by observers, Davis early showed a sense of daring and bravado that later served her well.[55]

Davis stayed at the settlement for three years, but her desire for further education remained unsatisfied. She left the College Settlement in 1897 to study political economy at the new University of Chicago. When Professor J. Laurence Laughlin interviewed her at the school, she confided to him her "reasons for giving up my work and coming to the University." (She left no record of what her motives were.) As a result of their conversation, she said, "he was suspicious of me ever afterward." She maintained that Laughlin suspected her of "some sort of socialism," presumably because she criticized the prevailing economic policy of laissez-faire and expressed interest in an activist approach to eradicating poverty.[56]

Whatever transpired, Davis apparently felt a strong desire to master the science of political economy. Part of fulfilling that wish included earning a Ph.D. Although by the 1890s a doctorate was of increasing value in the academic profession, virtually no other occupation required the degree. In fact, most *universities* were still staffed largely by professors whose formal educations ended when they graduated from college or seminary. Unlike Breckinridge, Davis did not simply drift into study at the University of Chicago; she set out to train herself in the fundamentals of political economy. With great purpose, at the age of thirty-seven, she eagerly took up this work, selecting as her mentor the iconoclastic Thorstein Veblen.[57]

III

In 1898, a year after Katharine Davis began her studies at the university, another young woman of considerable determination launched her graduate work at Chicago. Enrolled in the Department of Sociology, Frances Alice Kellor was a recent graduate of Cornell University. At twenty-five, she was younger than either Breckinridge or Davis, but unlike her two predecessors, Kellor had learned early on how to scramble for a living. In a childhood marked by poverty, she caught hold of an elusive dream, and with the help of benefactors, she managed to acquire an education.[58]

Born in Columbus, Ohio, in 1873, Kellor probably never knew her father. He had abandoned her family by the time Frances was two. Frances was the second of the Kellors' two daughters; her sister was twenty-seven years old when Frances was born. In 1875, Mrs. Kellor traveled with her two children to Coldwater, Michigan, where she made a new home for her girls.

Mrs. Kellor's choice of Coldwater proved to be fortuitous for "Alice," as Frances was then known. A town of tall, leafy elms, clear, cool lakes, and handsome Victorian homes, Coldwater seemed a quiet, rural community. But the town had a well-earned reputation for liberalism. It was known for its fervent abolitionists, who had aided the Underground Railroad that passed through the town. A public library and female seminary were further evidence of the community's progressive outlook and enthusiasm for education. Coldwater even boasted its own freestanding opera house, modeled after theaters built in Europe. Local luminaries included a native son, Cyrus Luce, who led the state's Granger movement and served as Michigan's "farmer governor." This lively local culture and proud history made the town an appealing place to live.[59]

The Kellors occupied a low rung on Coldwater's social ladder. To support her children, Frances's mother labored as a laundress and domestic servant. She washed the clothes of the wealthy, and locals later remembered "Frances as a little girl, collecting and delivering laundry in a little wagon." A fearless tomboy, adept at using both shotgun and revolver, Frances roamed the countryside hunting rabbits and other "fur-bearing animals" to augment the family income. Stalking the fields, accompanied by her hunting dogs, she fast earned the admiration of local boys and the envy of their sisters.

One girl recalled that she "disapproved" of Frances because she "wore her hair shingled and walked and talked like a boy." But the girl's brother saw Frances differently. He "thought her *outstanding!* He said she could play baseball, swim, and skate—She could whittle out a sling-shot and hit anything she aimed at." "Running and jumping" on the school playground, Kellor "could outdo any of the boys."[60]

In the classroom, it was another story. One pupil recalled that Kellor failed to keep up with her classmates, but was often observed "reading a book under her desk that was far beyond our interest." Bright and determined to secure an education, however bored she might appear, Frances joined her mother at the washboard in order to finance two years of high school. A lack of funds forced her to leave school in 1890 when she was seventeen.[61]

The previous year an accident occurred that altered the course of Kellor's life. While shooting targets in the woods with some local boys, Frances pulled back the hammer of her revolver only to see the gun suddenly discharge. The bullet tore through two fingers of her left hand and came to rest in a third. A jet of blood quickly soaked through the handkerchief hastily produced by her companions. Frightened by the gore, Kellor took off for home "across the fields with all the speed of a startled fawn." Not finding her mother there, she ran on toward the town doctor's office. Mary and Frances Eddy, the local librarians, spotted the young girl and helped her find a physician.[62]

After this accident, the Eddy sisters took Kellor into their home, apparently assuming the role of protective guardians of the young girl. They encouraged her social and intellectual development. Women of some means and culture, the Eddys freely shared their financial resources and their love of learning and books with Frances. Kellor gratefully accepted their care and their introduction to the impressive collection of books housed in Coldwater's public library. Before long, she began asking acquaintances to call her Frances, instead of Alice, emphasizing the middle name she shared with one of the women who had "adopted" her.[63]

Her appetite for learning and her quick intelligence earned Frances a position as a typesetter and then reporter for the *Coldwater Republican*, a local newspaper. In the summer of 1892, her beat included the Chautauqua summer program in Bay View, a northern resort on Lake Michigan. Kellor heard economist Richard Ely lecture there. In the fall of 1893, she traveled to Chicago with Frances Eddy for a visit to the World's Fair. It seems likely that she then saw for the first time the university she would one day attend.

Kellor's duties as a reporter kept her in the thick of Coldwater's busy community life for two years. The town well represented, in her words, "this age of organizations." A political equality club, several literary societies, a Twentieth Century group that sponsored talks on social issues, and a local chapter of the Women's Christian Temperance Union provided the young reporter with plenty of news. She seemed to relish local crime stories, especially those involving minor thefts. These misdeeds were described in a tone of heavy moralizing. But Kellor often put her fine sense of humor to work, as when she told a parable about a child who stole his dad's musket only to land his first shot "in the anatomy of a horse belonging to . . . [his] father."[64]

Kellor enthusiastically embraced the social gospel preached by Coldwater's influential Presbyterian minister, Reverend C. P. Collins. On Sunday, she accompanied the Eddy sisters to church, where Collins delivered inspiring sermons stressing Christian responsibility for social problems. The informal "sociological" discussions Collins led also intrigued Kellor. She spread the word in her newspaper column about local efforts to help the poor. She described in detail recent lectures on "national and political conditions and evils" designed to pierce "the lethargy of American rural citizens."[65]

With the encouragement of the Eddys and Celia Parker Wooley, another wealthy Coldwater woman, Kellor set her sights on a college education. She studied for, and passed, examinations that admitted her to Cornell. In mid-September of 1895, she traveled to Ithaca and was soon followed by Frances Eddy, the closest "family" she now seemed to have. Kellor selected law as her major subject, perhaps inspired by another Coldwater woman who had attended Yale Law School.[66]

When Kellor arrived in 1895, coeducation at Cornell was twenty years old, but women students still suffered from considerable discrimination. Excluded by male fraternities from many organizations and most social gatherings, the women of Cornell's Sage College fashioned their own community. Although segregation enabled the coeds to run their own student government and control the traditional college clubs, it delayed the social acceptance of women students at Cornell.[67]

Class differences between male and female undergraduates exacerbated these tensions. Unlike Wellesley and Vassar, Cornell drew large numbers of girls with few or relatively modest resources. But men of wealth increasingly attended the university as the institution developed its professional schools. At worst, the poorer girls were looked down upon by male students, and in the best of times they were only "tolerated and ignored." A year before Kellor arrived, the *New York Herald* quoted a Cornell faculty member's opinion of the university's female students:

> There can be no doubt that the large proportion of them (the coeds) are enti-
> tled to no social recognition whatever. Most of them are hard students, and
> some are really brilliant intellectually, but their personal appearance and con-
> duct in general show unmistakably that they would be out of place in fash-
> ionable college society.

A popular campus song expressed similar contempt more directly. "I'm glad all the girls are not like Cornell women / They're ugly as sin and there's no good within 'em."[68]

Within a few months of her arrival, Kellor challenged one form of sex discrimination at Cornell. She organized a group of women interested in rowing. Anticipating disapproval, the team would sneak out of their dorm at dawn and head for the lake. Kellor asked the physical education department to set up formal classes in crew for the Sage students. That request led to a summons by Cornell's president, who threatened to dismiss her. But Kellor stood her ground, and before long, defying the orders of the Athletic Council, a "women's eight" was formed.[69]

In spite of occasional hostility, many women who studied at Cornell in these early years of coeducation enjoyed themselves immensely. Florence Kelly, who later became a leader in early-twentieth-century reform circles, remembered with great warmth her days at Sage College in the 1870s. "As I look back over twenty years to my Freshman year," she wrote in 1896, "I see clearly that the most valuable thing in it was the life at Sage College; the long free talks with women in the upper halls, the meals with the men and women and the younger professors. If I must part with either, I would give the whole class-room work, and keep the University *life*." Kellor thrived in this environment as well. She applied herself to her studies in earnest; mindful, no doubt, of the debt she owed her patrons. Frances Eddy had followed her to Ithaca, and there could be no escape from the "great expectations" of her watchful benefactor.[70]

Her formal studies in social science began during Kellor's undergraduate days at Cornell. By 1894, social science had been taught at Cornell for ten years. The university's first professor in the field was Francis Sanborn, president of the American Social Science Association. The type of social inquiry introduced by Sanborn emphasized investigation of "practical" social problems. Under his tutelage, visits to institutions such as the nearby Elmira State Prison inspired student reports such as the "Relation of Insanity to Crime" and the "Duty of Aiding the Poor."[71]

Although Sanborn was gone by the time Kellor arrived at Cornell, a lively interest in social science remained. Her course work in law heightened Kellor's fascination with crime. After her graduation in 1897, she headed for Chicago, where her wealthy benefactor Celia Parker Wooley now lived. Appearing one morning at Wooley's door, Kellor announced her plans for the future, formed since she graduated. Wooley recalled that "she calmly informed me she had decided to be a criminologist." Baffled by these aspirations, Wooley nonetheless went about helping her young friend raise the necessary funds for graduate study. With the benefit of a special scholarship awarded by the Chicago Women's Club, Kellor began her studies with Charles Henderson in the University of Chicago's sociology department in 1898.[72]

IV

Four years later, in 1902, a young Nebraskan named Edith Abbott arrived in Chicago just as the university was about to celebrate its decennial. Throughout the school's first decade, the fame of the university had spread east and west. The distance from the flat prairie of Nebraska, where Edith Abbott was raised, to the teeming streets of Chicago was great in many ways. But a young woman captivated by the idea of a graduate education could make the mental journey with some ease by 1902. When Edith Abbott thought about continuing her education, she fixed her sights on the respected university that flourished in the greatest city of the Midwest.[73]

From early childhood, Edith Abbott had developed an appreciation of learning, a sympathy for social causes, and a familiarity with women's rights crusades. Othman Abbott, Edith's father, was the son of an "out and out antislavery man," who saw the Dred Scott Supreme Court decision as an omen of national suffering. As a young boy, Othman had traveled with his father and the rest of the Abbott family to DeKalb County, Illinois, where they began to farm. During his high school days in nearby Belvidere, Othman met his future wife Elizabeth Griffin, whose widowed mother also farmed in

DeKalb County. The Griffins were Quakers and ardent abolitionists who played a part in the Underground Railroad that ran through that section of Illinois. On the day John Brown was hanged, young Elizabeth was sent to school wearing black.[74]

Othman Abbott left DeKalb County to serve with the Union Army during the Civil War. Severely wounded in Nashville, he decided to forsake agriculture for law after a surgeon convinced him "the heavy work of farming would shorten my life." His brother later commented, "This rebel who shot you at Nashville, Othman, spoiled a good farmer to make a poor lawyer." But, in fact, Abbott enjoyed success in his legal career. Returning home after the war, he studied and gained admission to the Illinois bar. Traveling west with his brother in 1867, Abbott got as far as Grand Island, Nebraska, before running up against a government order barring Western travel because of "Indian hostilities." Abbott decided to settle in the frontier outpost on the Overland Trail, and to establish a law practice there.[75]

Land was easy to acquire, and there was plenty of work to do in building up the town, but Abbott soon "became lonesome in the prairie wilderness." He kept up a correspondence with Elizabeth Griffin, who was teaching school in West Liberty, Iowa. After a visit in 1870, Abbott returned to Grand Island engaged to be married. The wedding took place in the winter of 1873.[76]

Mrs. Abbott was an unusual woman in several respects. During the Civil War, she had attended college at Lombard University in Galesburg, Illinois, a rare accomplishment for a woman of her generation. When her brother was killed during the war, she left school and returned home to DeKalb County. Before long, however, Elizabeth Griffin had taken up her studies again, this time enrolling in Rockford Female Seminary, the Illinois school Jane Addams would later attend. She became a teacher after college, advancing to the position of a high school principal.[77]

Both Othman and Elizabeth Abbott embraced the cause of women's rights. Mrs. Abbott had been instructed in the subject by her mother, her aunt, and her uncle, who subscribed to early suffrage newspapers. During the Abbotts' courtship, Othman remembered, "she and I sent back and forth John Stuart Mill's Subjection of Women," filling the margins with notes. When Othman bought a house to prepare for his new wife's arrival in Nebraska, he put the deed to the dwelling in her name; a highly unorthodox move, given the limited legal rights enjoyed by nineteenth-century American women. "I had always felt that the wife should own the home," Abbott reasoned. "She was queen of the home and should own her domain in fee simple."[78]

Soon after their marriage, the Abbotts began their family. Edith, the second child of what would be two girls and two boys, arrived on September 26, 1876. By the time of Edith's birth, the Western migration had slowed. But as a young girl, she remembered, "the spirit of the Great Adventure was still in the air." Mrs. Abbott's mother had joined the household before Edith's birth, and the young girl was especially taken with her "Quaker grandmother." Surrounded by "men and women of courage, ability, and boundless energy who faced the difficulties of blizzards, droughts, and other hardships of the cov-ered-wagon days," Edith and her younger sister Grace acquired a pride in their Nebraskan heritage and a love of history that neither ever relinquished.[79]

Although "the endless distance of the western plains" seemed bleak to some, as a child Edith found her "prairie home" a source of fascination and pleasure. She looked with wonder on "the Pawnee Indian squaw who used to come back and work in our garden." Her mother, who felt "very sorry" for the Indian woman, explained "that in order to be near the land she loved, she was weeding the gardens of the interlopers who had dispossessed her peo-ple." To Edith, the squaw seemed "a romantic figure, reminding us all that the days when the plains had belonged to the Indian and the buffalo were not so far away."[80]

The landscape made it easy to recapture the spirit of that desolate time. Abbott liked to remember "the endless, frozen, pathless winters of those early years and the wonderful time when, at long last, 'spring came on forever.'" Summer months brought other wondrous sights, as when in "the long sum-mer twilights . . . we climbed high up in the cottonwood trees to watch the prairie fires creeping along the distant horizon." Although Mrs. Abbott clucked over her "poor benighted prairie children," Edith loved their games in the high buffalo grass and the searches for the "earliest, largest and thick-est" clumps of violets. Looking back, she and her sister Grace agreed that

> [if] we lived in Chicago a hundred years, we could never forget the call of the meadow larks along the roadside; the rustling of the wind in the corn; the slow flight of the sand-hill cranes over the prairie creek near our home; and the old Overland Trail, a mile from the main street of our town—where the wild plums were hidden and the bittersweet berries hung from the cottonwoods in the early fall.

Rich memories "of the pioneer days in our part of the Great Plains" long endured.[81]

In addition to the education they gained from exploring the prairie, the Abbott children also pursued formal studies. Mrs. Abbott hired a private teacher to instruct her children in German, the language of many local citi-zens. Edith excelled in the piano lessons also required, while Grace showed more aptitude in mastering *Pilgrim's Progress*. Collectors of books and mag-azines, the Abbotts urged their offspring to read the classics, but Edith espe-cially loved Mark Twain's *Adventures of Huckleberry Finn* and the cartoons in *Harper's Weekly* drawn by Thomas Nast. Rigorous religious instruction played a minor role in the Abbott children's education. Othman Abbott remembered that the family's independent beliefs made "life . . . none too easy for us in Central Nebraska in those early days because we did not go ourselves to the orthodox churches and allowed our children to play croquet on Sunday instead of going to the orthodox Sunday schools." Edith's formal classroom schooling began early. When she cried because her older brother

Ottie went off to first grade, Mrs. Abbott persuaded the local teacher to allow Edith to attend, even though she was only three.[82]

Mr. Abbott's active law practice added another dimension to his children's education. An interest in politics eventually led to his election as Nebraska's lieutenant governor. During Edith's childhood, her father encouraged her to observe activities in the county courthouse. Sometimes political conventions took the place of the normal docket; on other occasions the Abbott children "enjoyed the tense excitement of some of the important cases that were tried in the district court." From the balcony Edith had an excellent view, and she recalled: "father would look up and wave to us when we arrived, and some of the other lawyers would wave to us, too, or even come up to speak to us." The court became the Abbott children's "substitute for the modern 'movies.'" Edith remembered the courthouse as "a wonderful place." "It was," she said, "built almost on the prairie, and not in town but out where the town was expected to grow in some future day. And there was an old-fashioned wooden fence with stiles to keep the cows out of the open square around it."[83]

In spite of the remoteness of Grand Island, the Abbotts' interest in politics and their social standing in the community kept their household lively. Visitors traveling through Nebraska stopped overnight, and suffragists campaigning for their cause in the West received a special welcome. With her mother serving as an official of the Nebraska Woman Suffrage Society and her grandmother also supporting the cause, Edith was keenly aware of "the suffrage excitement." Among the Abbotts' guests were Lucy Stone and, later, in 1882, Susan B. Anthony. When Anthony visited Grand Island, Edith was six years old. Noting the cramped quarters in his house, Othman Abbott recalled: "one night while Miss Anthony was there the only way we could manage was to have our little daughter Edith, six years old, used as a bed fellow. She was very proud of it, particularly of sleeping with Miss Anthony." Only a few years later Anthony also touched the life of Sophonisba Breckinridge, who became Edith Abbott's partner throughout both of their distinguished careers.[84]

Her first break with the comforting circle of her family and local community came when Edith was twelve years old. Committed to providing her girls with the best possible education, Mrs. Abbott arranged for Edith to attend the private Brownell School in Omaha. The separation from all those she loved was traumatic for Edith, who especially regretted losing "the wonderful teaching that we got from mother and father and the educational values of the family group." Instead she struggled with new intellectual challenges, not all of which were pleasant. "U pity me Grace," she wrote to her sister. "Latin is the worst stuff I ever laid eyes on in my life."[85]

When Edith graduated from Brownell in 1893, she won honors from the high school and a trip to the Chicago World's Fair from her mother. On that visit, she saw the university going up near the fairgrounds. While her memories of the Exposition soon faded, her sight of the University of Chicago left a vivid impression for a long time to come.[86]

The Depression of 1893 foreclosed a bank Othman Abbott held an interest in—and any possibility of Edith's entering college. When the bank failed, Mrs. Abbott lost the money she had inherited from her mother in 1887. Like most of their neighbors, the Abbotts suffered during the depression, though not as severely as those who relied solely on farming for their family income. Edith's parents narrowly avoided bankruptcy and barely managed to hang onto their house.[87]

To help her family, Edith went to work teaching at Grand Island High School. Just sixteen at the time, she faced pupils who included older boys and girls and even her own sister Grace, only two years her junior. The job was burdensome for such a young girl. And when this was added to her father's financial troubles, a terrible drought throughout the Great Plains, and repeated crop failures in the region, the times seemed grim indeed.[88]

Reflecting the drive for further learning so characteristic of her predecessors at Chicago, Edith still found a way to continue her education. She took correspondence courses for a degree at the University of Nebraska. In the summer of 1897, Edith's savings permitted her to travel to Lincoln for summer school at the university. Times were still so hard that while she was there her parents wrote asking her for the rest of the money she had stored away. Her mother made this anguished plea:

> My dear Edith, I want you or rather Papa does to let him have your money
> for a little while only—I hope. He may get it from the bank . . . and then we
> shall not need to use it at all. . . . I hope he will be able to put back a good
> deal of it in the bank for you before you come home—My dear it is very hard
> for me to write this to you—but there seems no other way. . . . Answer, so I
> can get it if possible to-morrow morning—I have shed some tears over this—
> and Papa told me how much he hated to ask you for money. He has said you
> were having the house painted because he said he owed some and people
> would think he ought to pay before he painted the house.

Edith's loyalty to her family during this period of adversity moved Mrs. Abbott to tears. "You will always know Edith how much you have done for us all—. I can never think about [it] without wanting to cry."[89]

Not until a year later, with the help of a bank loan and what remained of her savings, could Abbott return to the University of Nebraska. The years of hardship did nothing to diminish her enthusiasm for college life, however. A senior now with all the credit she had earned from correspondence and summer school, Edith quickly gained the admiration of her teachers. Through them she met the writer Willa Cather and other Nebraska luminaries. Before her graduation in 1901, Abbott had won a Phi Beta Kappa key and admission to a campus sorority.[90]

After leaving the university, Edith returned to schoolteaching as a profession, this time in Lincoln. In the summer of 1902, she spent her vacation taking classes at the University of Chicago. When she arrived on the campus, Abbott was given a room in Green Hall. At that time women graduate students often earned their keep by living in the dorms and overseeing the activities of the house. Sophonisba Breckinridge served in this capacity at Green Hall. Abbott remembered that Breckinridge seemed "eager to help everyone to get what she wanted out of even a short period of residence in Chicago." Inspired by her example, and thrilled at the opportunity before her, Abbott plunged into course work at the university.[91]

Abbott studied political economy, and her clear intelligence once again attracted the attention of her teachers. She was encouraged by Veblen and her other professors to undertake full-time graduate study. The Department of Political Economy promised a fellowship if she would agree to enroll there. Returning to Nebraska to ask her father's permission, Edith must have approached her financially strapped parent with some trepidation. Delighted that his daughter's gifts had met with recognition, he vowed to send her back to the University of Chicago even if it meant sinking further into debt. One more year of teaching intervened. But when the fall of 1903 rolled around, Edith was on her way to Chicago to begin her graduate education.[92]

V

And so, from the southland of Kentucky, the prairie of Nebraska, a peaceful town in the Midwest, and the slums of Philadelphia, the four women came to the University of Chicago in its first ten years. Prompted by individual circumstances to leave familiar surroundings for an adventure in a city largely unknown to them, these women displayed enormous intellectual drive and a measure of daring. Each of them rebelled against prevailing nineteenth-century notions that woman's place was in the home. But all benefited from the rising challenges to such mores that were being increasingly voiced in the culture at large. Each at some point confronted aspects of "the cult of domesticity," but none fell victim to its most oppressive aspects. The pathways of their escape reveal a great deal about the fluid character of late-nineteenth-century America.[93]

Perhaps the most striking similarity in the lives of these women lay in the encouragement they received from family. At no point were they told by those they held most dear to stifle their ambition because it was inappropriate to their sex. How deep did the prevailing orthodoxy of "woman's proper place" run? Not very, in the family lives of these nonconforming women. While prescriptive literature continued to delimit roles for female children, some American families believed and acted otherwise. In so doing, they helped create new opportunities for their gifted girls.

The families of the future Chicago students also displayed a great regard for education. Books and learning were emphasized. Each was reared by parents and mentors committed to providing the best schooling they could afford. Education has always served as an important avenue of mobility in American society. This was especially true for these daughters of the nineteenth century. The Breckinridges clearly saw their child's schooling as a byway to success. Perhaps Kellor's mentors hoped that cultivation of her intellect could rescue Frances from her humble origins. The Davises and Abbotts certainly felt education to be an advantage for its own sake. Their faith in its power drove Katharine and Edith on their long quest to acquire college degrees. The prize to be won for intellectual achievement was intangible. No particular job nor material award awaited even the most successful female graduate. Yet each woman internalized a message passed on by the generation that lived through the Civil War. Knowledge and learning were keys to advancement whatever the tasks to be achieved. Deep within the culture, a powerful idea resonated: education was an avenue to success.

The prevalence of politics and the widespread interest in social issues among their local communities is another striking feature in the early history of Breckinridge, Davis, Kellor, and Abbott. Shaped by region, the great national issues reverberated in the towns where these women grew up. The social class of the Breckinridges and their prominent positions of leadership in Kentucky make their involvement in politics no surprise. Less expected, perhaps, is the impact of abolitionism among their Northern neighbors. Kellor could still hear stories of the antislavery cause in Coldwater: Abbott and Davis learned from their dedicated grandmothers about that noble crusade. All three women thus saw the legacy of the powerful national reform movement that had touched down like a storm in sleepy Northern towns. So transforming was its impact that the winds of abolitionism still swept their ancestors' memories. For both the conquered and the vanquished, the Civil War figured prominently in the older generation's experience. Their children and grandchildren, including the women who would travel to Chicago, grew up in a nation deeply changed by that bloody ordeal.

Class played a critical role in enabling the four women to pursue their educations. Each was able to tap financial resources that were essential in realizing her intellectual aims. Their stories make it clear that a college education was expensive and not easily come by for a person of moderate means. Years of work, scrimping, and saving were required if an ambitious girl hoped to do it on her own, and even then additional assistance was usually required. Even a relatively wealthy man, such as Colonel Breckinridge, felt the pinch of nineteenth-century tuition. To invest these resources in a daughter, who was most unlikely to ensure any financial return, required independence, sacrifice, and not a little love. If nineteenth-century Americans shared faith in education as a means of mobility, only the rich could reach that goal without sacrifice.

Finally, the personal qualities of Breckinridge, Davis, Kellor, and Abbott surely gave rise to their unorthodox goals. Each woman showed early evidence of an independent streak and an unusual aptitude for and enjoyment of learning that was recognized and rewarded by those around her. One senses, though, a lonely quality to their inner lives. Attached to their vague dreams and comforted by books, these women chose a harder road than the one society expected them to take. Much as they admired their grandmothers and mothers, they did not follow in their footsteps.[94]

They appeared to be mostly uninterested in the parties and social life that other young girls enjoyed. Their goals were more intangible, but to them, no less real. Their ability to persist in swimming against the tide eventually brought them other rewards. All that seemed far away, however, when they began their graduate studies. Had Chicago itself not been a product of the great forces that brought these students to its doors, the university might have claimed credit for their arrival. As it was, Chicago's first women graduate students appeared just in time to meet up with an institution on the threshold of realizing its own modern ideals. For the several women who were to study political science, sociology, and political economy, even the chance to make the trip already seemed a rich reward.

2

White City, Gray City

The women who traveled to Chicago in the 1890s discovered a university full of vitality and ambition. Its newness gave the institution a special air. As a young graduate student wrote on the evening of Chicago's opening in 1892: "In many ways the University of Chicago is wholly unique. It is at once an experiment and an assured success." Her confidence was inspired by the combination of President William Rainey Harper's mind and John D. Rockefeller's money. One had only to observe professors who had eagerly traded the rarefied atmosphere of the intellectual East for the rawness of "pork-packing" Chicago to sense that something momentous was afoot. Although revered traditions and cherished beliefs "hovered like a mist" over the new university and its members, there was about the institution from its start "a quiet strength, a consciousness of power."[1]

Several distinctive features of the university shaped the experience of the women social scientists who studied there. Among the most decisive were Chicago's commitment to graduate education, its acceptance and (tempered) encouragement of women students, and its interest in building a lasting relationship with the city that was its home. None of these aims was unique to Chicago: they evolved in a context of social and intellectual change that induced similar permutations in other academic institutions. Yet the opening of the University of Chicago in the 1890s gave particular force to the combined program of graduate training, coeducation, and public service. Like the city that had arisen from the ashes of the 1871 fire—indeed, like the nation itself—the University of Chicago boasted newness and freedom from the constraints of a weighty history. "The bigness of the plan" and the substance of the program made the university a true product of late-nineteenth-century America. For Breckinridge, Davis, Kellor, and Abbott, as well as their contemporaries, this was a zesty environment in which to learn.[2]

II

Nothing in the blueprints of Chicago seemed more contemporary than the stress placed on advanced study. Few would have predicted when Johns Hopkins University opened in 1876 that its goals of furthering scientific research and promoting graduate education would lay the groundwork for the modern American university. Yet by 1890 that foundation was in place. Graduate instruction now appeared, to reformers such as William Rainey Harper, to be the *sine qua non* for a university with pretensions to greatness. If graduate training captured the essence of what was modern in American higher education, Chicago, in its infancy, claimed special advantages. As Harper explained prophetically to Chicago's first graduate students, "At Yale and Harvard undergraduate work gives color to the whole university, owing to the history and the traditions of those institutions. *It shall not do so here.* Our record shall be from the top down, and the fame of this university shall rest primarily upon the quality of its graduate work." It required no special act of courage to include a graduate school in the plans of the new university. But to organize the life of the institution around research and scientific inquiry was still, in the 1890s, a daring decision.[3]

Equally (indeed perhaps more) audacious was the University of Chicago's invitation to women to join its exalted intellectual enterprise. Although educational opportunities for American women had expanded tremendously during the post–Civil War years, formidable obstacles remained for women who hoped to supplement their undergraduate training with advanced degrees. Until the 1890s, major graduate schools in the United States permitted only a few "exceptional" females to join male students in advanced study. Rarely at most universities would a tolerated coed be rewarded for her work with an actual degree, no matter how indefatigably she studied to meet all requirements. By the early 1890s, repeated attempts to cross such boundaries and increasing liberality among forward-looking administrators had helped to advance the cause of graduate coeducation considerably. Now, leading academic institutions, such as Yale and the University of Pennsylvania, agreed to admit women for graduate study. When Chicago opened its doors in 1892, the university courageously embraced a rapidly emerging orthodoxy with a timeliness that justified the institution's claims to adventure and acuity.[4]

By the time Sophonisba Breckinridge arrived in 1894, a distinct community of women had already emerged at the University of Chicago. Although the number of female students enrolled for graduate studies never exceeded that of men during the first ten years, women were a significant proportion of those in attendance. The year Breckinridge appeared, twenty-five women took their place alongside the eighty-five men registered for graduate study in the three social sciences of political economy, political science, and sociology. When Edith Abbott joined the university in 1903, the total number of social scientists in training had dropped to eighty-nine, but there were still seventeen women among them. Through most of the university's first decade, women made up nearly a quarter of the graduate students who claimed political science, sociology, or political economy as their major field.[5]

Living arrangements at Chicago enhanced a feeling of camaraderie among women who attended the graduate school. The all-female dorms were largely self-governed and served as a center for social activities. Many women scholars, including Breckinridge and Davis, met up with former college classmates in their dorms. The definable "Wellesley" presence evident at Chicago when Breckinridge was engaged in her studies was reported to her alumnae group by Elizabeth Wallace in 1899. "Five of us '86 girls are in or about the institution, while minor lights beam cheerfully." Katharine Davis noted that, upon arriving at the university in the fall of 1897, "I engaged a room on the campus at Foster Hall. Myra Reynolds, who had been in the English Department at Vassar when I was a student there, was head of the hall."[6]

Significant age differences among the graduate students contributed a special atmosphere to the school. When they met in 1902, Edith Abbott was twenty-six, Breckinridge ten years older. An observer noted in 1893 that "Nothing about the institution, perhaps, is more striking than the disparity of age among the graduate students. In nearly every class there is a sprinkling of gray-haired men and women, some of whom have been teachers and professors for years, and others to whom the advantages of special training have been denied, and who eagerly embrace this opportunity to broaden their knowledge."[7]

Dormitory living did nothing to detract from the mix of age groups. Katharine Davis noted that "Foster was inhabited by women of all ages and in all stages of their academic careers, from freshmen to students about to take the doctor's degree. This mixture made it very jolly, and kept us all young." Age was only one factor contributing to the diversity of women graduate students. Another young scholar observed: "Among the women graduates, nearly thirty different institutions of learning are represented, several of them European. In such a cosmopolitan assembly it may be imagined that there is much comparing of notes, much kindling of thought, much valuable interchange of ideas."[8]

Towering above the entire female community at the university was Marion Talbot, the dean of women. Initially appointed to assist Alice Freeman Palmer, Talbot quickly assumed almost the entire responsibility for women students at the university. From the moment she arrived at the university in 1892, Talbot labored tirelessly to provide women at Chicago with the best opportunities. She played a critical role in shaping the experience of several social scientists who trained at the university.[9]

Talbot's own career had been greatly influenced by the evolution of nineteenth century women's education. Born in 1859 to a wealthy and respected Boston family, she enjoyed unique advantages made possible by her parents' progressive ideas and their social class. Her father, Israel Tisdale Talbot, was an admired practitioner of homeopathy and the first dean of Boston University's School of Medicine. Emily Talbot, Marion's mother, focused her attention on educational reform, with an eye toward improving the schooling available to women. She organized a campaign to open Boston Latin School to female students, enjoying a partial victory when a "Latin School for Girls" began in 1877. This success came too late to affect Marion, who was educated first at home and then with future Harvard students at the predominantly male Chauncy School.[10]

An 1880 graduate of Boston University, Talbot experienced firsthand the postgraduate sense of aimlessness and uncertainty that was so common to college women of her class and generation. Observing her daughter's predicament, Mrs. Talbot suggested that Marion organize a gathering of college women to discuss issues of mutual interest. At this time Marion was beginning further course work in sanitary science with Ellen Richards at M.I.T. With Richards' assistance and the support of Wellesley's president, Alice Freeman Palmer, a meeting of recent female graduates was held at M.I.T. in the fall of 1881. Out of this initial gathering came the Association of Collegiate Alumnae (A.C.A.). The organization remained active and functioned as something of a lobby for women and education. Talbot served as the Association's secretary and then as president, never relinquishing her membership in the organization the A.C.A. spawned, the American Association of University Women (A.A.U.W.).[11]

Her graduate study at M.I.T. prepared Talbot for the teaching position in domestic science she obtained at Wellesley College in 1890. Palmer's great admiration for the young faculty member brought Talbot to Chicago soon after. While in residence, Alice Freeman Palmer somewhat overshadowed her younger assistant. From the start, however, Talbot gave clear indication that she would be an aggressive champion at the university of women's intellectual and professional rights.[12]

Before she even appeared at the university, Talbot had wrangled with the University of Chicago's president. In the summer of 1892, Harper offered her an assistant professorship in the "Department of Social Science" along with her administrative position as assistant dean. Instead of immediately accepting what was an extremely generous offer, given prevailing conditions, Talbot instead proposed that the University of Chicago establish a "Department of Public Health." There she would lecture and carry out work "in close harmony with the broad sociological and economical work which you have planned as a special feature of the University."[13]

She also pressed President Harper for a higher faculty rank. Talbot had yet to achieve the position of assistant professor at Wellesley. "May I suggest," she ventured with steely nerve, "that the proposed work as a member of the faculty and as an adviser is a very responsible and difficult one and it could be carried on with more ease as well as dignity in the grade of associate rather than assistant professor." Noting that "the acting heads of several of the departments of the university are only assistant professors," Harper denied her request, assuring Talbot that "the work assigned you, though responsible and difficult, can be carried on with ease and dignity" as assistant professor. While intrigued by Talbot's suggestion of a special public health department, Harper placed the assistant dean of women in the social science department "for the present." There she remained for the next twelve years. She attracted few students in the 1890s when young women graduate students seemed far more interested in the particulars of political economy, sociology, and political science than in the science of sanitation and domestic life.[14]

The boldness with which Talbot negotiated her own position at Chicago foreshadowed the unwavering attention she would apply to her charges at the new school. Asked by Harper to organize "the woman's work at Chicago," Talbot proved herself more than equal to the task. In countless ways, she worked to enhance the social and intellectual environment for women at the university. Her efforts resulted in an impressive set of formal organizations linking together women at the school. For graduate students, the Club of Women Fellows was among the most important of these associations. In monthly meetings, women holding university fellowships updated club members on the progress of their research. The Fellows also traded opinions on professional issues that troubled them, including "Dangers of Specialization," "Life in German Universities for American Women," and the "Value of Graduate Study for the Secondary-School Teacher."[15]

Perhaps nothing went further toward giving coherence to the female community at Chicago than Marion Talbot's annual reports to the president: "Women of the University." Every department head was required to submit a divisional report; Talbot seemed to relish this responsibility. Each year, she used the occasion to press the university for greater institutional support, to upbraid the president for any lapses, and to celebrate the various achievements of women students and faculty. With careful charts, elaborate graphs, and reams of statistics, Talbot made an annual effort to prove that "the presence of women did not mean the lowering of any standards."[16]

The reports provided dramatic proof that women were not just a tolerated and ephemeral presence at the University of Chicago. Instead, they emerged as a real and vigorous constituency integral to the special environment there. By 1904, William Rainey Harper referred as a matter of course to "the woman side of the University." Talbot's efforts helped account for the instant recognition evoked by that phrase. This impressive embrace of coeducation in the late nineteenth century enhanced the sense that the new University of Chicago exemplified the modern age.[17]

The trends of the 1890s also revealed themselves in the university's close ties to the city of Chicago. The links were formed with finance and secured by Harper's very definition of "the University plan." The contributions of wealthy Chicagoans to the new school proved critical to launching the whole endeavor. In the spring of 1892, a million dollars for the university poured forth within just ninety days from generous city businessmen and philanthropists. This support ideally suited the benevolent aims of the donors and reflected the changing nature of charity in Chicago, where gifts to institutions were increasingly coming to replace gifts made directly to the poor.[18]

Conspicuous among the university's many urban benefactors were affluent Chicago women. The buildings for women students they helped endow assured that coeducation would achieve permanence. Between May and June of 1892, three prominent women—Elizabeth G. Kelly, Nancy S. Foster, and Mary Beecher—each contributed $50,000 for a dormitory that would bear her name. The University of Chicago was a private school, but it owed a great deal to the city in which it was founded.[19]

Perhaps mindful of this debt to Chicago, William Rainey Harper created an educational program that drew on the university's metropolitan setting. Critics scoffed that situating a first-rate academic institution in primitive Chicago "would be only the next thing to putting it in the Fiji Islands." But Harper, a dedicated and active participant in the Chautauqua adult education movement, viewed the university's urban environment as an opportunity to enlarge his institution's scope and influence. A central feature of Harper's educational design revealed the president's wish to broaden the university and its public appeal. The "University Extension Division" was created to take professors out of their classrooms and into Chicago where they would teach those who would otherwise be deprived of opportunities for advanced instruction. In so doing, academics could give back to the city a measure of what they had received. A second ambitious goal of Harper's, to establish a university press, also rested on the notion that the public deserved to reap the benefits of the great intellectual advances he felt certain were impending.[20]

Chicago's public spiritedness evolved, in part, from the Baptist origins of the university, which contributed an evangelical temperament to Harper's bold scheme. The impetus for establishing a university in Chicago had come, after all, from Baptists concerned about the dismal state of educational affairs in the West. The scarcity of adequate Baptist colleges in the Western states meant that young Baptists were educated by other denominations, by secular schools, or not at all. A Baptist university centrally located in the thriving city of Chicago promised to attract students from all over the West. The founders hoped for "a school not only evangelical but evangelistic," a college that would both instruct the young and advance Christian principles.[21]

The choice of William Rainey Harper, a biblical scholar and Yale professor, as the university's first president elevated the plan. While the new school was to be open to students and faculty of all faiths, Harper infused the project with religious sentiment even as he promoted scientific inquiry and the advancement of knowledge. Here was a man who shared with other intellectuals of his generation a deep religiosity and a devotion to the pursuit of more secular ideas. In Harper's deft hands the founders' wish for a crusading school capable of saving souls took on a broader definition, one that blended scholarly and religious aims.[22]

Harper preached an intellectual's social gospel, urging the university community to pursue research, learning, and service to mankind. His contemporary message posed no contradiction between piety and verified knowledge, but traditional values were never slighted, either. Charitable duties and moral imperatives had their place in the modern university. As Harper put it, "the true university, the university of the future, is one the motto of which will be: Service for mankind wherever mankind is, whether within scholastic walls or without those walls and in the world at large."[23]

Harper's rhetoric echoed a refrain that resounded in the emerging universities of the late nineteenth century. The combined forces of philanthropic financing, institutional ambition, and religious sentiment helped to shape the contours of new academic institutions and prompted their interest in the world outside the university's walls. Public service was an ideal that captivated many university builders of the period, in part because a broad definition of purpose enhanced the university's prestige, enlarged its potential scope of influence, and, generally, added an air of importance to intellectual affairs. A shrewd academic planner, Harper, who was doggedly determined to put his untested institution on the map, made an intellectual virtue of his university's necessity. The public thus became an important and valued constituency.[24]

III

The new industrial society in which Chicago evolved, and to which the university owed its existence, gave shape to these civic goals. Although advanced study fulfilled few vocational prerequisites in the 1890s, the university felt the impact of sweeping social, political, and economic forces that were transforming American society. Theological training, a dabbling in the liberal arts, and a smattering of natural philosophy may have provided adequate sustenance for academies and colleges throughout much of the nineteenth century, but this intellectual diet proved to be meager fare for those who sought understanding of the world in the chaotic years that followed the Civil War. Complex technological advances, the rapid growth of cities, expanding industry, and proliferating social problems pressed on all but the most cloistered Americans. The discoveries of Darwin and the subsequent ascendance of scientific values rattled the windows of even the quietest and most placid of schools.[25]

Universities that sought a prominent public role, as Chicago did, could scarcely ignore the tumult besetting late-nineteenth-century society. If "service to mankind" stood at the center of Chicago's stated agenda, insulation from the unsettling and grim character of the times would be difficult, and even undesirable, to achieve. The evidence of turbulence was to be seen everywhere, nowhere more visibly than in the Chicago of the 1890s. There the last vestiges of what had been a prairie town were disappearing by 1892. Within just twenty years of the devastating Great Chicago Fire, the city's population swelled from 300,000 to over one million by 1890. Dilapidated housing, hastily constructed to quarter these city dwellers, lined Chicago's many unpaved streets. Near the stockyards, roughly 35,000 people made their homes jammed within a single square mile. Few of Chicago's residents enjoyed the comfort of a long association with local custom and habits: four-fifths were foreign-born or the children of immigrants. Black Chicagoans, over 14,000 strong, contributed to the city's racial and ethnic mix.[26]

The sheer strain of population growth alone would have severely taxed already inadequate and sometimes nonexistent city services. But Chicago's busy industrial and commercial sector added to the urban calamity. The Chicago River served as a reliable, if lethal, open sewer where garbage, animal carcasses, and similar refuse were carried to Lake Michigan—only to be recycled into the city's drinking water, which the large lake was then supplying. These practices bred catastrophically high rates of disease. Getting from one place to another was not usually life-threatening. But a ride on the city's crowded and unpredictable cable cars gave some citizens, it has been suggested, "cause to envy the cattle" who rode "in relative comfort to their death at the stockyards." Drays and wagons crowded Chicago streets, where mud and cobblestones made the passage treacherous for horses who carried heavy loads. A powerful stench emanated from the stockyards, and dust and grime from the railroads hung in the city's air.[27]

The industrial growth that accounted, in part, for these municipal problems continued in 1892 despite an impending economic downturn. Chicago was best known for its railroads, meat-packing plants, and foundries. Morris, Armour, and Swift created innovative business enterprises, and their efforts were matched by McCormick's American Harvester and Pullman's Palace Car companies. The Marshall Field, Sears Roebuck, and Montgomery Ward companies achieved commercial success by making available merchandise that filled what seemed to be ever-increasing consumer demand. In short, the city provided a showcase for American capitalism—and the price being paid for its advance.[28]

At the heart of Chicago's drama was an industrial working class that filled the bustling factories, breathed the city's fetid air, and bedded down in its ramshackle houses. The restiveness of labor had been amply demonstrated during the railway strike of 1877 and the Haymarket riot in 1886. As the University of Chicago opened its doors in 1892, the memory of that late disaster in Haymarket Square was still fresh in the minds of many citizens. When Governor John Peter Altgeld pardoned three anarchists in 1893 who had been convicted and jailed for throwing the bomb at the infamous labor rally, his action set off a storm of criticism that swept first the city and then the nation. Within a year, another dramatic clash between labor and capital would rock Chicago, this time at the Pullman Company. Attentive observers of the long chain of local events worried openly about the fate of the country itself.[29]

Yet liberal Chicagoans drew hope in 1892 from the city's many signs of vitality, including a lively circle of reformers who soon attracted considerable attention at the university. Focusing their energies on the underside of urban life, these social activists demonstrated a shared belief that concerted action would one day yield constructive change. Especially conspicuous for their idealism were the residents of Jane Addams' Hull House, who chose as their mission the redemption of one of Chicago's poorest neighborhoods, the Nineteenth Ward. In the shadow of the city's shipyards and slaughterhouses, men and women from the settlement offered basic human services, even as they struggled to comprehend the origins of the suffering they observed.

It did not take long for them to realize that slums and sweatshops thrived on political corruption and greed: the road from South Halsted Street led back to City Hall. No rose-colored glasses could transform the awful specter of child labor and "the boodle"; but formidable opposition to these evils appeared in the person of fiery Florence Kelley and in the "civic savior of Chicago," Jane Addams herself. Thus, as Chicago prepared to host a new university and a world's fair, its bright horizons seemed largely undimmed by the city's dark heritage and its unsettled recent past.[30]

I V

The World's Fair was the magnet that first drew Katharine Davis, Frances Kellor, and Edith Abbott to Chicago. Like millions of other Americans, they traveled by rail to the Fair's host city in 1893. There they discovered not only the dazzling "White City" that prompted their trip, but the university nearby, which had its own special allure.

It was a coincidence that the Columbian Exposition and the University of Chicago were launched simultaneously, but the physical proximity of the campus and fairgrounds created an indelible impression that would link the two great ventures in the popular imagination for many years to come. As university classes quietly got underway in October of 1892, the Fair was dedicated with a good deal more fanfare on a site adjacent to the college grounds. While the "White City" of the Columbian Exposition dwarfed "the gray city" of the university in size and apparent importance, the location of the Fair's popular Midway Plaisance with its giant Ferris Wheel ensured that interested observers of one spectacle would catch sight of the other. Indeed, the Midway provided an orientation point for at least one correspondent, who addressed a missive to "Professor Jones, University of Chicago, near the Ferris Wheel," and succeeded in having the letter reach its intended destination.[31]

That the university and the Fair shared more than common swampy ground was evident in the contributions architect Henry Ives Cobb made to both ventures. He planned the school's first gray, Gothic buildings and envisaged the campus's quadrangular design while preparing an intricate Fisheries building and a peculiar but popular "street in Cairo" for the Fair. Cobb's two worlds met in the summer of 1893 when the university leased space to Fair visitors eager for convenient lodging. Also on loan to the Exposition for display in an edifice devoted to "Manufactures" was a telescope recently donated to the university by Charles Yerkes.[32]

The "White City" extended services to inhabitants of the "gray city" as well, mostly by providing lively entertainment and diversion. One campus sage suggested in 1893 that "There were more profs than students, but then we didn't care; / they spent their days in research work, their evenings at the Fair. / And life upon the campus was one continual swing; / we watched the Ferris Wheel go round, and didn't do a thing." On at least one occasion the poet was right. Chicago's assistant dean of women, Marion Talbot, recalled the abrupt cessation of an administrative meeting in 1893 when one university official shouted, "The Ferris Wheel is moving!"[33]

Most of all, the university and the Columbian Exposition shared an historical moment. One could see in the civic goals of the university and the endless displays of technological progress at the Fair the intense optimism of the day. Exhibits at the Exposition showcasing locomotives, electric lights, heaps of coal, and modern kitchens seemed to be shrines to modernity. They swelled the popular enthusiasm for science that was finding professional expression in the halls of academe.[34]

Women were no less visible at the Fair than in the new university. During the dedication ceremonies of the Exposition, Chicago's leading socialite, Mrs. Potter Palmer, called attention to the congressional wisdom that had created a "Board of Lady Managers" for the Fair. "Even more important than the discovery of Columbus, which we are gathered together to celebrate, is the fact that the General Government has just discovered woman," she declared. Not far from where Chicago's female students took up their quest for advanced degrees, the Exposition's Woman's Building served up a curious mixture of traditional domestic values and contemporary feminist ideals in its gallery of progress. No wonder hopeful young women across the land believed, as one Smith College graduate proclaimed, "the clock of time" had "struck the woman's hour."[35]

The effort to create a forum for learned discourse amidst the celebrations of the Fair reflected another assumption of the times: namely, that organized understanding could speed the course of social progress. This idea would profoundly shape the quest for social knowledge at the university, as well. Surrounded by evidence of impressive advances, participants in the Fair's "World's Congress Auxiliary" paused to measure all that civilization still needed to achieve. The Auxiliary launched a series of intellectual symposia wherein "material triumphs, industrial achievements, and mechanical victories" took a back seat to "higher and nobler" aims. Planners of the Congress intended to gather together "eminent representatives of all interests, classes, and peoples" to survey the path of human progress. Yet the ease with which such interest groups could be identified might have justified suspicion about "the enlightened and progressive spirit of the present age."[36]

Indeed, concern for nineteenth-century social problems dominated the intellectual component of the Fair just as it would soon guide social inquiry at the nearby university. Throughout post–Civil War America, the ideal of using knowledge as a cure for the nation's ills thinly masked smoldering discontent about the prevalence of civic conflict. The Congress at the World's Fair proved to be no exception to this rule. Although the state of literature, music, and art came under scrutiny in several sessions, no subjects so dominated the Congress as did the great social issues of the day. The program of the Auxiliary offered an index to late-nineteenth-century American politics. Meetings devoted to "Woman's Progress" provided Elizabeth Cady Stanton, Lucy Stone, and Susan B. Anthony with an opportunity to press for female suffrage and equal rights. At a Temperance Congress, the Women's Christian

Temperance Union voiced its demand for moral uplift. Municipal government, banking, education, public health, copyrights, Catholicism, evolution,
the rights of black Americans, the problems of American Jews, and social
settlements all took their place among other controversial topics that
assumed center stage.[37]

It wasn't necessary to attend a Congress to learn about the prevalence of
social upheaval in Chicago. The Panic of 1893 created legions of unemployed
who wandered in the streets and scores of homeless people who slept in city
parks. These realities added heat and relevance to proceedings at the Fair. In
fact, the Congress on Labor took on characteristics of the phenomenon it
meant to explore. In August of 1893, participants convened outside for a
"mass rally" near Lake Michigan, where 25,000 others joined them to hear
Henry George, Clarence Darrow, and Samuel Gompers address the fate of
working people and the poor.[38]

Perhaps because religion seemed a reliable balm to national woes, no Congress attracted greater attention than the Parliament of Religions. Under a
"banner of love, fellowship, brotherhood," representatives of numerous religious sects assembled to consider theological mysteries and the power of religion in reforming the secular world. Among the invited speakers was a University of Chicago professor named Albion Small. Head of the first (and
newly established) Department of Sociology in the United States, Small
brought a message to the conference that mixed social analysis with social
gospel. One need not look beyond the nation's cities, Small claimed, to find
the true mission of the church. Vice, political corruption, unemployment, and
greed poisoned the uncertain promise of urban life. If an understanding of
social reality did not provide a starting point for the ministry of the church,
Small warned that religious sentiment would be based on nothing more than
"mythologies and riddles." Thus Small further narrowed the distance, at least
for a moment, between the scientific necessities of academic work and the
moral imperatives of the spiritual realm.[39]

As the World's Congress Auxiliary came to a close on October 28, 1893,
its chief architect, Charles Bonney, gave voice to a firm conviction that had
been bolstered by the high quality of intellectual discussion at the Fair.
Despite Frederick Jackson Turner's historic observations about the closing of
the frontier, Bonney sensed new vistas where "henceforth the armies of learning, virtue, industry, and peace" would vanquish "the hosts of ignorance,
vice, idleness, and strife" in America and all over the world. Within hours of
his speech, the first insult to Bonney's prediction was delivered right in the
host city of the Fair. That very evening Mayor Carter Harrison was assassi-
nated on the steps of his own house. Just a few days before, he had appeared
at the Exposition to acclaim the virtues of Chicago on "American Cities'
Day." The timing of the two events served as an ironic reminder of the violent and unpredictable nature of urban life. The World's Congress and the
World's Fair soon faded from existence, but the quest to heal social problems
with a dose of social knowledge had just begun for the women who studied
at the university that stood in the shadow of Chicago's great Fair.[40]

3

Scientists of Society

President Harper's broadly stated goal of serving society by advancing intellectual inquiry quickly found full expression in the University of Chicago's departments of political economy, sociology, and political science. There the preoccupations of the new university—graduate study, coeducation, and social concern—converged with the emerging interests of academic disciplines on the threshold of professionalization. The result was a lively environment where the women social scientists, and their male classmates, learned absorbing lessons about social reality and social reform.

The academic experience of graduate students at Chicago was shaped largely by the various professors who guided student work. Yet in all three branches of the social sciences a broad concern with scientific values and contemporary social problems was evident. As Sophonisba Breckinridge, Katharine Davis, Frances Kellor, and Edith Abbott embarked on their graduate studies, they met with different aspects of late-nineteenth-century social science. Personal interests drew them to divergent fields within the array of social science disciplines represented at the university.

But no matter whom she chose to study with or what she decided to research, each woman was exposed to an ethos that prevailed at Chicago. All four women were encouraged by their teachers to use the skills of a social scientist to address the pressing issues of their day. With a scholar's commitment to objectivity and an educated citizen's wish for enlightened reform, male and female students took up the ambiguous charge laid upon them by their professors. They struggled to balance the imperatives of academic social science with the lure of active social reform. At the University of Chicago, lessons in the meaning of society helped write a primer for reform.

II

It made sense that Chicago's departments of political economy, political science, and sociology displayed an interest in contemporary affairs. All three disciplines naturally touched on matters of public policy. But the practical value of social scientific inquiry might have lain dormant without the presence of other powerful catalysts that encouraged academic experts to assume a public voice. Political science, sociology, and political economy took shape at Chicago at a time when American social science itself was being defined. Professors who joined the university represented divergent strands that wove the tapestry of late-nineteenth-century social science. Together they designed a program that drew on both the amateur tradition of social inquiry in America and the rapidly professionalizing fields of academic social science. In so doing, they created an intellectual hybrid that prepared their students to use the science of society to address social policy.[1]

From the outset, the curriculum of Chicago's first social science departments reflected a scholarly preoccupation with modern social problems. In the political economy department, J. Laurence Laughlin lectured on money and practical economics in a class designed to provide "training in the Theoretical and Historical Investigation of Important Questions of the Day." Thorstein Veblen's instruction on socialism in 1893 balanced history with recent socialistic developments.

Edward Bemis, a young economist, went the furthest toward teaching an activist brand of economics in the university's first year. His course description of "Social Economics" promised that "schemes of economic reform will be studied and presented with a view to inform the student how they may be carried out into actual practice." Professor Bemis hoped to "familiarize" his students "with the process of organizing desirable movements of a philanthropic character in various parts of the community." This kind of daring cost Bemis his job at Chicago within another two years. The scientific study of pressing social issues was one thing; openly advocating "radical" causes without reference to scientific inquiry was another. When Bemis directly questioned the motives of the railroads during the Pullman Strike, criticism of the university followed fast on his heels. The economist quickly learned the limits of his employer's tolerance of social activism.[2]

Social policy, loosely dressed in a scientific form, remained a central focus of instruction in the Department of Political Economy. By 1899, "Practical" courses shared center stage with "Introductory" and "Theoretical" subjects. "Practical" courses made use of economic theory and logic but were "devoted mainly to the collection of facts, the weighing of evidence, and an examination of questions bearing on the immediate welfare of our people." Such courses very much reflected the pressing issues of the 1890s. One class was "Private (non-political) Attempts to Improve the Economic Conditions of Workingmen Who Are Not Highly Skilled." Another was "State Interference in the Distribution of Wealth," and included "immigration, labor colonies, factory legislation, insurance of the laboring classes by the state, and relation of government to monopolies and corporations." The "practicality" of such courses lay in their relevance to late-nineteenth-century public affairs.[3]

Civic problems surfaced, too, in courses offered by the Department of Political Science. One circular noted that "Political Science, as treated in the University of Chicago, relates to the organization of the State." Administrative law and legislation received heavy emphasis under the influence of Ernst Freund. His more conservative colleague, Harry Pratt Judson, taught a class on municipal government, using the city of Chicago as the setting for teaching modern politics. The course involved regular visits to public agencies and case studies of urban offices.[4]

The setting of Chicago shaped the instruction of sociologists. The Department of Sociology boasted in 1893: "The city of Chicago is one of the most complete social laboratories in the world. . . . No city in the world presents a wider variety of typical social problems than Chicago." With the great advantage of a corrupt city at their doorstep, professors urged students to get out of the classroom and into the teeming streets where social realities could be observed firsthand. According to one departmental brochure, settlement houses were "social observing stations" where students could "establish scientific conclusions by use of evidence which actual experiment affords." Yet Chicago's sociology department sharply distinguished its work from philanthropic activities: "Social programs . . . are without scientific credentials unless they are endorsed by social philosophy." And social philosophy was considered "invalid, unless it is chiefly constructed from data authenticated by the antecedent sciences." Course work in sociology led students to "work among social facts, and to test and form theory by experience."[5]

The social science departments at Chicago found their purpose, in part, by forging these links between scholarly inquiry and social responsibility. In the late nineteenth century, advanced degrees were only recently beginning to take hold as prerequisites for academic careers: they had little value as vocational training for anything else. New research universities such as Chicago had to build a case for the importance of extensive graduate training. Thus, social scientists made claims for graduate education that went beyond appropriate training for scholarly life. At the University of Chicago, the sociology, political science, and political economy departments agreed on the purpose of their academic plans. They stressed the importance of using scholarship to advance both knowledge and civic-mindedness.[6]

Public duties often surfaced in official departmental descriptions of their educational programs. The Department of Political Economy sought "to teach methods of work, to foster a judicial spirit, and to cultivate an attitude of scholarly independence." Even an elementary study of economic principles applied to practical matters would provide the student with "the knowledge necessary for the more intelligent discharge of the duties of citizenship." Political scientists envisioned their courses as a component of liberal education and of pre-law training, but added that their instruction would prove useful "for those who need a knowledge of Political Science for other ends." Albion Small and his fellow sociologists took as their charge the training of scholars, but they intended to professionalize the work of social reformers and charity workers, as well. The sociology department even dreamed of filling the country's theological seminaries with "a company of advanced students capable of the most comprehensive thought upon social philosophy" who could make "first-rate contributions to social doctrine."[7]

The scholarly journals quickly established by the university's social scientists addressed these public goals. Laughlin and Small, founders of the *Journal of Political Economy* and the *American Journal of Sociology*, respectively, launched their publications in terms that revealed careful attention to national affairs. When he introduced the *Journal of Political Economy* in 1893, Laughlin regretfully noted that the "influence of scientific economic thinking in the United States has little or no authority with the masses of people." Laughlin hoped that the journal would provide a "new means of communication between the investigator and the public." Unlike existing scholarly journals, the *Journal of Political Economy* would "lay more stress . . . upon articles dealing with practical economic questions." Professor Small explained the 1895 founding of the *American Journal of Sociology* in similar terms. He designed that journal "to assist all intelligent men in taking the largest possible view of their rights and duties as citizens." By writing about "familiar things"—such as public policy and national issues—academic sociologists might promote the well-being of society at large.[8]

Yet, in explaining their new academic journals, these professors drew a clear distinction between the work of social scientists and the tasks of social reform. The *American Journal of Sociology* and the *Journal of Political Economy* aimed to advance progress by illuminating the sources of social problems. Editors Small and Laughlin insisted that ignorance eroded social well-being. Laughlin tipped his hat to the many concerned citizens pressing for change in late-nineteenth-century America, but he observed that these idealists evinced "exceptional development of the heart without corresponding development of the head." He criticized leaders of the labor movement for not being "always wise, sagacious, or well instructed in our economic conditions," and leaders of the legislature for their "dense ignorance of cardinal doctrines of taxation." Albion Small echoed this scholarly critique: "If a little learning is a dangerous thing," he said, "jeopardy from that source is today universal."[9]

In stressing ignorance as a cause of unrest in industrial society, Laughlin and Small offered social knowledge as a remedy. Laughlin wrote: "It becomes very clear that possibility of change implies knowledge of the thing to be changed; that a knowledge of the existing economic system is a condition precedent to any ethical reform." Such an analysis clearly paved the way for scholars to assume an active role in advancing constructive social change. Small hoped to substitute "the order of investigation" for the "riot of instigation." Armed with weapons of "criticism, examination and judicial coolness," experts could tame public passions.[10]

The Chicago professors also credited scientific knowledge with the ability to cut across class lines. Noting the "popular unrest of our era," Small catalogued the diverse and often opposing figures of modern society: "Compatriot and alien, official and civilian, wage-earner and wage-payer, capitalist and landlord and tenant, union and non-union laborer, brain worker and brawn worker, industrial and criminal, rich and poor seekers of employment and shunners of employment." He looked to scholars, with their sweeping understanding of social phenomena, to see beyond such divisions. As Laughlin put it, "opposition disappears in breadth."[11]

Both the embrace of objective science and the enthusiasm for applied research were part of the growing pains of academic social science. For much of the nineteenth century, American colleges and universities treated social inquiry as an element of moral philosophy. Only in the late nineteenth century did political science, sociology, and political economy begin to emerge as separate and well-defined disciplines. At that time, a lively interest in social science also existed among reform-minded citizens outside of academia. A new generation of scholars brought social inquiry into the purview of academic life in the 1880s. These intellectuals shared the amateurs' interest in public issues. But they emphasized the place of theory and objective research in social science, as well.[12]

In their attempt to forge a professional identity and define their fields, the new academic social scientists tied their subjects and their purpose to contemporary national affairs. They stood to gain social influence and recognition in doing so. But the authority of scholars, and their special claims to expertise, rested on their adherence to scientific methods and values. Thus the new professors faced a dilemma. On the one hand, they sought to enhance their position and support their professional ambitions by addressing modern social problems. On the other hand, their authority to address such matters derived from their scientific detachment from the turmoil of modern industrial life. A tension was inherent in their aims.[13]

Scholars who launched the social sciences at the new University of Chicago bore witness to this ambiguous stance. Some asked their students to be involved in society but also stressed the necessity of scientific objectivity. No teachers waded more deeply in these waters than head professors Laughlin and Small. Laughlin's contempt for socialist agitators only slightly exceeded his distaste for "men of high abilities and scholarship" who had "little or no influence on thinking in general." Reform, he believed, "could be advanced only by the most rigorous, logical, and scientific investigation." Small criticized scholars with "eyes in the back of their heads" who had a "do-nothing" approach to contemporary problems, but he expressed equal disdain for popular reform. "The majority of contemporary social reformers act," he wrote, "as though society would at last have its foundation on the rock, if it would adopt this or that expedient—civil service reform, equalized taxation, the referendum, profit-sharing, government ownership, industrial arbitration." A well-trained Chicago social scientist might consider similar proposals, but he would weigh measures more carefully. "The most remote results that can be anticipated"—rather than immediate ends—would be explored. Method would thus separate the scientist from the philanthropist or agitator, with "primarily technical" and "scientific" research providing the underpinnings of responsible reform.[14]

III

The energetic scholars at Chicago who most influenced the four women students well represented the diversity of the new academic social scientists. Ernst Freund, J. Laurence Laughlin, Thorstein Veblen, Albion Small, and Charles Henderson were men of strikingly different politics, styles, interests, and temperaments. Yet collectively they shared with other intellectuals of their generation a set of experiences that led them to link social inquiry to contemporary social problems. German historicism, evangelical Protestantism, post-Darwinian scientific method and theory, and professional ambition stand out among the factors that inspired these men, and consequently, affected their students.[15]

An early arrival, Sophonisba Breckinridge began her graduate education a year after Ernst Freund joined Chicago's faculty in political science. Attracted to the academic discipline that made a science of her father's career, and her own dreamed-of profession, Breckinridge decided to concentrate her attention on law and politics. This led her to select Freund as a mentor. She recalled that in 1895 she spent a "wonderful year taking almost exclusively courses with Professor Freund." Anyone looking for Sophonisba in those days would have found her in Room 309 of Cobb Hall, Freund's favored classroom. "I got the janitor to shorten the front legs of one of the big chairs," she confessed, "otherwise my feet would not touch the ground."[16]

Her choice of Freund as a teacher proved to be intellectually decisive for Breckinridge. She learned from him a particular brand of political science, one that broadened the discipline's traditional focus on constitutional history to embrace an activist approach to law. These were the days that preceded Charles Merriam's arrival at Chicago (1900), and the university's heyday as a center for the study of modern politics. In 1895, Freund advanced a view of the discipline that emphasized jurisprudence. By 1902, these interests made the University of Chicago's new law school a more hospitable environment for his creative energies. During the years of Breckinridge's doctoral studies, Freund presented politics as a science that could point the way toward enlightened legislation and reform.[17]

The origins of Freund's views could be traced back to his legal education in the German universities of Berlin and Heidelberg and his course work in political science at Columbia University. In Germany, Freund was exposed to the historical school of jurisprudence that sought to place law in its social context. At Columbia's graduate School of Political Science, he absorbed the values its founder, John Burgess, had acquired in Germany. Scientism figured prominently in the new school, which promoted political study based on data collection, inductive analysis, and theory building. Freund gained from Columbia an education in jurisprudence, comparative history, an interdisciplinary approach to the social sciences, and, from Professor Frank Goodnow, his first exposure to administrative law. The last subject quickly captured his attention.[18]

When Freund joined the University of Chicago as a professor of jurisprudence and public law in 1894, his academic interests encompassed the most pressing public issues of his day. Freund clearly foresaw that modern industrialism would change the relation between the people and the state. Insistent cries for economic regulation and government intervention to promote social welfare promised to increase the authority of administrative agencies. The expansion of federal power raised questions about the rights of private citizens. For Freund, no subject proved more compelling than law within its social context. He labored to develop a science of legislation and fair principles of administrative law that reflected historical change. Through Freund, the molding of contemporary society achieved a place at the University of Chicago as a fitting subject for those who would lead the intellectual's life.[19]

Breckinridge's studies with Freund in political science included traditional courses devoted to Roman law, jurisprudence, and private law. But she became most fascinated with an "invaluable technique" Freund employed in his teaching. Freund's belief that law could be understood only within a social and historical context led him to direct his classes to study the historical record of judicial opinions and to pore over reams of legislation. In this legal labyrinth, Freund would ask his students to find the key principles involved in legal decisions. The task was then to summarize succinctly the opinions supported by judicial briefs. This approach helped Sophonisba to see how "large amounts of material could be presented within modest proportions." But just as important as Freund's innovative method of presentation were the political messages transmitted thereby.[20]

At the time of Breckinridge's studies with him, Freund was working out the ideas he would later publish in *The Police Power* (1904). Freund took a very expansive view of federal power. He stressed that government intervention "to secure and promote the public welfare" evolved in response to prevailing social, economic and political conditions. The police power conferred on the state by the Constitution was not, according to Freund, a fixed quantity. Rather, throughout time, governments had found it necessary to use powers of "restraint and compulsion" on individual liberty and property to achieve a greater good. The ever-changing nature of society mandated that "the police power must continue to be elastic, i.e. capable of development."[21]

Was legislation aimed at "the prevention of oppression" a legitimate use of the police power? This question, Freund maintained, was a vital one in the newly emergent American industrial society. Most would accept as legitimate, Freund noted, state action to ensure the protection of public welfare. But did the public welfare include economic interests? This, Freund said, was the debatable field.[22]

His belief in the dynamic nature of law led Freund to perceive social legislation as a proper exercise of the police power. The social and economic conditions that accompanied industrialism were creating, he wrote, "a new ideal of social justice." Even though legislation designed to neutralize "natural inequality" by expanding the power of the state departed from "older principles of justice," Freund stressed the importance of "the progress of law." "Under democratic institutions," he argued, "the courts cannot be permanently at variance with the matured and deliberate popular will." Laws that set maximum hours for labor, that upheld the closed shop, and that protected women workers were thus considered a "legitimate exercise of the police power." These causes would later be central to his student's interests.[23]

Breckinridge gained from Freund an understanding of the complexities involved in contemporary legislation and an interest in the historical development of law. She was also exposed to a vision of state power far more sweeping than the one that currently guided the American polity. Finally, she learned from Freund intellectual grounds that supported the use of law as an instrument of social welfare. These were powerful ideas that demonstrated the potential of legal activism.

Breckinridge also benefited from the political science department's use of the city of Chicago as a tool for teaching modern politics. In Professor Harry Pratt Judson's class on municipal government, the intricacies of governing late-nineteenth-century cities were explored. A required investigation of urban agencies brought students out of the classroom and into Chicago. Women students were expected to show as much diligence as men in pursuing field investigations. One of Breckinridge's contemporaries explained Judson's course to her father:

> I really think I incline toward the Police or the Health Departments and Mr. Judson says I could investigate either without the least trouble or impropriety. . . . Please advise me. In all these subjects there will be a good deal of compiling from records and *some* personal investigation. The design is to combine both.

In political economy, Breckinridge studied the financial history of the United States with Adolph Miller, who later served on the Federal Reserve Board. And she gained an appreciation for the compelling intellectual style of Thorstein Veblen.[24]

Veblen owed his position at Chicago to J. Laurence Laughlin, head professor of political economy. Yet his unique abilities, broad exposure to social thought, and rare brilliance contributed a depth to the political economy faculty at Chicago that Laughlin's presence alone could never have provided. This son of Norwegian immigrants had acquired an impressive education in political economy and philosophy: first at Hopkins, where he took courses with Herbert Baxter Adams, Richard Ely, and Charles Peirce; and then at Yale University, where he studied with two men at intellectual war with each other: the moral philosopher Noah Porter and the enthusiast of Spencer's evolutionary theory William Graham Sumner. After Veblen earned a Ph.D. in philosophy at Yale in 1884, his inability to secure an academic position interrupted his career. He drifted until 1891, when he showed up at Laughlin's Cornell office "in coonskin cap and corduroys," wishing to study political economy.[25]

Although Veblen came to Chicago as a teaching fellow in 1892, his intellectual maturity was already far above the low rung on the academic professional ladder he was forced to occupy. Within a year of his arrival, Veblen taught his own course and profoundly influenced Chicago's social science students. He brought to the university a great distrust of the deductive analytical methods Laughlin held so dear. Veblen's interest in anthropology, his enthusiasm for socialism, and his fascination with evolution led him to challenge the efficacy of purely abstract laws. Instead, he preferred to place economic behavior in its social and historical context. Applying such scrutiny, Veblen then sent many of the sacred cows of classical political economy, including private property, out to pasture. The questions Veblen chose to explore revealed a fervent interest in contemporary issues. But his rigorous allegiance to scientific method also clearly marked him as a product of his intellectual age.[26]

Relatively few students valued the eccentricities of Professor Veblen. His enrollments were chronically low, perhaps because many found his meandering lectures difficult to follow. The bookkeeping aspects of teaching bored him. Veblen rarely gave exams and satisfied the demands of the university registrar by giving everyone in his classes a C. "My grades are like lightning," he once said, "They are liable to strike anywhere." His razor-sharp wit could occasionally be turned against students, as on the day when Veblen asked a very pious, churchgoing coed to "compute the value of her church in kegs of beer." Students asking questions Veblen deemed foolish ran the risk of being embarrassed in front of the class. A young man who pressed the economics professor to distinguish "conjectural history" from "real history" got this response: "The relation is about the same as that existing between a real horse and a sawhorse." The best students persevered in spite of these deterrents, and Breckinridge observed that no one except John Dewey "so developed the situation of a master with disciples as was the case with Mr. Veblen."[27]

J. Laurence Laughlin played the central role in Breckinridge's political economy education. She credited him with providing "constant and generous sympathy" as he guided her studies. Laughlin exemplified a group of scholars in the new generation of American social scientists. His career and interests mixed traditional and modern aspects of late-nineteenth-century American academic life. On the one hand, Laughlin belonged to a small professorial elite who were among the first to undertake advanced graduate studies. He earned a doctorate in history from Harvard in 1876 when very few members of the academy could boast of such extensive academic training. On the other hand, Laughlin clung tenaciously to the tenets of classical political economy. Relying on deductive reasoning and wedded to the principles of laissez-faire, Laughlin appeared mostly unmoved by the ideas of German historicism that appealed to so many other young scholars of this age.[28]

Laughlin proved less resistant to another late-nineteenth-century intellectual temptation. Following his Harvard mentor, Henry Adams, Laughlin began early to put enormous value on knowledge that illuminated existing social and economic problems. Although his motives were conservative—he fretted about the dangers of populism and labor unrest—his interest in applied research was forward-looking. Laughlin's emphasis broke with a tradition that had dominated American academic institutions for most of the nineteenth century.[29]

Laughlin's civic-mindedness had a deeply conservative tinge. When Sophonisba began graduate school, her professor was attracting national attention for his heated exchanges with William "Coin" Harvey. In 1894, Harvey—a lawyer, speculator in silver mines, and publisher—issued a slim volume featuring lectures by a fictional character named "Coin" on the money question. In *Coin's Financial School*, the young men and great financiers of Chicago were treated to the wisdom of "the little lecturer," who claimed to understand the roots of the 1893 Depression that was causing such great suffering in the city and the nation. Coin spoke for "free silverites" in his insistence that most of the social and economic problems of the day could be traced to the demonetization of silver. His cure was an expansion of the money supply, and he attacked "hard money" advocates who favored adherence to the gold standard. J. Laurence Laughlin was among the experts "Coin" lampooned. Laughlin's academic interest in bimetallism and his outspoken opposition to free silver had attracted the attention of William "Coin" Harvey.[30]

Leaving behind the tranquil halls of the university and the rarified pages of professional journals, Laughlin often spoke out in public forums and published articles in popular magazines on the evils of "soft" money. He had achieved prominence, in short, as an academic expert who addressed controversial public concerns, and thus provided a perfect foil for the wise young child created by "Coin" Harvey. It was all made up, but the names of notables gave Harvey's parable a tone of authenticity. So popular was the book, and so convincing the artifice, that Laughlin felt compelled to deny that he had ever attended *Coin's Financial School*.[31]

Indeed, Laughlin found intolerable the suggestion that he—an expert in political economy—had been bested, albeit in literary form, by an unschooled child. He wrote a series of editorials for the *Chicago Times–Herald* repudiating Harvey's views. Later these articles were followed by an essay, "Coin's Food for the Gullible," and a popular book illustrated with cartoons entitled *Facts About Money*. The professor even agreed to engage in a public debate with Harvey. On March 17 of 1895 the awaited event took place. The goldbug political economist and the silverite publisher squared off before four hundred Chicagoans at the Illinois Club. A more accurate reading of history was on Laughlin's side, but Harvey showed greater sympathy for the human cost of a strict monetary policy. Laughlin's disdain for those caught in a cycle of debt and his lack of interest in the social impact of declining prices was evident.[32]

Laughlin's conservative political views also permeated his classroom at the University of Chicago. One student remembered: "There never was any doubt about where he stood on any question he discussed. To the student who wanted to listen and believe, this was downright dogmatism." Another agreed: "Laughlin was a 'publicist' rather than a 'scientist' and 'academician.' He could not forebear 'taking sides' and strongly supporting the 'side' to which he had given his conviction." To this young scholar, Laughlin's style stood in marked contrast to that of Veblen. "I am quite aware that Dr. Veblen had his preferences—not to say prejudices—relative to the subjects with which he dealt in class. But he very rarely discussed his own personal convictions in the classroom. . . . Dr. Laughlin, on the other hand, could not refrain from being 'the propagandist,' if you will, in class." While some students found his style oppressive, others perceived Laughlin as tolerant of dissenting views. Edith Abbott noted that Laughlin "gave each one of us an opportunity to disagree, and . . . apparently never cherished anything but kindly feelings toward those who refused his conclusions." But all agreed the professor's own opinions were never very difficult to divine.[33]

Breckinridge may have selected Laughlin to guide her studies in political economy because he was extremely sympathetic to women students. Even as a young professor, Laughlin earned a reputation for his kindness towards and encouragement of female scholars. At Harvard, he assisted young women enrolled in the Annex, as Radcliffe was then called, who wished to study political economy. By the time he was appointed a head professor at Chicago, the classical economist had extensive experience with coeducation, especially for a teacher of his generation. Breckinridge remembered that

> [he] was strangely lacking in any of the inhibitions which characterized so many able men in dealing with women whether as co-workers or as students. In a long life of association with men and women scholars Mr. Laughlin stands out as one of three or four who found it possible himself and made it possible for others to be wholly unconscious of the fact of differences of sex.

Edith Abbott felt the same way. "Professor Laughlin was," she said, "extremely generous about helping women students, at a time when women students were not particularly welcome in many Departments of Economics." Apparently as rigorous with women as he was with men, Laughlin managed to be challenging and supportive at the same time.[34]

Laughlin had a habit of snaring his students into research on monetary policy, but during her first years at Chicago, Breckinridge focused most of her attention on political science. Her studies with Ernst Freund led her to take *The Judicial System of Kentucky* as the subject of her master's thesis. Using her knowledge of legal history and her skill in analyzing court decisions, Breckinridge researched the evolution of courts in her home state. She completed much of her work at home in Lexington. After finishing a year of graduate school in 1896, a lack of funds made it impossible for Sophonisba to return to the University of Chicago for another year.[35]

More or less undaunted, she continued her studies on her own, balancing research on her thesis with domestic responsibilities to her family. In the spring of 1897, her brother Desha offered Sophonisba a vacation trip wherever she wanted. She long remembered her response to his generosity. "I said that I'd like to go to Chicago to take my examination, and he affectionately exclaimed, 'Well, go take your damned examination.'"[36]

Breckinridge passed her test with ease and the University of Chicago awarded her a master's degree in political science in July of 1897. With Marion Talbot's help and the support of Ernst Freund, she secured a fellowship in political science that permitted her to return to Chicago in the fall of 1897, and to continue studying for a doctoral degree.

To attain the status of Fellow required more than financial need. Fellowships were awarded on merit, and the holders were recognized as students of considerable distinction within their departments. Although many women received these awards, there was apparently some sex discrimination in determining the level of support. In the winter of 1897, Breckinridge explained the problem to her father.

> I don't believe there is any danger of my not getting my fellowship for another year; but I also think there is no chance of my getting the higher one—the $500. I don't believe they will ever give one of them to a woman again, except under extraordinary circumstances, when she has done a large amount of work and is fairly well on in years. A good many of the officers of the University are down on the women fellows for marrying off so, and I don't blame them, and I feel sure that no woman in our department will get a $500 fellowship for years.

The implications of the story are clear: a serious woman scholar would forego marriage. This was a sacrifice Breckinridge appeared willing to make. With funds from her scholarship, recognition for her talent, and a paying position as Marion Talbot's assistant, Breckinridge settled into a woman's dormitory and her life as an advanced graduate student. She was never again to leave the University of Chicago for more than a brief trip.[37]

When Breckinridge returned to Chicago in 1897, she continued her studies with Freund and Laughlin. As was the case with many other graduate students of her generation, she labored on a dissertation topic suggested by her head professor. Still in the heat of the battle over monetary policy, Laughlin urged Sophonisba to write a "history of legal tender doctrine in the United States."

The work that resulted drew heavily on Breckinridge's lessons with Freund. Using history and law, she traced the ways English and American governments had gone about "bestowing upon money the quality of being a legal tender." Her focus was on the power of the state; her interests "constitutional and legal" rather than economic. Can a government rightfully claim the power to determine legal tender? On what basis does the state justify its authority over currency? Does history show an abuse of state power so drastic that limits should justifiably be placed on government authority? These questions lay at the heart of Breckinridge's study.[38]

Such concerns seem archaic by the standards of our own time. But the questions Breckinridge posed about governmental authority and monetary policy engendered lively debate in late-nineteenth-century America. The financing of the Civil War through "greenbacks" and the sale of bonds set off a storm of controversy that lingered for years after Appomattox. How should the bonds be paid back? Were the paper notes convertible to specie? These questions were hotly debated in the aftermath of the war. Once the war debt was retired, larger issues about the direction of government monetary policy surfaced that turned on the question of whether an inflationary or deflationary policy should be pursued.

These issues pervaded late-nineteenth-century politics and bitterly divided several constituencies within American society. By the 1890s, much of the controversy focused on the coinage of silver and the gold standard. But the problem Breckinridge selected to study—legal tender—was still freighted with contemporary significance. The conferral of the status of legal tender touched on one of the most sacred of late-nineteenth-century rights: the freedom of contract. The privileges of creditors, the responsibilities of debtors, and the role of government in arbitrating the two generated a good deal of the heat engendered by the "money question."[39]

Breckinridge hoped to clarify the prevailing controversy "by reference to the facts of history, by an examination of the record of what has been done, what agency has been employed, what reasons have governed action." Thus "a proper setting" would be provided for an analysis of "economic aspects of the subject." Her purpose reflected Laughlin's oft-stated, if rarely fulfilled, ideal of using social scientific knowledge to provide a basis for informed public policy.[40]

For the most part, Breckinridge's dissertation was a straightforward, if dry, historical account of legal tender policy in England and America. Only in her discussion of Civil War finance did Breckinridge, in a flash of sectional loyalty, depart from her careful and seemingly objective analysis of monetary policy. She argued that congressional actions during the war far overreached constitutional powers. There was no constitutional provision for the issuance of the war's legal tender notes, she claimed, "because it was intended that neither in the state nor in the federal government should such a power reside." Breckinridge applauded the Supreme Court's 1870 decision in Hepburn v. Griswold that struck down the wartime Legal Tender Acts. But when a reconstituted Court reversed that decision just a year later, Breckinridge contended, it was "a deplorable incident in the history of the United States judiciary." To reverse so quickly a court decision because of a "change of personnel" ignored "all considerations of judicial dignity, of regard for precedent, of desire for the stability of law."[41]

Breckinridge opposed the government's issuance of paper money, because the notes "injured" a "private individual, the creditor," who "by a compulsory act of government" was "forced to share with the government, or bear for it, the cost of the conflict then being waged." This was a very conservative view. Indeed, Breckinridge believed that during the war, "an act as tyrannical as any act of Henry VIII in dealing with his coins found legislative and executive support and judicial sanction."[42]

In essence, Breckinridge's dissertation supported important aspects of Laughlin's sound-money religion. The rights of creditors were emphasized and the inflationary policy of the government during the war was condemned. In all, it was a conservative recounting of recent U.S. monetary history. Yet the style of the work added to its substance. Like her teachers, Breckinridge attempted to shed light on existing public controversies by means of scholarly research. She used history to provide distance on current debates and to demonstrate the evolution of political conflict. While the rights of the poor, instead of the claims of creditors, soon preoccupied her, the desire to address public problems by using scientific research and knowledge had already emerged.

Most important, her dissertation revealed that Breckinridge saw government power as malleable. She recognized that "considerations of a political and material character" influenced law. Although she criticized the "tyranny" of monetary legislation passed during the war, she issued no blanket condemnation of federal power. When government served a public good, she deemed sweeping actions justifiable. Like Freund, Breckinridge viewed as legitimate the exercise of federal authority in regulating economic affairs. This idea was an intellectual precondition for the modern welfare state Breckinridge would later endorse.[43]

IV

Problems of finance also claimed Katharine Bement Davis's attention when she began her studies in political economy in 1897. Unlike Breckinridge, Davis felt no special affinity for J. Laurence Laughlin or his political causes. She came to Chicago with her own ideas about social problems, and her well-developed "liberal" politics clashed with those of Laughlin. Although she took courses with the conservative political economist, Davis dismissively stated: "I did not get one single thing out of his classes that I could not have learned equally well out of books." She once described how Laughlin needled her by constantly challenging her comments in class and dissecting her term papers in search of socialist ideas. "There it sticks up its head!" he would exclaim when he thought he had hit pay dirt. "I did not mind this in the least;" Davis claimed, "on the whole I thought it rather funny."[44]

Davis took the finance course with Adolph Miller that was *de rigueur* among political economy graduate students. She found Miller "stimulating," but she felt little attraction to his subject. In retrospect, Davis observed that even though "finance was not especially in my line, I was thankful later on for what I learned."[45]

Her real mentor at Chicago was Thorstein Veblen. He was, Davis said, "the man from whom I got the most in the Department of Economics." Veblen never had problems drawing women students; many of them appreciated his quirky charm. His penchant for extramarital affairs eventually cost Veblen his job at Chicago, but several female graduate students remembered him as an always shy and proper man. When Edith Abbott's niece, an undergraduate at Chicago in the 1930s, heard the legendary tales about Veblen, she quizzed her aunt about her admired teacher. "He was always a gentleman with me," Edith Abbott stiffly replied.[46]

Davis found Veblen to be "rather shy of women." She tried to draw him out by inviting him to dormitory dinners, and the two quickly became "great friends." Their relationship endured when Davis left Chicago. After Veblen was fired by Stanford in 1909, again for involvement with a woman who was not his wife, he wrote to Davis asking her to keep her faith in him no matter what she heard.[47]

Davis chose Veblen to direct her work at Chicago because "he was sympathetic and made one think." It was hard to figure out where Veblen stood, and Davis greatly admired her professor's ability to lecture and teach about controversial subjects without ever revealing his hand. "It was said in the Department," she recalled, "that he was the only man in the world that the trustees and the faculty would dare permit to lecture on socialism, because no one knew when he got through which side he was on, and you couldn't possibly get it out of him by questioning!" Davis liked to tease Veblen about his convoluted style and his preference for polysyllabic words. Her own forthright manner countered her professor's marked tendency to withdraw. Theirs was an unusual and interesting student–teacher relationship, profitable and pleasurable for both.[48]

Davis's first research efforts as a graduate student clearly reflected Veblen's intellectual influence. During his early days at Chicago, the political economist taught a course on American agriculture at the university. In 1892 he wrote two articles for the *Journal of Political Economy* discussing farm prices. Davis published a scholarly article for the *Journal of Political Economy* in June of 1898, "Tables Relating to the Price of Wheat and Other Farm Products Since 1890," which followed up on Veblen's initial findings.[49]

The work of both teacher and student analyzed in technical terms the problems faced by American farmers. Veblen documented wide fluctuations in the price of wheat, and he pointed to the growing impact of industrial development on agriculture. Davis detailed the declining price of wheat and most other farm products since 1890, noting a drastic drop in 1894. That year, she explained sympathetically, wheat was at "a price at which the farmer claimed, undoubtedly with truth, that he could not afford to produce." Davis pointedly observed that United States consumers gained from worldwide depressed prices, "if there be any benefit to any one during a period of great depression." Although hers was a straightforward analysis of price data, Davis's sensitivity to the impact of falling prices distinguished her views from the classical laissez-faire economics advanced by Laughlin.[50]

Veblen encouraged his students to enlarge their understanding of human behavior by studying anthropology. Fascinated himself by the rituals and mores of obscure tribes, he believed that anthropology placed contemporary society "in perspective." When faced with a choice between political science and sociology, Davis selected sociology as her "minor subject." She did so "against Prof. Laughlin's advice" but probably with Veblen's blessing. She studied with Albion Small, George Vincent, and W. I. Thomas. Small especially reinforced with theory the intellectual style Veblen practiced in fact: he emphasized the importance of conducting objective research on real social problems. The accumulation of facts and the use of direct observation were encouraged as a way of understanding and improving "the social process."[51]

American sociology was still in its formative stage during the years of Davis's studies. In fact, the University of Chicago's was the first Department of Sociology in the United States. Head Professor Albion Small shaped the department and helped define the new discipline. Perhaps more than any other social scientist in the founding group, he unified in his career two major components of late-nineteenth-century intellectual life. Devoted to empirical study and attentive to reform, he brought to the university the influences of German historicism and evangelical Protestantism. Both played a significant part in shaping the course of sociology in Chicago's early years.[52]

The son of a Baptist minister, Small followed in his father's footsteps and prepared for the ministry at Colby College (then a Baptist school) and Newton Theological Institution. Though he chose the life of a scholar over that of a divine, Small's piety could be seen in the later stress he placed on ethics in the new science of sociology. Small's scientism owed its strength to other formative experiences. Like many students of his generation, he migrated to German universities to pursue a course of study unavailable in American academic institutions of this time. Between 1879 and 1881, first at the University of Berlin and then at Leipzig, Small served an intellectual apprenticeship that exposed him to the influential German historical school.[53]

From professors such as Adolph Wagner and Gustav Schmoller, Small quickly mastered principles that were transforming modern social thought. Fresh methods of investigation and a dynamic theory of social development were among the lessons he learned. Small left Germany a firm believer in empirical research. A "modern" scholar, he now placed his hopes for social understanding on the scientific methods of investigation, observation, and inductive analysis.[54]

Small's discoveries in Germany also cleared a path for him to put his social expertise in the service of reform. Thus he built a bridge between his old religion of Protestantism and Christian ethics and a recently acquired religion of science and reform. Professors Schmoller and Wagner again pointed the way. Believing that their social investigations uncovered scientific truths about reform, these men formed a *Verein für Socialpolitik* along with several other German scholars. The professors hoped to use their growing expertise to advance enlightened public policy. This kind of social action flowed logically from the tenets of the German historical school. Much impressed, Small enlarged upon these views. By the time he joined the faculty at Chicago, he believed that values could be established scientifically. Small credited social scientists with special expertise about reform.[55]

Davis's other sociology professors shared and enlarged on these views. George Vincent endorsed empirical research, but this son of the founder of Chautauqua liked to tie the mission of sociology to popular education. The aim of sociology, he wrote in a volume co-authored with Small, was "the development of social health." The man Veblen most admired, W. I. Thomas, focused his attention on comparative ethnology. Thomas was himself an early graduate student at Chicago; he earned a doctorate from the university in 1896. Although Thomas was then preoccupied with the innate characteristics of races, he shared Veblen's interest in the social meaning of customs, particularly those that evolved into modern life from their origins among "primitive people."[56]

Davis's dissertation topic drew on her work with Veblen and the sociologists. She proposed to study agricultural workers in Bohemia in an effort to understand the various causes affecting the standard of living and wages. With a fellowship from the New England Women's Educational Association, she set out for Europe in 1898. The year abroad added twenty pounds to Davis's frame and gave her a glimpse of royalty. She recalled that

> I felt that I knew Emperor William very well, for when I was a student in Berlin, a four o'clock seminar took me to the University several times a week, and always it seemed I reached Unter den Linden just as the Emperor returned from his afternoon horseback ride in the Tiergarten. He went accompanied by only two or three of his gentlemen-in-waiting. I stood on the edge of the sidewalk and waved at him anything I happened to have in my hand. He always saluted very politely and I daresay said to himself, "Another crazy American."

Studying in Germany at the University of Berlin and in Austria at Vienna, Davis gathered material for her thesis. The work that resulted explored factors that shaped the living conditions of farm labor in Bohemia: their lot was then compared to that of Czech immigrants who had settled in Chicago. In September of 1900, an excerpt from Davis's work was published in the *Journal of Political Economy*.[57]

Her essay, "The Modern Condition of Agricultural Labor in Bohemia," offered a compassionate portrait of Czech farm workers. As with Breckinridge's work, history was central to the young political economist's analysis. Davis traced the oppressive burdens imposed on peasants to feudal relations that persisted down to the Revolution of 1848. The "greed" of large estate owners, and the inhuman working conditions they imposed were detailed. Exploitation of child laborers had been rampant, Davis explained, and as a result, young Czechs grew ill and "stunted in their growth through the severe labor to which they were subjected." While conditions improved after the abolition of feudal servitude, vestiges of the old system remained. Davis saw land ownership as a crucial determinant of the standard of living among peasants.[58]

Davis relied on personal observation, public records, account books, government statistics, and interviews with workers and estate owners to construct her analysis of "modern" economic conditions in the region. These methods of research were groundbreaking. When W. I. Thomas used a similar approach in 1908, the work that resulted ten years later, *The Polish Peasant in Europe and America*, was considered a landmark in the study of sociology.[59]

In Davis's thesis, the availability of land, the supply of labor, the type of agricultural work available, and the quality of wages were all explored. Her sensitivity to the rigors of empirical research was apparent in her detailed discussion of "real wages." Her case study approach also incorporated much of what was modern in the lessons of her professors. Forsaking the untested laws of traditional political economy and the abstract hypotheses of social theorists, Davis met the Slavic workers on their own ground.[60]

There Davis's own values and preoccupations shaped her perception of Czech life. For instance, the Chicago graduate student took a special interest in female agricultural workers. "Women," she explained, "form a very important part of both the two classes of agricultural day labor" in Bohemia. From the account books of one employer, Davis determined that women labored nearly eight hours a day during the winter, and "12, 13, and 14, in summer, when 'overtime' means work until dark." As part of her duties, the Czech woman performed heavy farm labor, and for her efforts earned between six and ten cents a day. Using statistics, Davis calculated that male wages were "as a rule about one third higher than a woman's at the same time and place." This inequality had deep historical roots.[61]

Her study of nineteenth-century farm workers in Bohemia laid the groundwork for an analysis of immigration to the United States. Noting the "triple movement" of peasants from the country to the city, from one province to another, and from Bohemia to America, Davis spoke with sympathy of the plight of farm workers. She stressed the role of economic factors in luring farmers from the rural districts. In important ways, this perspective anticipated the conclusions W. I. Thomas would reach, with Florian Znaniecki, in *The Polish Peasant in Europe and America* (1918). Both student and teacher emphasized the influence of social, economic, and political forces in the lives of the foreign-born. When regarded in the context of nineteenth-century race theory, this perspective is forward-looking, because it stresses environmental factors in the social dislocation of immigrants, rather than blaming the foreign-born themselves.[62]

Davis's and Thomas's views stood in marked contrast to the shrill voice of sociologists such as Edward A. Ross, who wrote with a contempt unencumbered by sociological research of "the dull, fat-witted immigrant." Davis's experiences at the settlement house had given her a familiarity with immigrants and Eastern European cultures that informed her intellectual work. By the time her views found their way into the *Journal of Political Economy*, that earlier sensibility had been sharpened by "scientific" investigation and honed to academic respectability by social research.[63]

The distance Davis had traveled from the settlement house to the university was apparent in her embrace of the emerging professional standards of academic social science. In spite of her disdain for Laughlin, she gave credence to her professor's view that scientific knowledge was a superior avenue toward social understanding and enlightened reform. In a revealing review published in the *Journal of Political Economy* in March 1900, Davis praised W.E.B. DuBois's *The Philadelphia Negro* and a companion study, *Domestic Service*, by Isabel Eaton, issued with DuBois's work, for advancing understanding of the black community through empirical research. "It is a commonplace," she noted, "to say that any attempt at solving a problem should be preceded by a clear understanding of what the problem involves." But it was DuBois's masterful performance as a social scientist that allowed him to

> reach the facts of the case, to see them in their true proportions, to separate cause from effect, to trace out the action of special environment, and beyond this, to set forth the results of his study in a clear, concise, and scientific manner.

His impressive "intellectual training, tact, and sympathy," his "intensive study" of the Seventh Ward, his "statistical and historical material," and his use of "a house-to-house canvass" gave weight to DuBois's work. "The tone," Davis noted in words Laughlin and Small would have approved, "is not that of a reformer pleading for justice against a great wrong, but that of the scientific investigator who looks at things as they are and states what he sees without praise or blame." Such an accurate study, Davis concluded, "cannot fail to throw some light on the negro problem as a whole."[64]

Davis also approved of DuBois's analysis because it supported her own perspective on social problems. His study of black Philadelphians demonstrated that "the causes of poverty are largely historical in character. Low wages are explained when we consider the few occupations to which the Negroes are limited and the great competition that ensues." The information on black women workers unearthed by DuBois especially interested Davis. She quoted at length the Pennsylvania sociologist's conclusion that black women faced terrible restrictions in the labor market and suffered greatly from poor wages. Eaton made the trend even clearer in her analysis of the wages of domestic servants. Her study, Davis said, "shows that men in domestic service receive close upon 100 per cent more wages than women."[65]

Traditional notions about "uplift" could also be detected in Davis's views. Noting that "the prejudice of whites" was a central factor in the Philadelphia Negro's experience, she voiced special regret about housing discrimination. "Restricted to certain portions of the city inhabited chiefly by his own race, or by the lowest of the foreign white population," the black Philadelphian suffered from his lack of proximity to middle-class whites. "All the incentive that would come from living beside people whose standard of life is possibly higher than his own is lost." Davis invoked the sociological theory of "imitation, shown to be so powerful a force in molding a civilization," in warning of the dangers of such "herding together." Yet the greatest evils of "class prejudice," as she called it, were economic. "Class prejudice is . . . one of the chief causes which prevent the negro from acquiring experience and from gaining in efficiency by doing."[66]

Davis's research as a graduate student expressed interests and values that would pervade her later work. She perceived social dislocation largely as a product of poor economic conditions. Rather than blaming the poor for their misfortunes, she looked to the social and economic environment for the causes of contemporary unrest. Davis also evinced a special concern for the problems faced by women. She saw a commonality in the oppression of women workers—whether they were Czech peasants or black domestic servants. Both suffered the dual burdens imposed by sex and class. Finally, Davis embraced empirical research as the route to intelligent social understanding. Knowledge, she believed, was a precondition for reform.

V

Similar values were evident in Frances Kellor's work as a graduate student. During four years of graduate study, Kellor tried to contribute to the theoretical foundations and methodology of sociology in research on crime. Because the discipline of sociology itself was so new and ill-defined when she began her work in 1898, Kellor enjoyed considerable latitude in pursuing her interests. She studied mostly unencumbered by the weighty, and often conservative, intellectual traditions that Davis and Breckinridge faced in the Department of Political Economy.

But unlike her two contemporaries, Kellor never earned a doctoral degree. Her interests were largely in the wing of academic sociology most attentive to reform. The "practical sociologists" were still very much in evidence at Chicago when Kellor began her graduate training in 1898, with Charles Henderson and Charles Zeublein keeping that orientation alive. In spite of publishing major articles in the *American Journal of Sociology* and a book, *Experimental Sociology*, in 1901, Kellor left the university when new opportunities for applied study appeared in 1902. Still, she took with her a view of social inquiry and an approach to social problems that incorporated scientific values and reform.[67]

Among her teachers at Chicago were Albion Small, W. I. Thomas, and psychologist James Angell. An aggressive advocate of coeducation at Chicago, Angell was a functionalist who stressed the importance of experimental work. His teaching built on ideas Kellor had been introduced to by Edward Titchener at Cornell. A structuralist, Titchener probed the workings of the mind through various techniques, including word association. Kellor drew on these methods in her own experimental research.[68]

But Kellor's enthusiasm for criminology made Charles Henderson the natural choice to guide her studies at the University of Chicago. Henderson approached the fledgling academic discipline of sociology with an open commitment to reform: he came closer to advocacy than most of his colleagues

at Chicago. Outwardly he swore allegiance to the primacy of science in sociological method, but this Baptist minister inwardly felt a calling to social
action that flowed largely from the spiritual world. Henderson resembled the
kind of "expert" who figured centrally in the evolution of nineteenth-century
social science. Amateurs by the professional standards that soon emerged,
men such as Henderson added an evangelical cast to the alliance between
science and reform.[69]

Henderson's profession as a minister sparked his interest in practical
social investigations. An 1870 graduate of the "old" University of Chicago, a
Baptist school that did not survive, Henderson also attended divinity school
in the city. While still a student, he served in a church in the Chicago Stock
Yards. Henderson acquired a reputation as an expert on social problems during urban ministries in Terre Haute, Indiana, and Detroit, Michigan. Prisons
emerged as a special interest during these years as he investigated their conditions and their prospects for reform.[70]

Although Henderson earned a doctorate from the University of Leipzig
in 1901, he collected this academic credential only after teaching at the University of Chicago for nearly ten years. His appointment to the sociology faculty in 1892 demonstrated the nascent stage of professional development in
this academic field. In some respects, Henderson was like the architects of the
American Social Science Association, the organization that first displayed an
avid interest in organized social investigation.

Faith in the methods of natural science, concern over the advance of
industrialism, and dismay over the erosion of traditional religious values
determined the Association's course. The group considered social knowledge
a pathway to enlightened reform, but it also clung to classical nineteenth-
century notions that celebrated individual action. Education, civil service
reform, charities, and correction work emerged as favored causes. Henderson
brought many of these issues into the purview of academic social science at
the University of Chicago. The "practical sociology" he advanced blended
ethics, social theory, and pragmatic reform.[71]

Henderson found a forum for his interests as university chaplain and professor of sociology. While hardly enlightened by twentieth-century standards,
his ideas about poverty, mental illness, and crime differed in some important
respects from nineteenth-century hereditarian views. Committed by his religious principles to uplifting the "degraded" members of society, Henderson
searched for explanations of dependency and delinquency that lent themselves to human intervention. As a result, he expressed some skepticism
about the research of Cesare Lombroso, one of the most influential criminol-
ogists of the day.[72]

Lombroso insisted on the biological basis of criminal behavior. Those
who acted out their contempt for the law showed certain physiological characteristics, according to Lombroso, and anthropometric study could disclose
the distinctive, atavistic, "criminal type." Henderson accepted much of Lombroso's analysis, but he also stressed the role of social, psychological, and
environmental forces in the development of crime. Emphasizing the

"organic" nature of society, Henderson pointed to the similar drives shared by good citizens and offenders. "The wildest freaks of the criminal," he wrote, "may be understood by patient and sympathetic study. Theft is an evil direction of the universal desire for the means of satisfying physical and other wants. Erotic vices are exaggerations of sins not unknown in polite society. Tattooing is an expression of nascent aesthetic tastes."[73]

Henderson urged his students to employ direct observation as a method in their sociological work. Using his own experience as a model, Henderson advanced his case that academics had much to gain from being exposed to the realities of urban life, no matter how awful. "The University cannot neglect any phase of social life," he once wrote. "As in astronomy the study of perturbations in the movements of known bodies leads to the discovery of new worlds, so in social science the investigation of evils brings us nearer to an understanding of the good and helps us on the path upward." This required direct investigations of conditions, even among distasteful criminal populations and the thankless poor.[74]

Frances Kellor readily took up the challenge Henderson set before his students. On a visit to her benefactor Celia Parker Wooley, she explained her work in criminal anthropology. The socialite Wooley recalled: "First she unrolled alot of charts, done in red and black ink, mapping out the human brain and other portions of our mortal anatomy, showing where all our evil passions dwell . . . the delicate nerve-tracks. Next, she took from her bag a queer-looking apparatus, a system of weights and measurements." Wooley and a female friend were somewhat taken aback when Kellor mentioned that her next project would take her to the Illinois State Prison. "She said she was going to spend her vacation in Joliet, and she looked as pleased as if she was going on a pleasure trip to Europe."[75]

Within a year of arriving at the University of Chicago, Kellor published two major articles in the *American Journal of Sociology* on criminal anthropology in its relation to criminal jurisprudence. The essays demonstrated the young social scientist's wish to use scientific knowledge of crime in legal reform. Similar problems engaged her mentor, Charles Henderson. But his deep evangelicalism was nowhere to be seen in his young intellectual disciple. Without the humanistic luster of religious ethics, the dull motive of social control appeared more dominant in the new science of criminology. Whatever their limits as social science, Henderson's religious beliefs forged links between divergent members of human society. Kellor's secular views barely masked a powerful antidemocratic sentiment.[76]

Like Henderson, Kellor attempted to find some middle ground between environmental and biological explanations of crime. She accepted the importance of heredity in the evolution of society's misfits, praising Lombroso and other members of the "Italian School" for their "most elaborate and assiduous investigation, . . . supported by the prestige of prominent scientific names." But these researchers, she insisted, made excessive claims for their fledgling science. Kellor ridiculed Lombroso's assertion that he could identify criminals by looking at their handwriting, and she rejected another scientist's outlandish prediction that "at no distant day a criminal might be recognized and convicted by his physiognomy and the shape of his cranium." She especially regretted that "the hasty and extreme conclusions" reached by the Italian school had discredited other researchers. There was more to crime than biology.[77]

Kellor also found fault with the French school of criminology, which endorsed an environmental view of crime. Quoting Lacassagne's conclusion that "every society has the criminals that it deserves," Kellor explained that French scholars looked for the causes of crime within the social context. While admiring the rich perspective of these dissident scientists, Kellor criticized the lack of scientific rigor in their work. "No laboratory work has been done by this faction," she explained, "as the causes are not sought in the individual alone." The most balanced approach, Kellor argued, was to "consider crime as the result of multifarious causes—anthropological, physiological, and sociological."[78]

By using an integrative approach, the science could render "possible assistance in criminal-law reform." The young sociologist regretted that prisons and modes of punishment were not based on the findings of criminal anthropologists. Criminal anthropology, she said, was "the summit in the evolution of thought" regarding both crime and punishment. Indeed, the "sole purpose" of the discipline was to inform jurisprudence. Once social research established the factors that contributed to social deviance, steps could be taken to remove the most influential causes of crime. Hence, the "doctrines of criminal anthropology" would provide a new basis for reform; scholars would help craft a fair criminal justice system. The conferral of such sweeping authority on the social scientist was justified by the scholar's exhaustive "researches into history, the study of the individual in the laboratory and in society, and of social and legal institutions."[79]

Unbridled faith in scientific expertise held dangers that were fairly obvious in Kellor's discussion of criminal-law reform. Her knowledge-driven reform program had coercive implications. Indeed, in enshrining academic expertise, Kellor criticized basic American legal procedures designed to protect the rights of the accused. For instance, she characterized the jury system as being in a "degenerate condition . . . inconsistent with any theory of a scientific legal system." Ignorance of the circumstances surrounding a crime was considered a virtue in a jury pool, and the "most intelligent, trained, and thoughtful men" were sometimes excluded from service. Complex, modern trials "conducted upon a scientific legal basis" baffled the average juror. The Chicago student explained: "The criminal anthropologist believes that in modern times the common sense of the countrymen of early English history would not be capable of grasping and deciding the numerous and intricate questions discussed in criminal as well as civil actions."[80]

Kellor repeatedly stressed the greater needs of human society over the rights of individuals. The use of informants, the rule against self-incrimination, the plea bargain, and even the principle of presumed innocence, all received extensive criticism. Echoing some experts who would succeed her more than eighty years later, Kellor insisted, "Insanity should be no *defense*, although it may be an *explanation*."[81]

The social scientist envisaged a legal system wherein judges and lawyers received education in "medical jurisprudence and sociology." The election of district attorneys would also be radically changed "under a scientific legal system." A discussion of widely varying criminal codes among individual states paved the way for an endorsement of federal power. "The administration of criminal law," Kellor wrote, "forms a strong argument for the centralization of government power."[82]

There was also a humanistic side to Kellor's views on crime that surfaced in her harsh criticisms of the prison system. Kellor condemned both "the indiscriminate incarceration in prisons and jails of youthful and old offenders," and "the cellular system of imprisonment." She questioned the treatment of black inmates, commenting that "the number of negro prisoners . . . is entirely out of proportion to the negro population." And she noted the nation's "preeminence . . . as the exponent of lynch law." This interweaving of social concern and social coercion became a dominant pattern in Kellor's later work.[83]

Many of the themes explored in Frances Kellor's first essays on criminology were highly derivative. By the turn of the century, theorists of crime increasingly added social environment and psychological factors to their biological explanations of crime. Hereditarian thinking still dominated the field; fear of social disorganization clearly animated many researchers. Most notable in Kellor's early work was her insistence that the academic discipline of criminal anthropology be the guiding star of criminal justice reform.[84]

This view was entirely consistent with the broadly stated aims of the University of Chicago's sociology department. By drawing on Professor Henderson's dedication to reform and dropping his old-fashioned religious rhetoric, Kellor joined the "modern" school of social science that was emerging at Chicago. Wedded to empirical study and increasingly secular in outlook, these scholars nonetheless strove to make their work relevant to contemporary society. Their very definition of social problems ensured a prominent place for academic experts in the work to be done.

The perils of that worldview are well illustrated in Kellor's early research on crime. Her essays expose the intellectual arrogance in the perspective of social scientists who deified their own expertise. Insistence on objectivity acted as a fairly reliable brake on many scholars who addressed public concerns. But others, including Kellor, boldly staked their claim to leadership in public policy. When the subject was as volatile as crime, and the scholar's methods as ill-defined as an 1890s sociologist's, the pitfalls of academic advocacy were immense.

Kellor's unique intellectual contribution as a graduate student evolved from her experimental research on female criminality. During the summer of 1899, she traveled to five reformatories and prisons in New York, Ohio, and Illinois to investigate the female prison population. The results of her research were published in the January and March 1900 issues of the *Amer-*

ican Journal of Sociology. This research differed somewhat from her previous studies. Less concerned with the theoretical underpinnings of criminal anthropology, Kellor sought to contribute to the empirical base, and hence the respectability, of sociology. "One of the charges most frequently brought against sociology," she explained, "is that it consists only of theories, and these often of doubtful practicability. It is said its basis of fact is not sufficient to warrant its claim to the distinction of being a science."[85]

Kellor sought to ground her investigation of crime in scientific fact. On visits to institutions such as New York's Blackwell Island Penitentiary and the Illinois State Prison at Joliet, Kellor unpacked her anthropometric gear and set up a serviceable laboratory. She took physical measurements, conducted psychological tests, and pursued sociological research drawing on prison records, interviews with female inmates, and field visits to their home towns. As a control, Kellor performed similar tests on female college students.

Kellor rightly guessed that hers was the first attempt to compare female delinquents with women "from a different educational and social stratum of society." Lombroso had published a book, *The Female Offender* (1895), that found numerous physical abnormalities among women inmates. Until Kellor did so, no one in America had empirically tested his findings regarding female crime. Increasingly skeptical about the hereditarian theory of crime, Kellor incorporated sociology and psychology into her study to avoid the pitfalls of Lombroso's atavism theory. "The criminal has been regarded as a result, a finished product, rather than an individual in a state of evolution, as an organism responding and reacting to various stimuli," she wrote. Kellor believed the wider social environment deserved greater attention in studies of female crime. Referring to biological determinist views, Kellor wrote: "Were man's structure all, with these conclusions no fault could be found, but there remain the mental and emotional impulses, the tremendous forces of social and economic environment, to be reckoned with; for man's life is but the response of the former to the latter."[86]

Her research led to a scholarly critique of the Lombroso school. Careful measurements of college girls and criminals challenged the Italian criminologist's finding that prostitutes were "positive monsters of adipose tissue." The average female student, Kellor demonstrated, outweighed the average streetwalker by a few pounds. The "masculine voices and handwriting" Lombroso detected in his subjects were not apparent in Kellor's. "I found faces with hard expressions, and voices harsh and cynical, but they did not possess the peculiar masculine quality, and I do not believe that harshness, cynicism, coarseness make them masculine." National origin seemed a far greater determinant of physical type to Kellor than criminality. The personal habits and style of inmates also failed to support biological theories. When compared with "the classes from which these people come, who are not criminal, but who have the same cultural and educational acquirements . . . it is difficult to determine any marked differences."[87]

When psychological testing produced some differences among student and criminal groups, Kellor ascribed these variations to social environment. College girls gave evidence of better memories, but inmates suffered from "defective education and lack of practice." Prostitutes wore loud clothes for "economic reasons." Prison conditions themselves influenced the characteristics of female offenders. When the inmates scored lower on vision tests, Kellor interpreted the result in this way: "The irregularity of habits and excessive use of the eyes during night hours, often under glaring lights, must tend to weaken them, as does the use of strong stimulants."[88]

Sociological research into the backgrounds of women offenders suggested that economic factors contributed to crime. Employment available to poor and immigrant women, such as domestic work, was so inadequate that these jobs actually contributed to delinquency. Limited educational opportunity impeded chances for self-advancement, more readily available to those with good educations. Most inmates, she noted, "were idle when the crime was committed." Kellor thus concluded that a lack of useful work was "a predisposing factor, giving the opportunity for crime which a busy life would not permit." The notion that "the economic conditions of women render her liable to immorality" was endorsed. Observing the prevalence of married women with children in the prison population, Kellor dryly concluded that "forces stronger than a home and motherhood are in operation in sending women to penal institutions."[89]

Kellor even attacked sex role stereotypes for obscuring the true nature of female criminal behavior. It was, she wrote, the "prevailing opinion that when women are criminal they are more degraded and more abandoned than men. From the observation of the two sexes, this seems due rather to the difference in the standards which we set for the two sexes." Women offenders strayed further from societal expectations of proper behavior than men because they were measured against "the ideal of woman." While smoking and swearing seemed "bad habits" in women, "among men we should not consider them in the same light." For both men and women, crime grew out of a poor social environment. "The woman is not more degraded than the man." These bold conclusions were reached by a woman who had never accepted prevailing standards for female behavior. The tomboy from Coldwater now found in academic sociology a forum for views she had once only instinctively felt.[90]

Like many of her professors, Kellor published her research in popular, as well as scholarly, journals. For academics so inclined, this served the purpose of both educating the public and advancing the authority of professional social scientists. In 1900, Kellor detailed her investigations of female crime for the *Arena*. That same year *Harper's Bazar* printed a piece by Kellor entitled "My Experiments with the Kymograph," describing the instrument used in many of her laboratory tests. Always an endless source of fascination, the grisly subject of crime readily attracted the attention of readers. Literate Americans living at the turn of the century proved to be an especially receptive audience for literature on social deviants. Attuned to the great changes transforming their society, citizens of all stripes wondered about the sources of unrest and the roots of evils newly apparent. Kellor knew how to exploit these opportunities aggressively.[91]

She benefited especially from the social consciousness of female voluntary societies, such as the Chicago Women's Club. They provided the young graduate student with funds to extend her research on crime in 1900. Their support made it possible for Kellor to travel throughout the South comparing the inmates there to their counterparts in Northern states. Within a year, Kellor had collected enough material on crime to publish a book on her findings. Macmillan printed the manuscript in 1901 under the title *Experimental Sociology: Descriptive and Analytical. Delinquents.* Under her name on the title page, Frances Kellor was identified as a "graduate student in the University of Chicago." She was twenty-eight years old at the time.[92]

Acknowledging her intellectual debt to Albion Small, E. B. Titchener, and James Angell, among others, Kellor credited Charles Henderson with providing her with "much of the inspiration and guidance in so dark and forbidding a field." Henderson returned the praise in his introduction to the book. "Miss Kellor is one of the few women in the world," he wrote, "who have begun systematically to study those women who have been condemned for punishable offenses." Calling attention to his female student's unusual choice of subject, Henderson noted: "In a world that lies so far from that of respectable and cultivated life, so forbidding and dark, few educated women are willing to travel."[93]

Kellor's experiences in the field, and the unfriendly reception she sometimes encountered, magnified "the dark and forbidding" side of criminological research. Even though her studies were restricted to female prisoners, Kellor's gender sometimes got in the way. In some Southern states, convicts were leased to plantations for agricultural work. When Kellor attempted to study the inmates so employed, she ran up against considerable opposition from the keepers. "They seemed in constant fear that something would be discovered . . . All requests for visits to the convicts' quarters were met by assertions that it 'was no place for ladies,' although only women were confined there." Convicts sometimes treated Kellor with suspicion, balking at her peculiar laboratory tests and at her strange scientific instruments. One inmate being tested with the kymograph looked over the contraption and remarked, "I never seed such goings on and I've lived in New York nigh onto forty years, too." Kellor approached such resistance matter-of-factly: "Vanity, obstinacy and perversity have to be met," she said.[94]

Experimental Sociology was noteworthy for Kellor's compelling analysis of Southern prisons and black criminal offenders. The book presented information gleaned from her tour of Southern jails, a trip that took Kellor over 3,000 miles. Much of what she uncovered gave little cause for encouragement. Dilapidated buildings, chain gangs, exhausting farm labor, corporal punishment, contagious disease, and poor diet appeared to be the rule rather than the exception. Black prisoners suffered especially under these conditions. Kellor noted, "penalties in the south are extreme and negroes are serving life sentences for crimes which receive penalties of one to five years in the north." Highly critical of the unequal treatment of Southern Afro-Americans before the law, Kellor reported that "a negro may be seen serving a three-year sentence for stealing half a dozen ears of corn to feed his mule." Kellor rejected the notion that blacks possessed an inherent propensity toward crime. She blamed slavery for many of the difficulties besetting the race. If blacks were "several centuries behind the Anglo-Saxon race . . . for the loss of at least two centuries of this time the Anglo-Saxon is responsible." Although far from untainted by racial stereotypes, Kellor's perspective on the plight of black Americans was considerably more sympathetic than that of many of her white contemporaries. She stressed environment over heredity whether the subject in her lab was black or white.[95]

Kellor was also a good deal more explicit in *Experimental Sociology* about proposals for reform than she had been in her previous work. Her book advocated the "establishment of permanent laboratories in penal and correctional institutions" that would scientifically study crime and recommend treatment for offenders. Opportunities for recreation, exercise, religious worship, employment, and education ought to be afforded to prisoners. She also favored the abolition of corporal punishment and belittling forms of discipline, such as striped uniforms and shaved heads, that demeaned the inmates.[96]

Education once again stood at the center of Kellor's "Suggestions for Prevention of Criminality." Although increasingly aware of the social and economic roots of crime, Kellor still relied heavily on the traditional cures of knowledge and healthy community life as solutions to the problems she unveiled. If criminal sociology was a "systematic" science, it offered few sweeping structural remedies for reform. Instead, Kellor presented knowledge itself in various guises as a practical program of social change.[97]

V I

The line between objective social science and applied research, so thin in sociology during Kellor's years of study, could be readily detected in Chicago's Department of Political Economy when Edith Abbott arrived in 1903. By this time, some Laughlin graduate students, such as Wesley Clair Mitchell, were already making their influence felt in academia. And Veblen, in his usual iconoclastic fashion, had become even more outspoken about his discipline's outmoded traditions; as in one article entitled "Why Is Economics Not an Evolutionary Science?" Laughlin still exerted considerable control over the department; he proved to be an important force in Edith Abbott's intellectual development. Nevertheless, the method and focus of her work reflected the growing sophistication of economic science and the increasing importance to the discipline of quantitative techniques.[98]

Abbott's selection of a thesis topic integrated various interests and approaches represented at Chicago. Her thesis, *A Statistical Study of the Wages of Unskilled Labor, 1830–1900*, reflects this. The topic had clear social and political relevance, given the centrality of labor issues in early-twentieth-century America. Abbott's analysis of wages employed the historical approach so characteristic of the "new" economic science. Empirical research provided the foundation for her study. Unlike the investigations of Breckinridge, but similar to Davis's, Abbott's inquiry turned statistical data itself into a primary subject of study. Nevertheless, a familiar preoccupation with scientific understanding and contemporary social issues was evident in her research. Abbott's work followed in the tradition of Wesley Mitchell, who had written a dissertation on Civil War finance. Laughlin kept the focus on money, but it was Veblen who most influenced Abbott, Davis, and Mitchell in their precise studies of economic behavior and trends.[99]

Abbott soon demonstrated that she had a gift for quantitative analysis. Her skill as a statistician was amply evident in an article she published only one year after beginning full-time graduate study. Abbott's essay "Wage Statistics in the Twelfth Census," appeared in a June 1904 issue of the *Journal of Political Economy*. It was a incisive critique of a Federal Census Office report on wages issued with the 1900 Census of Manufacturers. The government study attempted to show the movement of wages from 1890 to 1900 for workers employed in manufacturing. Abbott lauded the aim, but she found fault with the government's statistical method.[100]

Her analysis of the census report demonstrated that Abbott had carefully studied the structure of the American industrial working class. While generally praising the schedule used by census workers, she suggested that the form obscured the prevalence of child labor. Data were collected on children working who were under the age of sixteen, but Abbott wished to know figures on child laborers under *fourteen*. (This was the minimum working age favored by prominent child-labor reformers.) A poor definition of occupations within given industries hid discrepancies in wage rates among workers of differing skills.[101]

What Abbott looked for, and found wanting, in the census report were *quantitative* conclusions about the direction of wages in the late nineteenth century. Failure to provide raw data on "actual rates on wages" prevented researchers from using the census results. Although the government's statistician justified his omissions by pointing to problems of convenience and expense, Abbott held him to a higher professional standard. The census report warned that "statistical art has its limitations." But its critic responded: "No one would question the statement that 'statistical art has its limitations,' but we are unwilling to admit that they are as great as the summary seems to indicate. No one who is familiar with Professor Mitchell's study of wages . . . can doubt the ability of the statistician to reduce the movement of wages to a quantitative expression."[102]

Mindful of the wider public, Abbott feared the government study would confuse the average citizen. The census report's conclusions, she wrote, seemed "temptingly definite, and many people will use the figures who do not stop to read the explanation." The volume suggested that wages had fallen in the United States since 1890. Abbott's apprehensions, however genuine, about the public's misuse of data were essentially conservative. She "regretted" the report did not offer to the discerning reader "any positive statement" regarding wage trends. Abbott believed real wages were stable from 1890 to 1900, even if "money wages fell slightly."[103]

Nothing more plainly suggested that Abbott had internalized the value of empirical research than her recommendation for reform in the Census Bureau. She noted that "no decennial investigation can ever show the real 'trend of wage.'" A ten-year report "would indicate an almost stationary condition," even in a decade that was scarred by severe depression, as the 1890s were. Wage statistics, Abbott asserted, needed to be collected annually; if not by the Census Bureau, then by the Department of Commerce and Labor. Abbott also hoped to see "such important classes of wage-earners as agricultural laborers, miners, and railway employees" included in the census wage reports. With more extensive information, researchers could accurately assess the economic condition of the working class.[104]

Similar intellectual issues informed Abbott's dissertation. In June of 1905, a long essay summarizing her thesis research was published as the lead article in the *Journal of Political Economy*. Entitled "The Wages of Unskilled Labor in the United States, 1850–1900," the paper reflected Abbott's growing interest in economic history and in the conditions of industrial workers. "The great unsettled questions of the day" inspired her investigation. Citing trade-union leaders and Karl Marx's *Communist Manifesto*, she noted that "complaints have not been wanting" that the industrial progress of the late nineteenth century had hurt the working class. Some critics charged to industrial capitalism the inequitable distribution of wealth, "de-skilling" of labor, and wage depression characteristic of modern society. Abbott asserted these problems were "no longer a subject for vague generalizations," since "expert statisticians" had demonstrated that wages had increased over the course of the nineteenth century. The most pressing question now was: Which groups among the working class gained from these economic trends?[105]

"The condition of the great army of the unskilled" was at the center of Abbott's concerns. Skilled workers "with their strong unions and their ability to earn wages" ought to command less attention, she said, than "the helpless masses of the unskilled." Abbott's observations about the plight of industrial workers called attention to structural factors in the American economy that other scholars were often content to ignore. Yet she echoed the views of conservative economists when she placed some blame on the personal inadequacies of working people for the burdens they bore. Cyclical unemployment, low wages, poor education, and inadequate technical training all contributed, Abbott maintained, to the "precarious existence" of common laborers. But the economist also suggested that a lack of "courage [and] divine discontent" kept unskilled workers in their lowly place.[106]

Whatever the origins of the problem, Abbott underlined the importance of facing it. Noting that "unskilled has come to be in a measure synonymous with unorganized and underpaid," she insisted that the circumstances of industrial labor deserved national attention. Workers who were "ignorant, incapable, and for the most part unorganized . . . cannot help themselves." To grapple with poverty, "society must face the question of doing something to help them." More than morality was at stake. "It must not be forgotten," Abbott reminded her readers, "that the unskilled are a dangerous class; inadequately fed, clothed, and housed, they threaten the health of the community, and like all the weak and ignorant, they often become the misjudged followers of unscrupulous men." Here was the familiar specter of loss of social control, never far beneath the surface of so much turn-of-the-century social investigation.[107]

Abbott raised the troubling issue of labor to explain the larger significance of her research on wages. She hoped to illuminate the condition of the working class and to lay the groundwork for a complete history of wages. Her purposes, in other words, were both practical and scholarly. Using information gathered from the U.S. Senate's "Aldrich Report"—*Wholesale Wages, Prices, and Transportation*—among other sources, Abbott constructed new tables revealing wage trends for unskilled workers. Measuring progress from 1860, Abbott concluded that common laborers saw their wages rise not at all from 1890 to 1900; from 1860 to 1900, their wages rose 37 percent. Abbott noted: "In 1899 the wages of this class had increased by only 4.1 per cent." "An extended study of prices and unemployment" would be necessary to determine changes in real wages, Abbott warned.[108]

Invoking the neutrality of a professional social scientist, Abbott avoided drawing conclusions about the important issues she had raised. "No attempt will be made here to discuss the significance of the changes indicated in these tables of wages, or to make any explanation of the causes of these changes. An effort has been made to present the facts as fairly as possible." Abbott hoped her data alone would determine "whether or not the unskilled man has been the victim of the industrial system evolved during the last century." Eighty years later, scholars still rely on Abbott's pathfinding work to document the conditions once endured by the unskilled.[109]

Her training in political economy gave Abbott a skill in quantitative analysis that served her well for the remainder of her professional life. As a graduate student, she learned to use empirical research and historical study to illuminate contemporary economic problems. Abbott rigidly insisted on objectivity: it was the scholar's duty to let "the facts . . . speak without comment." When this economist's voice was heard, the message carried some disdain for the working class. Nonetheless, Abbott chose to focus her intellectual energies on one of the most oppressed groups in the American economy. Her understanding of the working poor soon deepened. But Abbott never gave up her reliance on research as a method of reform.[110]

VII

Each of the women trained at Chicago internalized a set of values that shaped her approach to social inquiry and, later, to social change. All accepted the notion that scholars had a duty to address contemporary problems in their work. All agreed on the importance of empirical research. And all shared the belief that careful scientific investigation was a *sine qua non* for intelligent reform. These ideas owed a good deal to the intellectual and professional preoccupations of their professors—men who belonged to the first generation of modern social scientists in the United States.

The work of Sophonisba Breckinridge, Katharine Davis, Frances Kellor, and Edith Abbott differed very little in style from that of other Chicago graduate students in their departments in the decade from 1895 to 1905. Their classmates, male and female, conducted similar investigations that touched on the pressing issues of the day. Among the dissertations prepared at Chicago during this period were: "A Case Study of Delinquent Boys in the Juvenile Courts of Chicago," "The Development of Industrial Organizations," "The Economic Causes of Large Fortunes," "A Study of the Stockyards Community at Chicago," and even "The Garbage Problem in Chicago." Indeed, many of these theses involved more extensive exposure to reform. Yet the students who prepared these studies had in common a preoccupation with social science and an interest in laying the groundwork for sound social policy. This was the goal set before them by their professors.[111]

What *was* striking in the work of the female graduate students was their incipient intellectual interest in, and sensitivity to, the special problems faced by women. Of their mentors, only Thorstein Veblen and W. I. Thomas set any sort of example in this regard. In 1899, Veblen published an article called "The Barbarian Status of Women," and in much of his work he paid attention to the special roles assigned to the female sex. Thomas, too, struggled with the meaning of sex differences. The curiosity of the women students probably sprang from deeper roots. Their anomalous position as "women of the university" and their own unusual life experiences enhanced their awareness of gender. When mixed with their teachers' intellectual mandate, these subterranean concerns created a unique perspective with important consequences for their subsequent careers.[112]

4

"The Thing for Which You Are Well Fitted"

The freedom to pursue advanced training in the university's lively, support-ive, and challenging atmosphere provided the women social scientists at Chi-cago with an opportunity of inestimable personal and intellectual worth. But the professional advantage gained from graduate study turned out to be far more difficult to measure. At Chicago, academic social science drew life from the idea that power within American society should be derived from knowl-edge. This notion held both enormous appeal and limited practical signifi-cance for the women who joined the university in quest of advanced degrees. They had gained from Chicago a deep appreciation for the values and stan-dards of a profession from which they would be largely barred. After several years of study with outstanding scholars at a first-rate university, and the con-ferral of the highest degree any American scholar could hope to obtain, the women trained at Chicago faced the sobering task of forging meaningful careers.

The values they had internalized during their academic apprenticeship both made this undertaking more difficult and helped point the way. Their university experience sketched an ideal of the scholar as a detached social scientist and an involved social expert. Rigorous scientific research of timely political, economic, and social questions emerged as the central task of a modern social scientist. The pen and the mind, and the scientific principles that were to govern both, took shape as potential agents of social change.

Clearly, academic experts had a critical role to play in modern society. But the nature of their participation in the fray of contemporary affairs was left vague indeed. By their own example, professors at Chicago strongly sug-gested that the university was the place to work out these problems. After all, their positions in academia conferred upon scholars the authority to address modern social problems and the presumed objectivity that made their insight worthwhile. But academic careers at outstanding coeducational universities, such as the University of Chicago, were not readily forthcoming for Marion Talbot's much heralded "women of the university."

There were, however, unusual opportunities for Breckinridge, Davis, Kellor, and Abbott in early-twentieth-century public life. As each woman pursued her interest in contemporary social problems, her path intersected with various organizations and individuals involved in reform. Several influential men and women recognized the social value of the graduates' intellectual skills: they helped the social scientists find a place for their talent in civic affairs. It is ironic that in failing to enter traditional academic life, the women scholars ultimately took a giant step toward realizing the deeper meaning of their professors' goals.

II

The University of Chicago conferred its first doctoral degrees in the social sciences on women late in the 1890s. At that time, employment prospects for women in academia were far from encouraging. Coeducational universities were decidedly reluctant to include women on their faculties, and opportunities for teaching positions were few and far between. Of the nine women who earned doctorates in sociology, political science, and political economy during Chicago's first fifteen years, not a single one secured a regular faculty appointment at a coeducational university upon her graduation. Two thirds of their male classmates were so employed.[1]

The conditions women graduates faced when they left his institution disturbed Chicago President William Rainey Harper. Testifying before the Commissioner of Education in 1901, Harper commented, "So far as I can ascertain, during the past year the appointment of women, east and west, even in coeducational institutions, have [sic] numbered few—fewer perhaps than ever before. Is this progress? Or is it rather a concession to prejudices which, instead of growing weaker, are growing stronger?" Fifteen years later, the United States Government's *Biennial Survey of Education* reinforced Harper's pessimistic view. "In collegiate departments," the report read, "almost 79 per cent of the instructors are men. In professional schools and departments almost 98 per cent of the teaching staff consist of men. Altogether almost 81 per cent of all teachers in universities, colleges and professional schools are men. It is seen, therefore, that the teaching staff in these higher educational institutions consist largely of men, there being about four men to one woman." Looking back over records from previous years, the Bureau of Education concluded that "this tendency in these higher institutions is becoming more pronounced from year to year . . . in general the percentage of men instructors in colleges and universities has been steadily increasing since 1892, while the proportion of women teachers has decreased correspondingly."[2]

While its president expressed concern over the plight of women scholars, the University of Chicago itself had a poor record of hiring women. Although congenial about training them, the social science departments were not overly anxious to employ their female graduates once they had earned their advanced degrees. Some professors undoubtedly wanted their female students to enjoy good professional opportunities in academia, but many bowed to the accepted conventions of the day. Others, including Harry Pratt Judson, head professor of political science, subscribed to traditional notions of women's careers. When one of his graduate students, Madeleine Wallin, gave up her teaching post at Smith College for marriage, Judson congratulated her with these words.

> I am heartily pleased at the news you send me. In fact I am old-fashioned enough to think that no avocation for a good woman is higher than being a good wife for a good man—and it is my notion that only abnormal women think otherwise—in her heart of hearts no woman thinks otherwise. So you see the higher education in my opinion is by no means merely a device for fitting girls to teach or write. It is intended to make a woman more of a woman.[3]

Whatever its professors' attitudes, the University of Chicago reflected the discouraging trends the Bureau of Education detected nationwide. Aside from Marion Talbot, only one female held a faculty appointment in the social science departments during the university's first decade: Elizabeth Wallace was an instructor of political science for one year in 1892. Annie Marion Mac-Lean, who earned a Ph.D. in sociology in 1900, received an appointment as an assistant professor in the Extension Division: she still held the rank of assistant professor in 1931.[4]

MacLean's long service at a low rank was the rule rather than exception for women who found employment in American universities. In 1921, an extensive survey by the American Association of University Professors (A.A.U.P.) on the status of women in college teaching outlined in stark terms the low status and limited opportunities for advancement endured by academic women. At twenty-nine men's colleges and universities, only two women joined the nearly two thousand professors there employed. Among 104 coeducational schools, just over 1600 women were found in a professoriate that numbered nearly 13,000. Forty-seven percent of the schools polled by the A.A.U.P. "had no woman holding a professorship of the first rank in the academic faculty." The Association's report concluded that women faced grim chances for promotion, lower pay than their male colleagues, and clustering on the bottom rungs of the faculty.[5]

An extensive study of women Ph.D.s conducted in 1929 reinforced these conclusions. Emilie Hutchinson, a professor of sociology at Barnard College, noted that among the nearly six hundred women on college and university faculties in her survey, "those holding positions of professorial rank were more numerous in the college than in the university. In positions of lower rank the contrary situation was true." Hutchinson concluded that "to the woman with the Ph.D. degree the university offers an opportunity to teach as instructor or assistant or associate professor. Very few women became full professors in institutions for men and women."[6]

This seemed especially true for women in the social sciences. The figures compiled by Hutchinson, the A.A.U.P., and the Biennial Survey of Education included women who taught in the traditional female fields of education, home economics, and nursing. When women Ph.D.s were examined by discipline, Hutchinson noted that almost 50 percent of women with doctoral degrees in the social sciences found occupations in "administrative or executive work." Women social scientists accounted for the highest percentage of female doctorates in Hutchinson's study located in "miscellaneous positions," occupations that could not be easily categorized as college teaching or research. The study included women who had earned degrees as early as 1877 and as late as 1921. Among women who secured academic positions, "professors in the social sciences had had a shorter college or university experience than had those in other fields, their average experience covering a period of thirteen years."[7]

Employment prospects at women's colleges were more encouraging than those at coeducational schools. The 1921 A.A.U.P. study noted only 251 *men* among 989 faculty members teaching at fourteen major women's colleges. Women professors exerted considerable control over some of these academic institutions. At Wellesley College, the faculty was almost entirely female in the early twentieth century, and the institution had been ruled since its inception by women presidents. By 1908, President Martha Carey Thomas of Bryn Mawr was able to boast that "the old type of untrained teachers have practically disappeared from women's colleges . . . [being supplanted by] ardent young women scholars who have qualified themselves by long years of graduate study for advanced training."[8]

These schools often made significant, and excessive, demands on their female professors. It wasn't unusual to find teachers boarding in the dormitories where they supervised the students and their activities. Yet women's colleges provided young female scholars with the only really promising opportunity for advancement in academia. The chance to succeed carried costs that could spell failure. Low salaries, inadequate support for research, heavy responsibilities, and infrequent sabbaticals made it difficult to work one's way up the professional ladder and land at the center of one's field.[9]

Although the discouraging realities of employment in academia were gradually making themselves evident by the 1920s, they could not have been anticipated when the women trained at Chicago were earning their doctoral degrees. In 1892, the year Chicago opened, only about 3,000 men were enrolled as graduate students in all fields nationwide; fewer than 500 women joined their ranks. The number of doctorates conferred on both sexes by American colleges and universities was correspondingly low. From the time the first Ph.D. was conferred on three male scholars at Yale in 1861, until 1890, fewer than one thousand doctoral degrees had been awarded in the United States. Women accounted for fewer than three percent of the recipients. Only one woman earned a Ph.D. before 1880, while twenty-four women received the degree in the decade between 1880 and 1890.[10]

The 1890s brought dramatic growth in American doctorate production for both men and women. As the new universities began admitting women for graduate study, nearly eight times as many women earned Ph.D.s in the 1890s as in all the decades before. The degree was awarded to three times as many men in the 1890s as in the 1880s. Yet during the entire nineteenth century, only fifteen women earned Ph.D.s in the fields of political economy, political science, and sociology in the United States. One third of these were awarded by the University of Chicago, which had been in existence for only eight years. In short, Breckinridge, Davis, Kellor, and even Abbott (the last to earn her degree in 1905) were part of a very new phenomenon. No one could have predicted what the future held for a woman social scientist, whatever hopes she privately nourished or fears she uneasily bore.[11]

III

As dean of women, Marion Talbot began to get a good idea of what was in store as Chicago's first female Ph.D.s approached graduation. Katharine Bement Davis was the first of the four women to complete her doctoral degree. She received her doctorate in political economy *cum laude* in June of 1900 at the age of forty.

Davis had enjoyed her experience at Chicago. Designated a Fellow by her department, she had earned the respect of her professors and the affection of her classmates. Davis remembered a momentary feeling of unease as the only female graduate student in the political economy department.

> The men fellows used for working purposes a seminar room opening off the small library of the department. I had rather understood that they had not favored the innovation of a woman in the department, so I naturally hesitated about joining them there. But one day one of the young men, I think it was Herbert Davenport, now professor of economics at Cornell University came out to me and suggested that I bring my work in and join the other Fellows. I did. And from then on I had a beautiful time.

A contemporary of several of the political economy department's most distinguished graduates, she recalled being well treated by her male classmates. "There were some awfully nice boys there then, and there were several who had taken their degrees in the year or two previous who dropped in on occasion for friendly visits, among them Parker Willis and Wesley Mitchell, both now known to fame in their respective fields."[12]

Davis also profited from the community of women at the university. Sharing living space and seriousness of purpose, women scholars found occasion to delight in each other's achievements, as when Davis was about to complete the requirements for her Ph.D. She later recalled with affection the scene that awaited her after her doctoral examination.

At Foster Hall they had prepared a special feast to celebrate the occasion. I was very late, and the girls had begun to be afraid that something had happened. They had sent scouts out several times to see if they could hear anything. I must have been a sight as I approached! It was in the day of shirt-waists, stiff collars and neck ties—and it was a hot day. I have somewhere a snapshot that was taken of me as I stood on the steps, surrounded by Foster-ites. My cap was over one ear, my necktie under the other, creeping up over the top of my collar; I had a generally bedraggled appearance. But I had passed. To crown the feast which had been prepared was an enormous cake like a birthday cake, and in colored lettering on top was "K.B.D.—PhD."[13]

A few months before that festive day, Marion Talbot received inquiries about Davis from the president of the University of Missouri, R. H. Jesse. He was looking for an "unquestionably good woman" to teach *domestic economy*. But Jesse's letters to Talbot in pursuit of appropriate candidates reflected an ambivalent attitude toward female scholars. On the one hand, the president explained that his university hoped to find a professor who took a modern, scientific approach to her subject. "We want a woman that can develop Domestic Economy here making it include *finally* cooking and marketing." Yet Jesse was equally concerned to find "a woman both a lady and accustomed to good society," a professor who had acquired "from her mother a good head and a good heart." Still, this university president did not want his appointee to behave too much like a woman. "One objection that we have to getting women for anything," he explained, "is that if they come young enough to have a future ahead of them they are liable to get married about the time comes when they begin to become really useful."[14]

The Missouri president felt troubled over one candidate Talbot had nominated for reasons that gave evidence of the obstacles academic women faced. He wrote:

Frankly speaking she does not suit us, but there seems to be a good prospect of possibilities in her. In the first place her education has not been elaborate enough to suit me, and then she is I fear rather young. Further more it seems to appear between the lines that she is pretty. While men never hunt for homely women, and least of all Virginia men, it is not always an advantage to have them too handsome.

Katharine Davis's name might have come to Jesse from those familiar with her work seven years earlier at the World's Fair. Whatever he knew of her credentials, Jesse asked Talbot, "Will you kindly tell me if she knows anything about Domestic Economy, according to our needs here?"[15]

Talbot did play an important role in launching Katharine Davis's career. But the important contact was not a university president and the position was not in academe. Instead it was through Josephine Shaw Lowell, a noted New York charity worker and prison reformer, that Davis got her start. In March of 1900, Lowell asked Talbot whether she knew of suitable college women who might take up a variety of positions, including superintendent, in the new women's reformatory to be opened at Bedford Hills, New York. The reformatory was the third institution of its kind in New York, a product of a long campaign by women who advocated separate prisons for their sex.[16]

Lowell informed Talbot that "it is suggested to me that Professors Veblen, Small, Henderson, Zeublin and Vincent would all probably be interested in giving names of graduates from their sociological courses." Lowell's inquiry underscores the fact that sociological inquiry was increasingly perceived as relevant to social welfare. Some prominent social activists now placed a high value on those who could bring their university training to bear on social problems. The timing was fortuitous for Davis, who was just finishing her degree. Talbot promoted Davis for the job of superintendent, and Lowell responded with enthusiasm. She encouraged the Chicago graduate to take a New York civil service examination, which Davis passed with ease. Soon after, Davis's immediate future was secure. She won the appointment to the Bedford Hills post and left Chicago to begin her work there.[17]

Would Davis have preferred a teaching position in academia? No clear answer to this question emerges from records presently extant. It is possible that Davis always intended to use her intellectual training outside of academe. If this was the case, she certainly chose an unorthodox (and onerous) path to a career, since virtually no occupation, aside from college teaching, required a Ph.D. in turn-of-the-century America. To conceive of a doctoral degree in social science as an avenue of mobility required some imagination. Even though rapid professionalization made higher learning, hard-to-acquire academic credentials, and advanced degrees increasingly valuable commodities as time went on, there was still a long way to go in 1900.[18]

Whatever Davis's motives in pursuing a Ph.D., the most exciting opportunity that arose as she completed her studies came from outside academia. She found her calling in an institution that owed its existence both to the long tradition of female involvement in reform, and a more modern recognition by authorities that old social problems required new solutions informed by academic expertise.[19]

While constrained by the realities of sex discrimination in some sectors of the labor market, the women educated at Chicago reaped important benefits from the wider social and political environment of Progressive-era America. By the turn of the century, two decades of political unrest had coalesced into multiple and broad-based coalitions for social reform. Voluntary associations sprang up across the nation that focused attention on a range of public issues. Philanthropists and private charities bankrolled investigations into the causes of social unrest and funded programs designed to ameliorate social problems. Citizens displayed an appetite for social criticism; muckraking journalists were to make careers out of catering to this desire. Most important, state and federal authorities responded to the insistent chorus of discontent by launching their own investigations of civic problems and by creating new bureaucracies to deal with the realities of modern industrial life.[20]

This wider social climate had never been very far out of view during the years of the women's graduate training. And it was predictable that the vital setting of Chicago and a growing national movement for reform would play a part in shaping their careers. From the start, several factors ensured that the message of Chicago's social scientists would reach beyond classroom walls. Graduate education in the social sciences involved much more than lectures, courses, research, and exams. Students observed their professors translate an intellectual interest in social problems into active involvement with local and national reform. Albion Small joined the Civic Federation of Chicago, a liberal reform group of middle- and upper-class Chicagoans, and soon found himself on a special committee trying to arbitrate a settlement to the Pullman strike. Henderson was predictably among the most active of Chicago professors. But even J. Laurence Laughlin could be found helping his graduate students take the measure of a site for a University of Chicago social settlement.[21]

The city beckoned, and many young scholars, when free from their studies, joined the emerging urban coalition pressing for change. True to Harper's word, the University of Chicago encouraged this relationship by establishing special activities for socially conscious students that plunged them into Chicago's urban life. And the campus itself served as a meeting ground for veteran reformers eager to reflect on the greater significance of their battles for an audience of faculty and students sympathetic to, though somewhat removed from, their causes.

During the 1898–99 academic year, when Breckinridge and Kellor were both in residence at the university, Florence Kelley came to speak to the Sociology Club about her work with the Consumers' League. Titles of lectures by other visitors to the Sociology Club that same year included: "Practical Reform Measures for the Dawn of a New Century," "Recent Methods of Prison Reform," "Preventive Measures in Philanthropic Work," "Social Settlements," and "Sanity in Social Agitation." Lectures of this kind formed an important part of the intellectual ambience at Chicago. Many students could find common ground between these lively discussions and their own academic work.[22]

To be sure, the university was congenial to only a particular kind of social activism. Radical professors who criticized the monied interests that supported the university and the behavior of powerful businesses in the city risked, and at least in one instance lost, their jobs. Middle-class settlement workers, not impassioned anarchists, would have felt at home on their visits to the campus. Yet the ties that developed between some Chicago academics and key city activists resembled the alliances that when built nationwide would support a "Progressive Movement." Those who studied at the University of Chicago in its first decade could easily get a sense that social unrest lurked in the city, and that the moment to deal with it was at hand.[23]

For the young women scholars educated at Chicago, this stirring environment proved to be especially decisive. As one friend of Edith Abbott, her sister Grace, and Sophonisba Breckinridge remembered, "It was Chicago that made these three social workers. It was the University of Chicago that brought them to the city." The special atmosphere of reform so visible in Chicago enabled the women social scientists to find a calling. Although their university training had prepared Breckinridge, Davis, Kellor, and Abbott for a life in academia, they faced serious obstacles in realizing that goal. Their dilemmas were both internal and external; their predicament both of their own making and far beyond their power to resolve. Yet such was the historical moment that unique opportunities stood side by side with intractable impediments. Solutions could be forged that realized the deepest meaning of their graduate educations even while acceding to the regrettable limits the wider academic environment imposed. Crucial in shaping the experience of the female students at Chicago was a corps of active older women both on campus and in the city who helped the younger group to find their way.[24]

Women were at the center of Chicago's reform movements, and the city's many female activists provided a model for the university's students. Indeed, the most towering figure in Chicago reform circles was Jane Addams, with Florence Kelley running a close second. Addams' Hull House emerged as a hub of city activism, with many reformers, including Kelley, actually living in the dwelling on South Halsted Street. The founder of Hull House was a well-known figure at the university and a frequent visitor to the campus. Hull House proved to be a magnet for many of the university's teachers and students, who were drawn by the fascinating mix of working people, immigrants, and socially conscious reformers who often gathered there.[25]

One of the first female graduate students in political economy, Madeleine Wallin, described well the attraction Hull House had for her classmates at Chicago. During the university's first year, female students were housed in the Hotel Beatrice; and Wallin reported in a letter home: "Last Sunday afternoon I went to Hull House to a 'faculty meeting' as they are called for fun— a meeting of the residents of the House, and those who come from outside to teach classes. They have a conference once in a while about the work and Miss Addams invited me to come and bring my friends with me. So four of us went down from the Beatrice."[26]

The atmosphere in the settlement community deeply affected Wallin. As she sat at tea with Hull House residents and fellow Chicago students, Wallin savored the details of simple living and high culture she observed in Addams' home.

> Buttered bread was passed by a trim little maid, and tea was made at the table. We had sauce and cake besides. All was prepared in the kitchen and whisked onto the table in no time. We ate off beautiful blue plates—I have no doubt of fine name for the appointments of the house are nice. Pictures on the walls—most of them the private collection of Miss Addams and Miss Starr (founders of the place) and gathered by them in Europe.

Other students shared Wallin's enthusiasm. "Hull House is very popular," she noted.[27]

I V

Frances Kellor was one of the students who felt the pull of the settlement community. She visited Hull House often during her Chicago years, and even took up residence there when her studies allowed. Like Davis, Frances Kellor benefited from the social climate of which Hull House was a part. She moved rapidly toward reform activities after ending her university studies.[28]

Her reasons for leaving Chicago without earning her degree remain unclear, but financial considerations may have played a role in her decision. Unlike Breckinridge, Davis, and Abbott, Kellor never received a fellowship to support her graduate education. The sociology department seemed less inclined than political economy or political science to honor its female scholars with these awards. Between 1894 and 1899, only one woman received a fellowship from the department, even though seventeen were awarded to men. This in spite of the fact that of the three policy sciences, sociology attracted the largest proportion of female students. Nevertheless, Frances Kellor's professors demonstrated their high regard for her work by publishing four lengthy articles by the young graduate student in the *American Journal of Sociology*. Her academic achievements at Chicago were impressive. One of the few C's that marred an otherwise unblemished record was given, predictably, by Veblen for his course "The Economic Factors of Civilization."[29]

Kellor worked part-time while attending the university and depended, as she always had, on benefactors for additional help. Gertrude Dudley, head professor of women's physical education, helped Kellor finance her graduate studies by hiring her to teach gymnastics. An avid sportswoman, Kellor found in this job intense personal satisfaction, as well as financial reward. Dudley became Kellor's "close and intimate friend." Although little is known of their relationship, it reflected what was to be a lifelong pattern. Kellor formed strong emotional attachments to women, many of them wealthy.[30]

In the summer of 1902, Kellor left Chicago to spend a term at the New York School of Philanthropy and Civics, a social work training center. The summer school permitted Kellor to pursue her intellectual interests in social problems and her growing commitment to social reform. While in Chicago, Kellor had enjoyed her association with female reformers. She owed her graduate education to Celia Parker Wooley and the Chicago Women's Club. Thus it was natural for her to turn to women social activists as she struggled to define a professional career. Aggressive and well connected to prominent and wealthy women, Kellor soon secured the fellowship offered by the College Settlement Association to support social investigation. Now almost thirty years old, she moved into the College Settlement House and embarked upon her new research project. It was ironic, given the dilemmas the women social scientists faced, that the young sociologist chose to study unemployment. She decided to place special emphasis on the problems that beset poor and working-class girls.[31]

V

Davis and Kellor were willing to give up formal ties to academe in the interest of finding meaningful work that made use of their social scientific skills. For them, the future seemed promising, if not necessarily secure. But not all the Chicago women managed to make such a smooth transition from their graduate studies to a career. By the time Sophonisba Breckinridge earned her doctorate in 1901, she felt fully at home at the University of Chicago. Encouraged by her professors, respected for her research, and favored especially by Marion Talbot, who deeply valued the work Breckinridge performed as her assistant, Breckinridge enjoyed great success during her graduate schooling. In May of 1901, when she won her Ph.D. with high honors, J. Laurence Laughlin wrote her the following poem: "Now you're safely aer the bridge, Praise be the name of Breckinridge.—Here we come to say: 'Howdy'. Chanting *Magna cum laude.*"[32]

Once Breckinridge's years of intellectual apprenticeship drew to a close, her achievements seemed to open few doors in academia. Days of triumph as a social scientist in training gave way to years of struggle in realizing professional aims. Breckinridge's success as a graduate student was reflected in her attachment to the values most esteemed by her professors. She internalized the belief that a modern social scientist found his or her life's work in empirical research, teaching, and meaningful investigation of contemporary social problems. A professorship in a first-rate research university made such pursuits possible. But no appointment of this kind was readily forthcoming to Breckinridge. Her effort both to adhere to the values acquired at Chicago and to find meaningful work illustrates very plainly the problems faced by a woman with a deep commitment to academic life.

It was a measure of Breckinridge's ultimate creativity in forging a professional career that she was remembered as one who deliberately rebelled against the prevailing conventions in academia. Edith Abbott told the story this way. When Breckinridge's graduate studies came to an end,

> she had been eager to do something that was really useful and was unwilling to be absorbed into the quiet academic life. She responded eagerly to the appeal that swept so many men and women out of the academic current to face the great social questions of the day—the questions that brought one face to face with the inequalities of life and with all its social injustices.

Abbott claimed that Breckinridge, in fact, "led the way for many of us when she left the more comfortable way of life of the social scientist and went out to work on the new frontier." Charles Merriam, the Chicago political scientist who became a central figure in municipal reform battles, remembered Breckinridge in a similar way. At the end of her life, Merriam led a tribute at the university "to our departed leader," who, he said, "taught us the dangers of academic isolation—the social courage beyond the call of academic duty—and comfort."[33]

But Breckinridge remembered the origins of her unorthodox career differently. "Although I was given the Ph.D. degree magna cum laude," she recollected, "no position in political science or in Economics was offered me. The men in the two departments, Boyd and Miller and Ferty and Wesley Mitchell and S. J. Mitchell and others went off to positions in College and University faculties." In fact, virtually every one of Breckinridge's male classmates who completed the doctorate in political science secured an academic position. By 1931, all were full professors at respectable institutions, including the University of Minnesota and Yale. Wesley Mitchell, Parker Willis, Herbert Davenport, and Harry Millis, men who studied political economy with both Davis and Breckinridge, achieved great success in academe. Wesley Mitchell and Willis served as professors of economics and banking at Columbia, Davenport in political economy at Cornell, and Millis as chairman of economics—and Laughlin's successor—at Chicago. By the 1930s, Breckinridge, too, had achieved the rank of full professor at the University of Chicago, but her professorship was in social work. In fact, she owed her position to a professional school she had helped create.[34]

Marion Talbot took great initiative in trying to keep Breckinridge at Chicago. She pressured Harry Pratt Judson, head professor of political science, to create a place for the female graduate student. As Breckinridge described it, "Miss Talbot then got Mr. Judson to appoint me Docent but no one registered for such courses as I announced." Undaunted, Talbot continued to campaign on her associate's behalf. Throughout her graduate education, Breckinridge had served as Talbot's assistant. The stipend was small, and in December of 1900, a few months before Breckinridge was to graduate, Talbot asked Harper to give the younger woman a raise for the following year. Harper responded that he "made the effort, but failed" to persuade the trustees. "Nothing is being done for next year that is not absolutely necessary," he explained in a January 1901 letter to Marion Talbot.

> I could not say that this is absolutely necessary. Perhaps I ought to have said so. What shall we do about it? Will Miss Breckinridge continue her work next year on the old basis? It seems too much to ask her to do so, but I have nothing definite to propose.

Angered by Harper's indifference, Talbot scrawled her answer to the president's rhetorical questions on the bottom of his missive to her. "I think that if you are willing to quote me you *can* say this 'is absolutely necessary.'"[35]

Whether or not on the "old basis," Breckinridge continued to serve as Talbot's assistant, a position that included clerical duties. To earn her room and board, she also took on responsibilities as the assistant head of Green Hall, a women's dormitory. She resolved the larger dilemma of her career in a manner that had served her well in the past. She chose to pursue further study, this time enrolling in the University of Chicago's Law School, which opened in 1902. Breckinridge's legal studies permitted her to continue working with Ernst Freund, when he left the political science department to teach in the new professional school. Breckinridge held Freund in the highest esteem; the two were very close friends. During a summer trip to Europe in 1900, Freund wrote regularly to his graduate student, asking her to respond "if you feel like it" and advising her to "take me as an example and make the 'I' prominent in your letter."[36]

When the first class of law students graduated in 1904, Breckinridge was among them. She earned the first Doctor of Jurisprudence degree the University of Chicago conferred upon a woman. Reflecting toward the end of her life on her performance at the Law School, Breckinridge wrote: "the record there was not distinguished but the faculty and students were kind, and the fact that the Law School like the rest of the University in the words of the Charter accepted men and women students on equal terms was publicly settled." Others recalled a sparkling performance, including Breckinridge's admission to Coif, the law school's equivalent of Phi Beta Kappa.[37]

During the two years of Breckinridge's studies at the law school, Talbot made annual appeals to Harper requesting a salary increase and an elevated title for her assistant. Harper expressed his willingness to improve Breckinridge's position at Chicago, but he balked at the promotion Talbot had in mind. In January of 1902, Talbot pressed Harper regarding Breckinridge, arguing: "A regular appointment for her removing her from the clerical to the executive staff, would give great satisfaction not only in University circles but in many other quarters, as a fitting recognition of her high scholarship, peculiar executive ability and fine personal qualities." Talbot suggested that "she be appointed either Dean of Junior College Women or Junior Dean of Women at an initial salary of $1200 without room or board." Even more daring was Talbot's suggestion that Breckinridge be offered a faculty appointment. The dean of women's request to Harper made clear Breckinridge's deference to the professional values of her professors. "It is very desirable," Talbot wrote, "that she should offer at least one course but I know from her general attitude that she would not be willing to offer instruction except on the full and free wish of the department—either political science or political economy."[38]

A faculty appointment never entered into the realm of possibility from Harper's point of view. The Chicago president had difficulty enough with Talbot's request for another dean of women, and a larger salary for her assistant. "I regret that I cannot do so much for Miss Breckinridge as you suggest," he replied. "I am not sure about the appointment to a deanship, and in any case we could not find so large a sum as twelve hundred dollars." Harper agreed to double Breckinridge's present salary of $350 to $700, noting, "This, of course, is not much, but it would be necessary to squeeze some other things even in order to do this."[39]

Yet by 1903, Talbot, undaunted, was making another appeal. She told Harper that her deep affection for Sophonisba troubled her when she thought about seeking a more exalted position for Breckinridge at the university. "On the personal side I cannot urge her to remain in a position which has neither dignity nor authority, especially as there seems to be no early prospect of the appointment of a woman of even her exceptional training and ability to the faculty." Although women held professorships at the university, the departments of political science, political economy, and sociology remained an exclusively male domain. Such discouraging realities might have stilled a less persistent voice. "But when I consider what her leaving would mean to me as dean and to the University, I am convinced that I ought to speak more strongly of the value and need of her service," Talbot maintained. Again she asked that her assistant be made a junior dean with "a seat in the faculty."[40]

As Breckinridge's graduation from law school drew near, a solution to her dilemmas at the university emerged. Although William Rainey Harper had responded to Marion Talbot's proposal for a new Department of Public Health or Sanitary Science with favor in 1892, it took another decade before the dream of departmental status was realized. By 1902, Harper appeared more responsive to Talbot's ideas, and the new "Department of Household Administration" was opened at Chicago in 1904. Several factors may explain the president's increasing receptivity to Talbot's plans. An internal dispute over coeducation that pitted the dean of women against Harper's administration apparently played a role. The dispute coincided quite precisely with Harper's warming trend toward Talbot's new department.[41]

As early as 1900, a proposal emerged at Chicago to segregate men and women students in the "Junior College," as the first two years of undergraduate study were known. The idea reflected increasing concern about the "feminization" of the University: in 1902 women accounted for 52 percent of the freshman class. Some professors feared that male students were being overshadowed by the female presence. Talbot believed that the segregation plan was designed to curtail educational opportunities for women; she rejected Harper's notion that separate was equal. Nonetheless, the Chicago president's view prevailed, and sex-segregated instruction in the Junior College began to be put into place in 1903. The system never really worked, and within a few years it had all but disappeared on the campus. Yet the "experiment" left an unhappy legacy. Twenty years after the controversy, Talbot remarked that "the memory of the struggle, a bitter, heated and prolonged one, is still very vivid."[42]

In some respects, Talbot's Department of Household Administration, as the division became known, was consistent with the aims of segregation. The discipline created a special intellectual province for women, unlikely to be of interest to men. The department made an academic specialty of the home, woman's traditional domain. As Talbot admitted to Harper, "I have not pushed my own special line of work because I knew it would appeal chiefly to women." By 1902, many colleges and universities were finding a place for sanitary science, home economics, or household administration in their curriculum. Talbot argued, "there is a growing demand for it—which we ought to meet, if not lead." Harper now agreed.[43]

The Department of Household Administration incorporated many features of the public health program Talbot had proposed in 1892. But the discipline now also emphasized topics normally encompassed by home economics. The subject combined aspects of domestic science and social science, with an interest in "women's issues." Household administration offered students, the catalogue explained, "a general view of the place of the household in society as a means of liberal culture . . . training in the rational and scientific administration of the home as a social unit . . . preparation to serve as teachers of domestic science or as social workers in institutions whose activities are largely expressed through household administration."[44]

Talbot modeled her department after the other social sciences at Chicago. She requested funding for graduate fellowships and a professional journal that would "not only furnish suitable means for making known the investigations of the Department and of the best workers elsewhere, but would meet a need which is felt to be real by a large number of women scattered throughout the country." Consistent with the larger aims of the university, extension work was to be emphasized. Less orthodox were Talbot's requests for a "practice house" and a museum. The practice house would be "an actual household where special investigations might be carried on . . . to supplement the more theoretical instruction of the classroom." The museum, truly the product of the early twentieth century, would "show at all times all kinds of mechanical equipment for the household and demonstrate and test new appliances."[45]

Harper's receptivity to the discipline of household administration emboldened Talbot to seek a faculty appointment for Breckinridge in the new department. Harper understood that Talbot herself would serve as head professor while the venture got under way. Willing to consider expansion of the department "when we are able to see the new students come in for this work," Harper responded coolly to Talbot's requests on behalf of her associate. "I can understand that the presence of Miss Breckinridge will make it possible for you personally to do work in connection with the new department more satisfactory to yourself," he explained. "I have not thought that her connection with the proposed department was in any sense a vital one." Indeed, the president warned Talbot not to link her new venture to her demands for the appointment of the younger woman. "It would be quite a serious matter now to take a backward step in view of the fact that with the Trustees the case of Miss Breckinridge has never been a *sine qua non*."[46]

Harper's objections to Talbot's request did not stem from any personal animosity toward Breckinridge; rather, he felt compelled to hold the line with a dean whose priorities were not his own. While simultaneously warning Talbot away from making demands for Breckinridge's appointment to the new department, Harper mused aloud about the younger woman's value to the university. "I think myself that we should make an effort to hold Miss Breckinridge and I have been thinking on this subject since our interview." Harper expressed cautious optimism to Talbot. "I am hoping that we may be able to work out some plan. It may take a little time, but I have no doubt it will be accomplished." By the end of April, Breckinridge had been offered an instructorship in the new department. In a letter to Talbot, Harper wrote with pleasure, "I am glad to know that Miss Breckinridge feels disposed to remain one of us. There is a great possibility ahead."[47]

Talbot's persistence and creativity carved out a special province for women at the University of Chicago, and enabled Breckinridge to win a seat on the faculty. The new department offered professional opportunities for women who ran up against the constraints academic life imposed on their sex. To establish a new discipline was to circumvent the opposition women faced in more traditional departments. But the Department of Household Administration fell far short of providing the intellectual environment for which Breckinridge's academic training had prepared her. While the political scientist pursued research that resulted in an essay entitled "Industrial Conditions of Women Workers in Chicago Illustrated by the Packing Houses" in 1905–06, her colleagues in the household administration department wrote papers such as "The Relative Digestibility of Animal and Vegetable Albumen," "Loss of Nutrients in Beans Due to Soaking," "Comparative Richness of Gelatin-Yielding Material in Old and Young Animals," and "Pectin Bodies in Fruit Juices and the Effect of Temperatures and Density in the Setting of Fruit Jelly." Such concerns were far afield from the principles of law, political science, and political economy.[48]

Her desire to remain at Chicago, whatever her status, owed a good deal to the lessons Breckinridge had absorbed at the university. Commenting on the "unequaled opportunities at the University of Chicago," Breckinridge especially emphasized the "privilege of working with Mr. Freund and Prof. J. Laurence Laughlin." As long as she could be associated with Freund, Laughlin, and Talbot, she wanted to remain at the university. There were alternatives, as Breckinridge herself explained.

> For a time it was quite the thing to invite me to take positions as Dean of Women. Several colleges or university presidents came to interview me. Between my association with Miss Talbot and my Kentucky origin, I seemed to offer certain qualifications on which presidents of coeducational institutions laid stress. Salary and rank they could provide but not the opportunity for continued research combined with teaching and with the opportunity to develop new resources in the city that made life a continuous adventure.[49]

By 1903, the transition the women social scientists were making in their careers was evident in an event that took place in Chicago. The Association of Collegiate Alumnae's annual meeting brought together educated women from across the nation. One evening they gathered to hear the noted reformer Julia Lathrop put out a call for women "to offer themselves for public service, to learn the conditions under which public institutions exist, and to aid in efforts to release them from political control." Professor Charles Henderson stopped by from the university to say a few words about the importance of "professional education for social service." On the platform sat Katharine Bement Davis, now superintendent of Bedford Hills, who "urged that college women give their help particularly in state reformatory work for women and girls, and presented with great clearness and force the opportunities such work affords for philanthropic enterprise and educational ability." Davis's talk was described in such complimentary terms by another attendee—

Sophonisba Breckinridge. Two years later Frances Kellor paid a visit to the University of Chicago's Women's Union and delivered a similar message. She gave a lecture to those assembled entitled "The Opportunities for Women in Civic Life."[50]

V I

While Davis and Kellor found compelling work outside academe and Breckinridge found a sex-segregated niche within a coeducational school, Edith Abbott pursued a third path open to her contemporaries. After receiving her doctoral degree *magna cum laude* in 1905, Abbott worked and studied for two more years, and then accepted a faculty appointment at Wellesley College.[51]

Of all the early female graduate students in political economy, sociology, and political science, Edith Abbott displayed perhaps the most promise. Her research on wages broke new ground that was of recognized importance to other political economists working in the field. J. Laurence Laughlin took enormous pride in her work, and considered her among his most brilliant students. His admiration for Abbott was apparent in a formal report the head professor of political economy wrote to the University of Chicago's president in 1904–05. Describing a departmental seminar, Laughlin reported: "Probably the most important study presented has been that of Miss Edith Abbott, Fellow, on 'The Progress of Wages in the United States, 1850–1900,' a very elaborate economic and statistical study. The work will win her distinction." A brilliant defense of her doctoral dissertation in 1905 brought similar praise.

> dear Dr. Magna, *in futuro*. I had a feeling that I was responsible for you in a way; but the style with which you showed off makes me think some other had a hand in producing the result, chief of whom was your own self. Anyway, I am patting myself a little on the back just to have a share in the triumph.

But it was Sophonisba Breckinridge who led Abbott to secure her first job after finishing her graduate education.[52]

The two women had been fast friends from the moment they met in Green Hall in the summer of 1902. Abbott attended Breckinridge's course, "The Legal and Economic Position of Women," and their mutual admiration grew. By the time Abbott earned her political economy degree, Breckinridge was actively involved with city reform organizations. She had begun to get about "the city to an increasing extent," once her responsibilities to the university were sorted out. Margaret Dreier Robins had persuaded her to join the new Chicago chapter of the Women's Trade Union League, an organization devoted to helping working-class women organize and improve conditions in the workplace. In 1905, Breckinridge used her influence with the W.T.U.L. and with Carroll D. Wright, then conducting research for the Carnegie Institution, to find Abbott a position worthy of her skills. These contacts led to Abbott's appointment as both assistant to the Boston head of the

W.T.U.L. and researcher for Wright. In the fall of 1905, Abbott moved East. She resided in Denison House, a Boston settlement, and began to study the wages of industrial workers and the history of working women.[53]

The experience in Boston proved to be very demanding, and Abbott felt especially challenged by the Boston labor movement. W.T.U.L. president Mary Kehew expected more than research on the status of women workers. The economist was to work closely with women laborers, organizing them into trade unions when possible. For a young woman raised on the prairies of Nebraska, rough-and-tumble working-class Boston created considerable discomfort. In letters home she asked her sister to "tell Papa I haven't gone over to the Trade Unionists in any such way that he can forget he has a 'tall girl' though she is abroad in 'Bosting town.'" She admitted to being "very much afraid" of the labor groups, worried that they considered her "too conservative" and concerned that she would say the wrong thing. Still, Abbott felt secure enough to assert, "I won't do them any harm and shall get a lot of valuable information out of it."[54]

By the winter of 1906, Abbott was conducting her research in Washington, D.C., the Carnegie Institution's home. But by now she had also set her sights on an academic position. Laughlin encouraged her, and, realistic about the opportunities available in academia, he explored the possibilities at women's colleges. "I am glad that you are thinking of a college position. I shall of course write at once to the President of Mount Holyoke. If they have any sense they will jump at the chance of getting you."[55]

Throughout the spring of 1906, Abbott worked on a series of articles summarizing her research on working women. Laughlin approved of the direction Abbott was taking in her scholarship. He saw a professional advantage in the special topic—women's work—that his student explored. "It strikes me that your scheme is both attractive and worth doing," he commented in April of 1906. "An 'unworked field' is exactly what you want to show the world your investigative abilities. These results are sure to bring you a name, and to place you in a desirable college position."[56]

Before any college position materialized, a year abroad intervened. With funds from the Carnegie Institution, Abbott traveled to England, where she continued her research and her education, studying at the London School of Economics and living at St. Hilda's settlement in Bethnal Green. The year was an important one for Abbott, both personally and intellectually. Her studies at the London School of Economics exposed her to the thinking and forceful personalities of Sidney and Beatrice Webb, who were then teachers at the London School. The Webbs were at the center of London's community of Fabian socialists. More radical than Abbott's teachers at Chicago, they nevertheless also expressed a commitment to scientific investigation of social problems, laying stress on the importance of social reform. While Abbott undoubtedly recognized most of the principles Sidney Webb introduced in his "Methods of Social Investigation," she perhaps gained from Webb a more immediate sense of their political relevance.[57]

Two raging controversies in English politics captured headlines during

Abbott's visit, and she was influenced by her exposure to both. In 1905, the Royal Commission on the Poor Law and the Relief of Distress had been appointed to assess the need for changes in poor relief. Beatrice Webb's appointment to the commission ensured that the "Fabian-Labour" position would be heard. Throughout Abbott's London stay, Mrs. Webb's attention was focused on the commission's work, and there was much talk around the London School of the Poor Law debate. The Bethnal Green settlement, where some advocates of the current repressive law lived, exposed Abbott to the conservative side of the issue. Also compelling was Abbott's introduction to the radical English women's suffrage movement. Deeply moved by the activism of women textile workers in the feminist cause, Abbott grew more interested in the crusade that her family upbringing had led her to take somewhat for granted. In an article written for the *Independent* in November of 1906, Abbott explained her reaction. "To one born and bred a believer in woman's suffrage, but long accustomed to regard it apathetically as something which would come only in that long future which holds so much of truth and justice, the past week in London has been one of inspiration and new hope."[58]

Abbott's studies at the London School and her work at Bethnal Green increased her exposure to social problems, her involvement with social welfare organizations, and her familiarity with the populations they were meant to serve. While strongly affected by the plight of the working class and the poor, Abbott remained somewhat conservative in her views, skeptical of socialism, and disdainful of the chronically unemployed. In one letter to her father, Abbott reported that one British trade union leader "began life as wild as our Mr. Debs." She continued to blame some casual laborers for their own misfortunes. "They have done so much loafing that they aren't fit for anything else & when a man has lived on two or three days work a week for 20 years you can't suddenly transform him into a man of energy." These reports pleased her father, but their bravado belied a considerable degree of intellectual turmoil.[59]

Edith remained committed to social scientific values as she used her new experiences to deepen her research. An opportunity for some limited teaching experience arose when residents at St. Hilda's introduced her to the School of Sociology and Social Economics, a social-work education center. In all, Abbott's experiences in London enlarged her sense of the importance of social scientific inquiry, and the larger purpose it could fulfill.[60]

The long-awaited college position finally materialized in April of 1907, when Abbott was offered an appointment to the economics faculty at Wellesley College. Katharine Coman, chairperson of the department, had a fine reputation in her field, which made the job an especially attractive one for a young political economist. Laughlin was delighted with the news, as he wrote to Abbott in London. "I had already heard from Miss Breckinridge that you had 'arrived.' The appointment to Wellesley I think would be a great advantage both to you and to the College." For Laughlin, the achievement of a faculty appointment clearly meant success. But he urged Abbott to plan for the future, perhaps implying she would one day find a position at a major research university. "I hope that the courses Miss Coman hands over to you are the economic courses and not those in political science," he wrote. "I believe that the result of your work there will put you in the way of getting the thing for which you are really well fitted. Moreover, your work in various lines that you have carried on since getting your degree will be of great advantage to you in your college work." Carroll D. Wright also offered congratulations to Abbott on her achievement. "I am sure you will have a delightful experience there with my friend, Professor Coman, and the others."[61]

The community of women at Wellesley had a good deal to offer Edith Abbott. Among her colleagues there were Vida Scudder and Emily Balch, two women whose commitment to social action far outstripped Abbott's own nascent, though developing, social conscience. If all that Abbott wanted was an opportunity to teach economics and enjoy the company of like-minded women, Wellesley would provide considerable satisfaction. But instead she longed for Chicago. In the summer of 1906, a year before her arrival at Wellesley, Abbott already felt nostalgic about her university years. As her sister Grace attended summer school at Chicago, taking courses similar to the ones she had so enjoyed, and even living in Edith's old room in Green Hall, Edith wrote reflectively to her mother, "I never expect to be so happy again anywhere as I was my first year at Chicago."[62]

Once she was again in an academic environment, Abbott discovered just how great her loss was. The beautiful liberal arts college on Lake Waban turned Abbott's thoughts to the rugged university in Chicago. She longed especially for the air of importance, responsibility, and (perhaps) authority that permeated Chicago's academic community. She was appalled by the lack of seriousness in the Wellesley students.[63]

In a letter to Marion Talbot in October of 1907, Abbott described her impressions of Wellesley. "The most prominent one . . . is the one that struck me so forcibly going from Nebraska to Chicago—the *dignity* of the women students in Chicago as compared with Nebraska—the greater dignity of both places as compared with Wellesley." Especially ill at ease with the prevalence of Protestantism at the college, she complained that "the Christian Association and Sunday School Conventions loom large all over the place and take precedence of things scholarly!" Worst of all, in her opinion, was the behavior of the female students. "It is a constant shock to me . . . to see thoroughly grown up girls racing down the main corridors of College Hall—whistling themselves into the library or classroom—and coming to lectures in gymnasium shirts and shorts—wandering about the village on each other's shoulders."[64]

The opportunity to leave Wellesley and return to Chicago appeared before Abbott's first year at the college was out. While Abbott was still in England, Breckinridge had written to her former student in July of 1907 with some tantalizing news. "There are some interesting possibilities in the near future growing out of the Sage Foundation," she offered. "It looks as though they were going to make gifts for research centers in several places among which there may be one in Chicago." When funds from the Russell Sage Foundation materialized in the spring of 1908, Breckinridge invited Abbott to join the team of researchers gathering at the Chicago School of Civics and Philanthropy, an independent social-work training center that had received the Foundation's support.[65]

Abbott mulled over this new possibility and decided to return. She did so with some anxiety. Katharine Coman hit the roof when she learned of Abbott's plans, and other friends expressed outright dismay. Abbott worried most about Laughlin's reaction. But Breckinridge reassured her that their former professor was "delighted as can be over the fact that you are coming to Chicago. The fact that you are coming to the Institute has dignified it in his eyes as nothing else could." Noting that Laughlin was recommending another Chicago graduate student, Anna Youngman, to replace Abbott at Wellesley, Breckinridge commented: "I think he is recommending her partly for her sake; and it might do her real good, while it cannot do the students much harm, as I take it. She has fine standards of scholarship which perhaps the Wellesley girls need as much as a larger social consciousness."[66]

For her part, Breckinridge had little doubt that a social research institute in Chicago was a better place to be than a sleepy college town. Asked at the age of eighty "what single act in those 80 years she remembered with most pride: the passage of some law she had helped to frame[?] One of her many degrees from various universities[?] One of her courses, unique in our professional schools[?]" she answered without hesitation, "I brought Edith Abbott back to the University of Chicago from Wellesley. That was my best day's work."[67]

VI

Thus, in a short period of time, each of the women educated at Chicago found her way to a career that blended social science and social activism. Their departure from graduate school in the early twentieth century coincided with increasing opportunities for professional work, a growing appreciation of credentials in a modernizing society, and a new responsiveness by foundations, private charities, and social and political institutions to limited change. Their graduate training had inspired Breckinridge, Davis, Kellor, and Abbott to apply their social knowledge to social problems. Their advanced degrees made them attractive to organizations committed to "expert" reform. Although they failed to realize certain goals central to the academic profession, they never lost sight of the purpose of their graduate educations. In fact, they brought the impress of the University of Chicago to the vast world outside that institution's doors.

5

"A Most Scientific Institution"

When Katharine Bement Davis became superintendent of the Bedford Hills, New York, Reformatory for Women in 1901, she arrived with few credentials other than an advanced degree in political economy. Her years at Philadelphia's College Settlement had exposed Davis to the problem of urban crime, but she was in no sense an expert in criminology or an experienced penologist. Neither were most other prison wardens of the day. Yet American prisons, and indeed, the criminal justice system as a whole, were undergoing a metamorphosis during the Progressive era. Davis soon became an active participant in a sweeping movement to alter the nature of criminal punishment and custodial care. Within a decade her reputation as a national authority on prison reform was firmly established. By 1913, the Prison Association of New York looked proudly at Bedford Hills and brashly proclaimed that "under the progressive management of its superintendent, Dr. Katharine B. Davis, the reformatory is becoming perhaps the most scientific institution of its kind in the world."[1]

A year later, the New York State Board of Charities and Corrections was investigating the reformatory for its repressive methods of disciplining inmates. By that time, Davis had left the prison to assume new duties as New York City's commissioner of corrections. Yet in the years between 1901 and 1913 Davis struggled to create a model women's reformatory at Bedford Hills. In many respects, the institution she sought to develop drew on key elements of her academic experience.

The influence of Davis's training in the social sciences was most evident in her analysis of crime. She offered an intellectual explanation of delinquency that traced the roots of much wrongdoing to the social environment. In the genesis of female crime, she assigned primary roles to poverty, unemployment, and social unrest. This argument extended ideas that had informed Davis's earlier work on Bohemian immigration.

The empirical research on female criminality that stood out among Davis's innovations at the prison also reflected values that had been central to her academic training. Davis brought to her work at Bedford Hills firm convictions about the importance of social investigation. In creating the Laboratory of Social Hygiene at the women's prison, she attempted to institutionalize the use of social scientific research as a method of reform.

Finally, Davis's academic credentials helped her to win major philanthropic support for the reformatory's work. She advanced a pragmatic model of corrections reform that was rooted in social analysis and that responded to intense pressures for expedient change. Davis's "scientific" approach to crime appealed to several individuals who were capable of advancing her ideas. The result was an experiment that demonstrated powerful idealism, tragic miscalculation, and the dangers for foundations that would sponsor politically volatile research projects geared to practical social change.[2]

II

The New York State Reformatory for Women at Bedford, or "Bedford Hills," as it would later be known, owed its very existence to the nineteenth-century prison reform movement. By the 1870s, concerned state officials, charity workers, and citizens began to explore the reformatory as an alternative to the incarceration of criminal offenders in penitentiaries. The idea took root especially among those who advocated the establishment of separate prisons for women. When Bedford Hills opened in May of 1901, a reformatory for men at Elmira, New York, had been in existence since 1876, and two "houses of refuge" for women were operating at Hudson and Albion.[3]

Bedford Hills drew on the institutional design of its predecessors and benefited from their experience. When Davis assumed her duties in 1901, the reformatory consisted of "a large administration building, a reception hall, four different cottages, a laundry building, a power house, a gate house and a stable." Consistent with its rehabilitative aims, the setting was rural, and no high walls or fences scarred the landscape. The "cottages" where inmates lived were designed to resemble private homes. "Spacious and cheerful" throughout, each brick building included twenty-eight single rooms, a kitchen with modern conveniences, and even a flower garden outdoors.[4]

The prisoners who inhabited these quarters came from New York City and Long Island, and from Westchester County, where the reformatory was located. They found their way to Bedford Hills by committing relatively minor crimes, such as petty larceny, drunkenness, vagrancy, and, of course, prostitution. The reformatory also took women convicted of felonies other than first- or second-degree murder, if they were first offenders. Those incarcerated at Bedford Hills fell between the ages of sixteen and thirty when committed; most arrived with indeterminate sentences that stipulated a maximum stay of three years.[5]

From the start, Davis's intellectual interests and sensitivity to gender issues shaped her approach to prison reform. She came to Bedford Hills convinced that women's oppression derived from low wages, inequality, and inadequate employment. These theories assumed practical significance as Davis confronted the demands of corrections work. She quickly turned her attention to education and employment—issues that had been central to her own life.

The development of school programs and work routines for the women inmates were among Davis's earliest and most innovative decisions at Bedford Hills. These measures stood out in the array of plans that led Bedford Hills to be considered "the most active penal experiment station in America." Within two years of the reformatory's opening, several prison industries dependent on inmate labor were in full swing, and "palmetto hats and baskets and raffia work" were made on the premises. The most ambitious project was a fully equipped "modern" steam laundry, "where girls are taught the trade complete in both steam and hand work, and they are fully capable upon their release to take a position in any steam laundry."[6]

Although similar industries had long been a fixture in American prisons, Davis broke with tradition by introducing such work to a *female* reformatory. Instruction in domestic skills such as cooking and sewing constituted the usual training offered in women's prisons. Davis was determined to teach her charges that women could perform other kinds of work, whether society deemed it respectable for their sex or not. Davis's own experience had freed her from conventional notions about woman's "proper" domain.[7]

Nevertheless, many of the initial tasks provided inmates and the schoolwork offered emphasized nominally female endeavors. Inmates at Bedford Hills were taught to knit and weave, sing and dance, cook and can food. Special instructors were hired to hold formal classes, and physical exercise, now considered important to the well-being of "modern" women, was included in the curriculum. When the state commissioner of prisons visited the reformatory in December of 1903, he found good reason to praise the activities offered at Bedford Hills. "The educational features are splendid," he reported. "Aside from the regular grade work of the school room they teach physical culture, music and domestic economy with excellent results and manifest physical and moral benefit to the girls."[8]

Davis soon proved her willingness to go beyond the commendable to the truly unorthodox. Distressed by the legislature's plodding pace in improving the institution's buildings and grounds, and uneasy at seeing that young women were "'killing' their time with superfluous household activities or fancy work," Davis expanded her notion of "women's work" at the prison. She learned how to mix concrete herself, and then began to instruct the inmates in the process. Before long, prisoners were laying cement walks around the reformatory's grounds; and, to hear Davis tell it, they did so with gusto.

They excavated the earth, brought stones in wheelbarrows for the foundations, wheeled and spread the cinders after sifting them, mixed and laid the

three inches of concrete, then the inch of cement, all in the most approved
fashion, and so have made 700 linear feet of five-foot sidewalk in six weeks.

Ditches were dug, cement manhole covers were made, and concrete floors
were laid in buildings. The seasons provided few obstacles in carrying out
such ambitious "out-door work." The grading and seeding of lawns gave way
to snow shoveling, and even construction of an ice pond and house, where
ice was cut throughout the winter to supply the institution's needs. Soon a
working farm provided the reformatory with sausages from pigs slaughtered
on the premises. By the fall of 1905, a state inspector visiting Bedford Hills
reported that "this institution needs a building for the industrial classes, and
also a barn for the housing of implements and the institution teams."9

Book-learning at Bedford Hills was also oriented toward practical knowledge. Arithmetic was taught using data from prison expenditure and supply
books; inmates learned to keep accounts by documenting how their own
small income was spent. Lectures on law and democracy attempted, in Davis's words, "to impress the girls with the important factor women are in such
a democracy, though they may not vote or take part in the actual government." These lessons were reinforced by the creation of a self-governing
"Honor Cottage" where well-behaved inmates lived with (one visitor
claimed) "as much freedom as a boarding-school girl in a well conducted and
chaperoned school." Davis's were the "first systematic attempts to adapt the
school education to the particular needs of the reformatory population and
set an example for the later reformatories."10

Davis viewed Bedford's educational programs as important correctives to
the social and economic barriers delinquent women faced. The woman
offender, she believed, occupied an especially precarious position in American society. Female convicts faced much heavier burdens in returning to society than did imprisoned men. Noting that "immorality" was but "an accident
in the man's life," Davis insisted that "the reverse is true in the case of
woman. Her immoral life is the fact; the offense for which she is sentenced
to the institution . . . is an incident." A woman convicted of a crime was "a
social outcast and she knows it." Such disapproval tempted woman offenders
to return to their old ways when released, out of discouragement and
desperation.11

Davis believed economic inequality also hampered the rehabilitation of
female criminals. While men who "learned their trades in a State Reformatory have a way open to them when they go out," women enjoyed few ave-
nues of mobility. The only occupation open to convicted women, Davis
argued, was domestic service. A shortage of household help led some women
employers to overlook the backgrounds of delinquents. "So great is the
demand," Davis explained, "that one lady said to me, 'I don't care if she has
committed all the crimes in the decalogue if she can only wash dishes.'" By
rude experience, the superintendent learned that few other employers would
disregard a woman's criminal record. Davis vehemently rejected domestic
service as the only appropriate work for women. "Every woman is not

adapted to domestic service any more than is every man to the trade of tailor," she noted.[12]

The "out-door work" that was such a distinctive feature of the experiment at Bedford Hills was not an antidote, Davis recognized, to women's economic inequality. The grounds work and construction performed at the prison, she noted, "are not things the girls will be apt to do when they go out into this world. They are not learning a trade. . . ." Rather, the purpose of such industry was to expose incarcerated women to fresh air, to vigorous work, and to the sun. "When the women go out from us," Davis explained, "they will need every particle of physical strength we can give them, because they are going to have a harder fight than the men or boy criminals." The superintendent accepted an idea increasingly popular among the medical profession that life in the outdoors could bring back physical *and* "moral" health. Only when their well-being was restored could women offenders even begin to benefit from extensive vocational training and education in more appropriate fields of work.[13]

In a speech before the National Prison Association, Davis made a strong pitch for providing women with the "fresh air treatment" for their "moral disease." She urged prison officials to teach by example. Davis was especially proud of the reformatory's resident doctor, "a Vassar woman," who displayed considerable talent as a stonemason. And she delighted in explaining how she proved the skeptics on her staff wrong when they doubted that inmates were equal to the task of lawn work.

> Some of my officers laughed at me and our steward said it reminded her of a person trying to plow with a team of cats. It could be done if you could get enough cats and if you could make them all pull together. I succeeded in getting my cats to pull together and they filled, graded, and seeded the whole bank.

Anticipating criticism, Davis was careful to explain that she did not overwork the women inmates or subject them (or herself) to ridicule. The reformatory physician made sure that no "improper or unsuitable exertion" took place.[14]

Her acute awareness of the special problems faced by women prisoners led Davis to speak out publicly about their distinctive needs. Female corrections work, she argued, imposed unique demands and deserved the highest concern. "The general public," she noted in 1905, "does not understand the difference in reformatory work for women and similar work for men who are criminals, a difference which comes from the physiological, social and economic difference between them, based on the difference of sex." These differences required that separate institutions be established for women offenders.

At professional meetings Davis made reference to her gender to confer authority upon her views. She rose to address an evening meeting of the American Prison Association in 1906, and directly made note of the Conference's inattention to women's concerns.

> I have noticed that most of the speakers have talked about men prisoners and what they can do for the man while in prison or after he leaves it. I suppose

that is because most of the speakers know more about men than about women. I do not profess to know anything about men, but I do know something about women, and you will pardon me if I confine myself to the woman side of the question.

Davis's special perspective was a professional advantage in a social climate rife with fears about the decay of traditional values and sensitive to the moral depravity seen as endemic in crimes such as prostitution. Her ability to speak with authority about "the woman side of the question" made Davis an especially impressive speaker at national gatherings of corrections officials and charity workers. Her reputation spread, as well, among social reformers and politicians who considered correctional institutions and criminal justice an important item on their larger agenda of social concerns.[15]

III

To these reformers Davis offered a compelling analysis of female crime. In a 1905 address before the National Prison Association, and in many other speeches that followed, she departed from popular hereditarian views in emphasizing the environmental causes of delinquency. Women who broke the law, Davis argued, were themselves victims of destructive social and economic forces. Rehabilitation depended on recognition of this social fact.

Davis attributed crime to an array of evils in the social environment. Poor education, lack of economic opportunity, low skills, and an inability to cope with the demands of urban life were at work, she maintained, in producing an entire class of female criminal offenders. When the problems in American cities were resolved, Davis instructed, there would be "little need" for professional meetings devoted to methods of dealing with criminal behavior. Even juvenile delinquency could be traced, she argued, to inadequate housing, poor public health, child labor, and unemployment.[16]

This expansive view of crime reflected important elements of Davis's social scientific training. She linked deviance to sweeping changes in American society, and invoked the findings of sociologists to support her optimistic view of social reform. In a report, "Law Breakers," prepared for the National Conference of Charities and Corrections, Davis pointed to the "immense changes" brought about by the rise of industrialism, progress in arts, and in the applied sciences. "Sociologists," she wrote, "tell us that society is becoming self-conscious. We have reached a stage of civilization where we can in a measure direct our own evolution." According to Davis, advances in social knowledge proved that society was responsible for the law breaker. This was because "many things that we formerly regarded as within the will of the individual are now recognized simply as the result of the reaction of social conditions."[17]

The most striking feature of Davis's environmental conception of female crime was her rejection of nativist and racist explanations of criminal behavior. Eugenicists, who were boldest in advancing genetic theories of social deviance, often linked "bad traits" to racial and ethnic types. As a result, immigrants and black Americans frequently came under special attack for their supposed degenerate characteristics. Thus twentieth-century scientists who subscribed to eugenic theories helped fashion the intellectual arguments that were used to restrict immigration. Davis explicitly challenged the assumption that black and immigrant women made up the majority of incurable, and hence, "dangerous," criminal types.[18]

Her experience as a settlement worker and her research on Bohemian immigrants clearly shaped Davis's perspective on immigrant women who found themselves in trouble with the law. She recognized that many inmates had little control over their own life chances. Describing "all" the women committed to Bedford Hills as "victims of bad heredity or environment, or both," Davis expressed a good deal of sympathy for inmates who were foreign born. "From New York," she told the Prison Association, "we get a class of girls who are very hopeful. It includes the foreign element. They are girls who, in their own country, had no opportunity of training or education." Her description of these delinquents echoed her discussion of the impoverished Czech immigrants who were the subject of her dissertation.

> They come from the lower peasant class. They have come to better their condition, but do not understand the conditions of civilization which they find in a great city. . . . They are not necessarily criminal or vicious by nature, but they are lawless and have had no training. They are apt to be absolutely devoid of all education. Ten percent of all who come to us can not read. One-third can barely write their name and can not read a newspaper.[19]

Class, migration, and illiteracy were factors that figured in the analysis of Bohemian immigrants offered in Davis's doctoral dissertation. As a prison superintendent, she continued to view crime, at least in part, in sociological terms. Her remarks were not free of the condescending and paternalistic attitudes some Americans held towards the foreign born. Indeed, the superintendent managed to affirm a few prejudices even as she challenged others. Nonetheless, Davis went further than many of her contemporaries in her view that social and economic conditions, rather than genes, explained the problems faced by immigrants to the United States. Her social science training provided Davis with an explanation of delinquency that competed with biologically determinist views.

Davis applied a similar model to the black women incarcerated at Bedford Hills. The stress faced by immigrants was, she argued, "also true of the negroes who come from the South." Faced with the formidable task of adjusting to urban life and of finding work, and weighted with unrealistic expectations and dreams, these migrants found that "they can not earn what they thought they could and they get discouraged and fall into vice and are committed to prison." Davis's theory that black and white women differed little in their reasons for committing crimes was translated into practice when she refused to segregate inmates by race at the New York State Reformatory. This decision was unusual and controversial. Most prisons with any notable number of black inmates instituted a rigid policy of segregation. At Bedford Hills, black and white women shared quarters in the same reformatory residences. Davis came under fire for this policy, and her successor at Bedford reversed the procedure when Davis left.[20]

Davis's environmental analysis enabled her to find more similarities among her inmates than the accidental differences of race. Assessing the future of both black and immigrant criminal offenders, she stated: "Both of these classes are hopeful." Education and employment were all that was required to restore these inmates to good society. "Give them industrial and mental training and the colored girls realize their highest ambition and are satisfied; and the foreign girls when they learn our standards are willing to live law-abiding lives."[21]

Indeed, the most pessimistic prognosis of incarcerated women was reserved for native-born white Americans, the group most eugenicists and pseudo-scientists of race held up as exemplars of moral and biological purity. After rendering a hopeful judgment on the future of black and immigrant women at her reformatory, Davis expressed discouragement about the other group of prisoners there. "There is a class much less hopeful," she said, "and that is the girls who come from families of American parentage. They come largely with bad heredity. It is in this class that we almost always find these moral imbeciles." Still, Davis suggested that the social context influenced even these offenders in their turn to crime.

> I suppose in families of a higher class there may be girls who correspond to this class, but they are held in shape by convention. They are held upright by their parents, by their companions, and their fear lest they lose standing in their circle. Our girls have none of these artificial supports and they have nothing in themselves to supply the deficiency.[22]

Although Davis differed in critical ways from those who would attribute all crime to "mental deficiency," she never completely rejected prevailing intellectual fashions that ascribed criminality to inferior genetic strains. She drew a clear distinction between hopeless "moral imbeciles" whose mental defects prevented the development of a conscience, and relatively normal women who turned to crime when their social environment failed to provide for their needs. A 1906 address to the National Prison Association, "Moral Imbeciles," described girls of "bad heredity" at Bedford Hills who simply could not "distinguish between right and wrong when it concerns themselves."[23]

The punishment Davis prescribed for these delinquents was severe. Echoing the views of eugenicists who pressed a similar case in the early twentieth century, Davis argued that "it is the duty of the State to also segregate and colonize these women who are dangerous to the community who are moral imbeciles, just as we have colonized the mental imbeciles." Separate institutions for such "defectives" represented, for Davis, a kind of protective custody by which both society and the inmates who needed direction and supervision would benefit. But the coercive state intervention she endorsed clearly had less-than-benevolent aims. Custodial care, Davis suggested, would prevent feeble women from bringing "into the world children who, if there is anything in heredity, have only to look forward to a life of hopeless misery, such as their mothers have suffered before them."[24]

Davis's responsiveness to hereditarian interpretations of crime stemmed, at least in part, from the frustrations of running Bedford Hills. At the time she expressed her views on "moral imbeciles," the reformatory had begun to suffer the ill effects of overcrowding. An inspection in October of 1905 described an institution already filled beyond capacity "and in a somewhat congested condition, it being necessary to keep two inmates in a room on two corridors in the reception house." Most frustrating, the prison was filling up with inmates who had long criminal records and a history of stays in various state institutions. In spite of the stipulation that only first offenders be sent for reformatory care, the court barred only obvious felons from Bedford Hills. Repeat offenders convicted of lesser crimes appeared in growing numbers. And by 1906, the first "graduates" of Bedford Hills had been turned out into the world. Recidivism challenged Davis's idealistic notions that her reformatory would turn female lawbreakers around. Rather than question whether she had had unrealistic expectations of the curative value of reformatory programs, Davis concluded that some returning inmates were simply beyond rehabilitation. Her conclusions were typical of Progressive prison reformers frustrated when their ideas failed to yield effective results.[25]

Like many Progressives, Davis held "the state" responsible for the social cripples it created: it should invest resources, she believed, in helping struggling citizens. To her, this meant building and supporting custodial institutions that would house "in enforced seclusion" those who could not be restored to productive lives, and creating institutions that would educate and retrain those who were redeemable. This argument incorporated ideas that formed the essence of the Progressive approach. It recognized, for instance, that a modern industrial society could no longer rely on charity or local aid to provide for the welfare of growing numbers of needy citizens. It created a rationale for state intervention by arguing that such assistance was a wise economic decision. "As a cold business proposition," Davis wrote, "it is economy for the state to give its members the necessary training." Social control was embedded in Davis's expansive conception of state power. She invested experts with extensive authority to define and determine reformability. Most significantly, Davis's perspective on crime recognized the environmental causes of social problems even while it emphasized the treatment of individuals.[26]

Logic would seemingly dictate that if poverty, inequality, and unemployment created crime, a revamping of social, political, and economic institutions would help eradicate it. In the early decades of the twentieth century, many reformers could see their way to the first half of this equation, but not the latter. Attuned to the sweeping changes that were transforming their society, concerned activists such as Davis took a giant step forward by recognizing that social problems were intricately bound up with the emerging industrial order, and that the poor and the powerless were casualties of America's economic revolution. In this way, Progressives were forward-looking and modern because they broke the cycle of blaming the victim. Davis's social scientific training provided her with an important intellectual foundation for such environmental views.

Yet Progressive ideas about social problems produced a less-than-decisive approach to social policy. In part, this reflected the persistence of nineteenth-century political ideals. Although impatient with laissez-faire, most middle-class reformers did not yet fully envision or embrace a modern welfare state, even though many of their proposals for reform implied the need for one. Tenacious belief in the failed moral character of the poor also undercut new theories of public responsibility. Just as important in vitiating the power of Davis's social ideas were the exigencies of prison administration. At Bedford Hills, Davis was required to run an institution and to do so in a way that produced visible results; namely, the rehabilitation of individual delinquents. This imperative helped determine the superintendent's approach to prison reform.

Their unswerving faith in the power of education enabled Progressives such as Davis to reconcile their modern analysis of social problems with ameliorative programs that only vaguely addressed the deeper tensions their investigations had exposed. If existing institutions could play an educative role and if the public would attend to advances in knowledge, solutions to social problems could readily be found. Naturally, such a world view created a central role for educators and intellectuals. Davis herself readily wore the mantle of involved social expert. At conferences across the nation, she was almost always introduced as *Dr.* Katharine Bement Davis; in published articles, "Ph.D." inevitably followed her name. Her doctoral degree suggested expertise; it seemed of little importance that the penologist owed her title to a Ph.D. in *political economy*.[27]

I V

The Laboratory of Social Hygiene established at Bedford Hills in 1912 exemplified Davis's dual commitment to social investigation and reform. Although this center for research on female crime evolved gradually over the years of Davis's administration, it incorporated values that had long informed her work. The superintendent believed social inquiry and social scientific expertise were necessary preconditions for reform. This idea became reified in her founding of the Laboratory of Social Hygiene.

The plan for a research institute at Bedford Hills grew out of two related concerns. Davis's keen intellectual interest in female criminality had, of course, been apparent from the beginning of her tenure at Bedford Hills. Although charged with running the institution, providing basic custodial care, and helping to rehabilitate the inmates to society, Davis had always taken a deeper view of her responsibilities. The superintendent often likened the reformatory to an "educational institution" and referred as a matter of course to inmates who had left her care as "graduates." Consistent with that model, Davis sought to bring into the New York State Reformatory scientific experts who would, through their research, point the way toward rehabilitative goals.[28]

This ideal assumed greater urgency when Davis began to experience increasing difficulties in managing Bedford Hills. As the number of female offenders grew and as the Bedford reformatory received more attention for its innovative programs and its success, the prison's population rose steadily. By 1908, overcrowding had become a serious problem. Although two new cottages had been added since the reformatory's opening, 269 inmates and sixteen of their babies were confined in the institution when it was inspected that year. The original buildings, designed to accommodate 220, had already begun deteriorating, and a structure designed as a reception hall now housed 126 inmates confined to cells and double rooms. In 1909, over three hundred inmates were sent to Bedford Hills; the overflow was so great that inmates slept on cots set up in the hallways of residential buildings.[29]

Aside from the administrative nightmare of managing an overcrowded facility, Davis felt most distressed about the kind of inmates remanded to Bedford Hills. The new reformatories were designed to hold only criminals capable of rehabilitation. But little order seemed to prevail when judges and magistrates made sentencing decisions, partly because case histories of convicted women were often unavailable. Bedford gradually became filled with a diverse collection of female delinquents, many of whom were increasingly difficult to handle. Davis was dismayed when confronted with growing numbers of recalcitrant offenders and "mentally defective" women.[30]

The commissioner of corrections shared her concern about the latter group. He reported in 1909 that

> a considerable number of women has been committed to this institution who are feeble-minded, who should have been sent to some custodial institution; they are occupying the room here which should be given to the young women having mental capacity of educational and industrial improvement.

Bedford received a large number of women convicted in New York City, and its problems seemed greater than those at New York's other state reformatory for women at Albion. Most women sentenced to Albion came from rural communities; the inmates were less diverse, and there were fewer of them.[31]

For Davis, the most troubling result of overcrowding and dissimilarity among the prison population was the time "wasted in learning" how to identify the problems of individual inmates and the treatment they required. This process proved so over-whelming that "not enough time was left to accomplish anything like a re-education." Vexed by the lack of information at her disposal and committed to discovering a more "scientific" method of classifying offenders, Davis welcomed a visitor from the New York Public Education Association in the summer of 1909 who hoped to study the reformatory's inmates. The psychological tests conducted by this researcher interested Davis, and, as she described it, "in the constant consultations and discussions with her over the problems presented by these selected individuals came a crystallization of much of that over which I had been pondering."[32]

Davis was convinced that the assistance of skilled experts could make the entire system of criminal justice, and the organization of correctional facilities, more "rational." When the chief magistrate of New York City, Judge Russell McAdoo, toured Bedford Hills in the spring of 1910, accompanied by several other judges and officials of the Charity Organization Society, Davis explained her thinking to the group. The magistrates complained about the obstacles they faced in knowing where to send convicted women. In reply, Davis suggested that "the day would come when all cases convicted in the courts would be studied by experts before sentence was passed as a guide to the determination of the proper place of commitment."[33]

These remarks especially impressed a member of the Charity Organization Society who asked Davis to draw up a written plan for the system she envisioned. Soon after Davis drafted "A Rational Plan for the Treatment of Women Convicted in the Courts of New York City," which was published and privately circulated by the charity group.[34]

Davis's "rational plan" put enormous faith in the predictive value of research and in the panel of experts she hoped to empower. Proposing that courts be restricted to determining guilt or innocence, Davis advocated the establishment of a separate commission to determine the proper *treatment* of convicted female offenders. "Apolitical" in character, the commission would be comprised of knowledgeable citizens, a majority of whom would be women. Under its supervision, a "clearing house" staffed by doctors, psychologists, and other experts would thoroughly study every individual convicted by a court of law. Once provided with complete knowledge of the felon's case history, the commission would assign law-breakers to appropriate institutions for "treatment."[35]

This proposal reflected Davis's growing desire to bring scientific knowledge to bear on the practical problems faced by state institutions and municipal governments. It also incorporated a bold strategy for increasing the administrative authority of women. Yet the superintendent recognized that any large-scale reform of the criminal justice system would demand lengthy political agitation. Too impatient to wait for the legislature to see the light, Davis was already taking steps to improve her institution at Bedford Hills.

Determined to gain a better understanding of female criminal types, and motivated by a desire to gain surer control over the reformatory, Davis invited a Mount Holyoke College psychologist, Emily Rowland, to develop testing measures at Bedford Hills in the summer of 1910. Rowland's research uncovered a significant number of "mentally defective" women among the sample tested. These results convinced Davis that there was a real "possibility of using psychological tests to determine in a general way the group to which a young woman belongs so far at least as her mentality was concerned."

Hoping to add a more permanent research component to the reformatory, Davis sought and received funding from the New York Foundation to hire a skilled psychologist in the fall of 1910 to study the "mental capacity" of the women sentenced to Bedford Hills. The foundation's grant of $1,500 paid for the establishment of a modest "psychological laboratory" at the reformatory, as well as the psychologist's salary. A researcher from the Eugenics Record Office at Cold Spring Harbor and a "senior fellow" from the New York School of Philanthropy joined the team to help investigate the heredity of inmates at Bedford Hills.[36]

Davis relied on old school ties in selecting the psychologist funded by the New York Foundation grant. She chose Jean Weidensall, a Vassar graduate who had also earned a doctorate at the University of Chicago in 1910. A student of James Angell, Weidensall had mastered new empirical techniques in statistics and mental testing. She had studied at Chicago at a time when several young women scholars were conducting fast-breaking research in psychology. They pioneered in constructing a critique of the biological interpretation of sex differences.[37]

Most relevant to her new position at Bedford Hills was Weidensall's work with psychiatrist William Healy at the Juvenile Psychopathic Institute. Affiliated with the Chicago Juvenile Court, the institute administered a battery of psychological tests to delinquents in an effort to understand the origins of their criminal behavior. Healy subscribed to neither environmental nor biologically determinist views of crime. Instead, he focused his attention on individual cases, applying relevant theories as necessary, though often willing to ascribe juvenile delinquency to mental defects.[38]

Weidensall applied similar techniques to the adult women imprisoned at Bedford Hills. In 1911, the psychologist began a series of experiments designed to yield "a body of mental tests that could be applied after a woman's conviction and preceding her sentence and that would prove prophetic of her reformability." It did not require a Ph.D. in psychology to see that the undertaking was a dubious one. The issues of "what constituted reformation" loomed over Weidensall's investigation, and the possibility of actually predicting reformability seemed even more remote. With little help from the meager measures then available for psychological testing, Weidensall reluctantly decided to use the new Binet intelligence test on her subjects at the reformatory. She and Davis agreed that any woman could be reformed who was able to "learn a trade," support herself "industrially" and adjust "to ordinary social and industrial conditions." This definition clearly emphasized compliance rather than innate intelligence, but Weidensall and Davis were undeterred.[39]

As Weidensall suspected, the Binet tests proved to be ill-suited measures of intelligence when applied to adult "criminal women." Only one of the two hundred inmates tested proved to have the mental age of a twelve-year-old; everyone else scored lower. Davis seemed unsurprised by these results. She looked forward to the day when feeble-minded women would be placed in "permanent custodial care in institutions planned to give them the maximum

of pleasure consistent with the safeguarding of society from the dangers attendant on free propagation of defective offspring." Weidensall was much more
cautious. "Among those who failed to pass all the Binet tests," the psychologist reported, "was one who was an expert stenographer and another who
had been a successful teacher in the Brooklyn public schools for a number of
years." The tests were defective, Weidensall concluded, at least when used
among a highly diverse population of imprisoned women. Other measures of
reformability would have to be developed that would yield more encouraging
and reliable results.[40]

While Weidensall conducted her investigations, Davis renewed her search
for funds that would make it possible to establish a permanent research laboratory at Bedford Hills for the study and classification of female offenders.
As luck would have it, a man who belonged to the wealthiest family in America had only recently taken an interest in the problem of female crime. John
D. Rockefeller, Jr., son of the great oil baron, had been selected to serve as
foreman of a special grand jury, empaneled in 1910, to investigate prostitution in New York City. Once the jury disbanded, the philanthropist concluded that a "private organization" would be the most fruitful way of continuing investigative work.[41]

With the assistance of advisors Paul Warburg and Starr Murphy, Rockefeller drew up plans in the fall of 1911 to form a Bureau of Social Hygiene
that would support research into prostitution. The bureau was neither
announced nor incorporated, and ideas for its work remained tentative. Its
purpose was still undefined when Davis approached John D. Rockefeller, Jr.
Rockefeller had sought Davis's permission for a visit to Bedford Hills in the
spring of 1911, but "circumstances," whether of Davis's or of Rockefeller's
creation, intervened. Recalling Rockefeller's earlier interest, Davis wrote to
the philanthropist in September of 1911, testing the waters for a larger
scheme.[42]

With a letter of inquiry, Davis sent along a copy of her paper on the
"rational treatment" of New York City's female offenders. The prison head
noted that one of the greatest obstacles in dealing with women offenders was
a lack of knowledge about female criminality. "I believe," she wrote, "that
we will never come to a successful conclusion as to the best method of dealing
with them until we have, in the first place, made a more careful scientific
study of the types of women psychologically and physiologically who enter
upon the life of vice and crime." Davis also stressed the importance of the
pre-sentencing "clearing house" outlined in her paper, and the need for spe-
cialized institutions to care for various types of delinquent women. The establishment of a "criminalistic institute" charged with studying convicted
offenders, would go a long way toward meeting immediate needs, Davis
wrote. "I am writing you this, at length," she informed Rockefeller, "because
I know that the interest of a man of your position and influence would lend
weight to any such plan. We are making the beginnings of a scientific study
here at Bedford." Davis invited Rockefeller to visit the prison, where they
could discuss the ideas spelled out in her plan.[43]

The timing of Davis's letter was fortuitous. Not only did she raise an issue already of great interest to Rockefeller, she did so at a time when the Rockefeller philanthropies were being organized and defined. Although the Rockefeller Institute of Medical Research (1901) and the General Education Board (1903) had already been established, these organizations represented a "preparatory" phase in Rockefeller, Sr.'s, philanthropic plans. Since 1906 Rockefeller and his son had been developing plans for "a large trust" that would handle "considerable sums of money to be devoted to philanthropy, education, science, and religion." That trust became the Rockefeller Foundation, which was incorporated in 1913. In the years between 1910 and 1913, John D. Rockefeller, Sr., and his staff continued to work towards enlarging support for worthy ventures. Although the senior Rockefeller still controlled the purse strings, his son was the family member who played the central role in administering philanthropic support.[44]

In these early years, public health, medicine, and education commanded most of the interest, and money, proffered by the Rockefeller philanthropies. Once the Rockefeller Foundation was established, it was very slow to fund research in the social sciences. The creation of the Laura Spelman Rockefeller Memorial in 1918 inaugurated an active period in funding social scientific research. But Rockefeller support for a project such as the one Davis proposed was largely unprecedented in 1911.[45]

Nonetheless, Rockefeller looked favorably upon Davis's initial idea, particularly her proposal for pre-sentencing evaluation. At least part of his enthusiasm derived from his high opinion of the superintendent, whom he knew only by reputation. "The plan which you outline is most interesting," Rockefeller wrote; "your judgement in a matter of this kind ought to be unquestioned." Admitting he had "given relatively little study to the question," Rockefeller was especially impressed by the "wisdom and promise of so sane, scientific and humane a plan as yours seems to me to be." The philanthropist requested additional copies of Davis's article for outside evaluation. Starr Murphy, a Rockefeller lawyer and close advisor, encouraged his boss to have experts look at Davis's plan and pass judgment "upon its practical aspects." But Murphy agreed that Davis's article was a "most suggestive and stimulating document and on theoretical grounds at least it would seem to be almost ideal."[46]

Central to Davis's proposed research laboratory was the clearing house for convicted offenders that would make practical use of the scientific studies conducted there. For all involved, both elements of the proposal were inextricably linked. Davis's brief for applied social science appealed to her backers precisely because it promised to produce tangible reforms. Although the laboratory's larger goal was to uncover the roots of female crime and the best methods of treating delinquency, its immediate goal was to evaluate women convicted by New York courts and to make recommendations on the institutions to which they should be remanded. Barely concealed in such a definition of purpose was an effort to screen out the irredeemables and foist them off on the state for permanent custodial care.

After Rockefeller paid a visit to the reformatory in the early fall of 1911, serious negotiations ensued. Davis pressed her case hard, arguing that "the establishment of the research laboratory and clearing house would be the most important step ever taken in this country for the scientific study of prostitution and criminology among women." She passed along a letter to Rockefeller from British sex researcher Havelock Ellis, who described Davis's plan as "admirable, absolutely sound both on the scientific and on the practical side." Ellis even grandly predicted that the proposed facility "would be a model for the world to follow." Less enlightened, Davis told Rockefeller, was the New York State Legislature, and any program of mandatory pre-sentencing evaluation would require legislative approval. "The doubtful quantity is always the state legislature," she explained, "which as you know, is composed of men who have neither a philanthropic or a scientific outlook on life." In short, they had little in common with Rockefeller or herself.[47]

The negotiations over the laboratory or "criminalistic institute" reflected dilemmas that bedeviled early-twentieth-century reformers. On the one hand, only state action could alter existing procedures in any broad or lasting way. On the other hand, to go the ambitious route of political change was to confront the panoply of opinions represented by elected officials and to invite the interference of various interest groups. The democratic process itself became an obstacle to change for activists who invested experts with superior wisdom about public affairs. Both Rockefeller and Davis appeared to be mindful of these dilemmas, but Rockefeller saw little problem in circumventing the political process. Of Davis's proposal, he asked, "would it be necessary to enact the legislation therein suggested now? Could that not be done later after the scheme was in operation? Would there not be enough material coming to the reformatory through the ordinary channels as at present?" Rockefeller expressed his "hope that some day the plan in its entirety may be adopted," but he was willing to proceed with a more modest approach.

Davis drew up an "alternative" plan that was "framed with a view to as little legislation as possible." But she still wanted some legislation passed, at least for New York City, that would make it possible to prevent the poor and mentally ill from being sent to her institution. She sought, as well, to make it incumbent on the state to aid women who did not belong in a reformatory but who were too ill or indigent to support themselves. In spite of such daunting problems, Davis expressed great confidence in her proposed project. Ever the social scientist, she reminded Rockefeller that "the time seems to be ripe for a beginning. Thinking people everywhere are realizing the dangers of prostitution and a double standard of morals, an investigation and definite knowledge *must* precede concerted action to make it worthwhile or its results lasting." Here was the familiar reliance on scientific knowledge that had long guided her work.[48]

Mindful of the political constraints imposed by unenlightened state legislators, Davis and Rockefeller agreed that the laboratory should be constructed with private funds, on land adjacent to the existing reformatory at Bedford Hills. Both superintendent and philanthropist viewed the project as an experiment that would demonstrate its value to the state. Both assumed that the laboratory's success would guarantee future political support, and plans were made that looked for the research facility to be taken over by the state of New York in five years' time. "No one can foresee what the attitude of the state legislature or the city's authorities will be five years from now," Davis warned Rockefeller. "That would be one of the points which would have to remain open." But Davis felt certain that the laboratory would prove its worth.

> Personally I have no doubt of the success of the experiment. If it is conducted in the right way, I am sure it is the next step. I have faith to believe that it may be the nucleus for the first really scientific institution for the study of crime in the world, but whether or no we can convince the state authorities of that effect remains to be seen.[49]

Davis's success in convincing *Rockefeller* of the merits of her plan owed a good deal to her reputation as a highly trained expert. In a letter to advisor Paul Warburg, attempting to persuade him of the worth of Davis's plan, Rockefeller spoke of his recent visit to Bedford Hills with Starr Murphy and their reaction to the reformatory's superintendent. "We were both deeply impressed with the work she is doing there and think her a woman of unusual mental endowment. She is a college graduate, has done post graduate work in this country and in Europe." It did nothing to diminish her reputation that Davis earned her academic credentials at an institution Rockefeller's father had endowed. Yet more impressive to the philanthropist than Davis's affiliation with the University of Chicago was her distinctive approach to the vexing issue of crime. Rockefeller valued Davis's scheme because it carried the impress of science *and* addressed contemporary public problems. As he described it, "this plan seems to me to be generally a most scientific and at the same time practical suggestion." The work of the proposed laboratory was at once broad, theoretical, and best of all, "feasible." "I regard it," Rockefeller confessed, "as the most important step in penology which has been contemplated in this country."[50]

At least part of Rockefeller's enthusiasm could be traced to Davis's affirmation of a theory regarding female crime the philanthropist himself cherished. A man of largely Victorian sensibilities, Rockefeller found it difficult to view wayward women as inherently evil, yet very easy to think of females in sexual terms. On his tour of Bedford Hills, Rockefeller took great interest in the causes that led to the inmates' downfall, and he derived considerable satisfaction from Davis's explanation. "Miss Davis told us that while the girls in her institution are committed there for various crimes, practically all of these crimes were committed as a result of or in connection with their being prostitutes." This reductionist argument appealed to Rockefeller, perhaps because it preserved his notion of women while simplifying and rendering more manageable a complex social problem. Whatever its allure, Rockefeller deemed Davis's theory worth supporting. As he explained to Warburg: "in other words, her experience would go to prove that the one crime of woman is prostitution. All the other crimes are simply incidental thereto."[51]

Rockefeller proceeded with caution before committing any funds to Davis and the laboratory at Bedford Hills. He sought the views of public figures "whose opinions would be weighty": a group that included three college presidents, several professors, and social workers such as Jane Addams, Graham Taylor, and Edward Devine. Davis had suggested Addams' name, telling Rockefeller that "it would be a good thing to get Miss Jane Addams' endorsement. Anything that she says carries weight."[52]

Rockefeller's letter to these luminaries began with an introduction of Katharine Davis, the hub around which all other aspects of the project revolved. "The State Reformatory for Women at Bedford, New York," Rockefeller began,

> is one of the best, if not the best reformatory in this country. Miss Katharine Bement Davis is its head and has been since its establishment eleven years ago. She is a Vassar graduate, has done post graduate work at Chicago, and also in several cities in Germany. She was also head worker of a settlement in Philadelphia for several years. She is a woman of rare mental endowment, combined with deep human sympathy and an unusual amount of common sense and knowledge of practical things.

After describing Davis's proposed "criminalistic institute," Rockefeller asked for help in evaluating the idea's merits. The enthusiastic response of those consulted brought the project one step closer to realization.[53]

Upon Rockefeller's suggestion, Davis also tested the waters with officials, including New York judges and John Glenn, head of the Russell Sage Foundation. She began to search for "competent women" to begin the initial phase of research. At Jean Weidensall's suggestion, Davis looked again to the University of Chicago for two of its graduate students in philosophy and psychology, Jessie Taft and Virginia Robinson. Rockefeller wondered whether "some physician would be better fitted" to carry out the planned investigation of prostitutes incarcerated at Bedford Hills (and elsewhere). But he ultimately deferred to Davis's judgment, and the two Chicago students were hired.[54]

Robinson and Taft promised to offer precisely the kind of trained, scientific, and detached approach that Davis so admired. But there were competing voices to contend with. When the Woman's Prison Association learned that the Bedford Hills superintendent planned an in-depth study of prostitution, they made inquiries that left Davis uneasy. The Woman's Prison Association had been planning to introduce legislation calling for a fact-finding study of prostitution, they told Davis, and they did not want to duplicate her work. Davis voiced her frustration with these amateur social activists to Rockefeller. "I should be sorry to have any legislation pushed by this organization," Davis wrote, "unless the various other people interested along these lines found that their plan was wisest."[55]

Although the W.P.A. had been an effective lobby in the past (it had played a role in the creation of Bedford Hills), Davis looked upon its members with obvious condescension. The association dated back to 1850, a time when many female antebellum reformers broke with male-dominated organizations uninterested in the unique problems faced by their sex. A voluntary association, the W.P.A. differed from the professional prison activists whom Davis represented. Her dispute with the association bore witness to the divide that separated nineteenth-century activists from their twentieth-century successors. As Davis explained to Rockefeller, "in confidence, the organization is composed of women who are far past the prime of life and who with every desire to keep abreast of the times, have, it seems to me, failed to get new blood into the organization." Assisted by the ablest young women researchers available to her and freed from the necessities of battling the state legislature, Davis hoped the new research institute at Bedford Hills would prove to be a thoroughly modern, scientific endeavor.[56]

At the beginning of April 1912, John D. Rockefeller, Jr., committed himself to donating up to $200,000 for the establishment of "an experimental criminalistic institute known as Miss Davis's 'Alternative Plan for the Treatment of Women Convicted in the Courts of New York City'" at Bedford Hills. Under the aegis of the Bureau of Social Hygiene, Rockefeller agreed to provide $150,000 for an "investment in land and buildings," as well as "a total annual expense of not to exceed $10,000 a year for from two to five years, as may be necessary in order to fully work out the problem involved." The bureau resolution creating the research center at Bedford explicitly and optimistically addressed the issue of eventual state ownership.

> While the state of New York could not itself carry on such an experiment, it is understood that if the experiment proves a success the board of managers of the New York State Reformatory for Women will recommend to the legislature that it take it over, at an agreed price.[57]

The necessary endorsements were gathered, and with by-now-typical hyperbole, the bureau announced the project. Davis's plan was, it said,

> a piece of scientific research which is fully in line with the purposes of the Bureau; an experiment of vital importance, the results of which promise to be both far reaching and revolutionary as regards the treatment of criminals, not only women but also men and children, in this country and in all countries of the world.[58]

Rockefeller's decision to finance Davis's scheme was, in many respects, an extraordinary one. In effect, a private citizen was agreeing to bankroll a venture launched by state officials and tied to a public institution. The philanthropist assumed a risk on behalf of the state by funding an experiment in social reform with the full expectation, if not a written guarantee, that success would lead to state adoption. Well aware of the sensitive nature of such a move and attuned to political appearances, Rockefeller attempted to mask his own central role in the Bedford project by emphasizing the sponsorship of the Bureau of Social Hygiene.[59]

The issue of proper appearances was critical, for, in order to succeed, the Bedford Hills project would require extensive publicity. Rockefeller explained his thinking to Davis in this way. "The more generally the people are interested in it the easier will it be for you to get the judges to commit a larger number of girls to Bedford and subsequently to get whatever additional legislation may be needed." On the other hand, close scrutiny of the project's financing was less welcome. The purchase of land and buildings was involved, yet the ostensible buyer, the Bureau of Social Hygiene, didn't exist in the eyes of the law. This problem was circumvented by having Starr Murphy, the bureau's secretary, take the deed to any property acquired in his name and then lease it to the New York Reformatory for Women. Rockefeller instructed Davis, "if anyone asks just who is putting up the money for the financing of this plan, it may be truthfully said that it is being subscribed by several members of the Bureau and some of the friends of the Bureau." In fact, this explanation was not really truthful at all, as Rockefeller was well aware. The "'friends' referred to," Rockefeller admitted to Paul Warburg, were only one friend—his father. The truth was that the laboratory to be established at Bedford Hills owed its existence to the resources of a private citizen.[60]

The first practical outcome of the Bureau of Social Hygiene's beneficence was a study, *Commercialized Prostitution in New York City,* conducted by George Kneeland. In January of 1912, Kneeland, a former chief investigator for the Chicago Vice Commission, was set to work explaining the structure of prostitution in New York. Jessie Taft and Virginia Robinson joined the project in April of 1912, and they worked closely with Kneeland, "observing the prostitutes soliciting on 14th Street or being brought into night court." Interviews were conducted with female prostitutes detained at Bedford and at other institutions in New York. By 1913 the results of the women's investigations with Kneeland were published in book form. Rockefeller himself wrote the introduction to Kneeland's study, and Davis penned a lengthy chapter reporting the results—"A Study of Prostitutes Committed from New York City to the State Reformatory for Women at Bedford Hills."[61]

The Kneeland work proved to be a classic in the large Progressive-era literature on prostitution. A thorough study of the "business" of prostitution, Kneeland's book detailed the highly structured world of New York City vice. Police corruption, the exploitation of women by male pimps and procurers, and the grim setting in which it all took place were scrutinized. Like much of the investigative literature of the Progressive era, the Kneeland book linked the social problem it explored to a wider climate of corruption and greed. In truth, the most damning thing that could be said of prostitution was that it was a business. During the early twentieth century, social critics especially condemned human exploitation in the interest of commercialism. The Kneeland study leveled this charge. "The evidence submitted," Kneeland wrote,

> proves that prostitution in New York City is widely and openly exploited as
> a business enterprise. . . . Most of the wreckage, and the worst of it, is due to
> persistent, cunning and unprincipled exploitation: to the banding together in
> infamous enterprise of madame, pimp, procurer, brothel-keeper, and liquor
> vendor to deliberately carry on a cold-blooded traffic for their joint profit.

Such an analysis pointed to the necessity of eradicating, rather than regulating, the immoral industry.[62]

Davis's contribution to the Kneeland study examined the "victims" of
vice, the prostitutes themselves. Using records of nearly 650 prostitutes who
had been sent to Bedford Hills, Davis attempted to construct a portrait of
women who engaged in prostitution. Her method of social analysis was similar to the approach she had employed in her dissertation research. Place of
birth, family history, education, records of employment, religion, age, and
nativity were among the variables considered. Analysis of birthplace and parentage showed that the vast majority of streetwalkers confined to Bedford
Hills were "American-born whites." Black women had the lowest rates of
prostitution; they made up only 13 percent of the inmates convicted of the
crime. Foreign-born women accounted for just 24 percent of the prostitutes
remanded to the reformatory.[63]

Davis's conclusions were notable, once again, for the weight they placed
on social environment in determining the causes of prostitution. She stressed
the problems faced by single-parent families whose mothers worked long
hours for low wages as domestics and laundresses. While many studies of
prostitution drew a direct causal relationship between domestic service and
prostitution, Davis had a different perspective on this issue. She viewed
domestic service as an economist might, emphasizing the broader context of
the female labor market. Her conclusions echoed her earlier findings on Bohemian farm workers. "Domestic service for women under existing economic
conditions corresponds to casual labor for men," she wrote. "It is the job
where training and education are unnecessary in order to find work." Very
few of the women incarcerated at Bedford earned more before entering "the
life" than the nine dollars a week "generally conceded to be the minimum on
which a girl can live decently in New York city." Most earned much less. But
it was *underemployment*, rather than low wages, that played the greatest role
in turning women toward prostitution. That conclusion may have owed as
much to Davis's own preoccupations as to the realities of incarcerated wom-
en's lives.[64]

Research conducted at the reformatory also uncovered "degenerative
strains" in 20 percent of the women convicted of prostitution. A history of
family alcoholism, venereal disease, epilepsy, insanity, tuberculosis, and
criminality suggested, to Davis, the importance of heredity. But Davis
approached these data cautiously, arguing that without comparison to a control group of girls "who had not gone wrong," nothing definitive about the
causes of prostitution could be said. Nonetheless, Davis's growing fascination
with intelligence testing and with medical analysis of imprisoned women surfaced in her 1913 analysis of prostitutes at Bedford Hills. Binet and Wasser-

mann tests, the latter conducted by a doctor from New York's Health Department, provided the superintendent with tangible scientific data on female offenders. This information was very appealing, in part because it was quantitative, and, therefore, presumably accurate.[65]

The tests also told Davis what she wanted to hear. The low scores of inmates on intelligence tests seemed irrefutable proof that many of the women sent to Bedford Hills were incapable of being reformed. The most difficult disciplinary cases at Bedford performed poorly on the Binet test, a fact that supported Davis's view that these troublesome inmates simply could not "stay good" or develop any "moral sense or continuity of purpose." In all, nearly 30 percent of those tested for mentality proved "decidedly mentally defective," a statistic Davis considered "an extremely conservative estimate." Nearly 90 percent of the convicted prostitutes gave evidence of some "venereal infection," as well. These grim findings gave further evidence, Davis believed, of the importance of the new laboratory's work. "With the facilities which we are to have in the Laboratory of Social Hygiene under the auspices of the Bureau of Social Hygiene, we expect to get much more definitive results," she promised.[66]

While the Kneeland study was under way, construction of the Laboratory of Social Hygiene at Bedford Hills began. For $75,000 Rockefeller purchased over seventy-one acres of land that abutted on the reformatory's grounds, and an architect drew up plans for several buildings, a sewerage system, and roads. In November of 1913, the project was completed, and a new cottage, named after prison reformer Elizabeth Fry, opened with single rooms for fifty inmates. The building served as a "reception hall" where new prisoners were housed for up to three months while "scientific" studies were conducted and decisions about their future treatment were made. The laboratory itself was built nearby; it housed equipment and office space for the all-female scientific staff, which included a psychologist, statistician, a sociologist expert in eugenics, and "two field workers." A home for the laboratory staff completed the physical plant.[67]

To circumvent the unseemly arrangement of a private citizen's assuming financial responsibility for state wards, the buildings and grounds were leased to the state of New York for four years. Of course, no rent was charged: the state paid only for the "maintenance" of inmates housed at the Elizabeth Fry cottage and the salary of the matron who looked after them there. Rockefeller paid for everything else, including the salaries of the laboratory staff. The fact that several of the laboratory's researchers were academic women influenced the salary structure. University of Chicago professor James Angell, who served on the laboratory's advisory board, instructed Rockefeller about appropriate compensation. "Inasmuch as you are likely to have to compete in part with academic salaries, I should think the standard salary of the better women's colleges might serve as criteria."[68]

Under psychologist Jean Weidensall's supervision, the Laboratory of Social Hygiene quickly commenced its study of new arrivals at Bedford Hills. Although the research center was committed to exploring the broader problem of female criminality and to testing the feasibility of a clearing house, the practical matter of helping to classify prisoners at the reformatory assumed initial importance. In weekly meetings, researchers at the laboratory were to share their findings with staff members at the reformatory.

The real ordeal was reserved for the inmates, who had to endure the invasions of privacy and self the testing often entailed. A stay at the laboratory soon became an important part of reformatory routine. Upon arrival, a new convict would be "quarantined" in the Elizabeth Fry Hall. Stripped naked, searched, bathed, and if necessary deloused, the inmate immediately received a routine physical examination by the resident physician. With an issue of prison clothes, she would then retire to her solitary room to await further exams. The isolation of her single room prevented the new arrival from learning about the testing that awaited her.[69]

The quarantine period benefited researchers. As Weidensall explained it,

> Most important of all, perhaps, after three or four days of confinement, the women were so lonesome that it was a great boon to be taken to the laboratory, which was some distance away. If, during the test, a subject's interest flagged or her attention wandered, it was only necessary to say, "Are you tired? Shall I take you back?" or "If you will do this test as quickly and as well as you can, I will bring you back this afternoon and let you try some others." . . . When they are told that, if they do well in these tests, it will help them to an early parole, they are vitally interested in doing their best.

Using information provided by the inmates and employment and education records, studies of the offenders' social environment were also undertaken. Inquiry into family histories provided researchers with possible clues about the role of heredity in producing criminal behavior. Standard physical tests measuring height, weight, strength, and agility were administered. But the bulk of research entailed psychological and mental tests. The laboratory incorporated modern methods of empirical investigation, often at the expense of the inmates—the defenseless subjects of Bedford's social scientific research.[70]

V

Work at the Laboratory of Social Hygiene had barely gotten off the ground when Katharine Davis came to a momentous decision that profoundly affected both her own career and the Bedford Hills Reformatory. Approached by New York's newly elected reform mayor John P. Mitchel in late 1913 with an offer to become commissioner of correction in his new administration, Davis readily accepted. Mitchel knew of Davis's work at Bedford Hills, and he called on John D. Rockefeller, Jr., to ask what he thought of the superintendent's fitness for the job of commissioner. Rockefeller replied, "Dr. Davis is the cleverest woman I have ever met," and the choice was sealed. Davis asked for, and received, a leave of absence from the reformatory's Board of Managers, probably to protect herself if she became a casualty of shifting political winds in New York City.[71]

Mitchel's appointment of Davis was unprecedented: when she took office in January of 1914, Davis became the first woman to hold a cabinet-level office in the history of New York City. The new mayor's generosity may have been influenced by his perception that women's suffrage would not be far away. In 1910, the National American Woman Suffrage Association established their headquarters in New York, and springtime brought annual and well-attended pro-suffrage parades to Fifth Avenue. Mrs. Carrie Chapman Catt galvanized loyal supporters: a sense that change was imminent (it was not) was in the air.[72]

Whatever the mayor's motives, his selection of Davis startled some. Not only was the political barrier against women commissioners broken, traditional notions of women's work received another trouncing as well. As the city's commissioner of correction, Davis assumed responsibility for roughly fifteen prisons and the 125,000 inmates these institutions held each year. Conditions in New York's many prisons were abysmal, as Davis herself knew very well. Some commentators doubted that a woman was equal to the task of managing the depressing facilities. The *New York Times* described Mitchel's appointment of Davis as "appalling." "Handling the hardened criminal," the newspaper elaborated, "is a man's job." Other observers looked beyond Davis's gender to her reputation as a prison superintendent and expressed more optimism. The *Brooklyn Eagle* wrote with enthusiasm of Davis's selection.

> The appointment of Dr. Davis as Commissioner of Correction is not a chivalric or quixotic effort on the part of Mayor Mitchel to recognize the interest which women have in city government, nor is it a tribute to the capacity of the sex in general. It is the appointment of a prison executive, who has conspicuously "made good" in her own field, to larger opportunities.

The range of reaction compelled Mitchel to defend his decision. "Dr. Davis has been requested to come into the administration," he said, "not because she is a woman, but because she has the training, the experience, and the point of view that I desire for the Commissioner of Correction."[73]

Davis's new position represented an important evolution in her career. Ideas and programs tested at the state reformatory now entered the realm of New York politics through Davis's administration of the prison system. Davis brought many of the methods she had tried at Bedford Hills to her new responsibilities as commissioner. Among her earliest reforms was the abolition of striped clothing for prison inmates. On her first visit to Blackwell's Island, Davis caught a glimpse of prisoners laboring on the docks in the familiar black and grey prison garb. She turned to her deputy, Burdette Lewis, and the collection of reporters that accompanied them, and spontaneously recited: "When first he saw the zebra, the donkey wagged his tail. Good gracious was his comment, that mule has been in jail." Similar wisecracks and jokes won the press over, and Davis enjoyed considerable publicity delivered by an intrigued, and sometimes delighted, press.[74]

But her quips about prison stripes quickly gave way to action. Davis announced: "I believe strongly in the psychology of clothes. As for a woman, she always has more self-respect when she has on her best clothes. . . . You cannot reform a woman who is wearing bed ticking." The decision was made to do away with New York City's traditional prison clothes, and newspapers reported that "convict stripes are going to be abolished as soon as Commissioner Davis can get rid of 18,000 yards of stripes." Predictable jokes about the female commissioner's dress reforms circulated in the city, but the change lasted, and it remained one of Davis's best-remembered innovations.[75]

Davis's training as a social scientist soon came into evidence during her early days as commissioner. Interviewed upon her appointment, Davis revealed her plans "to study all the laws which concern my position" and to "take up a study of the financial end of my work." Davis's course work in finance with Adolph Miller now came in handy as she took on responsibility for a large city budget. The new commissioner carefully went over the books of her department at the outset. Of her cautious preparatory work, Davis said, "I have a statistical mind that always has to count noses before I draw a conclusion."[76]

A similar desire for reliable information emboldened her to make a more unorthodox early move. Davis instructed two researchers on her staff to get arrested: they succeeded, and were sent to the Tombs for three weeks. While there, they observed an incredible scene of drug dealing, alcohol smuggling, and corruption. Bribes and payoffs greased the system, and inmates with money regularly gained special favors and more comfortable conditions. These firsthand reports led Davis to crack down hard on prison procedures. Food and tobacco were no longer permitted to be brought in from outside, since she claimed both served as conduits for illegal drugs. Guards were instructed to treat all prisoners alike, and one infamous inmate was remanded to a regulation cell. A city newspaper greeted this change with unbridled enthusiasm. "If this be feminism, let us have more of it." Tours for city sightseers through the Tombs came to an abrupt halt, as Davis declared, "no longer shall the prisoners there be gazed upon as wild beasts in cages."[77]

The Bedford program of outdoor work also proved compatible with the city prison system. Early in her administration Davis saw to it that a new farm school for boys was constructed in Orange County that provided an alternative to the dingy New York City Reformatory on Hart's Island. The new facility was to provide young men convicted of misdemeanors with vocational training and agricultural work. Steady in her belief that fresh air and farming cured the soul, Davis began work on the project not long after assuming office in January of 1914. By March, the first twelve boys were transferred from the city reformatory to the new farm; by summer, the fields there were already being cultivated. Less easily accomplished was the construction of a new facility for convicted women awaiting court appearances. Davis felt strongly that women inmates should be physically separated from men to prevent ill treatment and abuse; she also wanted to protect women accused of misdemeanors from being thrown in the Tombs or Blackwell's Island with hardened prisoners. As commissioner, Davis lobbied hard for the construction of a new house of detention for women. But the facility was not opened until 1932.[78]

As was true at Bedford Hills, Davis also drew on the expertise of fellow graduates of the University of Chicago. When the position of superintendent of Blackwell's Island opened up, Commissioner Davis appointed a good friend and classmate from her graduate school days, Mary Belle Harris, to the job. Harris had earned a doctorate from Chicago in the field of Sanskrit, even more remotely connected to penology than Davis's degree in political economy. Nevertheless, Harris's appointment as head of Blackwell's Island launched what was to be a distinguished career in corrections work. Harris's success in upgrading conditions at the New York City prison led to her subsequent appointment as superintendent of New Jersey's Clinton Farms Reformatory for Women. In 1927, Harris, lauded as "a woman both of broad scientific training and much practical experience," became superintendent of the first federal prison for women in the United States, established at Elderson, West Virginia. There she re-created many of the innovative programs she had learned from Davis; thus extending Davis's legacy to the federal corrections system. Among the practices that found their way to the women's prison at Elderson were outdoor work, practical educational courses, and social and psychological study of individual inmates as a first step in developing treatment plans.[79]

A severe test of Davis's leadership came just seven months into her administration when a full-scale riot broke out at the Blackwell's Island prison. The disturbance followed the indiscriminate punishment of a group of men suspected of drug smuggling and was complicated by the participation of several Wobblies (members of the Industrial Workers of the World) who had been incarcerated in the city prison. Ironically, Davis happened to be returning by boat from a meeting of the Political Equality Association at the Belmont estate in Newport the day the revolt began. As Davis passed by Blackwell's Island, she could hear the sounds of insurrection as wild "cat calls and shrieking" filled the air. To the amusement of journalists, Davis arrived at the prison dressed to the nines with, it was said, a parasol.[80]

She exhibited no signs of timidity, however, as she attempted to quiet the storm. Walking through the cell block, Davis patiently answered the shouted demands of the inmates for food. She expressed her willingness to negotiate, asking prisoners to yell out the numbers of other inmates they wanted to represent them. In a show of solidarity with her staff, and in spite of potential personal danger, Davis set up office at the prison during the riot. When Sunday arrived, the commissioner took it upon herself to lead separate religious services for Catholic, Protestant, and Jewish inmates, and she used her homilies to instruct the men in her moral principles. When the riot was soon quelled, Davis had earned new respect for her abilities as a commissioner. Yet she spoke of the inmates to the press with a familiar mixture of concern and condescension. She compared the prisoners to children, referring to them alternately as "bad boys" and "strong individualists." She insisted that "a social consciousness is asleep in the criminal as it is in a child. In both it must be awakened and after it is awakened trained." Yet she worked hard to offer the prisoners better food, and sought to improve the medical care available to them.[81]

As she had during her years at Bedford, Davis did not hesitate to turn to private philanthropy when frustrated with government bureaucracy. In the fall of 1915, Davis developed a proposal for a drug treatment center on Riker's Island. Aware that the city would not underwrite the expensive project, she turned to private donors. She quickly succeeded in raising $10,000 for the hospital from Mrs. William Vanderbilt. She then asked John D. Rockefeller and the Bureau of Social Hygiene for additional help. With a promise from them of $18,000, Davis enlisted the services of architect Franklin B. Ware, who drew up plans for the facility at no charge. The anticipated snag developed. City officials refused to authorize construction until various municipal committees approved what was to eventually become municipal property; meanwhile, prices for labor and materials rose with each passing week. Soon the estimated costs of the building far exceeded available funds, and Davis reluctantly dropped the idea.[82]

A year after the Blackwell's Island riot, Davis's administration was rocked again, this time by charges levelled against the city prison system by New York reformer Frank Tannenbaum. He attempted to expose the degrading procedures and harsh conditions that were the norm in the city's jailhouses. The State Prison Commission launched an investigation that came down hard on Davis and her leadership as being "too severe, harsh, and repressive." Mayor Mitchel stood by his commissioner. He blasted the report, and accused Davis's critics of playing politics. Other reformers shared his sentiment, and Davis survived that imbroglio with her job, if not her fine reputation, fully intact.[83]

Throughout her term as commissioner of correction, Davis continued to press for broader reform in the criminal justice system. She became increasingly outspoken about the importance of probation, parole, and of a truly indeterminate sentence. Still concerned that too little was known about offenders before their sentencing took place, Davis stressed the importance of careful study by scientific experts of alternative methods of supervision and treatment.[84]

By 1915 she could point to the Laboratory of Social Hygiene at Bedford Hills as a model. More loyal than ever to her idea of a state clearing house, Davis sought to place in the hands of experts, and take out of the hands of judges, wide discretion in determining which lawbreakers were suitable for probation. This vastly increased the authority of such officials, but Davis's naïve faith in the power of their expertise extenuated what should have been reasonable doubts. A thorough investigation of the "social, economic, and

The Midway of the World's Columbian Exposition, as seen from the Ferris Wheel. The gothic, gray buildings of the University of Chicago are visible in the background. *(The University of Chicago Library, Department of Special Collections)*

Wellesley College's Class of 1888 in their junior year on "Tree Day." Sophonisba Breckinridge is standing second to the right of Dr. and Mrs. Lyman Abbott, seated under the window. President Alice Freeman and Professor E. Horsford are in the window. *(Seaver Photo, Wellesley College Archives)*

Sophonisba Breckinridge around the time of her Wellesley graduation, 1888. *(Photo by Pach Brothers, Wellesley College Archives)*

Sophonisba Breckinridge, late in her career, professor and founder of the School of Social Service Administration, the University of Chicago. *(The University of Chicago Library, Department of Special Collections)*

Breckinridge as a graduate student at the University of Chicago, circa 1900. *(The University of Chicago Library, Department of Special Collections)*

Edith Abbott as a graduate of
Brownell Hall, wearing her
Scholarship Medal. *(The University of
Chicago Library, Department of
Special Collections)*

Abbott as a graduate student at the University of Chicago,
circa 1902–1903. *(The University of Chicago Library, Department of Special Collections)*

bott in her academic robe at the start of her reer. *(The University of Chicago Library, Department of Special Collections)*

A formal portrait of Edith Abbott as a young woman. *(The University of Chicago Library, Department of Special Collections)*

Sophonisba Breckinridge (left) and Edith Abbott (right), colleagues at the School of Social Service Administration, the University of Chicago. *(The University of Chicago Library, Department of Special Collections)*

Kellor in her twenties, photographed in the kind of natural setting she so enjoyed. *(The Schlesinger Library, Radcliffe College)*

Kellor (left) with her companion, Mary Dreier. Their relationship endured for nearly fifty years. *(The Schlesinger Library, Radcliffe College)*

Kellor relaxing and fishing off the coast near the Dreier summer home in Stonington, Connecticut. *(The Schlesinger Library, Radcliffe College)*

Frances Kellor, late in her career, when she was Vice-President of the American Arbitration Association. *(The Schlesinger Library, Radcliffe College)*

Katharine Bement Davis, superintendent of the Bedford Hills, N.Y., Reformatory for Women. *(The Library of Congress)*

Katharine Davis, Commissioner of Correction, New York City, and her Deputy Commissioner, Burdette Lewis, circa 1914. *(The Library of Congress)*

Commissioner Davis (far left), Blackwell's Island. *(The Library of Congress)*

Davis with several of the children
at Hart's Island, July 1914.
(UPI/Bettmann Newsphotos)

Katharine Davis receiving an
honorary degree from Yale
University, 1915. *(UPI/Bettmann
Newsphotos)*

Marion Talbot, Dean of Women at the University of Chicago. *(The University of Chicago Library, Department of Special Collections)*

Professor Ernst Freund, mentor of Sophonisba Breckinridge. *(The University of Chicago Library, Department of Special Collections)*

J. Laurence Laughlin, Head Professor, Department of Political Economy. Abbott and Breckinridge credited him with supporting their intellectual aspirations. *(The University of Chicago Library, Department of Special Collections)*

Professor Charles R. Henderson, sociologist and teacher of Frances Kellor. *(The University of Chicago Library, Department of Special Collections)*

Albion Small, Head Professor of Sociology, shaped Chicago's unique department. *(The University of Chicago Library, Department of Special Collections)*

Political economist Thorstein Veblen influenced all four women social scientists. He was the teacher "from whom I got the most," Katharine Davis said of her graduate studies at Chicago. *(The Bettmann Archive)*

Cobb Hall, the University of Chicago. Sophonisba Breckinridge spent most of her days as a graduate student there, taking courses from Ernst Freund. *(The University of Chicago Library, Department of Special Collections)*

moral status of the candidate for probation," she believed, would lead to intelligent decisions. "The members of the staff of a clearing house being but human, mistakes would be made," Davis admitted, "but these would be reduced to a minimum, and in the event of a given person's being found unfit for probation, he should be returned to the clearing house for further study." Davis supported the liberal use of probation for those who were mentally and physically healthy, capable of work, and convicted of first or accidental offenses, as well as for young offenders newly before the court.[85]

Parole likewise figured prominently in Davis's vision of criminal justice reform. Davis likened the goals of prisons and reformatories to those of educational institutions. She saw reflected in the varying approaches to rehabilitation all the major schools of thought regarding education. She favored a model that first taught inmates how to govern themselves, permitted them to gradually practice what they learned inside the prison, and then allowed them a point of "considerable freedom" prior to parole. The indeterminate sentence was critical to this approach. If the aim of institutions was to "train" prisoners for their "readjustment to society," no prior constraint should be placed on the superintendents who were responsible for an inmate's reeducation. The only real test of rehabilitation was behavior on parole.[86]

As commissioner of correction, Davis lobbied hard for legislation that would enact an indeterminate sentence and parole law for New York City's workhouse and county penitentiary. Along with other reformers, she favored the creation of a parole commission, which would determine when inmates were fit to be released. This campaign was successful, and in 1916 the New York State Legislature passed a bill creating the New York City Parole Commission. Mayor Mitchel rewarded Davis with the chairmanship, and in December of 1916 she gave up her position as commissioner of correction to assume her duties on the parole board.

Davis's departure gave rise to considerable praise for her record. The *New York Tribune* credited her with bringing "the city's penal institutions to a stage of modernity in theory and practice hitherto unattained and the public is the gainer thereby." Although not without its challenges, work on the Parole Commission removed Davis from the constant glare of publicity and the continual turmoil that went along with responsibility for the city's correctional institutions. But her chairmanship of the Parole Commission proved to be short-lived. When Mitchel was turned out of office in 1917, Davis's career as a city official also came to an end.[87]

Throughout her days as a prison superintendent and a member of Mitchel's cabinet, Davis found time for some participation in politics. An ardent suffragist, she took an active part in that movement, often addressing feminist groups and marching in suffrage parades. In 1914 she served as Vice-President of the National American Woman Suffrage Association. Her loyalty to the Republican party was tested by her affinity for Theodore Roosevelt and the Progressive cause. Davis defected to the Bull Moosers, as the Progressive party enthusiasts were known, in 1912. But like many of the renegades, she returned to the fold in 1916 and campaigned aggressively for Charles Evans

Hughes, riding on the special "women's train" to the West. Organized politics always took a back seat to Davis's demanding career. Firmly rooted in the here and now, she found little time for religion, either.[88]

VI

Davis retained an intense interest in the Laboratory of Social Hygiene at Bedford Hills during her three years in public office. When she left the reformatory in 1914, she continued to serve as an active member of the Bureau of Social Hygiene. Indeed, Davis functioned as a go-between for the laboratory staff and its benefactor, John D. Rockefeller, all during her years of service in New York City. Nothing illustrates more plainly the tragic failing of Progressive reform than the unravelling of Davis's bold experiment at Bedford Hills. As much as Davis believed in the soundness of her ideas, she couldn't help but see the limits of the program she enacted. The sweeping power of scientific expertise proved all too vulnerable to the vagaries of administrative changes and the torpor of the state.

Davis's timely departure from Bedford Hills prevented her from bearing the brunt of the disaster that almost immediately befell her institution. With each successive year, officials from the State Commission of Prisons had voiced increasing concern about conditions at the reformatory. Much of their criticism focused on the inaction of the state legislature in making money available for necessary improvements. The vexing problems of overcrowding, run-down facilities, and unattended repairs all depended on state attention to the reformatory, rather than the superintendent's handling of the facility under her care. Yet, as early as 1912 commissioners reported with concern that the inmates at Bedford were not being taught very "useful" trades. They hoped to see more "domestic employments" taught, including sewing, embroidery, basket weaving, and light farm work. These mild complaints provided little indication of the storm of criticism that was to follow.[89]

When Davis left Bedford in January of 1914, the dam burst. Well before her departure, rumors had circulated that "immoral and other improper conditions" existed at Bedford Hills. But the superintendent's complete control over the institution and her excellent reputation among correction officials may have prevented any formal inquiries from being undertaken at that time. Within days of Davis's departure, the State Board of Charities sent an inspector up to Bedford Hills. As a result of her week-long visit, a sharply critical report was submitted to the State Board of Charities in March of 1914.[90]

Inspector Dieckmann's report catalogued the well-known fact of overcrowding and the poor, though familiar, conditions in reformatory buildings. But laxness in discipline was now added to the list of the institution's failings. Children over two were allowed to stay at the prison with their mothers in violation of a state law that called for their removal. When "harmful intimacy" was discovered among inmates, officers did little to punish the participants. Davis's refusal to segregate black and white prisoners rankled some state authorities. Dieckmann renewed the call to separate black women in their own cottage to prevent "an unfortunate attachment formed by the white women for the negroes." She also reported that the "heavy outdoor work," so touted by Davis, was burdensome for some of the inmates at the institution, and that others learned no useful trades.[91]

The Dieckmann report led to a further inspection of the reformatory and extensive discussions with Bedford's Board of Managers. Davis's successor had little hesitation about segregating prisoners by race, even though Davis had warned that "it would be impossible to officer it with white officers in colored cottages." In late September of 1914, the Prison Association of New York noted that the original receiving building of the reformatory was in a state of complete disrepair, and was "without a doubt a blight to the institution." Steel cells provided a stark contrast with the homey cottages that comprised most of the reformatory dwellings. "The cement floors in the rooms containing the cages are in a wretched condition and add much to the gruesomeness of the section." Inmates were forced to eat with cracked and broken utensils; the building had no fireproofing. Worst of all, the ten cells in the reformatory's "disciplinary building" prevented inmates confined there from breathing fresh air.[92]

These rumblings were a prelude to the blast delivered by State Commissioner Rudolf Diedling on a visit to Bedford Hills in late October of 1914. Diedling came as close as he could to calling the reformatory a total loss. He criticized the very ground on which it was built as inadequate and advised that "not another dollar should be expended in extending the property of the Bedford Reformatory." Conditions in the disciplinary building, Diedling wrote, seemed "better suited to one's ideas of a medieval dungeon than to a disciplinary building in a modern reformatory for women in the great state of New York." Among the "horrors of this disciplinary building" were inmates shackled hand and foot for two weeks at a time and fed only with bread and water. Excessive punishment seemed the rule. Superintendent Moore did not try to defend herself to Diedling; she said that "she merely continued a system that was in vogue when she assumed charge."[93]

Moore's excuse may have had some merit. Davis was not above withholding food from unruly inmates: she provided only bread and water during the riot at Blackwell's Island as a form of punishment. There is no question that Bedford suffered from overcrowding and disrepair during her tenure there. But her successor's regime seemed to bring a dramatic turn for the worse. Simmering problems suddenly came to a boil: Moore quickly earned a reputation for being harsh and difficult. Her administration became more directly involved with discipline than had Davis's. Whether her staff was also more abusive is difficult to know.[94]

Whatever the truth, when Diedling's report hit the press, a storm of controversy was unleashed. The State Board of Charities inaugurated public hearings in November of 1914 to investigate the charges raised by Diedling that continued into January of 1915. The special committee that led the investigation concluded that "the defects in the management of this institution . . . have been largely due to the congestion of population." Much of the committee's report reiterated demands Davis herself had made long ago. Removal of "feeble minded" inmates to asylums and a reduction of the reformatory's census led the list of suggested reforms.[95]

Virtually untouched in the two years of scrutiny by state officials was the new Laboratory of Social Hygiene. Diedling expressed support for the goals of the research center, although his report contained an implied criticism of its staff. Discussing their classification work, he wrote: "Care must be taken to treat this matter in a systematic way rather than in a cold, harsh, purely scientific manner; and not by persons who assume airs of distant superiority." The State Board of Charities endorsed the laboratory without hesitation, referring to the "promise of excellent results." Indeed its special investigative committee concluded their report on Bedford with lavish praise of the research center. Yet all was far from well beneath the surface appearance of brave experimentation. For Davis and the Bureau of Social Hygiene, the laboratory became a troubling reminder of the limits of reform.[96]

Only a little more than a year after the laboratory opened, the existing facilities already seemed inadequate to the task at hand. The large number of "psychopathic cases," considered by the staff neurologist neither insane nor fully normal, troubled researchers who were baffled about how to treat this unruly group. These "borderline" inmates were seen as very difficult to manage; they often posed the most serious disciplinary problems confronted at the reformatory. Davis, now commissioner of correction but still actively involved, explained to Rockefeller that the laboratory wanted to discover what "mental or physical pathological conditions" caused the psychopaths' unrest and "whether, if handled in a scientific way, there is hope of restoring them to normality." Davis proposed that the Bureau of Social Hygiene build a "psychopathic cottage on its property opposite the present laboratory" where special research on these troubled inmates could be conducted. With space for twenty patients, five staff members, and the necessary equipment, total cost, Davis estimated, would run to $34,500.[97]

Davis's request to Rockefeller again plainly stated her desire to circumvent the state bureaucracy. There was greater reason than ever to avoid the legislature now: she made her proposal in January of 1915 just as the Board of Charities was wrapping up its investigation of Bedford Hills. Davis believed it imperative that the hospital be tied to the Laboratory of Social Hygiene. In the (unlikely) event that the legislature could be persuaded to construct the facility, Davis warned, "it would not be possible for the scientific workers to have full control and direction in matters of discipline." Her concern clearly reflected a growing rift between the laboratory's staff and that of the reformatory. In a passing and sarcastic reference to Diedling's report, Davis noted that "even Dr. Diedling, whose recent visit of forty minutes to the Bedford Reformatory has resulted in an investigation, recommended in his report that a pathological ward be established."[98]

Rockefeller's enthusiasm for the Laboratory of Social Hygiene was apparently undampened by the scandals surrounding the reformatory. After the usual period of study in July of 1915, he authorized that $51,759 be appropriated to establish the psychopathic hospital at Bedford Hills. When the facility opened in 1916, it provided impressive quarters for psychiatrist Edith Spaulding and her staff. (Like her predecessor Jean Weidensall, Spaulding had also worked at Chicago's Juvenile Psychopathic Institute.) Rockefeller's generosity permitted the hospital to employ two psychiatrists, several psychiatric nurses, and an array of service workers. The entire facility was "splendidly equipped," although Rockefeller balked when Spaulding asked for additional money to establish a "hydriatic dept." Yet by May of 1917, even that division was being built.[99]

The new venture reflected an important change in the modern approach to crime: criminality was beginning to be understood as a mental illness. Where once a poor social environment, bad genes, or a lack of intelligence were pointed to as causes of crime, now psychiatric disorder became the favored explanation of wrongdoing. This "modern" theory served the needs of weary administrators whose efforts to rehabilitate and reform consistently fell short of their goals. Troublemakers who performed well enough on intelligence tests to outwit mental testers now faced the hydrotherapy favored by prison psychiatrists. At the new psychopathic hospital some patients received eleven baths a day, with immersions that could last up to two hours each. For a while, with Davis's amazing ability to win support, Rockefeller's unlimited resources, and a persistent supply of criminals, the laboratory at Bedford Hills was a chameleon that changed in response to the latest modern views of deviance and unrest. Eventually, however, all the variations began to pall, and as early as December of 1915, clear doubts about the venture had emerged.[100]

That month, plans were being made to gather the men and women who served as advisors to the laboratory for a meeting. The Laboratory of Social Hygiene was overseen by an "advisory board" that included University of Chicago professor James Angell; the well-known psychiatrist Adolph Meyer; Dr. Abraham Flexner, a close Rockefeller associate; and Davis herself. When Angell realized he could not attend the upcoming meeting, he wrote a long letter to Starr Murphy articulating his concerns. Angell expressed real doubts about the future of the laboratory, and his message to Murphy presented the problems there as a true crisis. The crux of the matter involved the relationship between the reformatory and the laboratory. Angell explained that Superintendent Moore felt "personal animosity towards Miss Davis," which led her to undermine those aspects of the reformatory that most clearly bore her predecessor's stamp. Moore had, Angell claimed, "brought it about that in every possible way the general program established by the latter, is discredited and put under fire, sometimes openly, but more often subtly and surreptitiously."[101]

Moore's attack on the Laboratory of Social Hygiene was one of exclusion rather than direct assault, Angell maintained. The superintendent ignored the laboratory as much as she could, preventing the research staff "from rendering any practical service to the Reformatory." Although the laboratory continued to compile a social history of new arrivals, and psychologists administered mental tests, the reformatory made no effort to use the information with which they were provided. Most frustrating, researchers never got a chance to work with the troubling disciplinary cases. A study of this group, Angell said, might have enlarged the laboratory's understanding of crime and provided Bedford officials with some real assistance in dealing with the most recalcitrant offenders. Instead, the reformatory's administration spent more and more time attempting to control the most unruly inmates. And they became increasingly isolated from the rest of the staff as they strove to do so.

Angell's remarks made it plain that an intensely hostile climate prevailed at Bedford Hills. "Instances are not wanting in which a matron has been told by the Superintendent that it would be of no value to her to be on friendly terms with the laboratory." The prison doctor found it difficult to be civil to staff members of the laboratory. With the research center's influence "now reduced to zero," valued assistants, such as the "sociologist" Virginia Robinson and neurologist Dr. Guibard, had left. Superintendent Moore had none of Davis's scientific interests or enthusiasm for academic expertise. As Angell explained:

> the abler and better trained of Dr. Davis's administrative appointees are one by one being eliminated, and in their places are being appointed persons who are entirely unsympathetic to the scientific spirit, and so far as I can judge in large measure quite unprepared to appreciate any of the more enlightened methods of scientific work in its relation to reformatory problems.

Laboratory head Dr. Mabel Fernald was a woman of great integrity and ability, but Angell warned that without some intervention "the whole situation must speedily go to shipwreck."

Angell had little to offer Murphy and the Bureau of Social Hygiene in the way of solutions. The laboratory had to either cut its ties with the reformatory and function as a group devoted to pure research, or the present prison administration had to go. The new psychopathic ward promised only to add to the "chaos." Angell foresaw bitter struggles between the prison superintendent and laboratory psychiatrists over who controlled the disturbed inmates. In all, the Chicago professor felt gloomy about the laboratory's prospects. "I confess that I am quite hopeless of any ultimate cure," he wrote, "short of the return of Dr. Davis or some other equally intelligent and rational person to the charge of the institution as a whole."[102]

Angell's discouraging assessment of the once-promising experiment at Bedford Hills plainly reflected the frustration scientific experts felt in establishing an institution responsive to intelligent reform. As long as Katharine Davis ran the state reformatory, it was possible to believe that scientific researchers could join hands with those who kept the inmates at Bedford Hills. Davis firmly believed that scientific investigation provided the best avenue for practical reform. But she saw the prison's work from an unusual vantage point. She appreciated the imperatives of broad-based research as well as the necessity of using knowledge for rehabilitative ends. Her perspective was clearly open to serious question. But she made her staff believe the brave experiment could succeed. When Davis left the reformatory, the staff at the Laboratory of Social Hygiene learned a painful lesson. The strength of the superintendent's ideas vanished with her presence. The pathway to "enlightened" reform depended on the sure footing of a sympathetic guide.

Two weeks before Angell voiced his dismay about the laboratory and its future, officials at the Rockefeller Foundation had already begun to formally question the mission of the Bureau of Social Hygiene. With the Bedford Hills project much in the news, there was every reason for these men to examine the wisdom of funding applied research in the social sciences. Enthusiasm was growing for ventures that did not carry political costs.[103]

A recent and unhappy experience with another Rockefeller-supported project heightened concern. In 1914 the services of W. L. MacKenzie King had been secured to direct a new research venture in industrial relations. Unfortunately for the Rockefeller Foundation, at about the same time a company run by the Rockefellers, Colorado Fuel and Iron, was rocked by a violent strike. The walkout followed the deaths of eleven children and two women, a tragedy long since remembered as the "Ludlow massacre." The United States Commission on Industrial Relations launched an investigation of the debacle in 1915, and the foundation came under intense scrutiny in the process. Searching questions were asked about the connection between the Rockefellers' philanthropic interests and their financial empire.[104]

At a conference held on December 7, 1915, to discuss the Bureau of Social Hygiene, two sentiments gained strength among foundation officials. While there was a clear desire to probe deeper into a wide array of pressing social issues, there was also intense concern about how such forays should be made. One can see in the discussion intelligent men feeling their way toward a solution that in later years became standard at the Rockefeller Foundation. Jerome Greene spoke enthusiastically of academic research in the social sciences and the value of funding individuals who would investigate timely problems. The great advantage in such an approach, Greene seemed to suggest, was that the Rockefeller Foundation could be well insulated against political fallout and administrative failure.[105]

In one exchange Greene put it this way:

> There is no limit to the amount of such fundamental studies as the Rockefeller Foundation can make. It is not like giving away to charitable agencies all over the country. The only limitation it seems to me on such study is the capacity of seeing the need but such a study does not commit us to anything. It has no by-products that are conceivably anything but good when you have got the important problem well defined and the man to take it up. You could stop at any point and not lose the work already accomplished. It could be taken up again by anyone at that point. We could do as much or as little in this field as we are advised.

One colleague questioned Greene's assumptions. "You say that you could do as much or as little in this field as you are advised. Is that exactly true? For instance if the Foundation should take up some investigation such as this it would not only take it up but would try to make it fruitful all over the country and it would be an established agency. If you suddenly stopped off. . . ." But another colleague immediately sensed Greene's meaning. Abraham Flexner interrupted, "Are you trying to show that it was not like setting up a model prison, Mr. Greene?" "That's it, exactly," Greene replied.[106]

Consultants to the Laboratory of Social Hygiene also began to warn the foundation against incautiously authorizing any further work for the research center. When a proposal emerged in 1916 to expand the Laboratory of Social Hygiene's investigations beyond Bedford to other institutions, Adolph Meyer expressed great reservations. "I should reduce the amount of expansion into such a large number of institutions unless I had an idea of reform influence, and on that point the laboratory force has not proved very successful at Bedford." Meyer's perspective reflected the ascendancy of a new profession—medicine—in corrections work. Now the impressive credentials of psychiatric experts made the first professionals to become involved in prison work, such as Davis, appear second-rate. Meyer did not hesitate to call into question Davis's competence. Referring to the problems at the laboratory, he said, "It makes me deplore again the absence of a thoroughly trained head of this Research Department. I admire Dr. Davis, but I consider her problem and ambition very vague."[107]

Bringing more medical professionals into the research venture clearly meant a challenge to the almost entirely female laboratory. Dr. E. E. Southard recognized this, and apprised the Rockefeller Foundation of his views. The psychiatrist wrote: "I feel that the problems of the female delinquent are not problems for women alone to investigate; that the developments at Bedford Hills have suffered from their execution almost entirely by women." Where Davis and her associates were once hailed as experts because they possessed Ph.D.s, now their academic credentials withered next to the seemingly more modern and valuable expertise of those who held medical degrees. This change reflected a fundamental shift of authority that accompanied professionalization in the early twentieth century. Women such as Davis who had forged careers as activists outside of academe, in the face of barriers to success in university life, were now too marginal to conform to the standards of academic life. They were also becoming very isolated from the centers of knowledge modern social scientists believed were essential to effective corrections work. Fortunately for Davis, John D. Rockefeller, Jr., himself was a man of the nineteenth century. He remained intensely loyal to her and to her work, and he continued to support the Laboratory of Social Hygiene at Bedford Hills.[108]

Perhaps most difficult for those involved in the Bedford Hills project was the disappointment they faced when New York State failed to fulfill their expectations by taking charge of the experiment. In 1916 a plan was drawn up to transform the Laboratory of Social Hygiene into a "State Clearing House for Women Convicted in the First, Second, Third, and Fourth Judicial

Districts of New York." The proposed legislation called for the study of convicted women before sentencing, to determine the sort of institution to which
they should be remanded. The clearing house, which would be created out of
the presently existing laboratory at Bedford Hills, was to be an independent
state institution, with a board of managers appointed by the governor.[109]

All involved knew that winning the passage of such sweeping legislation
was not going to be easy. In discussions with Starr Murphy and Mabel Fernald in April of 1916, Davis stressed that the success of such a campaign
depended on demonstrating the practical value of criminology research to the
state legislature. This could only be done, Starr Murphy guessed,

> if we can show to the legislature that in the absence of such a clearing house
> a great deal of public money is wasted by endeavoring to give education to
> women who, by reason of mental deficiency, are unable to profit by education
> . . . it may lead the legislature to see the importance of providing such a clear-
> ing house as a matter of economy of public funds.

It seemed clear that the state of New York saw little value in pure research.
Murphy explained, "Miss Davis was very strongly of the opinion that no legislature would ever take over the institution as a purely scientific
institution."[110]

Davis herself took the lead in lobbying for the bill. In December of 1916
she drew up an outline of the legislation and submitted it to Rockefeller for
his endorsement. A strategy for winning approval of the bill was also laid out.
She suggested that the support of influential judges, charity organizations,
prison reformers, state agencies, and elected officials be secured. Rockefeller
apparently approved the plan and took it upon himself to personally
approach the governor of New York, Charles L. Whitman. On February 15th
of 1917 the bill was introduced to the New York Senate as "an act to amend
the state charities law in relation to the establishment of a state clearing house
for delinquent women." But the timing could not have been worse. The
beginning of February brought the increasing likelihood of war as Germany
announced its intention to resume unrestricted submarine warfare. President
Wilson severed diplomatic relationships with Germany in February, and
heightened preparations for war followed. The New York Legislature had
more important matters to consider than a clearing house for delinquent
women. And in spite of some "favorable" sentiment, the bill was tabled for
the entire session.[111]

Nevertheless, Davis expressed great optimism to Rockefeller that a year's
delay would result in "favorable action by the state." The problem was that
the Bureau of Social Hygiene's contract with the Bedford Hills Reformatory
was due to expire in September of 1917. Davis asked Rockefeller to carry the
laboratory through for another year. Acknowledging in May of 1917 "the special situation of the state finances owing to war preparation," Rockefeller
announced that the Bureau of Social Hygiene would appropriate additional
funds of up to $30,000 until July 1, 1918. But the grant was made with the

explicit "understanding that if further delay should occur on the part of the State, the Bureau will not be expected to go on with the work after that date."[112]

Davis was in a good position to prevail upon the generosity of Mr. Rockefeller. In August of 1917 she had accepted Rockefeller's offer to work full time as general secretary of the Bureau of Social Hygiene when she gave up her chairmanship of the parole board at the end of the year. But persuading Rockefeller was one thing—moving the New York legislature was another. Again in 1918 the state failed to take over the laboratory at Bedford Hills, and in August of that year even Rockefeller's limits had been reached. With nearly $200,000 spent on what was to have been a compelling experiment, the Laboratory of Social Hygiene and the Psychopathic Hospital closed.[113]

The closing of the laboratory did nothing to abate the ghastly problems of Bedford Hills. In 1919 the State Commission of Prisons was once again investigating the reformatory as reports of cruelty and abuse of patients surfaced. The prison's administration found itself on the defensive yet again as inmates testified of being "strung up," doused with water, and starved. Overcrowding had become a desperate problem; the prison barely resembled the institution Davis had walked into in 1901. Typically, officials at the reformatory blamed the "psychopathic cases" for much of the trouble, a charge that led the state commissioner investigating the facility to stress the importance of having a working hospital on the grounds. With utter shamelessness, Commissioner John S. Kennedy made an incredible appeal to John D. Rockefeller, Jr., in November of 1919 to "loan" the defunct hospital and adjacent buildings he owned at Bedford Hills to the state. Davis had been asked to make this overture to Rockefeller, but she declined. As she explained to the philanthropist, "it seemed to me that the State had its chance to avail itself of the facilities of the Laboratory but had not taken it." In denying Kennedy's request, Rockefeller took the opportunity to resurrect the original clearing house plan. He told the commissioner he would be glad to make his facilities at Bedford available "if the legislature . . . should shortly vote to acquire this property for State purposes, appropriating the necessary funds for its acquisition and maintenance and having in mind its use as a clearing house . . . for the care of mentally defective women." The state had no intention of doing so, and the deal was not struck.[114]

In the spring of 1920 a bill finally made it through the legislature that created the Division for Mentally Defective Delinquent Women at Bedford Hills. Although the plan had Davis's support, the new department bore very little resemblance to the dreams the idealistic young superintendent had nourished twenty years before. Under the new law, all "enfeebled" women in the state were to be remanded to the new division, where they would serve out their time in quarters away from the rest of the reformatory's inmates. Davis felt optimistic about the arrangement in part because "a new superintendent, with some experience in dealing with mental defectives, has just been appointed at Bedford." Yet, gone from the blueprints was the elaborate research institute Davis so desired. Nonetheless, she and Starr Murphy urged

Rockefeller to lease his property at Bedford to the state for one dollar so that the requirements of the new law could be carried through. Rockefeller agreed, and finally, in 1924, the buildings were sold to the reformatory for good. By that time Bedford had become the institution of choice for judges sentencing "mentally defective women and those addicted to narcotics." A male psychiatrist headed the reformatory. Davis spent the rest of her career at the Bureau of Social Hygiene, in essence a paid employee of the Rockefeller Foundation.[115]

VII

Throughout her long career in corrections, Davis never abandoned her compelling vision of social problems and her optimistic view of social reform. She brought ideas that had been forged in the quiet of the university to the volatile realm of American prisons. In so doing, Davis helped to broaden contemporary views of crime, taking special pains to advance a new understanding of female delinquency. The methods of intellectuals yielded far more ambiguous results when they were used to guide prison administration. Research and scientific expertise provided no clear blueprint for rehabilitation or reform.

Instead, prisoners were victimized by ill-conceived treatment methods based on dubious theories of crime. Neither the state nor private philanthropists ultimately had much patience for the slow process of social research. The model of applied social science Katharine Bement Davis helped advance made her one of the most influential women in the corrections field. But it could not solve the terrible problems confounding American prisons. This was the disappointing reality of Davis's innovative experiment at Bedford Hills.

6

"If Sex Could Be Eliminated"

Public service, private philanthropy, and hard-nosed politics shaped the destiny of many reformers who hoped to change American society in the early twentieth century. Few had a keener sense of this reality than Frances Kellor. From the moment she left graduate school in Chicago and settled down in New York, Kellor began to build a career around a series of causes. Her experience underscores the tremendous challenges faced by activists in the era that preceded the welfare state. Those who believed that government bore a responsibility for the welfare of its citizens needed to persuade both the public at large and those who wielded power to expand the state. They relied on the support of voluntary associations and private benefactors to finance their public relations campaigns. And they readily resorted to practical politics to realize their vision of a just society.

For Frances Kellor, these tasks were more than a means to an end. Her entire professional existence was based upon her advocacy of social change— a feat made possible by her own special talents and the extraordinary times in which she lived. Kellor's impressive academic training and her highly developed social research skills proved valuable commodities in the crowded marketplace of early-twentieth-century reform. The rapid progression of the sociologist's career brought her ideas about social problems, her intense interest in women's issues, and her vision of social change to private organizations, state government, and national party politics. The result was a complicated, and uneasy, fusion of social-scientific values and state-centered social reform.

Kellor's activities on behalf of Progressive causes evolved in roughly three stages. In the earliest phase of her career, she joined forces with several voluntary associations. Kellor's research and writing were designed to heighten public awareness of unemployment and mobilize political support for legislative reform campaigns. This was muckraking, but of a very special kind. Kellor offered an environmental analysis of social problems that highlighted the special concerns of women and that justified active intervention by the state. Through the efforts of like-minded social activists, these ideas found a place in the political language of reform.

Kellor's views were grafted onto state government in the second stage of her career. As chief of New York State's Bureau of Industries and Immigration, she sought to expand public responsibility for immigration. Kellor's perspective on social problems and her commitment to social research soon found expression in her administration of the state bureau and in her aggressive pursuit of federal immigration reform.

In the most extraordinary period of her career, Kellor managed to exert some influence on the substance and form of Progressive politics. She became one of the first American women to penetrate the inner circle of a national political party. During the tumultuous campaign of 1912, she wielded a power in organized politics that was nearly unprecedented for a woman of her own, or any previous, generation. Close advisor to Theodore Roosevelt, member of the Progressive party's National Committee, and head of the Bull Moose's innovative Progressive Service, Kellor rose to these dizzying heights at a time when American women could not vote. The vitality of early-twentieth-century public life permitted her ascendance in all of these endeavors, just as surely as it ordained her fall.

II

Kellor's New York career began in a way that made quick use of her extensive training in the social sciences. Under the auspices of a College Settlement Association Fellowship, she embarked on a study of unemployment in 1902. This issue first captured her attention when she was a graduate student. Her investigations of female offenders had convinced Kellor that unemployment contributed to criminality. During summer studies at the New York School of Philanthropy in 1902, she decided to focus her attention on New York's employment agencies. Their practices, she believed, deeply affected the city's destitute who turned to these offices out of desperation. The grant offered by the settlement group permitted Kellor to expand her study to Boston, Philadelphia, and Chicago. Arriving in Chicago in the fall of 1902, Kellor stayed at Hull House, and found time to sit in on Charles Henderson's sociology classes at the university. Her initial research findings seemed promising, and the Settlement Association renewed Kellor's fellowship in 1903 to give her an extra year of work.[1]

By the spring of 1903, Kellor's investigations had captured the attention of New York's Woman's Municipal League. Josephine Shaw Lowell, the ubiquitous reformer who had helped place Katharine Davis at Bedford Hills, was the founder of the league. Initially formed in October of 1894 as part of an anti-Tammany campaign in New York City, the Woman's Municipal

League kept up its interests in city politics and reform. Margaret Dreier, head of the league's legislative committee, worked to advance laws that addressed various social welfare issues. Dreier's interest in the corrupt practices of New York's employment agencies led her to Kellor, whom she knew from the New York School of Philanthropy and from the settlement house community. Dreier encouraged Kellor to return to New York and focus her study there. The sociologist readily agreed, and for much of the following year she prepared an important book on unemployment, *Out of Work*, which was published in November of 1904. While in New York, Kellor made her home at the Rivington Street College Settlement House.[2]

Out of Work was one of the first studies in the United States to analyze unemployment as a social problem. Well into the early twentieth century, faith in economic mobility and expansive opportunity militated against a critical perspective on this troubling feature of industrial capitalism. Without a structural view, academics and laymen alike relied on explanations of unemployment that blamed the idle for not being more aggressive in pursuing work. Kellor's previous sociological research on crime, her exposure to prisoners, and perhaps her own life experience, led her to examine the social and economic context of joblessness. She approached her study of employment agencies convinced that "abuses were common," and determined to advance "further knowledge" of unemployment through her own investigative work.[3]

Much as she had during her graduate school years, Kellor quickly embarked on risky field research in an effort to gain firsthand knowledge of her subject. Along with eight assistants, she disguised herself as both employer and employee, personally visiting various agencies and even assuming a job as a domestic in a private home. To ensure objectivity, she also played the role of potential agent, asking for advice on setting up her own business and seeking out entrepreneurs who made a living from placing domestic help.

Kellor justified this deception as being in the interests of science; she insisted that it was impossible to acquire honest answers without using devious techniques. "Does not the end justify the means?" she asked.

> Is it not expedient and right to employ this, the only accurate method of investigation, rather than to continue the present conditions, which, beyond doubt, are at least partly responsible for the doubling of wages, the dissatisfaction of employees ... the swindling of penniless, homeless, but worthy men and women out of fees and positions, and the misleading of ignorant immigrants and innocent city and country girls to the number of many thousands a year?

Nevertheless, the masquerade sometimes led to ticklish situations, as when "we came straight up against an old acquaintance who was looking for a maid and were sent in to her to fill that place." In all, Kellor and her staff visited over seven hundred employment agencies in Boston, Chicago, New York, and Philadelphia. "Intelligence offices" that handled domestic servants and agencies supplying help for various businesses received the most attention.[4]

Kellor's research on domestic work exposed a vast, largely unregulated, and exploitative network of agencies in each city that prospered from the misfortunes of immigrant, black, and migrant women. Located above saloons, in three-room apartments, dingy tenement houses, and even in the corner of one barber shop, the employment offices were generally clustered in areas of the city where transients wandered in search of lodging. Many offices provided room and board for those seeking work. In so doing, the agencies filled a void left by poorly developed municipal welfare systems. "In no city," Kellor noted, "are adequate provisions made for such homeless women, and their predicament is particularly acute, for their friends are often household workers who cannot extend the hospitality of their rooms." Beds offered by the agencies were often "dirty and alive with vermin," but few tenants could expect to sleep alone. Kellor found the rooms filled with "old and young, sober and drunk, clean and unclean, good and bad ... innocent fresh girls and old hags." The scene was grim, and all the more troubling to Kellor because the owners of the agencies were frequently women.[5]

Agency owners resorted to virtually any method that yielded profits, Kellor discovered. The outright trickery of flimflam artists separated young girls from their money with costly promises of employment: the agent departed with the cash and the job never materialized. Excessive fees and inflated promises were the rule in many offices. Employers who used such agencies learned the hard way about their limitations. In their eagerness to acquire fees, agents rarely screened those in search of work. Sometimes the results were no more serious than incompetent workers; on other occasions domestics robbed employers of their most valuable possessions.

Larger social and economic forces, Kellor argued, created conditions ripe for such exploitation. Poverty and racial discrimination made black Americans especially vulnerable to employment agencies. Ruthless white operators preyed on Southern black women, Kellor noted, promising them lucrative employment in the North. The migrants discovered upon arrival that nothing more than domestic service was available to them. This was, Kellor insisted, a "system of slavery" whereby black women were controlled and "kept at offices until sold." Kellor quoted her classmate from Chicago, Katharine Bement Davis, when describing black women deceived by agencies that acted as procurers for houses of prostitution. "The Superintendent of the Bedford Reformatory says: 'Almost without exception the negro girls at my institution have been brought North by some employment agency.'" Kellor's study repeated some of the racial and ethnic stereotypes that had surfaced in her research as a graduate student. But she harshly condemned the ill treatment and oppression of minority groups by white employers and agents.[6]

Kellor also stressed the suffering of immigrants in her description of household work. Migration created a pool of vulnerable young women who traveled from American farms to cities in response to well-organized recruitment drives, only to be exploited by urban employment offices. The offices circumvented immigration laws and located foreign women through advertisements in European newspapers. Once these immigrants landed in the

United States, agents took advantage of their ignorance of American customs and cities. Male researchers investigated firsthand the conditions endured by immigrant men. They discovered a routine of excessive fees, false advertising, illegal contracts, low wages, and unbelievably long hours. One staff member, Gino C. Speranza, exposed the inhuman methods used by *padroni*, Italian labor bosses who manipulated immigrant loyalty to home and community by luring their fellow countrymen into harsh labor camps. Kellor explained the Italian immigrant's vulnerability to such schemes in sociological terms. Community life among southern Italian peasants revolved around local leaders who could provide assistance in times of need. An immigrant newly arriving in America "being apparently ignorant, though really intelligent" turned to the padrone for assistance as a matter of course.[7]

Corrupt employment agencies flourished, Kellor believed, because a large market for servants existed without a rational system of acquiring help. While lambasting offices for mistreating jobless men and women, Kellor insisted that the agencies exemplified problems that were deeply rooted in American society. The public considered employment agencies as "factories where household workers may be manufactured." In reality, an agency could only be, at best, "an intermediary—a medium of exchange." The offices could "never be a solution to any problem whose roots go deep down into social and economic life." At the very heart of "social and economic life" was the need for adequate jobs and decent working conditions. "Lack of employment," Kellor asserted, was

> more vitally related to crime, immorality, vice, dishonesty, degeneration, and conditions vitally affecting national life, than any other one condition, and this is true of professional men and women as well as of general laborers.[8]

As in her studies of crime, Kellor placed great emphasis on gender in her analysis of household work. Like Katharine Davis, she challenged the notion that domestic employment was ideally suited to women's special needs. Both women were acutely sensitive to sex segregation in the labor market. Their personal experience as professional women led them to reject traditional views of women's work. Household labor, they suggested, offered modern women little in the way of status, wages, or self-esteem. In fact, Kellor insisted that the very structure of domestic service contributed to the exploitation of women workers. "The conditions of household labor," she wrote, "are responsible for about all that the offices are not." Dividing her analysis into a consideration of "health, economics, and sociability," Kellor found domestic service wanting in all three respects. Long hours, low wages, heavy labor, incessant and unreasonable employer demands, inadequate food, and insufficient living space belied the popular notion that "housework is more healthful than any other kind of occupation."[9]

Kellor hoped to elevate domestic service by mandating fair contracts that stipulated wages, duties, and hours. Only then would household labor deserve the attention of women workers. Indeed, *Out of Work* displayed a markedly prolabor stance in several respects. Kellor praised organized labor for providing important safeguards against the rampant exploitation of unemployed men. Local unions that took an active role in helping members find work staved off even more widespread distress. "The dangers which beset the unemployed, unskilled laborer at employment agencies would, we believe, exist more extensively for skilled workers if trade unions did not prevent them." Unions had their own motives for putting their rank and file to work. Every employed union member, Kellor noted, meant greater influence for the organization. But this fact did not trouble the sociologist in the least. She wrote of the unions with respect: "the incentive is not money but power." Indeed, her only criticism of trade unions was their choice of meeting-place— saloons. A temperance advocate, Kellor disapproved of exposing working men to alcohol's temptation. But she softened even that mild criticism by pointing out that "wherever settlements or individuals have been able to offer desirable rooms, unions have expressed themselves as more than willing to meet there."[10]

Kellor's analysis of unemployment emphasized themes that had figured prominently in her previous research on crime. She again stressed the importance of race and ethnicity in determining one's life chances: in American society joblessness fell most heavily on oppressed racial and ethnic groups. Gender was as important a variable in Kellor's study of unemployment as it had been in her assessment of crime. Women operated within a distinct labor market, she argued, that made them especially vulnerable to exploitation. Finally, Kellor placed responsibility for unemployment on social and economic forces rather than on individuals. As a result, she looked to the state for reform.

Out of Work advanced a program of change that relied primarily on scientific knowledge, state intervention, and government centralization. Kellor had emphasized all three approaches in her prior research on crime: they would remain persistent themes throughout her career. She considered social inquiry a precondition for reform, as did Katharine Davis. Both women developed similar models for bringing about institutional change. Kellor held up the Boston-based Women's Educational and Industrial Union as a "most representative and progressive association" because its Domestic Reform League used "scientific" research into "household problems" as a basis for reform. The league served as "a practical clearing-house for labor and an educational centre." Kellor hoped to assign similar responsibilities to the state.[11]

Kellor endorsed the creation of state "Bureaus of Information" that would investigate existing problems and direct employees to respectable employment and decent housing. (Later, Kellor lobbied for a federal Department of Labor.) The informational "clearing-houses" she envisioned resembled Katharine Davis's "rational" plan for treating criminal women in New York. Both models attempted to institutionalize social research, placing considerable authority over social policy in the hands of experts. Although the investigative bureaus were to be "educational centers rather than a final aid or solution in themselves," Kellor assumed their research would result in intelligent policy recommendations.[12]

The clearing house idea responded to two political realities. It was designed, first, to circumvent New York's disgraceful machine politics. Although organizations thriving on the unemployed required regulation, existing statutes often were inadequate in scope or poorly enforced. Law, Kellor observed, seemed to bend under the weight of shifting political allegiances. During reform mayor Seth Low's administration more careful supervision of employment agencies began, but that changed quickly when Low was turned out of office. "In New York, with the Republican state office in the midst of a Tammany-governed city," any state commissioner attempting to regulate these agencies faced "tremendous" odds. In short, the corruption of municipal politics prompted Kellor to lobby for statewide reform.[13]

Kellor's employment clearing house reflected not only her disenchantment with local politics, but her attraction to state power. She hoped to expand government control over labor policy: the clearing house was intended as a first step in that direction. German national employment bureaus provided Kellor with an attractive model, even though she did not consider that system practical in the United States. "Its whole atmosphere is business rather than politics." Since the same could not be said of New York, Kellor pressed for a compromise. She favored state legislation regulating employment agencies with municipal enforcement. That approach had the advantage of assuring state supervision while offering city officials some power to police local conditions. As Kellor put it, "this method ensures the interest of the state, gives the law more permanency, and makes it possible to utilize all of the city machinery in its enforcement. It also vests some discretionary power in the Chief Executive."[14]

In 1903, Kellor took the advice she freely dispensed, and launched a campaign to enact strict regulation of employment agencies. Under the auspices of the Woman's Municipal League, Kellor and Margaret Dreier drafted legislation for New York State to correct the abuses uncovered in Kellor's study. The bill called for strict licensing and supervision of employment agencies in New York's major cities. Enforcement would be provided by a new commissioner of licenses, appointed by the mayor. Agencies would be monitored, in part, through bimonthly visits by inspectors selected through the Civil Service.

Dreier and Kellor lobbied aggressively for passage of their model law. During two years of research, Kellor had worked in silence, refraining from publicizing her findings in any way. Now she and Dreier called together municipal officials and representatives from key employment agencies for a dramatic unveiling of Kellor's findings. The proposed bill was offered as a convenient remedy. Kellor leaked the results of her investigation to the press, and copies of all supporting evidence were sent to New York City's mayor. This media blitz worked. Major newspaper editors endorsed the bill; extensive publicity stimulated public interest. In one sensational story penned for the *New York Tribune*, Kellor played the part of muckraker by telling an extreme tale of exploitation that ended with an immigrant girl's death in an insane asylum.[15]

Some powerful agencies objected to Kellor's findings and to the Municipal League bill, but Dreier, especially, proved a very shrewd lobbyist. She built a coalition that included political figures and leading employment agents, who recognized that some regulation was now inevitable. In hearings that preceded the bill's introduction to the New York State Legislature, compromise on controversial aspects of the proposed law was achieved. By the time the measure was presented for discussion in Albany, no one voiced opposition. The bill passed unamended with just four dissenting votes cast.

The victory was a heady one for Dreier and especially for investigator Kellor, whose research provided a foundation for the reform campaign. Proven was the young sociologist's conviction that informed study could guide effective social action. Reflecting on the struggle, Kellor concluded that "success seems primarily due to two things: an indisputable knowledge of conditions; and second, the willingness to cooperate, and find out under what regulations the agents themselves could work most honestly, and to grant any fair demands." "Facts" gathered by scientific investigation, Kellor concluded, could serve as powerful political instruments for social change.[16]

Kellor and Dreier knew enough about New York politics to recognize that passage of a regulatory law would not eradicate the problems endemic to household work. As a result, they proceeded with Kellor's idea for an informational clearing house that would conduct further research and disseminate investigators' findings. The two women brought together representatives of the Women's Educational and Industrial Union in Boston, the Association of Household Research in New York, and the Civic Club of Philadelphia to form an "Inter-Municipal Committee on Household Research." The committee was charged with coordinating local organizations in each city. The College Settlement Association (C.S.A.) and the Association of Collegiate Alumni (A.C.A.) agreed to provide funds for a research fellow. This was fortuitous for Kellor, whose stipend from the College Settlement Association ran out in June of 1904.

Although she seemed the logical choice for the new fellowship, Kellor required a decent salary to live on, unlike wealthy Margaret Dreier and her activist sister Mary. When she expressed reluctance about accepting the modest salary offered by the C.S.A. and the A.C.A., the Dreier sisters appealed to the Woman's Municipal League. Its officers needed little persuasion, and Kellor was soon appointed to oversee the organization's various committees. The league had long functioned as a voluntary association: Kellor's new job made her one of only two paid employees in the women's group.[17]

Her association with the Dreier sisters also marked a decisive turn in Kellor's personal life. By the winter of 1904 she had formed a close bond with Mary Dreier, and in 1905 she moved into the Dreier home in Brooklyn Heights. Thus began a relationship that would endure for forty-eight years—until the end of Kellor's life. In many respects, Mary Dreier was Kellor's opposite. Free-spirited, passionate, comfortable with herself and with her life, Dreier gave her friend a level of emotional (and financial) stability that Kellor had probably never before experienced.

The relationship was clearly romantic; whether it was also sexual is impossible to know. However she expressed her love, Kellor herself saw the start of her association with Dreier as the end of an important phase of her life. At thirty, she experienced a painful personal crisis that brought self-acceptance. "Fighting against a certain temptation for years has depleted my strength," she confessed to Dreier. "Now that the temptation is overcome . . . I find myself something of a wreck . . . and strange as it may seem somewhat at a loss—that part of my life is finished. . . . There is a great deal I must do, but there is no longer one single great thing to overcome." Sustained by Dreier's warmth and affection, Kellor faced her future as a single woman and redoubled her commitment to her career.[18]

As "general Secretary" of the Inter-Municipal Committee, Kellor worked closely with Margaret Dreier, who served as treasurer, and Mary Morton Kehew, head of the Women's Educational and Industrial Union, who agreed to act as chairperson. By the time *Out of Work* was published in November of 1904, the Inter-Municipal Committee had already recruited supporters who included such luminaries as Edward Devine, president of New York's Charity Organization Society, Grace Dodge, treasurer of the Woman's Municipal League, settlement leader Lillian Wald, social worker Mary Sim-khovitch, and the most-impressive Florence Kelley, leader of the National Consumers' League, who now lived in New York. As secretary of the Inter-Municipal Committee and director of research for the Woman's Municipal League, Kellor continued to investigate labor issues. The work was rewarding, particularly when her studies led to successful legislation such as the Prentiss-Tully bill, which tightened enforcement of child labor laws.[19]

The publication of *Out of Work* enhanced Kellor's reputation as an expert on social problems and served as a springboard for her increasing involvement with other reform campaigns. Although many social activists knew how to passionately argue their cause, Kellor's adroit use of social research enabled her to present her personal convictions as social "facts." That talent impressed several public officials, including New York Congressman William S. Bennet, who happily complied when Kellor asked him to introduce her to President Theodore Roosevelt. Bennet considered Kellor "a fine woman, highly intelligent, alert and energetic." As he recalled the meeting with Roosevelt:

> I understood his psychology quite well. So I said, "Mr. President, I am pleased to present Miss Frances Kellor, author of the well-known book 'Out of Work.'" That put me right out of the picture, as I knew it would. An appointment was made to come and talk to him about the book. The President and Miss Kellor became close friends.

Roosevelt took great interest in Kellor's research. "I have just read the chapter on Household Work," he wrote to the reformer in 1906, "and I wish it could be distributed as a tract among just about four fifths of those who hire household servants!"[20]

In 1905 Kellor was also welcomed as a member of New York City's Committee of Fourteen, an organization seeking to eradicate the "Raines Law Hotels" many believed encouraged vice. As secretary of the committee, Kellor oversaw the research and writing of the group's report. When its findings were issued in 1910, as *The Social Evil in New York City: A Study in Law Enforcement*, it took an analytical approach to the "white slavery" problem. The study recommended further exploration of the links between real estate businesses and prostitution, the low wages paid to women and the growth of vice. It stressed the environmental causes of prostitution and the importance of scientific work, a perspective Kellor readily endorsed.[21]

Long-standing intellectual interests began to reappear as items on Kellor's reform agenda. She acted on one persistent concern in 1906 when she founded the National League for the Protection of Colored Women. Designed to prevent the abuse of black women migrating North, the league also reflected Kellor's evolving political views. Her quest for "inter-municipal" cooperation was giving way to efforts that cut across regional boundaries.[22]

The organization attempted to provide black women with social services, housing, and decent employment. Its membership was biracial. At headquarters in New York and Philadelphia, assistants were dispatched to areas frequented by new arrivals. The league also operated in Southern cities that often served as departure points. Pamphlets warning young women of false promises and dangerous con artists found their way into Southern black churches and schools. The league worked closely with the White Rose Working Girls' Home, established by black activist Victoria Earle Matthews, though it relied for money on the Inter-Municipal Committee. Active until 1911, the league then merged with two other groups devoted to helping black Americans into the now well-known National Urban League.[23]

Few white Progressive reformers shared Kellor's consistent concern for the plight of black Americans. Like Katharine Davis, she was unusually attentive to the issue of race. Childhood influences most likely shaped the sympathies of both women; they grew up in communities that had been much affected by abolitionism. Davis's Philadelphia settlement work and Kellor's field research in Southern prisons gave each woman personal knowledge of black Americans. Both women were deeply touched by the injustices they witnessed at first hand. Kellor and Davis also embraced an intellectual worldview that competed with racist ideology. Their environmental view of social problems challenged reactionary interpretations that attributed causality to race. Finally, Davis's and Kellor's compassion for black Americans owed something to their experience as women. They seemed to identify with victims of the social order; finding, perhaps, in other oppressed groups some reflection of their own lives. Taken together, these forces inspired an uncommon commitment to racial advancement and an unusual effort to broaden the focus of reform. But it was Kellor's growing focus on the problems faced by immigrants that launched her career in government.

III

Few aspects of Kellor's unemployment research had shocked her more than the pathetic situation of poverty-stricken immigrants in American cities. Kellor felt especially moved by the suffering of immigrant women. Acting on her sympathies in a predictable manner, she organized a major research project on immigration in 1906, again under the auspices of the Woman's Municipal League and the Inter-Municipal Committee on Household Research. The study examined the treatment of the foreign-born in New York, Boston, Philadelphia, and Chicago.

Kellor had an uncanny sense of political trends that paid rich dividends when she decided to devote her energy to immigration. Before 1906 was out, her research project had drawn the attention of New York's new reform governor, Charles Evans Hughes, and of President Theodore Roosevelt. Soon Roosevelt was promoting Kellor as an expert on immigration law. In December of 1906 the President instructed members of his cabinet, including Secretary of Agriculture James Wilson and other federal department heads, to receive Kellor with courtesy, and to pay attention to what she had to say. After reviewing the accounts Kellor submitted to them, Roosevelt requested his staff to "report to me the results of your investigation and action thereon." When a bulletin on Kellor's research entitled "The State and the Immigrant" was published in 1907, Roosevelt requested the first available issue.[24]

Kellor's perspective on immigration closely resembled her approach to unemployment and crime. She again stressed the issue of gender. Immigrant women, she noted, enjoyed "no advantage in laws or trade over men, and are at a disadvantage politically." At times she acceded to dominant prejudices toward ethnic groups even as she championed their cause. Southern and Eastern Europeans, she wrote, were "difficult to assimilate" because they came from countries with "experiences, traditions, superstitions, and suspicions of a middle age progress and opportunity." (America, on the other hand, was "an advanced civilization.") Her stress on acculturation often carried frank overtones of social control, as had her previous studies of criminal justice and labor reform. Yet, as always, these regressive views were blended into a stinging critique of prevailing social and economic conditions. Kellor strongly indicted the rampant exploitation of immigrants in the United States. She especially condemned the low wages paid to foreign-born domestics and their treatment as indentured servants.[25]

The most striking aspect of Kellor's approach to immigration was her direct appeal for a government "system" to "protect" the foreign-born. This was essential, she said, "not for dependents or for those needing charity— not for rescue work, for most immigrants do not need this upon arrival, but for the average normal healthy immigrant who wants to work and to be a citizen." Kellor's emphasis was unusual. The year 1905 ushered in a period of resurgent nativism in the United States. At a time when Congress was debating (yet again) hostile, restrictive legislation, Kellor called for a national immigration policy that addressed social welfare concerns. The sheer magnitude of immigration and the complexity of modern society made it "impossible that this should be continued effectively by philanthropy alone." Community efforts and local relief suffered from lack of uniformity and inequalities in services. Even progressive state laws were insufficient measures without "a federal law" to address "inter-state abuses." "The protection of immigrant women," she once explained, "is the business of a people, not of racial philanthropies, of a state, not of a corporation; and of mankind, not of a few individuals."[26]

In spite of such expansive rhetoric, Kellor's vision of state action incorporated few structural remedies for social and economic dislocation. Instead, the social activist relied on familiar intellectual values and emphasized education and knowledge as *methods* of reform. She hoped to provide immigrants with information about American laws and customs, English language instruction, and rudimentary civic lessons. Most important was the creation of state departments of immigration, which would "primarily protect, educate, and distribute the immigrants within the state and not merely seek laborers." Kellor pressed for a federal system of this kind, as well.[27]

Kellor's growing insistence on state and federal intervention derived, in part, from her continued frustration with municipal politics. The hopeless corruption and intractable power of Tammany-like machines discouraged social activists, who soon grew weary of fighting on local battlegrounds. Reform mayors rarely stayed in office long enough to bring about enough constructive change to satisfy their constituents. Even when regulatory statutes were signed into law, widespread corruption made a mockery of their enforcement provisions. The success of the Republican party statewide made appeals to Albany a much more encouraging process. With Theodore Roosevelt in the White House, even the most ambitious dreams of reformers seemed within reach. Yet, as always, Kellor warned that enlarging the state's role in social welfare required a campaign based on research and knowledge. "Back of all of this legislation for protection are groups of citizens and individuals who have gathered the facts and created a public sentiment for the protection of immigrants."[28]

In spite of her nationalist ideals, Kellor focused on achieving reform in New York State during the early years of her career. She pressured Governor Charles Evans Hughes to appoint a special investigative committee on New York immigration in 1908. Hughes readily acceded to her demands and those of fellow lobbyists, including Lillian Wald. Within months he had won the legislature's approval to appoint the "Commission to Inquire into the Conditions, Welfare, and Industrial Opportunities of Aliens." Kellor served as secretary to the nine-person board, whose members included Wald and other representatives of New York's reform, business, political, and labor communities. When the group gathered to discuss their mandate in August of 1908, Kellor predictably urged members to commit themselves to a full-scale research project. She hoped to include personal visits to immigrant neighborhoods, tenement houses, and surveys of labor camps, as well as general inquiry into issues that affected immigrants, such as unemployment, public health, law, and education.[29]

Kellor took the lead in carrying out this investigation. For seven months, she wandered through depressing labor camps and climbed rickety stairs that led to grimy tenement apartments. She personally witnessed the dangerous working conditions in crowded factories and the exhausting labor performed by aliens who worked on outlying farms. By now an old hand at conducting such sociological research, Kellor accumulated a mass of evidence detailing the dismal conditions under which New York's immigrants lived and worked. Her firsthand observations were supplemented by material accumulated in thirty-seven commission hearings.[30]

By the spring of 1908, the group had prepared its report. It recommended a variety of state programs for immigrant education. Yet its chief request was for a new state agency that would make permanent key aspects of the commission's work. The report proposed that a Bureau of Industries and Immigration be established within the state's Department of Labor. The bureau would research problems that beset immigrants, locate employment, inspect "contract labor camps," and disseminate information useful to immigrants and to the various organizations that had contact with them.[31]

Hughes felt favorably disposed to the commission's ideas. His own commitment to administrative government easily accommodated a new state agency that would run on the engine of expertise. The New York legislature required some convincing, however. When the Immigration Commission's report appeared too late to permit any action in 1909, lawmakers in Albany found it an easy matter to ignore its recommendations.

But Kellor lobbied aggressively to prevent the commission's proposed bureau from being remanded to the bureaucratic wasteland. To keep up the pressure, she joined forces with others on the by-then-dissolved commission to campaign for the new legislation. The group formed a New York branch of the Boston-based North American Civic League to legitimize their activities and to give coherence to their cause. The Boston league had been formed by a somewhat reactionary group of businessmen opposed to immigration restriction but obviously concerned about the threat of unassimilated foreigners. A New York branch of the league would, however, enjoy wide latitude in defining its work. Kellor took on the job as secretary when the committee came together in December of 1909.[32]

Like all the private organizations that advanced Kellor's career, the New York Committee of the North American Civic League required financial backing. And once again, the committee's purposes meshed perfectly with those of its rich benefactors. Businessmen concerned about the stability and productivity of labor and eager to show their commitment to public service displayed growing enthusiasm for the efforts of moderate social reformers. Kellor discovered, as did Katharine Davis, the considerable advantages of such philanthropic support. With the help of Lillian Wald and Mary Dreier,

Kellor easily bagged wealthy banker Felix Warburg of Kuhn and Loeb, and Frank Trumbull, head of the Chesapeake and Ohio Railroad. Trumbull agreed to be the committee's vice-chairman assisting Chairman John Hayes Hammond, a mining engineer and an associate of the Guggenheims. Frank Vanderlip, president of New York's National City Bank, served as treasurer. Prominent women also endorsed the committee's goals. Mrs. E. H. Harriman donated funds; Ann Morgan, sister of J. Pierpont Morgan and an activist in the Women's Trade Union League, agreed to join the cause.[33]

The committee succeeded in persuading the New York legislature to carry out some of the most important Hughes Commission recommendations. In April of 1910, a bill was passed creating a new Bureau of Industries and Immigration within the state's Department of Labor. Hughes selected Kellor to serve as the new division's chairperson; she began her duties at the start of October 1910. Like Katharine Davis's ground-breaking appointment as a city commissioner, Kellor's selection shattered old barriers. At thirty-six, she achieved distinction, not only as the first woman to head an executive department in New York, but as one of the youngest administrators of either sex to serve as division chairperson.[34]

For the next two years, Kellor worked hard to give the bureau a strong identity, to address the issues she believed most pressing, and to expand her authority as division chief. Kellor's administration incorporated her distinctive ideas about reform. As always, she placed a high priority on research. With a budget that fell just short of $10,000, Kellor still managed to hire four investigators, a lawyer, and a staff of volunteers recruited from settlement houses. From offices in Buffalo and Brooklyn, the bureau quickly began to carry out an ambitious program of study. Kellor established four separate departments within the bureau that focused on administration, conciliation, investigation and inspection, and education and publicity.

The bureau had far-reaching authority to enforce state laws protecting the foreign-born, including three statutes passed in 1910 that regulated the conduct of bankers, steamship ticket agents, and notaries public. But the agency earned its reputation by devising individualized remedies for various social and economic wrongs. Immigrants could file complaints with Kellor's bureau that entitled the aggrieved party to an "impartial" hearing attended by interpreters and followed by a thorough investigation of any accusations made. The conflicts often involved wages and working conditions. Once grievances were aired, the bureau attempted mediation: extralegal dispute settlement thus formed an important dimension of the agency's work. In 1912 over 1,100 complaints were heard, and all but seventy-eight were resolved. The remainder required formal legal settlement.[35]

While the bureau undoubtedly helped some immigrants secure justice, it also served the interests of the industrialists who employed them. By mollifying mistreated laborers, business could avoid costly litigation, undesirable publicity, and intervention by the courts. Arbitration also affirmed the integrity of existing political institutions, thereby undercutting the challenge of labor militants. As its name implied, the Bureau of Industries and Immigration sought a peaceful relationship between workers and businessmen—one that would stabilize the labor force and the industrial economy.[36]

The bureau was also charged with proposing additional laws mandated by its ongoing investigations. Kellor warmed to this task and turned out reams of protective legislation for consideration in Albany. Among the bills enacted were measures that widened state intervention on behalf of social welfare, as in a statute that called for state inspection of labor camps. The bureau lobbied for a workman's compensation law and a state agency on unemployment.

For Kellor the goal was not simply to prevent the exploitation of immigrants, but actively to encourage a "healthy" adjustment to American life. This kind of social engineering gave evidence not only of Kellor's broad view of state power but of the antidemocratic impulse implicit in her conception of reform. If social policy was best formulated by experts, average citizens could do little more than attend to the superior judgment of those in command. Immigrants became objects of various ameliorative programs, rather than participants in a process that determined their particular needs. Not surprisingly, legislative measures proposed by middle-class reformers often most clearly addressed the architects' concerns. Some of Kellor's programs as division chief were coercive, as when New York's Department of Labor was empowered to trace immigrants through "ships' manifestos." The information was used to monitor compliance with compulsory school laws.

The bureau's Education and Publicity Division ensured that its successes received considerable attention. This, in turn, promoted the legislature's good will. In her two years as bureau chief, Kellor saw her budget double in size. Pamphlets prepared in foreign languages spread word to immigrants of the bureau's resources and success in adjudicating cases, as did notices in foreign-language newspapers. English classes organized by the bureau also forged links with the foreign-born.[37]

Kellor's experience at the Bureau of Industries and Immigration sharpened her vision of immigration policy. When the Federal Immigration Commission issued its report in 1911 favoring some restrictive measures, she noted a dominant ambivalent attitude towards the foreign-born. She placed herself among a more progressive minority.

> To that small group of dreamers who had expected the promulgation of a domestic policy, who had waited for the constructive note, who had hoped that the government might be urged to accept some of the responsibilities which it now leaves to benevolence, the overwhelming negative position of the Commission is a disappointment.

Kellor especially criticized the nation's preoccupation with immigration restriction. The greatest matter before the public, she argued, was the welfare of immigrants once they arrived in the United States. "No matter how strict these laws are made, they will not solve the problem already confronting the nation and States."[38]

Kellor's concern for the social welfare of the foreign-born sharply distinguished her views from those that were gaining currency in the second decade of the twentieth century. Although nativist groups temporarily failed to win sweeping restrictive measures, anti-immigrant sentiment grew in many quarters. Congress itself was bitterly divided about the direction of national policy. Kellor believed the foreign-born deserved to be considered as more than a "labor asset"; immigrants brought with them to the United States an "inheritance which will enrich our national life." She noted in 1911 that

> there exists in very many localities and among very many classes of people an unreasonable prejudice, amounting to the feeling and belief that foreigners are a different kind of people from "our people," and that they are, therefore, warranted in according them different treatment not sanctioned by the Golden Rule.

To Kellor, this hostility made it plain that the "native born American" required assimilation "as well as the alien." That assertion reflected the social activist's usual impatience with mass politics and her willingness to make policy making the province of some ill-defined, though ostensibly more knowledgeable, elite.[39]

The tension between democratic values and Kellor's rather authoritarian conception of reform became ever more apparent in her studies of immigration. By 1911, she envisioned an immigration policy of sweeping social welfare measures structured around "fair industrial opportunity, distribution, protection, education and equal protection of the laws." Immigrant workers, she argued, were "the poorest protected of all humanity in this country . . . even worse off than the children." Their uplift required state regulation of labor camps, "the elimination of home work," and "the establishment of minimum wage schedules beyond which it is agreed no person can maintain a decent standard of living." Mixed in with these modern proposals was a brief for a government "distribution" plan that would direct immigrants to areas offering education and adequate jobs. While designed to relieve unemployment and urban poverty, the system involved a high level of state control and, indeed, coercion.[40]

Kellor boldly assigned to the states and federal government responsibility for immigration reform. Only "national legislation" and uniform state laws would ensure better conditions for immigrants and a more enlightened attitude among the native-born. Her experience in state government had led Kellor to become even more emphatic in her demands for *federal* regulation. In a letter to Theodore Roosevelt, Kellor described "the perils of our big country, and how helpless New York State is to deal with international and interstate problems." State immigration bureaus, such as the one she directed, ought to be overseen by a federal agency that would "deal with interstate matters, naturalization, stimulation of educational facilities in remote communities, distribution and protection." This could be done, she argued, without interfering "with State rights in any way." Her brief for federal activism appealed to Roosevelt. "Off hand I can say that I am absolutely in accord with you," he averred.[41]

IV

Kellor's growing conviction that significant reform required federal power, her cordial relationship with Theodore Roosevelt, and her enthusiasm for women's suffrage easily drew her towards the National Progressive Party in 1912. When Roosevelt broke with the Republican party in June of that year, and agreed to run for President on a third-party ticket, many social reformers saw an opportunity to press their reform agenda on the new political party. Roosevelt's "New Nationalism" promised support for a broad range of reform measures, including woman's suffrage, and the use of federal power for an array of social welfare measures. Neither the Republican nor the Democratic Party, William Howard Taft nor Woodrow Wilson (their respective nominees), were willing to go quite so far as Roosevelt. While some social activists remained loyal to their party affiliations, others, including Kellor, were convinced their moment was at hand.[42]

For women reformers, the Progressive party held a special allure. Roosevelt once admitted that he had "favored woman suffrage . . . only tepidly, until my association with women like Jane Addams and Frances Kellor." The former president felt personal affection for both women. "I think Miss Kellor," Roosevelt once wrote, "is just one of the finest souls I ever met." Addams and Kellor both stressed that women needed the vote to bring about "social and industrial justice." The argument appealed to Roosevelt. He promised to endorse suffrage and include women in the new party's leadership.[43]

The Progressive party's convention in Chicago in early August of 1912 provided dramatic evidence that Roosevelt had kept his word. "More than a score" of women delegates took their seats at the convention, after a huge parade of suffragists escorted them through the streets of Chicago to the Coliseum. In the first car were Kellor and Mary Dreier, members of New York's delegation. The participation of so many women in a national political convention was unprecedented in American history. And newspapers made much of the extraordinary new phenomenon. A political cartoonist for the *Chicago Tribune* sketched a woman lecturing her husband at the breakfast table, as their infant played with a toy "Bull Moose." "In the future, Henry, Please do not refer to me as the 'Missus': Call me the moosus."[44]

For many suffragists, the highlight of the convention was Jane Addams' speech seconding Roosevelt's nomination. It was an unusual moment in American political history. How amazing to see a woman speak to the packed convention hall! The Coliseum erupted in wild demonstrations as Addams' speech drew to a close. A similar spectacle had followed Roosevelt's "Confession of Faith" the day before. Reporters marveled at the women delegates who "followed state banners in excited procession up and down the convention aisles." Later, Roosevelt thanked Addams for her support and affirmed the importance of women to the new Progressive party:

> In this great National Convention starting the new party women have thereby been shown to have their place to fill precisely as men have, and on absolute

equality. It is idle now to argue whether women can play their part in politics, because in this convention we saw the accomplished fact, and moreover the women who have actively participated in this work of launching the new party represent all that we are most proud to associate with American womanhood.

At a meeting of the party's National Committee on August 8, Kellor and Addams were appointed "members-at-large."[45]

For the next two years Kellor dedicated herself to advancing the new Progressive party. She participated first in the lively back-room debates over the platform. The document that emerged reflected the influence of many social reformers. At a June 1912 meeting of the National Conference of Charities and Corrections, Owen Lovejoy had presented the report, "Social Standards for Industry." Conference members who joined the Progressive party wanted a national platform modeled after this document, and, to a significant degree, they prevailed. Kellor drafted an immigration plank that endorsed, in a rather general way, the use of federal power to protect the foreign-born. Never before had an American political party stood behind such a policy. Kellor also made sure, along with other feminists, that the party unambiguously supported woman's suffrage. Shot through with the ideas of academics and social activists, the platform showcased issues Kellor had long held dear. Workman's compensation, the abolition of child labor, and a minimum wage for women stood out among the Progressives' many social welfare concerns. The platform of the Progressive party, she proudly told a rally, was the product of "political and sociological experts."[46]

When the convention was over and the "herd" of Bull Moosers dispersed, Kellor returned to New York to begin active campaigning for Roosevelt. In the fall of 1912, she worked closely with reformer Henry Moskowitz to galvanize party support in New York State while serving as national director of publicity and research.

As a national committeewoman, she handled the suffrage appeal, along with Jane Addams. Kellor made it plain that she believed the Progressive party offered a unique political opportunity for women. Their participation in the Bull Moose cause, she said, would increase their power in American politics and win converts for the vote. "For the first time we are in the inside of a great political party with all the machinery of that party at our disposal." But not all feminists agreed. Jane Addams' endorsement of Roosevelt at the Chicago convention unleashed a storm of criticism. The National American Woman Suffrage Association was supposed to be nonpartisan. Because Addams was serving as NAWSA's first vice-president when she seconded Roosevelt's nomination, some suffragists believed her actions compromised the principles of the suffrage group.[47]

Among Addams' most vocal critics was Ida Husted Harper, who bitterly attacked the settlement leader in a letter to the *New York Times* on August 10th of 1912. Harper's hostility towards Roosevelt provoked a sharp response from Kellor. She begged Jane Addams to put the woman in her place.

> Without making it a personal matter of Mr. Roosevelt can you not write a
> statement showing the partisan attack on Mr. Roosevelt, the absence of any
> attacks or even mention of Mr. Taft's or Mr. Wilson's attitude, the curious
> attack by suffrage officials on a party or on candidates standing for them and
> point out the essentials of a non-partisan attitude.

Unlike many suffragists of her generation, Kellor felt no hesitation about getting involved in the mean business of party politics. Her many years of social
activism, her experience in state government, and her rewarding associations
with several elected officials drew her toward American politics. Kellor put
her loyalty to Progressive principles and, perhaps, her own ambitions before
allegiance to a nonpartisan style. She had little sympathy for other suffragists
who felt disdain for the Progressive party.[48]

The recalcitrance of some suffragists especially vexed Kellor because she
had held out their support as a lure for male Progressives who doubted the
political wisdom of the suffrage plank. She was embarrassed when important
feminists failed to rally to the Progressive party cause. "It seems to me so
very shortsighted for suffrage to be opposing the one party that is for them
and ignoring the ones against them," she confessed to Addams. "I am not so
concerned about not getting the women or the organizations but I fear we
shall lose many a good strong vote we have won. Men are already asking what
we can expect from such women within the ranks." Ever optimistic about the
value of sound intellectual argument, Kellor advised Addams that "a strong
educational analytical statement from you . . . might help very much."[49]

Kellor herself did not bother to mince words. When a referendum on
women's suffrage was badly defeated in Ohio in September of 1912, she
wasted not a moment in rubbing salt in the feminists' wounds. In a letter to
women's suffrage organizations, she wrote:

> Woman suffrage and the holding by women of certain political offices in Ohio
> have been defeated. The two old parties, hostile to suffrage and dominated by
> the liquor interests, have deprived women of their political opportunity. In
> spite of the magnificent fight put up by WOMEN OUTSIDE OF PARTY
> LINES, they have lost.

This appeal for support for the Progressive party was so baldly stated that
even sympathizers of the cause were taken aback. After reading Kellor's
broadside, Jane Addams was quoted as saying she "would never have the
courage to send this out, but Miss Kellor apparently has." The letter reflected
Kellor's aggressive personal style. A slender woman with flashing dark eyes,
Kellor never really lost the tough persona she exhibited as a child. She bluntly
spoke her mind, often ignoring the middle-class conventions observed by
more polite women reformers.[50]

Throughout the campaign, Kellor monitored the suffrage issue on two
fronts. She constantly prodded Theodore Roosevelt to emphasize his commitment to women's rights. "Whenever in your speaking campaign or in your
mail, women offer their services or cooperation will you have their names
and addresses sent to . . . National Headquarters," she instructed the candi-

date. "*Also don't forget to speak for suffrage,* telling the people how the women are organizing and working." On another occasion, she pressed Roosevelt to include women on a local campaign committee. "We have such splendid women in our ranks. Lillian Wald, Mrs. Nathan, Mrs. Simkovitch + Miss Morgan, Miss Marbury. . . . If sex could be eliminated these women are among our [finest] citizens." For the converted, she offered political broadsides addressed: "To the Women Voters of the United States from the Women in Political Bondage. Vote the Progressive Ticket and Make Us Free."[51]

The Progressive appeal to women focused on the party's support of suffrage and its "program to secure social and industrial justice." These issues were presumed to be of greatest interest to American women. But Kellor advanced a third argument based on political pragmatism that addressed other female social activists. "Women's work is largely done with the election or defeat of Mr. Taft or Mr. Wilson; women's work is but begun with the defeat or election of Mr. Roosevelt," she wrote in *The Progressive Bulletin.*

> Women in the old parties can then go on, as women have always done, with their philanthropic, welfare and civic work, and have the chivalrous support of their political friends where public or political policy does not interfere. They will be a good deal like the unorganized laborer, dependent upon the popularity and wealth and sympathy of their friends who believe in their cause, and can get a hearing.

By 1912, Kellor had become convinced that no lasting reform could be achieved outside the political process. While the Republican and Democratic parties represented "the classes and not the masses," the Progressives offered women a unique "opportunity" to find a national voice.[52]

Most Progressives knew very well that their party could not win the election in 1912. When Woodrow Wilson rolled up an unambiguous victory, it was still hard for Progressive loyalists not to be disappointed, however. "We have fought a good fight; we have kept the faith; we have gone down in disaster, " Theodore Roosevelt wrote to Jane Addams. But their defeat did not lead to a regretful surrender, as the organization of the National Progressive Service so amply demonstrated. In December of 1912, leaders of the Progressive party gathered in Chicago to discuss the organization's future strategy. Among the proposals discussed was a plan—largely the brainchild of Frances Kellor—to establish a research bureau within the party devoted to important political, social, and economic issues.[53]

V

The National Progressive Service was the apotheosis of Kellor's persistent effort to fuse scientific expertise and social reform. After the party's electoral defeat, Jane Addams had drawn up a "Plan of Work" that committed the Progressives to both "political organization and social education." Kellor's

Progressive Service addressed the latter imperative. With the help of leading authorities in various fields, the Service would conduct ongoing investigations of critical social and economic problems. Its findings would then be used to draft model remedial legislation. Public support for the proposed bills was to be mobilized through extensive publicity. Since the Service was designed to advance Progressive goals between elections, it would be an integral part of the party organization, answering to the national committee. State Progressive Services would also be launched to carry out the party's reform agenda.

The idea of the Service provoked some criticism from Progressive leaders. But stalwarts such as Roosevelt and Charles Merriam approved, and the Service won endorsement from the party's executive committee on December 19, 1912. At that meeting, the Progressives divided their work among four separate bureaus: Finance, Organization, Progressive Service, and Publicity. Kellor was appointed chief of the Service, and given a seat on the party's national Administrative Board. She resigned as chief of New York's Bureau of Industries and Immigration, and took up her new duties early in 1913.[54]

Kellor's new position with the Progressive party was a powerful one, perhaps the most prominent yet afforded to any woman within a political party. Her organization included a maze of subdivisions and committees. The Service had four departments: Social and Industrial Justice, Conservation, Popular Government, and Costs of Living and Corporation Control. (Each addressed a major plank of the Progressive party platform.) Still more committees proliferated under the authority of each division. And the Service added a Bureau of Education and a Legislative Reference Bureau to advance the findings of the various research groups. Kellor's budget exceeded $40,000 in 1913.[55]

Most extraordinary was the array of talent represented by the National Progressive Service. Gifford Pinchot, who had served as chief of the U.S. Forest Service, headed the Department of Conservation. The highly successful political reformer George Record led the Department of Popular Government. Jane Addams agreed to take the Department of Social and Industrial Justice, while Robert G. Valentine, Roosevelt's Commissioner of Indian Affairs, directed the Department of Cost of Living and Corporation Control. William Draper Lewis, dean of the University of Pennsylvania's law school, chaired the Legislative Reference Committee; Chicago reformer Donald Richberg directed the Legislative Bureau's work. Columbia professor Samuel Lindsay guided the Bureau of Education.

Even more impressive was the parade of social welfare leaders, academics, and public figures Kellor assembled to serve on departmental subcommittees. John Dewey headed a group interested in "public education problems," while Booth Tarkington directed the Division of Motion Pictures. Edith Abbott served on a subcommittee investigating women's labor under the guidance of Chicago settlement worker Mary McDowell. Kellor herself agreed to launch a committee on immigration, whose members included Wellesley professor Emily Greene Balch, writer Jacob Riis, and Edith Abbott's sister Grace, then head of Chicago's Immigrants' Protective League. Chicago professor Charles Merriam, U.S. Commissioner of Corporations Herbert Knox Smith, settlement leader Lillian Wald, juvenile court innovator Judge Ben Linsey, George Kirchwey, dean of Columbia's Law School, and *Survey* editor Paul Kellogg were among the other luminaries who served under Kellor's direction on National Progressive Service committees.[56]

Most of those who joined the Progressive Service had been enthusiastic supporters of the Progressive party. But not all had been. The Service won new friends by crafting an approach to reform and partisan politics that had deep appeal for a variety of early-twentieth-century social activists. In many respects, Kellor's conception of the Progressive Service reflected her matured understanding of political necessity. But to a far greater extent, the Service brought to life a way of looking at the world that had deep roots in her university experience.[57]

For Kellor, the key reality of American political life was that political parties failed utterly to provide intellectual and moral leadership. Because she was a woman, excluded not only from the inner circles of the two major parties but even from casting a ballot, Kellor easily perceived the limits of early-twentieth-century politics. Of the years before the Progressive party, she once wrote:

> Politics in America had become a question of nominations and elections. Patronage was the key to success and power the hand maiden of the boss. Party lines were drawn, not by issues and policies laid down in platforms to be carried out, but by men who controlled conventions and competed for office.

To win public support, political parties needed to "do something besides mark time between elections." The party itself, rather than its candidates, should lead the way in reform. By downplaying the emphasis on candidates, Kellor enlarged the potential role of women.[58]

Her appeal for reform in party organization also reflected Kellor's understanding of early-twentieth-century society. Industrial capitalism, she argued, had transformed the nation and created a need for social welfare "administration and legislation." Proper measures for "relieving the results of . . . our social and industrial system" required prior scientific investigation. Although universities, private groups, and, to a limited extent, new government fact-finding commissions had taken the lead in providing this "correct information," political parties had failed to follow suit. As a result, the public had grown disaffected with party politics. Progressive reforms such as "the direct primary, the abolition of conventions, fusion in municipal affairs, the commission form of government and similar movements" had further weakened the party system. Soon, Kellor predicted, campaigns and elections would be reduced to "mechanical details," highly regulated by statute and "largely supported by state funds and taxation." To wield any significant power, political organizations would have to embrace a new field of work: social research.[59]

Kellor wanted to reconstruct modern political parties in a way that would preserve partisanship and address the contemporary need for scientific expertise. No individual office holder, private philanthropy, or social welfare organization could alone provide the necessary leadership. But a politics of substance rather than of personalities, a political party guided by experts rather than self-interested hacks, could benefit from the shifting base of authority in American society. She proposed that political parties become "laboratories" of social research whose work would be "defined by scientific laws and . . . manned by experts." A political laboratory would be at once scientific, objective, and useful in achieving the public good. "Social research will be its method and it will constitute a general clearing-house for information, as well as a power for the most intelligent and courageous government action." Very similar logic had inspired Katharine Davis's Laboratory of Social Hygiene at Bedford Hills.[60]

In truth, Kellor had in mind the kind of applied social science she had long sought to graft onto public affairs. She argued that social research was comparable to experimentation in the natural sciences. By applying scientific techniques to the platform of a political party, the practicality of reform measures could be tested.

> If, for instance, the laboratory shows such a plank as mothers' pensions to be unworkable in practice, by bringing together the experience of the country, the evidence is presented and a substitute measure recommended. Platforms worked out in this way would leave the candidate little excuse for not living up to his pledges, and would make political activity wholly intelligent.

So sweeping was Kellor's faith in scientific knowledge that she imagined research would provide a single solution for the terrible social and economic problems she herself viewed with a clear eye.[61]

Obviously Kellor's plan for "party organization" gave academics and social scientists a central role in guiding public policy and political life. The notion that a highly organized, rationalized, and efficient system of government could provide a substitute for an inefficient, corrupt, and disconnected party politics captured the imagination of many Progressives, including Theodore Roosevelt. As he explained to one loyal supporter in 1913:

> Let me add that I most cordially agree with what you say as to the type of party which we should create by changing the type of party control. We must have politicians of the right stamp, but the working party instrument should be such as to unite with these upright and competent politicians trained men and women from our colleges, labor unions, civic clubs, and business and professional offices so as to get a political party with the sociological viewpoint and passion. It is because of this that I have devoted so much of my time to the Progressive Service.

Roosevelt went even further in a speech before a Pennsylvania State Progressive Conference that year. "We intend to realize the new freedom for which this nation strives, by social research, in which information is the keynote; and then by immediate translations of the knowledge thus acquired into action." But the Service proved to be a sorry example of what happened when social science directed political reform.[62]

The Progressive Service's first year was full of encouraging signs. In 1913 committee members worked long hours establishing state bureaus, conducting social investigations, and preparing propaganda on cherished causes such as workman's compensation, child labor, protective legislation for women workers, and unemployment. The Service had sent out "30,000 pieces of literature" by the start of April 1913. A typical broadside described how the organization intended to realize its goals.

> First: By studying scientifically political and social conditions. Second: By prescribing remedies in the form of *laws*. Third: By arousing public opinion through an *understanding* of the *conditions* revealed and the *remedies* proposed.

The Service office was located in New York at the Progressive party's national headquarters. The pace of activity there was incredible; one staffer commented that "usually work ceased at midnight only because the elevators stopped running."[63]

Alternately frustrating and gratifying was the time-consuming process of drafting model legislation. The Service provided to state Progressive leaders involved in reform campaigns preformed bills, supporting evidence, and even experts to testify at public hearings. In many states, the alliance worked well, and Progressive legislators managed to win approval of impressive reforms that included workmen's compensation and hours legislation in Maine and Vermont; election reforms in Vermont and Oregon, and a minimum wage (creation of an Industrial Commission regulating hours, wages, and working conditions); and a commission to oversee immigration and housing issues in California.

Working closely with "Progressive Congressmen," the Service also developed a series of bills in the spring of 1913 that embodied key elements of the Progressive party platform. The "Progressive Congressional Program" included sixteen bills that called for, among other things, the barring from interstate commerce of any goods created by child labor, the creation of the Tariff Commission, and the establishment of a Federal Trade Commission with broad enforcement powers to break up monopolies and prevent unfair trade.

Although doomed from the start, these measures together made a powerful national statement about the intent of the Progressive party. The Education Bureau organized public speeches and a lecture series, and the Progressive Service often lent its name and numbers to groups who were engaged in public battles over righteous causes. In the winter of 1913, Roosevelt himself met with striking workers of the International Ladies Garment Workers Union in New York to dramatize the Service's support for their cause. Suffrage groups often benefited from the vocal support of the Progressive Service, as well.[64]

Yet in spite of such enthusiasm, the Progressive Service was racked with dissension from the very start. The organization was highly bureaucratic and complex, and Kellor rigidly attempted to control her entire domain. Some young reformers chafed under this inflexible rule, and no staff members were more rebellious than key associates Donald Richberg and Paxton Hibbens. (The two men had been classmates at Harvard.) Richberg, who headed the Legislative Reference Bureau, resisted reporting to Kellor. He considered William Draper Lewis, director of the Legislative Reference Committee, his boss.

Kellor's imperious attitude made her difficult to work for. She aggressively fought even the smallest battles, arguing with secretaries over the disposition of mail, the use of space in party headquarters, and, on one occasion, payment of a $21 phone bill. She was highly sensitive to slights that involved any deviations from the proper chain of command. It is doubtful that fault for these persistent conflicts belonged solely to Kellor. Not many staff members were used to taking orders from a woman. Kellor may have overreacted to minor sins of omission or thoughtlessness because she knew some employees rejected her command. But the person who knew her most intimately admitted Kellor was terribly "high-strung." Whoever was to blame, the atmosphere in Service headquarters was often tense.[65]

The turbulence within the Service was amply evident in the "Navy Day" debacle of July 1913. With the Newport Progressive Club, the Service sponsored a conference in Rhode Island that featured an address by Theodore Roosevelt. R. K. Forsyth, general secretary of the Service, and Daniel Leroy Dresser of the Newport Club handled—or rather mishandled—arrangements. At the end of an exhausting day, Donald Richberg sailed back to New York with Roosevelt. Richberg lashed out at the "chief culprit" behind the disorganized day—Dresser. "Oh, Mr. _____ is just a jackass," Roosevelt philosophically replied. "But it was our mistake in trusting him. Now it's a beautiful moonlit night on the water. The night will atone for the day."[66]

But it took more than a moonlit night to repair the damage of Navy Day. When Dresser attempted to pass the entire cost of the conference on to the National Service, Kellor was enraged. Vendors who had provided various services for the event secured legal counsel and then pressed the National Service for compensation. In a letter to Paxton Hibbens, Kellor observed: "Dresser's intention is apparently to have us sued alone. Well the sooner the Service does a crook like that the better. Even if we have to pay it's worth showing him up." She instructed Hibbens to find a good lawyer to represent the Service, "gratis if possible," and then to surreptitiously do some investigating of his own.

> Will you see Forsyth and find out the general nature of the correspondence. Then wouldn't it be a good plan to drop up there in Newport quietly and carry off all the correspondence of the Navy Day Committee. We can then introduce it to show Dresser and his committee had charge and contracted the bills. Forsythe may still have a key. I think you can perhaps do this better as it better not be bungled.

Once he gained entry to the Newport office, Kellor instructed, Hibbens might as well grab all the "Service furniture" and bring it back to New York with the purloined papers.[67]

The battle over financing Navy Day underscored a central tension within the Progressive party. The treasury just wasn't large enough to support the organization. As a result, the party's internal departments engaged in a Darwinian struggle for financial control. Kellor enjoyed some advantages in this regard. The Progressive Service succeeded admirably in raising private funds. But not all of its wealthy benefactors supported the Progressive *party*. To ensure their continued support, and to protect the Service budget, Kellor strove to make her organization as financially independent as possible from the national party organization. This did not sit well with George Perkins, chairperson of the party's Executive Committee.[68]

Perkins, a former partner of J. P. Morgan, was the *bête-noire* of social reformers in the party who had sought to oust him since 1912. Many questioned the millionaire's commitment to Progressive principles. The alliance between the party's social activists and its political managers was never easy. But Kellor was among those who were, at first, willing to give Perkins a chance. And he made an effort to treat her fairly, as well. When one of his associates complained in May 1913 that "Miss Kellor's attitudes toward 'the party' are all puzzling me," Perkins dismissed the man's concerns. Explaining the division of labor between Kellor and Executive Committee member Walter Brown, Perkins wrote: "One is running the political end of the organization and the other the Service and naturally they are working along different lines, but for the main results, namely putting through the Progressive principles . . . they are a unit."[69]

During the off year of 1913, the party's political organizers and social activists worked fairly well together. As plans got underway for the election of 1914, however, the alliance between the two party wings became very strained. At issue was control over the direction of the party and its financial resources. Astute Progressive political strategists realized that the very survival of the party depended on an immediate show of strength at the polls. Social activists also wanted to win elections. But they were just as committed to advancing the Progressive program. The Service itself made it possible to promote issues independently of candidates, although ideally Progressives wished to encourage both. Social activists were accustomed to slow progress. The methods of intellectuals—knowledge, research, and education—required patience. They offered no quick fix. The party's political pragmatists could not wait for results that would be achieved in some future day: they insisted on tangible electoral results now.[70]

In this context, relations between Perkins and Kellor deteriorated badly. Skepticism about the Progressive Service's worth began to be voiced early in 1913. One party leader told Roosevelt that year: "[I]t is my belief the Progressive Party has become too academic. It would please me to see the organization snuggle up to practical politics a little more, and perhaps, when it appears in public, to appear a little more as a political party, and a little less as a cult." By the end of 1913, Perkins shared this view.[71]

Kellor sensed that her control over the Service was slipping away in the winter of 1913. She fired Paxton Hibbens in late November, and an office memo announcing the decision made it plain a siege mentality prevailed at headquarters. Hibbens, Kellor ordered, "is not to have the facilities of this office and no material of any kind connected with the Service is to go to him." Her dismissal of Hibbens destroyed for good her relationship with Richberg; other staff members also felt alienated from their embattled chief.[72]

When the party's Executive Committee met in January of 1914 to discuss the upcoming year, Perkins began the process of dismantling Kellor's organization. The Progressive Service's Legislative Reference Bureau had completed its mission in 1913, Perkins suggested, "and was in comparatively slight demand now." Therefore the bureau ought to be disbanded, Perkins ventured. He got little argument from the pragmatic politicians who dominated the party's Executive Committee. After transferring the "Speakers' Bureau" from the Service to the Progressive Organization Committee, Perkins and his associates proceeded to slash Kellor's budget as well.[73]

These proved to be mortal wounds for the Progressive Service. The abolition of its Legislative Service, its dwindling funds, and her own impatience cost Kellor many of the organization's brightest and most creative young workers. She carried on for much of 1914, but the Progressive party's crushing defeat in the November election seemed an ominous sign not only for the Service, but also for the party. Fighting for her department's survival, Kellor made a bad mistake. She persuaded Mrs. Gifford Pinchot to ask George Perkins for a favor. Would he put before the Executive Committee the possibility of "relieving" Kellor from turning over to the national organization any money she raised for the Progressive Service? Under such an arrangement, the Service would be free of the party's direct control. Certainly, Perkins replied, he would present the idea. When the December 1914 meeting was over, Kellor was relieved of her offices at party headquarters, any further ties between the Service and the Progressive party, and even the right to use the name of the organization she had founded.[74]

Although Kellor had set herself up for this defeat, Perkins had behaved underhandedly. Jane Addams left the Executive Committee meeting early, after being assured by Mrs. Pinchot and activist Raymond Robins "that the matter of the Progressive Service had been postponed until the next meeting." Instead, the issue was taken up after Kellor's ally had departed.[75]

Perkins gave Kellor until February 1 to vacate her offices: New York State's Progressive organization would then take over the Service's place. But Kellor resisted, and in an icy reply to Perkins she wrote:

> I have your letter of the 14th to Colonel Roosevelt, who will doubtless communicate with you on the subject of the removal of the Service from headquarters. I shall act in accordance with his decision in the matter. . . . I am unwilling to assent to your order in this matter unless Colonel Roosevelt advises it.

Kellor knew that she would have to leave, but she wanted to keep the Service's name and mission alive. Roosevelt stood by her. "I most emphatically think that Miss Kellor is entitled to take the Progressive Service with her and to keep the name 'Progressive Service.' It is Miss Kellor who has done everything for the Service," he admonished Perkins. "Its work has been done entirely by or through or under her and I very strongly feel that she is entitled to keep the name." Perkins backed down; Kellor could, he told Roosevelt, "at least temporarily keep the name." But, he instructed the former President, "you ought not to let Miss Kellor put you in the position of being an arbiter in her matters."[76]

Kellor tried to keep the Service going by running it on her own, relying, once again, on the assistance of private individuals. Roosevelt helped her raise money. But without the link to the Progressive party, the Service became just another organization with an ambitious reform agenda. There was no shortage of such groups in Progressive-era America. The party was the lifeblood of the Service, just as the Service had invigorated the party. The political organization could go on, driven by the reform agenda Service workers had provided. The Service had lost its meaning, however, without the promise of political triumph at the end of the battle for reform. This time Kellor's best efforts weren't enough. With virtually no publicity, "the Service," as one active participant put it, "was chloroformed and buried privately."[77]

The unraveling of the Progressive Service revealed persistent tensions inherent in Kellor's conception of reform. Kellor believed social research would produce a successful prescription for reform. Yet the Progressive Service failed to ensure a victorious Progressive party. Kellor's patience in defeat suggested that intellectual ideals, rather than political imperatives, animated her organization. In spite of her deep affection for Theodore Roosevelt, she offered her greatest loyalty to a set of abstract ideas that were of limited appeal to, and doubtful practicality in, American party politics. Scientific inquiry might deliver greater social knowledge, but it could not ensure the triumph of a political party. High-velocity political campaigns could not wait on the snail's pace of social research. Finally, party regulars would not defer to the wisdom of a self-appointed intellectual elite. As some Progressive politicians feared, Kellor's faith in social scientific research methods and her belief in academic expertise ultimately exceeded her commitment to any single issue, any individual candidate, or even to the Progressive party.

VI

The collapse of the Progressive Service did little to diminish Kellor's interest in reform. But her experience with Progressive politics did affect the tone and substance of her ideas about social change. Kellor's demands for federal action were now voiced in the spirit of Roosevelt's New Nationalism; regulation became the watchword for reform. The theme of government intervention surfaced often in a revised and expanded edition of *Out of Work* that appeared in 1914. The book took a much broader approach to unemployment than it did in its previous incarnation. Rather than focusing on employment agencies as exploiters of those without jobs, Kellor called attention to the persistence of chronic unemployment in American cities and to the permanent army of unemployed in the United States.

As always, Kellor offered a strikingly sympathetic perspective on unemployment that emphasized the suffering of individuals. In a February 1914 issue of *The Survey*, she reported observations made while trudging around the New York City inhabited by the poor.

> I saw a saloon that set out every night in the barroom a counter of sandwiches and a tank of hash, and witnessed the mad rush of men who had been without food for days, other than picking from ash barrels. The saloon expects, when times are good, that the men will repay the favor.

Kellor insisted "these thousands of people are not mendicants nor crooks, but honest working men and women." Yet the social activist coupled her expected appeal for human compassion with an unusually harsh indictment of business leaders. Kellor claimed the "timidity of capital is now equivalent in New York City to the starvation and homelessness of thousands of men and women."[78]

Only government regulation of the economy, she now argued, could solve the unemployment crisis. As Kellor put it, "the business of government is to support the work of industry, to supervise and to regulate it." This meant forcing business to accept responsibility for displaced workers so that "it may not close its doors without a moment's notice at its own sweet will, without considering its workers, without giving a public account of its actions and its grounds." Lasting reform involved organizing the labor market in a rational way.[79]

Yet Kellor continued to view social research as the first step in rectifying the unemployment problem. Her argument was logical. In fact, there *were* no reliable statistics detailing the rate of unemployment. When the Committee on Industrial Relations issued its report in 1916, the group could only repeat in a general way that joblessness seemed to be a major problem in the United States. Kellor observed that months before the harrowing winter of 1913–14 "any intelligent government by consulting the employment agencies ... could have seen what was coming." Instead the problem was ignored, a fact that led Kellor to ask:

> Now what is the matter with our labor market that we let men freeze and starve before we know what is happening? What is the matter with our city that, with its abundant resources, those who have jobs and supplies and those who have neither miss each other within the circumference of a few blocks? What is the matter with our state and nation that a laborer can not go to the place where a job is waiting?[80]

Kellor recommended the creation of an unemployment research fund that would gather information on present conditions in the labor market, the rate of unemployment, the effect of seasonal work and of worker displacement, opportunities for "industrial training," appropriate legislation, and unemployment insurance. She hoped that eventually this knowledge would pave the way for a "Bureau of Distribution" within the United States Labor Department. To achieve this end, the North American Civic League for Immigrants offered three bills for consideration by the Department of Labor in 1914 that called for a distribution bureau, regulation of employment agencies that handled unskilled workers engaged in interstate commerce, and the licensing of steamship ticket agents.[81]

Kellor's increasing focus on national reform produced the most dramatic results in her work on immigration. Throughout her two years with the Progressive party, she had served as executive secretary of the now expanded New York–New Jersey Committee of the North American Civic League for Immigrants. In the spring of 1914 Kellor joined other members of the New York branch in breaking away from the Civic League's parent group. Labelling themselves the "Committee for Immigrants in America," they now attempted to act as an informational clearing house for those interested in the problems of the foreign-born. Although officially holding the office of Vice-chairman, Kellor was the central figure in the new organization that emerged.[82]

From its inception, the Committee for Immigrants in America sought to draw the federal government into an activist immigration policy. Perhaps the most extraordinary consequence of this campaign was the creation of the new Division of Immigrant Education within the federal Bureau of Education. Kellor had long considered lessons in the English language, vocational training, and classes in civics important methods of assimilating immigrants. Throughout her years as a social activist, she had emphasized the role of knowledge and education in reform. These two approaches merged in her perspective on immigration. Not content to let immigrant education be handled on a "semi-philanthropic" basis, Kellor pressed hard for more organized programs on the local, state, and especially national, level. Her committee approached Secretary of the Interior Franklin Lane in April 1914 to propose a United States Board of Education program on immigrant education.[83]

Lane liked the idea: he brought the Committee for Immigrants in America together with Commissioner of Education P. P. Claxton. Plans were made for a Division of Immigrant Education within the Bureau of Education. But no funds to finance the work of the new division were forthcoming from the federal government. Frances Kellor responded to this reality in her usual manner. She approached private individuals for support. The chief financial backers of the Committee for Immigrants in America, most notably Frank Trumbull and Felix Warburg, agreed to underwrite the new federal agency under the auspices of the Committee for Immigrants in America. By July of

1919, the committee had provided the government division with close to $90,000.[84]

The Committee for Immigrants in America provided the Division of Immigrant Education with more than just financial support. Kellor's committee recommended staff members for the division. Social investigators so appointed quickly launched ambitious research projects. Early studies explored the problem of illiteracy and potential resources for retraining immigrants.[85]

Highly reminiscent of John D. Rockefeller, Jr.'s involvement with the New York State Reformatory at Bedford Hills, this arrangement seems extraordinary to the modern observer. But until 1917, no law prevented the federal government from accepting such contributions from private groups. In fact, agreements of this kind represented an important transitional phase in the history of the welfare state. Activists who tried to persuade the government to accept greater responsibility for social welfare found it much easier to win a show of goodwill than a commitment of taxpayers' funds. In the past, private charities and philanthropic groups had often underwritten efforts to aid the poor and needy. As a halfway measure, reformers such as Kellor and Davis tapped the traditional willingness of philanthropists to fund ameliorative social welfare programs in order to lower the stakes for the elected officials they were attempting to persuade. In this way, they were able to harness the power and authority of government to their cause.[86]

World War I cemented the alliance between the United States government and various organizations committed to immigration reform. American interest in immigration was still largely focused on restriction when hostilities broke out in August of 1914. That emphasis changed quickly as concern about the loyalties of foreigners living within the United States led to intense debate about immigration policy. By the spring of 1915, active efforts were being made to speed up the assimilation of immigrants into American society by various artificial means. The U.S. Bureau of Naturalization sponsored a public ceremony in Philadelphia, attended by President Woodrow Wilson, during May of 1915, which heightened public interest in its naturalization campaign. Suddenly the unthinking faith that immigrants would somehow naturally become Americans one day gave way to aggressive assertions that the foreign-born required "immediate Americanization." Organizations devoted to achieving that transformation began to proliferate.[87]

Kellor instantly recognized that an opportunity was at hand to ride the crest of this new wave. In March 1915 the Committee for Immigrants in America launched a new publication edited by Kellor, *The Immigrants in America Review*. In a lead article Kellor announced that "the most important subject before the American national government today is the adoption of a domestic immigration policy, with adequate official machinery to carry it into effect." She called for changes that included better transportation and distribution for newly arrived immigrants, secure employment, adequate housing, a decent standard of living, education, and "uniform state naturalization laws."[88]

Yet where Kellor had once made her case for these reforms by stressing their inherent justice, she now pandered to the growing public fear of the unassimilated foreign-born.

> Every effort should be made toward an Americanization which will mean that there will be no "German-Americans," no "Italian quarter," no "East Side Jew," no "Up-town Ghetto," no "Slav Movement in America," but that we are one people in ideals, rights and privileges and in making common cause for America. We are far from that ideal citizenship today, how far the European war has brought vividly home to us.

While Kellor emphasized that "government, business and philanthropy" needed to forge an intelligent immigration policy, she also described the role citizens could play. She argued that only individuals could "eliminate race prejudice and class distinction." This plea for toleration, however, was now directly tied to the motive of social control. An involved and helpful American, Kellor pointed out, "is the natural foe of the I.W.W. and of the destructive forces that seek to direct unwisely the expression of the immigrant in the new country, and upon him rests the hope and defense of the country's ideals and institutions."[89]

To capitalize on the growing zeal for "Americanization," the Committee on Immigrants in America organized a "National Americanization Day" for July 4th of 1915. Designed to bring immigrants and native-born Americans together in a common expression of "loyalty" and "patriotism," the idea quickly took hold with the help of Kellor's planning committee. Massive publicity spread word of the impending event; Woodrow Wilson expressed his enthusiasm for the day, as did Theodore Roosevelt. Posters advertising the celebration appeared at railroad stations, and Tiffany and Company created special citizenship buttons, a gift of Mrs. Cornelius Vanderbilt, to commemorate the day. Kellor also saw to it that cities and towns were provided with literature emphasizing the importance of Americanization. Using data from state immigration commission reports, these pamphlets sympathetically described the burdens shouldered by the foreign-born.

Over a hundred cities participated on the designated day. In Pittsburgh, ten thousand turned out to witness the spectacle of a thousand children standing in a formation that resembled the American flag. Across the country, similar rituals took place. Successful advertising in the foreign-language press brought out huge numbers of immigrants. Indeed, Kellor reported that "it was symbolic of the day that in some localities, Americans forgot to decorate their home with the Stars and Stripes while the shops of nearby immigrants carried them."[90]

The success of Americanization Day advanced Kellor's career. After the festivities, a National Americanization Committee emerged that subsumed the Committee for Immigrants in America. With Kellor's assistance, the new organization attempted to carry on the work of Americanization by educating the public, and pressing a broad agenda that mixed coercive measures aimed at homogenizing the foreign-born with ameliorative measures geared to moderate social reform. Kellor continued to emphasize social welfare issues. In September 1915 she was still pressing the case of the unemployed because they suffered so terribly in American society.

> How much more do we need to know to do something more fundamental than start bread lines, temporary workshops, or asking full time men to work half time or to receive less pay? How much longer will we rely upon charitable societies and relief funds collected by personal appeals, fetes, dinners, balls, and other entertainment to feed and clothe the unemployed? Is it not ironical that we depend so largely upon *entertainments* to keep people from freezing and starving to death? The proceeds of a circus are today paying the wages of helpless women in New York City, and this is typical of the country.

But her appeal now often played on fears of radicalism and demands for industrial discipline as it stressed the larger context of the war.[91]

When the "preparedness" campaign to arm and ready the nation for World War I gathered steam in 1916, Kellor jumped on the bandwagon. Claiming that "American employers create the immigrant standard of living in America," Kellor focused her appeal for reform on business and industrial interests. Intensely hostile to the Wilson administration, she had become discouraged about the prospects for federal leadership in immigration reform. Now she turned to the U.S. Chamber of Commerce, proposing that a special committee on immigration be formed to implement Americanization programs in the workplace. The business organization agreed in December 1915. Kellor served as assistant to Frank Trumbull, who was appointed chairman of the new Immigration Committee.

The committee ran on funds donated by the Chamber of Commerce and the National Americanization Committee, and it followed the usual pattern of organizations in which Kellor had a role. A brief was made for the scientific study of existing conditions; a program of research soon followed. Conditions in industrial areas throughout the country were surveyed. Some of the severest problems facing the foreign-born were analyzed in an intelligent way. Yet to the increasing dismay of organized labor, the committee followed an example being set by other Americanization groups. It attempted to use the workplace as a setting for teaching the foreign-born the "values" of American society, including compliance, and the essential strength of American institutions, most notably laissez-faire capitalism.[92]

As debate over American intervention in the war increasingly dominated national politics, Kellor's remarks on Americanization took on an increasingly militant tone. She railed against the government's failure to prepare itself adequately for war. In some ways, the war represented Kellor's greatest opportunity, for she found in the global conflict a rallying point for the United States. "Thanks to the war, we have been freed from the delusion that we are an united nation marching steadily along an American highway of peace, prosperity, common ideals, beliefs, language, and purpose," Kellor wrote in 1916. In a strident book entitled *Straight America*, Kellor made a sensational appeal for "military preparedness," "industrial mobilization," "universal service," and "Americanization." Concern for the welfare of immigrants began to take a back seat to insistence on stricter naturalization procedures, compulsory education programs, and a coercive nationalism.[93]

This shift in tone reflected, in part, Kellor's growing dependence on business and industrial leaders. The organizations she created relied on the support of powerful financial interests for their very livelihood. And they captured public attention only by appealing to the national mood. In other words, Kellor had no independent institutional base from which to advocate reform. Nor could she rely on widespread enthusiasm for reform by World War I. Progressivism was in eclipse. The Progressive *party* no longer existed. As public opinion shifted to the right, Kellor moved with it. Nor was Kellor a pacifist, unlike other female activists of her generation. Without an ideological commitment to peace, she became a willing captive of the preparedness drive and the extreme nationalism that accompanied it.

Kellor's long-held ideas about social problems did little to check her conservative views. In fact, they proved remarkably compatible with the social activist's belligerent stance. Kellor's enthusiasm for state planning, the antidemocratic nature of her allegiance to elites, and the strong element of social control that had always figured in her writing were consistent with her wartime Americanization drive. The model of applied social science she endorsed clearly accommodated a wide range of political beliefs.

Perhaps most apparent in Kellor's wartime writing was a keen disappointment that her desires for national reform had not been realized. In one discussion of political life, Kellor made reference to the Progressive Service. "It failed temporarily," she said, "because the average voter does not yet respond to national issues in the absence of danger and conflict; of controversy and emergency.... This attempt to realize an ideal ahead of its time has suffered defeat but temporarily." Describing the efforts of the Division of Immigrant Education, Kellor repeated her disappointment that the wisdom of experts failed to guide national policy. Their efforts "could be wiped out tomorrow by a single order. It is makeshift, not policy."[94]

Kellor saw in the campaign of her former patron Charles Evans Hughes an opportunity to change the direction of national politics. She campaigned vigorously for Hughes in 1916, riding on the women's train and giving speeches that attempted to rally suffragists to Hughes' side. The election badly divided Progressives, who split over the issues of peace and war. When Hughes lost the election to Woodrow Wilson, Kellor managed to express both anger and a philosophical attitude in an article for the *Yale Review*. She believed that women who voted for Wilson made a mistake because the President did not support a federal woman's suffrage amendment. Yet she also criticized the Woman's Party for trying to defeat Wilson "by negative action and sex appeal"[!] In a blistering attack on the Republican party, Kellor accused its National Committee of failing to make good use of its women supporters.

> The Republican Party did not think of these women voters as a vital factor in the campaign and obstinately to the last refused to consider them as an integral, vital, self-respecting part of the electorate to be dealt with in an intelligent organized way.

This was an especially disappointing contrast to the "Bull Moose" party of 1912.[95]

Kellor had no illusions that woman's suffrage would "elevate" politics. She described the Women's Bureau of the Democratic party as "a model national feminine Tammany hall." The group, she said, left "a trail of misrepresentation, class hatred, race prejudice, and questionable campaign methods which the country will be a long time overcoming." Her only praise was reserved for the Women's Committee of the National Hughes Alliance, a "courageous little band of independent women of both Republican and Progressive faith" who tried to advance "women's national political work." Kellor praised the Hughes Alliance because they proved "there is no such thing as sex loyalty and that women approach politics from exactly the same human, individualistic angle as men and will vote for precisely the same reasons that men vote." Looking forward to 1920, she predicted that the triumphant party would be one that gave women power and trusted "them with leadership." Her prediction was not fulfilled.[96]

After the war, Kellor's ties to the business community defined her professional existence. With the assistance of wealthy industrialists, many of whom employed large numbers of immigrant laborers, she formed the "Inter-Racial Council," designed to carry on the work of Americanization. When the council acquired the American Association of Foreign Language Newspapers in 1918, Kellor became its chairperson. The association controlled advertising in the immigrant press and used this power to spread propaganda attacking "Bolshevism" and emphasizing the virtues of life in the United States. Although the Inter-Racial Council rejected the tactics of rabid Americanizers, it bore little resemblance to the amicable social welfare groups that Kellor led in the early phase of her professional work. Education, information, and knowledge remained central themes in her intellectual arsenal. But how empty these methods seemed when stripped of the Progressive promise that had given life to Kellor's remarkable reform career.[97]

VII

Through the efforts of Frances Kellor, academic social science found a place in the political drama of Progressive reform. Along with other social activists, she used her skills in social research to advance knowledge of early-twentieth-century social problems. Her ground-breaking studies of unemployment, with their environmental analysis of social and economic distress, helped broaden the parameters of contemporary debates. Her deep commitment to women's advancement produced an extraordinary literature of social exposure that highlighted women's concerns. Her insistent pursuit of woman's suffrage and her forceful advocacy of social welfare reform helped shape the Progressive party. Yet Kellor's impressive achievements went hand in hand with troubling ideas about the dynamics of social change. She hoped to invest experts with the power to define social problems and direct social policy. If successful, those plans would have augmented the powerlessness of the very groups Kellor intended to serve. Indeed, when her ideals came to play a part in immigration reform, the lessons derived from scientific investigations wound up advancing the interests of the state.

7

"The School Is Yours"

The struggle to balance social inquiry with social activism attained one of its most lasting expressions in the work of Edith Abbott and Sophonisba Breckinridge. Unlike their two contemporaries, Abbott and Breckinridge maintained close ties with academia while pursuing their many interests in reform. They held faculty appointments, conducted scholarly research, and published in academic journals. Yet their success in blending careers as social scientists and social activists was a measure of their professional ingenuity rather than their adherence to any predetermined avenue of advancement. Wedded to the values of the university but relegated to the margins of the academy, Abbott and Breckinridge sought to create a new setting within the university that would permit them to address public issues and advance social research. In so doing, they helped professionalize social work, a field they first adopted, and then worked to make their own.

Abbott's and Breckinridge's compelling approach to social change incorporated key elements of their training as social scientists. Their ideas about social problems built on their previous social research. Breckinridge drew on her education in law and politics to construct powerful intellectual arguments justifying a modern welfare state. Abbott used her skill in quantitative analysis, her understanding of economic history, and her knowledge of the industrial working class to advance an array of Progressive causes. Like Frances Kellor and Katharine Davis, Abbott and Breckinridge offered an environmental analysis of social dislocation that emphasized the suffering of indigent men and women. Their dexterous use of social research and their groundbreaking studies of urban problems made the two women imposing figures in early-twentieth-century reform movements.

Abbott's and Breckinridge's university experience was also reflected in their favored method of reform. Both women considered social knowledge and scientific research to be prerequisites to informed social policy. As a result, they sought to advance legislative change by conducting investigations that exposed the dangers of industrial life. To Abbott and Breckinridge, no victims of the social order seemed more at risk than women and female children. In books and articles detailing the stress of the urban environment, the two women focused public attention on the oppression of their sex. Their research on women added intellectual weight to suffrage and Progressive campaigns.

Abbott's and Breckinridge's intellectual approach was institutionalized in the University of Chicago's School of Social Service Administration. Their innovative design for the school reflected ideas and values that had been central to Edith's and Sophonisba's academic training in the social sciences. If the founding of the school brought to fruition professional and scholarly ideals, it also represented the final stage of the women's metamorphosis from social scientists into social workers. That evolution was influenced by Abbott's and Breckinridge's enduring commitment to social inquiry and social welfare reform.

I I

From the start, Abbott and Breckinridge drew inspiration for their intellectual and political work from the city of Chicago. Their scholarship and social activism were deeply influenced by the urban, industrial setting in which they lived. The costs of industrialization had been high in Chicago. Political corruption and mismanagement had exacerbated the inevitable tensions that accompanied urban growth. Private charities and municipal welfare services could not begin to meet the needs of the city's poor. These tragic conditions quickly became the focus of Abbott's and Breckinridge's research.

Their collaboration began when Abbott was a graduate student at Chicago and Breckinridge her professor. Breckinridge's course on the economic status of women opened a new area of inquiry virtually untouched by most male scholars. The class made a tremendous impression on Abbott. In 1905, Breckinridge helped Abbott extend her statistical studies of industrial labor to incorporate women workers. That initial research effort led to a jointly written essay, "Employment of Women in Industries—Twelfth Census Statistics," which appeared in a January 1906 issue of the *Journal of Political Economy*. The article was the first of several investigations into women's industrial work undertaken by the two scholars.[1]

The essay introduced a way of looking at social problems that persisted throughout much of Abbott's and Breckinridge's later careers. Their emphasis on gender was particularly striking. Neither Abbott nor Breckinridge had been especially attentive to women's issues in her graduate research. But women's economic and political oppression became a personal and intellectual preoccupation soon after they had earned their degrees. In addressing the economic barriers faced by women, the scholars pursued an issue that had great relevance for their own lives.

Indeed, they invoked modern debates over "woman's position in the economic world" to explain the purpose of their research. In an environment where "the factory system is on trial because of its abuses," discussion of women's work had become particularly heated. Some workingmen wanted to keep women out of industrial jobs; many middle-class Americans hoped to prevent women from working (outside the home) at all. The controversy, Abbott and Breckinridge maintained, was making women "self-conscious and irritable." Men reacted by being "sometimes obstructive, frequently incredulous, occasionally patronizing, and often unsympathetic."[2]

These responses, the social scientists believed, reflected widespread ignorance of women's economic lives. In a classic affirmation of the importance of objective research, they expressed dismay that there had been no rigorous study of women's employment.

> The problem has not been definitively formulated; observations have not been systematically made; conclusions and convictions rest on *a priori* reasoning, illogical analogy, and limited personal experience.

Abbott and Breckinridge offered a statistical analysis of women's labor force participation to advance more reasoned debate.[3]

Their study of women's employment emphasized the persistent growth of women's work, the segregated labor market in which female laborers were employed, and the exploitative conditions women industrial workers endured. Women were entering the labor force at an unprecedented rate, Abbott and Breckinridge concluded. But they faced constant inequality and grueling conditions in their pursuit of industrial work. Some critics attributed economic dislocation to "competition between men and women" for employment. Others demanded "the same wages for the same work." In fact, women industrial workers rarely worked "side by side at the various processes" with men; they thus comprised a largely "non-competing group." Anticipating the modern controversy over comparable worth, the researchers asked, "in the face of facts just presented . . . where is the same work to be found under present conditions?"[4]

The social scientists made little attempt to conceal their reaction to the injustices their research uncovered. Working-class women were broken by the very structure of industrial work; the current division of labor was "unendurable." A "rational system" would provide women with "tasks peculiarly fitted to them" and a decent wage. But this meant social recognition of physiology "as the basis for pecuniary return." Since that goal seemed far out of reach in 1905, Abbott and Breckinridge endorsed open competition between men and women as "the only plan compatible with the continued self-respect of working women." "Women," they wrote, "must enter upon industrial life in a workman-like spirit, have opportunity to achieve necessary skill, and overcome the obstacles to practice of a craft after it has been acquired."[5]

Abbott and Breckinridge recognized that self-help could do little to bring about industrial reform. Yet they credited social research with significant power to advance social change. This sentiment led them to an early, and successful, reform campaign in 1905. After completing their initial research on women's employment, they began to lobby for a major federal study of women industrial workers. Breckinridge's legal training and her work with Ernst Freund had made her especially sensitive to the limits of nonuniform state laws. A congressional inquiry into female employment, she believed, would be more than an expression of political concern. It promised to uncover national trends. A government report might also mobilize public opinion for legislative change.

Over dinner one evening, Abbott, Breckinridge, and Chicago settlement leader Mary McDowell decided to mount a campaign to win congressional support for the federal research project. They persuaded Jane Addams to approach Theodore Roosevelt with their idea. Organizations such as the new Women's Trade Union League, the General Federation of Women's Clubs, the American Federation of Labor, countless settlement workers, and church groups were enlisted, as well.[6]

In spite of such allies, winning congressional approval was no easy task. Roosevelt agreed to endorse the investigation in his December 1905 address to Congress. But before he could do so, a bill appeared before the House that called for the appointment of a similar commission to study child labor. McDowell, Breckinridge, Abbott, and other key supporters of the women's employment project now concentrated on getting women included in the child labor investigation.

Aggressive lobbying of important government officials, including the commissioner of labor, members of the Census Bureau, and various congressmen, paid off. In the spring of 1906 legislation calling for an investigation of women *and* child laborers was introduced in both houses of Congress. By December, the Senate had approved the measure; the House vote approached. At the eleventh hour, McDowell, working frantically to see the legislation through, instructed Breckinridge to pay a visit to one influential congressman. "If possible size up the situation for me," she advised. The Kentuckian moved easily among powerful legislators, some of whom were family friends. With her connections, and McDowell's sharp attention to detail, the reformers triumphed. Roosevelt signed the bill into law on January 31, 1907.[7]

Three years later the first of nineteen volumes of investigation and analysis appeared. *The Report on the Conditions of Women and Child Wage Earners in the United States* immediately became a critical resource for researchers; it remained so for many years to come. In 1911 Breckinridge reviewed the sixth volume for *The Survey* with great satisfaction. *The Report on the Beginnings of Child Labor Legislation in Certain States*, she noted, supported important findings previously made by Edith Abbott. "It may be," she optimistically wrote, "that the revelation of conditions prevailing in the states will suffice to secure substantial protection in terms made real by effective factory inspection."[8]

Their conviction that social knowledge advanced reform inspired Breckinridge and Abbott to continue their scholarly research on industrial problems. Breckinridge focused her attention on legislative remedies and issues involving the police power, an approach that reflected the intellectual influence of Ernst Freund. At a very early date, she began to construct legal arguments that justified government intervention on behalf of social welfare measures. In a 1905 article for the *Journal of Political Economy* Breckinridge described two decisions relating to organized labor handed down by American and British courts that upheld the closed shop. A similar essay written in 1906 examined protective legislation for working women. Breckinridge noted that laws limiting the hours of work and prohibiting women's labor in certain industries were "not enacted exclusively, or even primarily, for the benefit of women themselves." The state, she insisted, had an interest in safeguarding the "physical well-being" of women who were "the mothers, actual or prospective, of the coming generation."[9]

Breckinridge supported protective legislation for women as a step in the direction of elevating all workers. In a detailed analysis of a 1910 Illinois Supreme Court decision upholding the state's ten-hour law, she noted with approval that the statute was deemed "a justifiable exercise of the police power." The case was significant, Breckinridge explained, because the court accepted arguments that a relationship existed between "the health of women workers and the public health, and second, between the public health and public well-being." The decision opened the door for other legislative remedies if evidence could establish "the bearing of any other industrial abuse upon the public welfare." The case, she wrote, "removes a doubt which paralyzed all activity in the direction of legislative control of industry for the improvement of working conditions" by invoking standards that went beyond "bodily safety and reasonable decency." Unfortunately, the court decisions affected only women industrial workers in certain trades. Others were "allowed the privilege of being employed as many hours of the twenty-four as the conditions of their trade and their economic weakness dictate." But Breckinridge felt optimistic that protective legislation for women would hasten the day when men won a shorter day and additional trades were regulated, as well.[10]

Abbott's studies in economic history provided the foundation for an extraordinary book tracing the evolution of women's industrial work. Beginning in 1906, sections of the manuscript began appearing as essays in the *Journal of Political Economy*. By 1908 Abbott's study, *Women in Industry*, was complete. Breckinridge played an important role in bringing her friend's book to fruition. She criticized Abbott's drafts, helped her find a publisher (D. Appleton and Company), and wrote an introduction to the work when it appeared in December of 1909. Most of all, Breckinridge had, early on, legitimized research on women as a worthy area of scholarly inquiry. In recognition of Breckinridge's help, Abbott dedicated *Women in Industry* to her loyal friend.[11]

The book built on Abbott's dissertation and her previous research with Breckinridge. But it also reflected the author's experience at the Carnegie Institution and the London School of Economics. Abbott's exposure to trade unionism and British textile workers had clearly heightened her understanding of economic stratification and deepened her sympathy for the poor. Professor Laughlin might have raised an eyebrow, but by 1906 Abbott's analysis emphasized class. Indeed, Abbott used her own achievements to illustrate the narrow-mindedness of those who trumpeted modern woman's advance.

> It has . . . been too often assumed that the conspicuous broadening of the field of opportunities and activities for educated women during the latter half of the nineteenth century has been a progress without class distinctions in which all women have shared alike. But the history of the employment of women in professional and industrial life has been radically different, and the fruits of the long struggle of the last century for what is perhaps nebulously described as "women's rights," have gone, almost exclusively, to the women of the professional group.[12]

Women in Industry remains a brilliant piece of work, perhaps the most important study of women industrial workers ever written in the United States. Abbott added a new chapter to American economic history when she described "the history and statistics of the employment of women in America." In *Women in Industry*, Abbott confronted the challenge her professors had so often posed. The book was offered "not only as a contribution toward the history of an important subject, but because of the practical bearing it may have upon the problems of women today." Abbott sought the middle ground between popular, and unscientific, discussions of women industrial workers, and studies that were excessively "theoretical," ahistorical, and inattentive to contemporary affairs. The economist's personal experience as a young professional woman surely animated her study. She wrote with feeling of the "restriction of opportunity" and "equal work for unequal pay" middle-class career women faced. But her intellectual passions were with industrial working women "wronged . . . because of the pseudo-democratic refusal to recognize class distinctions in discussions of the woman question."[13]

Abbott used her skill in economic history to construct a powerful analysis of women's industrial work. There was nothing new, she argued, about female participation in the industrial labor force. Colonial Americans "rigidly insisted" upon women's work. Their heavy use of women and children in domestic manufactures set a precedent that led to work outside the home when workshops for spinning and weaving appeared. "The tenement workers of the so-called 'sweated trades' today," she pointed out, were the "direct descendants of the women who were employed in weaving or in making cards for the 'manufactory' of the eighteenth century." In the early nineteenth century, a scarcity of labor, the persistence of a Puritan work ethic, and fears of the social cost of idleness ensured that "no social prejudice" interfered with women's participation in industrial work.[14]

These conclusions were supported by empirical research. Rejecting economists' views that no complete study of women's participation in industry before 1860 was possible, Abbott applied statistical methods developed in her dissertation to census returns. The results thoroughly refuted the notion that women had only recently entered the industrial labor force. Abbott discovered that female labor was both common and "an important factor in a large number of industries." Over one hundred industrial occupations employed women between 1820 and 1840. *Women in Industry* offered a thorough history and statistical profile of the five industries employing the largest number of women. In separate chapters, she explained the wages, hours, and working conditions women confronted in textiles, clothing, cigar making, shoes, and the printing trades.[15]

This was ground-breaking research. Until Abbott, few economists or historians considered women's employment worthy of such detailed study. Abbott's description of the early-nineteenth-century "Lowell mill girls" anticipated by at least twenty years the fascination these factory girls would hold for historians. Her rendition romanticized, in some ways, the "daughters of New England farmers" who filled the first cotton mills. These hardy pioneers, the Chicago graduate wrote, were educated women who suffered from having "no field of employment . . . and opportunities for training." But Abbott did not idealize conditions in the mills. She described the poorly lit, underheated, "badly ventilated" and crowded factories in stark terms, and she carefully chronicled the long hours operatives were forced to work. The only thing "superior" about the early cotton mills, in Abbott's opinion, was their "unique body of operatives," whom she greatly admired.[16]

Abbott's history of women industrial workers was a story of exploitation, occupational segregation, discrimination, and unequal wages, bluntly told. The economist maintained a tone of neutrality throughout, but her account emphasized the obstacles women factory workers faced in various trades. She pointed to the tremendous wage differentials between men and women in shoe manufacturing, the grueling sweatshop conditions endured by Bohemian cigar makers, and even the "jealousy of men" toward women in the printing trades. The structure of modern industry as it evolved in the late nineteenth century created many of these evils, Abbott argued. She underscored the impact of technology, the "de-skilling" of labor, and the deliberate exploitation of workers by employers as causes of these trends.[17]

Although *Women in Industry* offered no prescriptions for reform, Abbott hoped her research would persuade the public to address the needs of working women. At the very least, she asked that women's work outside the home be acknowledged as a social and historical fact. When workers were needed to tend the new machines that launched America's industrial revolution, the economist pointed out, women "quietly" left their homes and went to the factories. "This was not only the natural thing for them to do but it was demanded of them by the public opinion of their day, and there was no voice lifted then to remind them that woman's proper place was at home." She hoped the lessons of history would still the voice of public moralists who contributed to women's economic oppression. In that sense, *Women in Industry* was itself an effort to advance reform.[18]

Abbott raised the issue of economic regulation in her discussion of wages. But she stopped short of endorsing specific legislative changes. Instead, the economist suggested that organization provided the best hope for "an improvement in women's wages." A "growing class consciousness" leading women "into the labor movement," the demands of trade unionists for equal pay for men and women, and "the effects of the woman movement" all gave reasons for hope. Female workers, Abbott believed, could look confidently to these social movements to "do away with influence of custom and tradition which have had so depressing an effect on their economic condition." In a long appendix describing the history of child labor, she argued that an absence of regulation had led to terrible abuse.[19]

Abbott's and Breckinridge's early essays on social problems were scholarly studies that adhered closely to the standards of "objective" social scientific research. Yet their intellectual work was driven by a powerful sense of injustice that grew out of contemporary realities. Their analysis of political and economic trends focused on the victims of industrialization. That emphasis would become more pronounced as the women found a place for their talents in the arena of Progressive reform. Ideas and methods cultivated in the university would produce a compelling analysis of social problems and a familiar approach to social change.

III

Unlike Katharine Davis and Frances Kellor, Abbott's and Breckinridge's careers as social investigators and social activists developed in the context of an educational institution. That fact had a significant impact on Edith's and Sophonisba's involvement with Progressive reform. Neither woman faced the political pressures imposed on Davis and Kellor. They avoided public service and hence escaped public accountability for their vision of social change. They made an intellectual contribution to early-twentieth-century reform, as did Davis and Kellor. But their administrative responsibilities were exercised primarily in academia. Nevertheless, Abbott and Breckinridge also struggled to institutionalize social knowledge as a method of reform. They found their "laboratory" for social research and social welfare policy in the Chicago School of Civics and Philanthropy.

The School of Civics was the first setting that really enabled the women social scientists to practice their "craft." Breckinridge had begun teaching at the school in 1907, while serving as assistant professor in the Department of Household Administration at the University of Chicago. Edith Abbott joined the staff in 1908. Before long the women were staking a claim to the social work training center. They tried to transform the School of Civics into a graduate school that realized their intellectual, professional, and political ideals.

The school owed its existence to Graham Taylor. A dedicated leader of the Chicago Commons settlement house and an ordained minister animated by the social gospel, Taylor resembled the "Christian sociologists" from whom Albion Small was so eager to distinguish modern sociologists. As a teacher at the Chicago Theological Seminary and a part-time lecturer in sociology at the University of Chicago, Taylor consistently advanced the view that effective social action required reliable social knowledge. Much influenced by a growing movement to provide effective training to young men and women engaged in social work, Taylor met with President William Rainey Harper in 1903 to explore the possibilities of university sponsorship of such a program.

Taylor's idea meshed perfectly with Harper's vision of the University of Chicago's Extension Division. The president agreed to announce a course of social work in the Extension bulletin and 'to provide classroom space in downtown Chicago. Taylor named the new endeavor the "Social Science Center for Practical Training in Philanthropic and Social Work." In reality, when the center opened in the fall of 1903, it consisted of one course, "Dependency and Preventive Agencies," taught by Taylor and Charles Henderson. Neither instructor received payment for his services, and the class met just one evening a week for three months. But twelve students, "all of whom were actively engaged in social work," attended: the venture was launched.[20]

The following year, Taylor's Social Science Center acquired more students, offered several new courses, and enlarged its staff. Visiting lecturers included Hull House resident and charity worker Julia Lathrop, social critic Robert Hunter, Chicago sociologist Charles Zeublein, Cook County circuit judge Julian Mack, and Jane Addams herself. By 1905 the school was known as the "Institute of Social Science and Arts." Harper now offered Taylor a stipend for serving as director, and guest lecturers were also paid a modest honorarium. Taylor hoped that Chicago would absorb the institute and give it standing as a professional school within the university. But this never figured in Harper's plans. The minister was shocked to learn when Harper died in January of 1906 that the institute's small budget had come from funds the Chicago president himself had privately raised.

After Harper's death, the university let Taylor know it would not follow the founding president's precedent in supporting the school. The minister then turned to the trustees of the Chicago Commons; they agreed in 1906 to underwrite the school, now christened with its third name in as many years: The Chicago Institute of Social Science. The Institute's budget grew considerably, and a summer school added to regular winter and spring offerings. Over 150 students enrolled for classes. The school's short-term future, at least, seemed secure.[21]

When news came in 1907 that the institute would receive one of the grants the Russell Sage Foundation was awarding to social work training centers, Taylor's wildest dreams seemed about to be realized. The grant provided a $10,000 stipend for five years to establish a program of social research. The Sage Foundation's interest in social welfare and social analysis reflected new developments in philanthropy that had benefited Katharine Davis and Frances Kellor. They now advanced Breckinridge's career. Taylor persuaded Julia Lathrop to join the school as director of the new Research Department and co-director of the institute. She hired Breckinridge as her assistant. The two women knew each other well from Hull House where Breckinridge was a frequent visitor. Indeed, in 1907 the Chicago professor began spending her vacation quarter from the university at Addams' settlement house. She continued to do so for another fourteen years.[22]

By the time Edith Abbott joined the school in 1908, it had another new name. Incorporated in May 1908 as the "Chicago School of Civics and Philanthropy," the school was now overseen by a board of leading public figures in educational, philanthropic, and reform circles. Wealthy Chicago women such as Mrs. William F. Dummer and Mrs. Emmons Blaine served as trustees, along with University of Wisconsin economist Richard Ely, University of Michigan sociologist Charles Cooley, industrialist Charles Crane, and Chicago businessman Edward L. Ryerson. Taylor and Lathrop combined membership on the board of trustees with their duties as president and vice-president of the school. The institution's charter issued a broad mandate that stressed social betterment. The School, it read, was to "promote through instruction, training, investigation and publication, the efficiency of civic, philanthropic and social work, and the improvement of living and working conditions."[23]

Taylor had always envisioned the new school as a practical training center for social workers. He hoped to develop an educational program that responded to the growing demand for "efficient helpers, in charitable and reformatory service, both public and private, and in all endeavors to improve industrial, civic, and social conditions and relationships." Public and private agencies often asked settlement houses to provide them with trained welfare workers, but the settlements had trouble maintaining their own staffs. A special school for social workers might replenish the ranks with highly skilled recruits.

Taylor and Lathrop formulated a program of study at the School of Civics and Philanthropy that emphasized "technical preparation," field work, and practical social service. Students served apprenticeships at various Chicago agencies, including the juvenile court, the Chicago Bureau of Charities, and the Relief and Aid Society, as well as settlements, insane asylums, hospitals, and orphanages. Course work often focused on specific methods of assisting the needy. In the summer of 1908, Julia Lathrop offered instruction in occupational therapy for workers employed at mental institutions. Similar courses soon broke new ground in social-work education.[24]

The Department of Social Investigation, where Breckinridge taught, formed a parallel area of study within the School of Civics. Students enrolled in this division took an introductory course on "methods of social inquiry" designed to teach the fundamentals of research. Then they embarked on intensive investigations of social problems with the guidance of Lathrop and Breckinridge. Edith Abbott helped out by teaching statistics. When Lathrop relinquished her position as director of the department in the fall of 1908, Breckinridge took over her post. Abbott then assumed responsibilities as Breckinridge's assistant. Lathrop remained deeply involved with the school, continuing her membership on its board of trustees, and lecturing to students from time to time. But Breckinridge soon began to fill the void in leadership left by her predecessor. By 1909 she had been appointed dean.[25]

Breckinridge and Abbott made a distinctive contribution to the School of Civics and Philanthropy. Social-work education was then in its infancy, and there were few models to follow in developing a professional school. Breckinridge and Abbott drew on their graduate educations as they organized the research department. Both women encouraged their students to carefully study the social sciences. They prodded them to pursue detailed investigations of contemporary social problems. They emphasized empirical study as a superior method of social research. And they helped students publish their findings as a way of advancing enlightened reform. In short, they tried to offer their own students the kind of training professors at Chicago had once offered them.

The women social scientists' style contrasted sharply with that of Graham Taylor. While Taylor enjoyed teaching and lecturing in a casual manner that made heavy use of personal stories, Abbott and Breckinridge took a much more rigorous, formal, and theoretical approach. Taylor liked to develop his courses around guest lectures, a practice that confounded students who heard from "almost as many different people as they were sessions in a series." Breckinridge and Abbott rejected this format; their special department became known for its tightly organized courses offered by one professor alone.

As enrollments grew rapidly, and the school became a regular two-year professional training program, its students were more often college graduates. Slowly the School of Civics began to resemble a graduate school. Graham Taylor himself credited the "rare and distinctive service" of Breckinridge and Abbott with much of the institution's success. He later recalled

> the scientific thoroughness of the training thus offered to graduate students in methods of social investigation and research; the wide range, statistical accuracy, and practical value of the publications reporting these investigations; and the exacting positions for which graduates were sought and in which they rendered public service—all contributed much to the growing reputation of the school.[26]

IV

Breckinridge's and Abbott's penchant for joining academic research to social activism also attracted attention to the school. By 1908 Breckinridge had become a an important figure in Chicago reform circles. She had served as a factory inspector in 1906, and, like many liberal professors at the university, had taken an interest in municipal reform battles. But Breckinridge's link to other female activists cemented her commitment to social welfare campaigns. At local meetings of the Women's Trade Union League and through countless evenings in the drawing rooms of Hull House, Breckinridge joined a community of women deeply committed to Progressive causes. Emotional need, intellectual sympathy, and professional ideals converged. Breckinridge found her place among the women activists of Chicago. When Edith Abbott returned to the city in 1908, she followed the example of her colleague and her younger sister Grace.[27]

Breckinridge's growing stature in Chicago led public officials to the School of Civics and Philanthropy. Shortly after Edith Abbott joined the staff in 1908, Chicago's chief sanitary inspector, Charles Ball, approached the social-work center for assistance in surveying city housing. The two women readily agreed. The project would offer students a chance to undertake social research that might coincidentally improve conditions in the city. This was precisely the kind of applied social science Breckinridge and Abbott hoped to advance.[28]

Their experience at Hull House had prepared both women for their investigation of living conditions in Chicago. Breckinridge had witnessed the grim circumstances in which many immigrants were forced to live. In fact, her knowledge of the settlement neighborhood played a part in the 1907 founding of Chicago's Immigrants' Protective League. The organization tried to assist the foreign-born in adjusting to urban life by helping new arrivals find work, housing, and education. The league also sought to prevent the exploitation that was rampant in the city. Breckinridge brought several colleagues into the organization, including Ernst Freund, who served as president; Samuel Harper, the son of Chicago's founding president and a Russian expert at the university; and Professor George Herbert Mead, who agreed to be vice-president. Although Breckinridge was devoted to the group, she refused to give up her work at the university when Jane Addams asked her to lead the organization. Instead she advanced Grace Abbott, Edith's younger sister and a political science graduate student at the university, for the job. Grace accepted, and Breckinridge stayed on as secretary of the Immigrants' Protective League.[29]

Edith Abbott's association with Hull House also well prepared her for the School of Civics housing survey. She had moved into the settlement upon returning to Chicago, and with her sister Grace, she remained for many years. Edith later recalled the tremendous impression this experience made on her.

Hull House and the old West Side were still a part of a vast city-wilderness when Grace and I went there to live in 1908; and "getting over to the West Side" was not easy in those days, when automobiles were still in the future for common use. The streets were atrocious—badly paved or not paved, rarely cleaned or never cleaned; there were horses everywhere, and filthy, rotting stables and undescribably filthy alleys; the tenements, many of them wooden shacks that had been built on the prairie before the "Great Fire," were beyond description; and there were sweatshops and "home finishing" on every side of us as we came or went. Great foreign colonies had been established, where English was seldom heard. We were in the midst of an Italian neighborhood adjoining a large Greek colony with a "Pantheon" restaurant and a "Parthenon" barber shop across the way. There was a large Bulgarian colony along Halsted Street to the north, and the old Ghetto to the south, as

picturesque as it was unsanitary. Immigrants were pouring into Chicago, and
the West Side offered shelter to large numbers.

The scene fascinated Abbott. She was no stranger to the underside of the city
exposed in the School of Civics housing study.[30]

The research project Breckinridge and Abbott designed was impressive in
scope and methodology. It incorporated empirical techniques that had been
stressed in their graduate training. The city now became a laboratory for students at the School of Civics. They conducted an exhaustive door-to-door
canvass of tenement lodging that included visual inspections and interviews
with residents. The Chicago River cut the city in three, and efforts were made
to study systematically key districts on the North, West, and South sides.
Wards were broken down into streets, then blocks, and finally buildings; individual visits were made to hundreds of tenement houses.

The Chicago Health Department provided investigators with official
badges that permitted entry into private dwellings. Breckinridge and Abbott
worked closely with Chief Sanitary Inspector Ball in targeting areas of study
and exchanging information. A talented team of students carried out most of
the door-to-door canvass, keeping careful records of what they found. They
compiled statistics, constructed tables, and drew extraordinarily detailed
maps that illustrated their findings. This material, along with a series of
graphic photographs, illustrated the articles Breckinridge and Abbott wrote
for the *American Journal of Sociology* between 1910 and 1911 describing the
study's results.[31]

Much of the impetus for the housing investigation derived from concerns
that were essentially conservative. Immigrants and the poor lived in conditions, the researchers feared, that made "traditional" family life an impossi-
bility. In a report on "furnished rooms," Breckinridge and Abbott described
a city transformed by the desperate circumstances of the poor. In Chicago,
they reported,

> there are now large sections of the city in which houses intended for families
> of one type have been taken over by families of another, and serious evils
> have arisen through the attempted adaptation of houses which were, in the
> sixties, seventies, and eighties, the dwellings of well-to-do and dignified fam-
> ilies, to the present uses of families that are unfortunate, incompetent, pov-
> erty-stricken, and often degraded.

Once-stately homes were broken up into cheap rented rooms. Tenants lived
in windowless hallways, with little air, without plumbing. Parents ill with
tuberculosis shared a bed with their children.[32]

Breckinridge's and Abbott's assessment of urban poverty repeated themes
that had surfaced in Frances Kellor's and Katharine Davis's research. Like
their classmates, they measured what they found in Chicago's slums by middle-class values. Abbott and Breckinridge shared Davis's and Kellor's grave
concerns about social disorganization. In fact, they seemed even more threatened by the "degraded" circumstances of the poor. Yet they also believed

their research illustrated important truths about the character of American society.

Abbott and Breckinridge used their training in the social sciences to set Chicago's problems within a wider social context. They linked urban poverty to industrialization, thereby offering an environmental analysis similar to that of Davis and Kellor. "Modern industry," Abbott and Breckinridge wrote, "dominates all the aspects and conditions of life for those who are of the pecuniarily incompetent grade." The incursion of business and industry into once respectable neighborhoods had driven out middle-class dwellers, who left their abandoned homes as inadequate shelters for the poor. Breckinridge and Abbott blamed unemployment, low wages, the alcoholism and irresponsibility of men, and the helplessness of women for the poor's "disorderly manner of living." They placed responsibility for improving these conditions on the public.

The municipal regulation favored by Kellor had an equally prominent place on Breckinridge's and Abbott's reform agenda. Like many Progressives, they considered imperative the enforcement of health and building codes, police protection, and a crackdown on criminals who preyed on the poor families. In ascribing responsibility to public officials, Breckinridge and Abbott shifted the blame for these evils from the victims of industrial society. Thus immigrants were seen as the "respectable tenement population" who deserved to have their neighborhoods rid of prostitutes and thieves. The only workable solution in the long run, the women concluded, was to provide decent housing and rooms for the poor.[33]

No chapter in their brief for reform was more dramatic than Breckinridge's and Abbott's description of the Chicago Stock Yards district. In a lead article for the January 1911 *American Journal of Sociology*, they reported the gruesome life researchers discovered "back of the Yards." The district, bounded by "city dumps, brickyard, and Bubbly Creek on one side, and the greatest slaughterhouses in the world on the other," had commanded public attention since Upton Sinclair exposed its underbelly in *The Jungle* (1906). The area was still home to large numbers of Chicago's poor, it had a high infant mortality rate, and it continued to breed terrible rates of disease. Investigators for the school visited over fifteen hundred families who boarded in "typical homes of this neighborhood." There they found a community of Slavic immigrants nearly uniformly exploited, paying "the highest rents for the poorest apartments."[34]

The Stock Yards survey uncovered the now-expected conditions of overcrowding and poor sanitation. Paternalistic attitudes towards the foreign-born were evident in Breckinridge's and Abbott's reference to their "un-American standard of living." The women blamed the very business of the Stock Yards, with its omnipresent "suggestions of death and disintegration," for the "demoralizing" atmosphere there. Yet their harshest indictment fell on the city's "niggardly public policy," which refused to grant the Health Department adequate appropriations to enforce existing codes. Empty legal reforms failed to bring about any sort of lasting change, the social scientists warned. "To substitute the shadow for the substance in dealing with the problem of city housing leads quickly to criminal neglect." Once again, they offered their research as an instrument for reform. "It is hoped that this brief statistical summary will speak more forcibly than words of Chicago's long neglect of duty in making proper provision for the maintenance of modern standards of housing and public health."[35]

Throughout their research on Chicago's housing conditions, Breckinridge and Abbott balanced broad sociological study with attention to individual human needs. Although they recognized the structural origins of urban poverty, they tried to mobilize public welfare services on behalf of the city's poor. Information about especially dangerous health violations was passed to Sanitary Inspector Ball. He pressed the social workers to keep him informed of the housing investigation "in the hope that it may prove useful to us in the immediate future." They happily complied. In a typical report, Breckinridge disclosed findings at 4500 Paulina Street. "Cellar floor covered with sewage water. Man claims four feet in some places. Needs attention at once. Plumbing in whole house bad." The health commissioner appointed Breckinridge "Tenement Inspector in the Department of Health, without salary" in November of 1909, ordering her to "act as an investigator in connection with the studies made by the School of Civics and Philanthropy."[36]

But the social worker required no official title to prompt her social conscience. When a visit to one tenement family revealed an infant suffering from "diseased eyes," Breckinridge wrote to the United Charities of Chicago asking them to help the child. The district superintendent soon assured her that "an attendant" had been dispatched to take the mother and baby to the Illinois Charitable Eye and Ear Infirmary. The Relief Board thanked Breckinridge "for calling our attention to this matter," and promised to "follow up the case." Concerned about the welfare of children set to work picking up rags at the city dump, Breckinridge pressed the state factory inspector to track down the perpetrators. Their continual exposure to terrible human suffering and dangerous public health problems led student investigators to similar actions. Breckinridge's assistant William Chenery, later an editor of *Collier's Magazine*, directed the study of city dumps. In the midst of his research, he sent preliminary findings to Chicago professor and city alderman Charles Merriam in the hope of securing public action.[37]

Breckinridge's singular contribution to the housing survey was her intervention on behalf of black Chicagoans. Like Katharine Davis and Frances Kellor, she was unusually sensitive to the issue of race. Breckinridge insisted on including black neighborhoods in the tenement survey even when the Health Department told her the areas weren't worth canvassing. And in 1913, she wrote a compelling article for *The Survey* describing what she called "the color line in the housing problem." The burdens shouldered by black Americans were perhaps most obvious in the South, she wrote, but they were not restricted to that region. Northern urban blacks faced serious problems, as well. "In the face of increasing manifestations of race prejudice," Breckinridge noted, the black city dweller "has come to acquiesce silently, as various civil rights are withheld from him in the old 'free north,' which was once the Mecca of his race."

> He rarely protests, for example, being excluded from restaurants and hotels or being virtually refused entertainment at the theater or the opera. There are three points, however, which he cannot yield and in regard to which he should not be allowed to yield. He must claim a decent home for his family in a respectable neighborhood and at a reasonable rental, an equal chance of employment with the white man, and education for his children.[38]

Breckinridge recognized that black Chicagoans faced barriers even the most reviled immigrants escaped. They were often barred from housing regardless of their economic or social class. In Chicago, poor blacks faced "extortionate rents and . . . dangerous proximity to segregated vice." Police usually ignored prostitution in areas that abutted on black neighborhoods. "The segregation of the negro quarter is only a segregation from respectable white people. The disreputable white element is forced upon him." Careful investigation proved that black districts had the worst housing in the city.

> In no other neighborhood were landlords so obdurate, so unwilling to make necessary improvements or to cancel leases so that tenants might seek better accommodations elsewhere. Of course, to go elsewhere was often impossible because nowhere is the prospective colored tenant or neighbor welcome.

Black Chicagoans living in dilapidated apartment houses paid rents that were among the highest in the city for "an ordinary four room apartment."

Breckinridge blamed these realities on "race prejudice," arguing that "persecution" had created "the special Negro housing problem." This was an unusually sentient perspective on the relatively new black ghetto of Chicago. The patterns of segregation and restricted opportunity that soon defined the city were still in the making in 1913. Most white Chicagoans, including some members of the spirited reform community, ignored the tragedy of race discrimination and the urban poverty that accompanied it.[39]

Yet Breckinridge's trenchant analysis was accompanied by an idealistic belief that ignorance permitted these conditions to exist. Only a "small minority" of whites, she claimed, harbored race prejudice. Discrimination went unchecked because "the great majority are completely ignorant of the heavy burden of injustice that the Negro carries." The social activist admitted that a few powerful racist whites could make life very difficult for black Americans. But she felt even more concerned about "the acquiescence of the great majority who want fair play." Perhaps research on the problems shouldered by black Americans would facilitate change. "It seemed worthwhile to collect and to present the facts relating to housing conditions in the Negro districts of Chicago because one must hope that they would not be tolerated if the great mass of white people knew of their existence."

Like many Progressive writers, Breckinridge used this argument as a rhetorical device. She hoped to galvanize her readers by appealing to their public conscience. But the tactic reflected a genuine belief that broad knowledge of social conditions could ameliorate even the harshest social realities. This unfaltering faith in education as a method of reform had deep roots in Breckinridge's intellectual and life experience. Her academic training helped nourish an incisive perspective on social problems and a much less concrete approach to social change.[40]

In her own life, Breckinridge went beyond providing simple lip service to the ideal of racial equality. Like Frances Kellor and Katharine Davis, she took practical steps to end the exploitation of black Americans; albeit with varying degrees of success. Breckinridge joined a variety of organizations committed to racial advancement, as had Frances Kellor. An active and early member of the Chicago branch of the N.A.A.C.P., Breckinridge also devoted time to the Association of Colored Women. She worked hard to get the black Wendell Phillips Settlement off the ground, using her influence with Sears Roebuck magnate Julius Rosenwald to ensure the settlement's financial stability in 1913. Rosenwald agreed to provide the community with 25 percent of its budget. The philanthropist also acted favorably on Breckinridge's request for two scholarships to the School of Civics for black women. Breckinridge hoped the recipients would learn lessons that would assist them in directing the Phillips Settlement House. Sophonisba herself served as the settlement's president for a time. Along with Edith Abbott, she played a major role in the founding of the Chicago Urban League. As always, Breckinridge readily lent her expertise to a fact-finding commission on Chicago race relations appointed after a brutal riot in 1919. She also put her students to work conducting investigations to enhance the commission's report.[41]

Breckinridge met with less success in her efforts to confront racism at the University of Chicago. When a "very able and learned 'woman of color'" sought dormitory housing in 1907, Marion Talbot left the problem to her assistant dean. Several Southern women threatened to move out, but Breckinridge "agreed" the black woman "had every right to stay." Sophonisba offered to help the white students find other accommodations. But a few days after they had departed and Georgiana Simpson was settled in the dorm, Breckinridge was "summoned to the President's office."

> President Judson told me that the halls were for white students and Miss Simpson must leave. I pointed out that the announcements distributed by the University with reference to the Houses said nothing of this, but he was immovable and Miss Simpson moved out.

(Simpson later earned her doctoral degree.) Breckinridge told Edith Abbott that she had at least "got Miss Talbot and the women on record on the side of admitting her which was worth a good deal." But she could not provide, she later conceded to W. E. B. DuBois, "any brief for the treatment offered the colored students by the University of Chicago." Katharine Davis had enjoyed greater success in integrating a prison than Breckinridge had achieved in academe.[42]

V

By 1912, Breckinridge and Abbott had waded deeply into contemporary social policy issues. That year a second major study came out of the Chicago School of Civics and Philanthropy's research department. *The Delinquent Child and the Home* was an ambitious investigation of Chicago's juvenile court. As in the housing survey, Breckinridge and Abbott made extensive use of student researchers in the juvenile court project. Interviews with the families of delinquents and probation officers and analysis of court files yielded a massive amount of material that revealed important facts about the social origins of young offenders.

The book provided the intellectual underpinnings for a Progressive approach to juvenile delinquency. It also secured Breckinridge and Abbott's reputations as experts on children in trouble with the law. Their painstaking social research added weight to arguments advanced by many child welfare reformers. Yet apparent throughout *The Delinquent Child and the Home* were a set of intellectual values that shaped the authors' perspective on reform.[43]

Illinois was the first state in the country to enact a juvenile court law. It mandated a separate system of justice for children in 1899. Late that year the nation's first juvenile court opened in Chicago. The court handled dependent or neglected children, truants, and delinquents. They were treated as wards of the state rather than as criminals, and their cases were often resolved with probation. Chicago reformers had played a major role in creating the juvenile court system; the idea quickly caught on in other areas of the country. By 1920 only three states in the nation had failed to make provisions for a separate children's court.[44]

Breckinridge's and Abbott's study of the delinquent children handled by Chicago's juvenile court had a dual purpose. The women hoped to assess the court's effectiveness and to enhance "understanding of the needs of all children" by providing "more exact knowledge" of children under stress. They hoped to achieve those ends by conducting exhaustive social scientific research. With the cooperation of the court, they gained access to the records of every case that came before the court in its first ten years, a number that exceeded 11,000. Since official court records revealed little about the social backgrounds of accused children, home visits were made to a representative sample comprised of delinquent boys brought before the court in the year 1903–1904. Plans for a similar study of female juvenile offenders were aborted when families objected to investigators' questions about their young daughters. Instead, case histories of delinquents committed to the State Training School for Girls were examined. When completed, *The Delinquent Child and the Home* included extensive statistical data, numerous tables, and a truly extraordinary map of Chicago that marked with a dot the home of nearly every child appearing before the juvenile court between 1899 and 1909. This data helped sketch a vivid portrait of delinquent children. Less detailed was the analysis of the institution charged with rehabilitating them.[45]

Abbott's and Breckinridge's approach to juvenile delinquency followed the pattern of their previous research. As in the housing survey, they stressed the environmental causes of social dislocation. Children had no innate propensity to do wrong. Rather, the unstable circumstances in which they lived accounted for their criminal behavior. Careful study of delinquent children proved that "poverty in itself is often a direct and compelling cause of delinquency." Most children brought before the court belonged to indigent families. Put to work at a young age, they rebelled against their heavy responsibilities by stealing or running away. Impoverished mothers who worked long hours for low wages could not adequately supervise their children. The tenement districts in which needy families lived offered few safe opportunities for play. As Breckinridge and Abbott explained:

> When we see all the wide background of deprivation in their lives, the longing for a little money to spend, for the delights of the nickel theater, for the joy of owning a pigeon, or for the glowing adventure of a ride on the train, it is not hard to understand how the simple fact of being poor is many times a sufficient explanation of delinquency.

Young children who had lost a parent, become homeless, lived with an alcoholic father or mentally ill mother struggled with tremendous hardships that could easily explain delinquent behavior.[46]

Although the vast majority of cases brought before the juvenile court involved children of immigrants, Abbott and Breckinridge rejected nativist explanations of delinquency. They insisted, as did Katharine Davis and Frances Kellor, that immigrants were no more "criminal" than the native-born. Instead, they attributed misconduct to social forces beyond the immigrant's control. The trauma of adjusting to life in the United States, and the bigotry of Americans, Abbott and Breckinridge suggested, accounted for many appearances before the court. "The child in a crowded immigrant quarter who does wrong, quickly comes to the attention of neighbors, police and probation officers; and his offense, though perhaps more trivial than the American child's, may involve much more serious consequences." Immigrant children who were dependents wound up being treated as delinquents when they stole food or wandered unattended in the city. The parents of many juvenile offenders had migrated from rural areas where they performed agricultural labor. Plunged into American cities and factories, these men and women struggled with "the difficulty of adjustment." Their heavy burdens had a tremendous impact on their children.[47]

The Delinquent Child and the Home reflected the middle-class values of its authors. Abbott and Breckinridge offered moral judgments about the behavior of the poor. They placed an extraordinary emphasis on education as a remedy for the grinding poverty the book detailed. Those who worked to support their families instead of attending school, the social scientists warned, lost their best chance to improve their life circumstances. Families struggling with alcoholism, parents who had themselves been convicted of crimes, those who lived in run-down dwellings, made, the authors wrote, "degraded homes." In such a setting, delinquency became "almost inevitable." Abbott and Breckinridge shared Katharine Davis's worries about moral contamination. Young female prostitutes, they feared, threatened other children with "both spiritual contagion and physical infection."

Indeed, the researchers were surprisingly inconsistent in their assessment of male and female delinquency. Young boys frequently appeared before the court, they noted, for crimes that varied in gravity from thefts of large sums of money to lifting "candy, gum, pigeons, and similar articles of special value to the small boy." Both types of misdeed could land a child before a magistrate. The two women likened such innocent stealing to "the long tolerated privilege which the country boy enjoyed of swiping melons and pumpkins in neighboring gardens." These crimes were "not vicious" but "performed in the spirit of harmless adventure." Other petty misdemeanors labeled "incorrigibility" were dismissed as trivial by the researchers. Incorrigibility, they wrote, was "a word apparently coined of despair." Parents who could not control their boys, but had the economic resources and good health to do so, deserved "to be disciplined and possibly placed on probation as delinquent parents." A variety of offenses committed in the railroad yards could be eliminated by elevating the tracks and fencing and guarding the yards.[48]

But Breckinridge's and Abbott's relatively relaxed attitude toward mischievous young boys shifted dramatically when the two considered female delinquency. In this case, court officials considered "incorrigibility" behavior better labeled "immorality." The researchers asserted that

> 80 percent of the delinquent girls are brought to court because their virtue is in peril, if it has not been already lost. To put it another way, in less than 20 percent of the cases is there a first charge not involving imminent moral danger.

While many more boys appeared before the juvenile court than girls, young female offenders received harsher punishments. The two researchers accepted this double standard without criticism. Girls, they explained, only came to the attention of the court after grave concerns about them had surfaced. Thus, a delinquent girl was "in peril which threatens the ruin of her whole life, and the situation requires immediate action," while "the delinquent boy . . . is frequently only a troublesome nuisance who needs discipline but who, as the probation officer so often says, is not really a bad boy and with a little watching he is sure to come out all right."[49]

Breckinridge and Abbott may have acceded to these prejudices because they felt a stronger affinity for female children. Certainly they hoped to galvanize public interest in the welfare of disadvantaged girls. Yet the potential sexual acting out of female juveniles clearly troubled the two women. Their aversion to the sexual exploitation of children requires no explanation. Their belief that delinquent girls represented a more serious social threat than wayward boys reflected a heightened sensitivity, appropriate or not, to the vulnerability of their sex. This was a concern Davis and Kellor also shared.[50]

Like most enthusiasts of the juvenile court system, Breckinridge and

Abbott approved of giving judges extensive discretionary authority in delinquency cases. Both women accepted as a given the state's responsibility for
"care of the weak and defenseless." This expansive view of governmental
authority paved the way for nearly unrestrained judicial power. The court,
they believed, simply acted as an agent discharging the state's duty to protect
child welfare. They were untroubled by the limits the court's authority
imposed on parental rights. Breckinridge explained the legal reasoning for
such intervention in this way:

> In a community which has abandoned slavery as a possible human relation-
> ship, power exercised by one person over another must be exercised in behalf
> of and for the benefit of that other, and the community must always be able
> to judge whether or not it is in any particular instance being so exercised.

This was a principle she had been introduced to years earlier by Ernst Freund.
Breckinridge invoked the police power to justify active intervention by the
state.

Neither Breckinridge nor Abbott favored unthinking interference with
family life. In removing a child from the home, they wrote, "the court under-
takes as difficult a task as has ever been attempted by the community through
any agent." But when a child was being abused or cruelly exploited, they
wanted to see swift and decisive action. "As a major operation is undertaken
by a surgeon, amputation should be resorted to in these cases and the child
promptly and permanently removed from the contaminating influences."[58]

The operation, the social scientists believed, was best performed by
experts versed in social research. Only extensive knowledge of a delinquent's
social background and family life could determine what constituted a threat
to the child. Probation officers needed to be "efficient, well equipped, and
thoroughly grounded in the principles of relief and of sound family life."
Women were most experienced in social welfare work, and they deserved a
greater role in running the juvenile court. "Even when the judge is a genius
at understanding the child, or devotedly kind and genuinely sympathetic,
there is often the need not merely of advice from a woman, but of deciding
power exercised by a woman."[59]

Breckinridge's and Abbott's model of criminal justice reform closely
resembled Katharine Davis's design for Bedford Hills. All three women
wished to use social scientific research as a basis for judicial action. They
sought to expand the role of experts in the criminal justice system. And they
hoped to increase female authority in corrections work. Similar imperatives
informed Frances Kellor's agenda for reform. Though many Progressives
embraced similar goals, these proposals were laden with intellectual and professional significance for the academic women. They suggested that the skills
of women social scientists were indispensable to the business of the state.

Abbott and Breckinridge were less daring in proposing structural remedies
for the causes of delinquency. Although they insisted poverty and inequality
created most social problems, they endorsed few economic reforms in *The
Delinquent Child and the Home*. A stronger child labor law, enforcement of

compulsory school statutes, a better educational system, vocational training, and improvements in the school curriculum would assist endangered children. Still, the women reminded their readers that these measures were ineffective antidotes for disease in the social environment. "The only way of curing delinquency is to prevent it." This required the eradication of "conditions" that "are feeding into the court thousands of delinquent children every year."[60]

Their recognition of the social origins of delinquency did little to dull Abbott's and Breckinridge's enthusiasm for individualized child welfare reforms. Both women served on the board of directors of an important Chicago organization that tried to prevent delinquency. The Juvenile Protective Association was both a social casework agency that followed up reports of abuse and complaints of truancy, and a lobby for protective legislation. The association established several offices in city neighborhoods and launched an extensive program of public education on juvenile delinquency. Edith's sister Grace also worked briefly for the agency in 1908 performing what she called "a sort of police duty in the interests of children."[61]

The "police duty" performed by juvenile protective agencies and the juvenile court had complicated results. Intervention undoubtedly shielded some children from neglect and abuse. But the expansive powers exercised by some child welfare authorities created a "dragnet effect" that weighed heavily on the poor. The children of working class families, immigrants, and indigent city dwellers most often came before the court, sometimes for relatively trivial offenses. Often their misconduct was evaluated by class- and culture-bound behavioral standards. Although Abbott and Breckinridge criticized this bias, they did not really challenge the wide discretionary authority that legitimized unbridled intervention by the courts. In fact, the reformers sought to expand the state's power over child welfare. They believed "scientific" research could isolate those truly in need. Yet their own investigations suggested empirical study produced no simple explanation of delinquency, nor many specific measures for reform.[62]

VI

The Delinquent Child and the Home proved to be only the start of a long inquiry by the women social scientists into the fate of problem children in Chicago. After they completed their research on delinquency, Breckinridge and Abbott hoped to investigate truants handled by the juvenile court. Preliminary study led them to shift their focus from individuals to the wider problem of urban school attendance. They sought to assess the effectiveness of compulsory school laws and child labor legislation. The study was again conducted under the auspices of the School of Civics' Department of Social Investigation. It took several years to complete. But in January of 1917 the project reached fruition in a book published by the University of Chicago Press, *Truancy and Non-Attendance in the Chicago Public Schools.*[63]

Like *The Delinquent Child and the Home*, Breckinridge's and Abbott's report on truancy stressed the environmental causes of absences from public schools. The women poignantly described the tremendous hardships borne by poor families and the understandable neglect of their children's schooling. Some parents literally could not afford to send their children to school; either because they relied on their offsprings' meager wages to feed the family, or because they had no money to buy shoes or decent clothing. Upon visiting the homes of truant children, investigators often discovered youngsters who were caring for ill parents or babysitting for children only slightly smaller than themselves. The authors presented an unending parade of tragic case histories that proved that children's "willful absence" from school was "a relatively unimportant factor in non-attendance."[64]

Instead, they argued, "poverty is . . . the real excuse for non-attendance." Absent children were, overwhelmingly, poor children. A ten-year-old Polish girl who had missed nearly two months of school

> was found at home in a rear basement apartment of two rooms, taking care of her mother, who was lying on a mattress in the kitchen. . . . It was learned that the mother was usually able to support herself and the child by washing; but when she was ill she was compelled to keep the child at home to care for her.

At another dwelling, researchers discovered a truant child "home sick, lying on the floor by the stove. His mother was always working, and there was no one to look after this child or the three smaller children who were at home."[65]

While sympathetic to the plight of impoverished families, Abbott and Breckinridge insisted that the state had a responsibility to protect children and to safeguard their future. Parents might keep their children home for a variety of understandable reasons, "but it is clearly wrong that in such cases the heaviest cost should be paid by the child." Education, in their opinion, represented the child's only real hope for the future. It was imperative, they believed, to mobilize state charitable agencies to intervene on behalf of distressed families. Compulsory school and child labor laws needed to be rigorously enforced to prevent children from being forced to assume adult responsibilities. In caring for children, the state should, they wrote, "be relentless in demanding that the child's future must not be jeopardized."[66]

Their study on truancy indicated that Abbott and Breckinridge were growing increasingly aggressive in their search to find effective "administrative machinery" for reform. That effort was clearly driven by frustration with local authorities and lax enforcement of protective legislation. In a long historical summary of compulsory education laws in the state of Illinois, the women described how slow progress was in persuading the state to educate children. They recounted the bitter struggle to pass an effective child labor law. Victories won in Illinois were credited to "the little group of social reformers" affiliated with Hull House. Chief among them, Breckinridge and Abbott wrote, was "Mrs. Florence Kelley, who for nearly a quarter of a century was to be the embodiment of the public conscience on the subject of child labor and its attendant evils." Her "impetuous fire" lit the crusade for child labor reform, but their own research proved that what was "a brilliant piece of social legislation for that time" was inadequate for contemporary needs.[67]

In *Truancy and Non-Attendance in the Chicago Public Schools,* Abbott and Breckinridge moved closer to endorsing principles integral to the welfare state. They repeatedly held up the example of progressive English laws, an indication that the British approach to social welfare still exerted a powerful hold on Edith Abbott. Public schooling, they insisted, was a *national* concern. In a "few states," the women reported, all children were given free books. "In a few countries," schools provided poor children with free dinners. "It is doubtful," they wrote, "whether free dinners will ever be acceptable in this country unless like free education and free books, they are made free for all." Abbott and Breckinridge considered it a hopeful sign that Americans would reject "assistance for which they are singled out solely on the ground of their poverty." But even if books and dinners were as free to children as instruction, the cost of "maintaining" children who were no longer permitted to work remained. "Obviously, the only solution in accord with the standards of a democracy is such a permanent lifting of the wage levels as will make possible the higher standard of living that is, in practice, demanded by the State."[68]

Their study was a brief for state activism in public education. Because "constitutional limitations" stood in the way of federal reform, it was imperative that "radical changes" be made in state child labor and compulsory education laws. For Breckinridge and Abbott, that meant requiring school attendance without exception for all children under sixteen, and prohibiting anyone under that age from working. The social workers proposed that "a state board or department of education be created which shall have, among other functions, the duty of supervising and standardizing the enforcement of the school attendance laws in all portions of the state."[69]

These measures admittedly fell far short of the modern welfare state Abbott and Breckinridge would later embrace. In 1917, they still sometimes looked to state and local charitable agencies for solutions to the terrible social dislocation suffered by truant children's families. Hence, this naïve description of reform:

> If, then, there could be a good social worker attached to every school, not only cases of neglect but extreme poverty, sickness, incapacity on the part of the mother of the family, and unfavorable home conditions of many other kinds would be discovered at the earliest possible moment, and if there were in the communities agencies for dealing with such cases, their aid could be promptly secured, or, if special forms of need could not be met, the attention of the community could be effectively called to that lack. In this way a great step forward might be taken toward the prevention of destitution in the next generation and a great deal of present suffering might be relieved.[70]

Indeed, Breckinridge and Abbott themselves launched a program of this kind at the School of Civics. A "small employment bureau" was established at the school to assist fourteen-year-old boys just released from state reform schools. Efforts were made to help the children secure appropriate part-time work from "good employers" and further schooling. The program, of course, also provided the research department with subjects for further study. It appealed to the women precisely because it would "add to the results of the investigation and because a genuine service might be rendered to the children." A growing number of poor and handicapped children found help through the school as settlement houses and local charity organizations began sending children there. Chicago female reform groups, including the Women's Club, a local branch of the Association of Collegiate Alumnae, and the Women's City Club provided funds to hire a "special investigator" to assist young girls especially.[71]

Soon Chicago's superintendent of schools, Ella Flagg Young, paved the way for the program to be extended into the city's public schools. In June of 1911, all the children about to drop out from a large academy on the West Side were interviewed by investigators from the School of Civics. This active intervention impressed local school officials, and a "joint-committee" took over responsibility for the project from the School of Civics after a year. By March 1913, the experimental vocational program had proved its worth, and Chicago's Board of Education lent its support.

The Board of Education agreed to provide office space, a secretary, and a telephone. It placed responsibility for the project in the hands of "one of the district superintendents." But private organizations continued to pay the new bureau's staff. Breckinridge and Abbott noted that this "Bureau of Vocational Supervision" had a "peculiar semi-public semi-private character." These arrangements were very much in keeping with the style of other Progressive-era reform campaigns, including Davis's research laboratory at Bedford Hills and Kellor's proposed Division of Immigrant Education. The Chicago agreement lasted until March 1916 when the city finally began to provide salaries for the bureau's staff. Anne S. Davis, Breckinridge's and Abbott's student at the School of Civics and the project's chief investigator, became head of "the Bureau of Vocational Supervision in the Chicago Public Schools."[72]

Their efforts to advance state welfare reform and local social services reflected Breckinridge's and Abbott's enduring commitment to social activism and their new identity as social workers. By 1916 they had gained much recognition for their achievements at the School of Civics. As social work educators, they assumed responsibility for the training of caseworkers. They built alliances with public and private welfare agencies while finding placements for their graduates. Breckinridge's and Abbott's struggle to advance a new profession secured their reputations, not as social scientists, but as social welfare workers.

Yet the women's intellectual abilities, commitment to academic values, and deep interest in reform contributed a rich dimension to their work. Both women sought to advance social knowledge through their research and writing on social problems. Breckinridge's and Abbott's direct contact with indigent families and public welfare agencies had only heightened their concerns about local relief. They would never have been satisfied with ameliorative efforts that addressed only individual needs. Edith's and Sophonisba's extensive involvement with Progressive causes reinforced their allegiance to broad-based social welfare reform.

VII

Abbott's and Breckinridge's duties at the School of Civics proved remarkably compatible with the demands of Chicago's vigorous reform community. Their intellectual skills and endless social investigations made the two women valued members of a large band of dedicated activists in the city. These men and women knew each other well, exchanged ideas and favors, were recruited as supporters for each other's causes, and perhaps most of all, were nurtured by each other's company. During Abbott's and Breckinridge's tenure at Hull House, Florence Kelley would pass through; Alice Hamilton, a trailblazer in industrial medicine, often shared their table. Hull House was the workshop where many ideas were forged; Jane Addams was the common bond of those gathered round her. The settlement provided Edith Abbott and (at times) Sophonisba Breckinridge with a home. It always bolstered their spirits and their sense that they belonged to a community of like-minded souls. Unmarried, far away from their own families, and immersed in their exciting work, Abbott and Breckinridge found great comfort in the familiar house on Chicago's West Side.

Both women, in turn, left their impress on the settlement. Hull House was created out of the special qualities of its many diverse residents. Addams credited Abbott and Breckinridge with helping the community achieve its "best results" in social investigations. With others who shared their penchant for research, the Chicago women brought the special perspective of a social scientist to bear on practical problems that made up the settlement's daily work.

The "academic" approach was especially apparent in a memo Sophonisba Breckinridge wrote to Jane Addams in March of 1911 "suggesting a plan to be proposed by the Relief Committee for the care of tramps who ask for food at Hull House." Breckinridge complained that "the most unsatisfactory part of the work of the Relief Committee last winter was the failure to get any sort of data" about the tramps who came to the settlement for food. To really assist these hoboes, and to meet the public's high expectations for Hull House, required more than alms-giving. Breckinridge instructed:

> It is, of course, a very easy thing to give a man who asks for a meal some food and send him on, but it is very bad for the man. If we are going to feed him, we ought, of course, find out why he is tramping, and after investigating put him in a way of getting work. This requires, however, a good deal of special knowledge and organized effort.[73]

Breckinridge was close to Jane Addams, who prized the Chicago professor's advice. Breckinridge readily served as Addams' secretary in 1912, answering correspondence and dealing with the many issues Addams trusted her to resolve. The mistress of Hull House's familiar greeting to Breckinridge was an excited "Dear Lady!" She especially relied upon Breckinridge in matters regarding race and the South. "Dear Lady!" Addams wrote on October 1, 1912, "I don't know why I developed the habit of sending you all these southern things—possibly because you are so good-natured about them and I don't know what else to do with them but send them along!" On another occasion Addams pleaded, "The enclosed letter is from a Kentucky lady—rather an incoherent one, I am afraid. Perhaps you can decipher it better than I can!" Occasionally the exclamations were more personal. "Dear Lady," Addams wrote, "I am 52 years old today!"[74]

Addams had a profound influence on Breckinridge. It seems likely that Addams helped bring the Kentuckian (a previously loyal Democrat) into the Progressive party in 1912. The settlement chief persuaded Sophonisba to run for alderman on the Progressive ticket along with several other city women in 1913. (Needless to say, the slate went down to defeat.) Although she was not a pacifist, Breckinridge joined Addams and her associates in forming the Woman's Peace Party in 1915. The party vocally opposed American intervention in World War I. Breckinridge served as treasurer of the Women's Peace group and took her place among a delegation of Hull House women (including Addams, Grace Abbott, and Alice Hamilton) who sailed to The Hague in the spring of 1915 for an International Congress of Women. When that gathering led to the formation of the Women's International League for Peace and Freedom, Breckinridge enthusiastically joined the new association.[75]

Abbott and Breckinridge also belonged to a tight group of University of Chicago professors who had high visibility in municipal reform circles. These men and women used their credentials and their expertise to challenge the city's political machine and to advance various worthy causes. They formed a coalition of "bloody but unbowed" urban reformers. Among the women's compatriots was their former professor Ernst Freund, who used his legal skills to advance legislative reform. When Alderman Charles Merriam agreed to direct the Chicago City Council's study of crime, he pressed Edith Abbott into service as principal researcher. Abbott predictably concluded that many of those arrested in the city made up the ranks of Chicago's poor. "It is not that the poor are more criminal than the rich, but that their offenses bring them so easily within the reach of the law," she wrote.[76]

Breckinridge played a similar role in a dramatic confrontation in 1910 when 25,000 Chicago garment workers went out on strike. A group of city reformers formed a citizens' committee to investigate the workers' complaints. Chicago professors George Herbert Mead, Charles Henderson, and Breckinridge were asked to carry out the inquiry. When their subcommittee submitted its report in November of 1911, the professors supported the striking laborers. Dismal shop conditions, speed-ups, and the employers' callous lack of interest legitimated the walkout, they concluded. The best solution to these problems, the committee proposed, might be "some form of organization among the workers in the shop." The day after the citizens' committee endorsed this report, one major manufacturer came to terms with his workers. When other industrialists failed to follow suit, Breckinridge and Mead joined another member of the subcommittee in blasting the businessmen's behavior. "The community demands that industrial struggles should be ended by arbitration, and that either party that refuses to submit its case to arbitration must meet the just condemnation of the community."[77]

With results that (initially) seemed more promising, Abbott and Breckinridge also participated in reform movements that moved beyond the boss-ridden city of Chicago and swept across the nation. Both women saw the Progressive party as a tremendous opportunity for social reformers. At the Chicago "Bull Moose Convention," Sophonisba joined Kellor, Addams, and other women reformers in persuading Roosevelt to enthusiastically embrace women's suffrage. Breckinridge and Abbott contributed to the crucial 1912 meeting of the National Conference of Charities and Corrections that shaped the Progressive party platform. Edith Abbott was thrilled to hear Jane Addams' speech at the convention endorsing Roosevelt. She sat in the gallery cheering wildly with her sister, heartily lending her voice to the chorus of conventioneers who sang out "Onward Christian Soldiers." Addams invited Edith, her sister Grace, and Sophonisba to a back-room meeting with convention delegates to discuss strategy.[78]

When the convention came to a close, Abbott and Breckinridge campaigned energetically for the Progressive party ticket. Breckinridge put her name to a revealing broadside: "A Comparison of the Platforms of the Progressive Party and of the Social Scientists—as to Social and Industrial Justice." The handout showed the close similarities between the Progressive program and the recommendations of Owen Lovejoy's committee at the National Conference of Charities and Corrections.

The Progressive platform, the broadside read, was based on the ideas of "recognized leaders in their respective fields of social service, of great social, economic and industrial problems." Presumably unsullied by the corrupt motives that pervaded party politics, these social experts were above the fray. "The earnestness and sincerity is not open to question. They constitute a group of specialists in human welfare and speak with the highest authority when they undertake to recommend remedies for the evils and injustices of the present day." With Jane Addams, Margaret Dreier, Mary McDowell, and Graham Taylor, Breckinridge publicly pledged herself to "work unceasingly in state and nation" for workman's compensation laws, minimum safety and health standards, organized labor, social insurance, and a host of other Progressive causes. After the party's defeat in 1912, Edith Abbott joined a subcommittee of Kellor's Progressive Service, where she contributed her expertise on women's employment.[79]

The women's suffrage movement attracted both women; each made her own distinctive contribution to the cause. Breckinridge reluctantly agreed to serve as vice-president of the National Woman's Suffrage Association in 1911, a troubled year for the organization in which it suffered from tremendous infighting. Breckinridge always emphasized the importance of the ballot as a means of achieving social justice. In 1914, she published an article in the *Annals of the American Academy of Political and Social Science* arguing that an important connection existed "between lack of political equality and this double under-payment of women workers." Employed women, she noted, suffered from "at the one end of the scale . . . exploitation based on youth, lack of training, and helplessness; at the other, exclusion." Women required the vote to legislate decent wages and working conditions. Some suffragists' single-minded dedication to the vote led them to ignore the ends the ballot could achieve. Breckinridge condemned that attitude.

> Those who see clearly the end sought and who therefore desire urgently to possess the most efficient instrument are often prevented by their very eagerness from seeing the more remote but more far-reaching and really important aspects of the claims of women to be admitted to full political equality, because of the important bearing of their political on their economic status.[80]

Edith Abbott devoted her energy to proving that enfranchised women would be "a force for good government." In 1915, she prepared a careful statistical analysis of municipal election results for the *National Municipal Review* to demonstrate the power of women's suffrage. In a recent Chicago Republican primary, Abbott reported, women favored the progressive fusion candidate (Municipal Court Chief Justice Harry Olson) over the victorious William Hale Thompson by a "decisive plurality." She concluded: "if the men had stayed away from the polls on the day of the primary and left to the women the business of choosing a candidate, the fate of Chicago would have been different." Olson's defeat led to a mayoral election between two "machine candidates," and, Abbott noted, "men and women alike had to do the best they could with the hopeless situation created by the men voters." Women endorsed the "least undesirable" candidate, again to no avail. By July of 1916, Abbott declared, Chicago was once again "in the hands of the spoilsmen." Reformers enlisted women voters to prevent the ascendance of what Abbott described as "one of the most vicious political machines that ever controlled the administration of a great city." But "the horse has been stolen and . . . it is now too late to lock the stable door." She called upon women to engage in "trench warfare" against the spoils system by electing decent aldermen to the city council.[81]

Although not one for public displays, Abbott marched in a huge Chicago suffrage parade during the Republican National Convention in 1916. Participants hoped to make a powerful statement that would lead the party to support the suffrage amendment. Grace Abbott organized a large contingent of foreign-born women, newly made citizens, to join the parade of ten thousand. Edith assisted her sister by helping a group of Lithuanian women get in line. But as the procession began, pandemonium ensued, and Abbott found herself walking alone holding high a banner that read "Lithuanian Women Want the Vote."[82]

Throughout their involvement with suffrage and Progressive campaigns, Abbott and Breckinridge kept the focus on social welfare reform. Each woman continued to use her unique intellectual abilities to advance their common cause. The legal treatment of the poor inspired a Breckinridge lecture to the National Conference of Charities and Corrections in 1914 about the evils of the 1907 federal immigration law. The measure provided for the deportation of immigrant paupers; Breckinridge insisted that the law was being abused. Immigrants were being deported for "insufficient cause." Foreign-born workers who labored in the United States for several years, fell victim to industrial accidents, and sought relief were threatened with expatriation. "My point," Breckinridge said, "is that, however short the period of their stay before they fall into distress, however alien the tongue and distant the former home, the same principle should govern every case in which aid is asked or distress is to be relieved as rule in the treatment of the American family whom we are serving." Out of similar concern for industrial workers, Edith Abbott kept a close watch on English reform legislation and reported with great optimism the "progress of the minimum wage in England." In a 1915 issue of the *Journal of Political Economy*, she pointed out that most employers had adapted easily to the minimum wage ruling set by the English Board of Trades in 1909. This fact gave encouragement to those who wanted to see similar measures passed in the United States.[83]

Abbott invoked English welfare measures as a model for the United States even more insistently after World War I. Concerned that anti-German sentiment might shatter support for national welfare measures, Abbott sought to demonstrate that "social insurance" was neither Germanic nor antidemocratic. She characterized mid-nineteenth-century British protective labor laws as "superior to our twentieth century standards in the U.S." For its admirable "measure of state control" over public welfare and democratic concern for its citizens, America ought to look to England "for lessons in social reform." England's early regulation of children's work, and a recent U.S. Supreme Court decision striking down a federal child labor law, suggested "our constitution is . . . less subject to democratic control than the English constitution." British protective legislation for women workers, Abbott wrote, far surpassed American standards. The Illinois ten-hour law Breckinridge once considered progress was now described as "reactionary" by her colleague. Minimum wage legislation, old-age pensions, national health insurance, and national unemployment insurance demonstrated the superiority of England's system. Abbott especially praised Britain's social insurance plans for including "aged women" and for freeing pensioners from making contributions to support the system.[84]

VIII

Abbott's and Breckinridge's compassion for dependent women may have been deepened by their own struggle to survive as professionals. Between 1908 and 1915, their Department of Social Investigation at the School of Civics ran largely on the Russell Sage Foundation's grant. When these funds dried up, the financial instability that had long plagued the School of Civics became acute. In spite of the school's steady growth, expenses had always outstripped fees. Upon Graham Taylor fell the unenviable job of raising funds critical to the school's very survival. Julia Lathrop was appointed head of the United States Children's Bureau in 1912. She used her authority to help the School of Civics secure federal grant money. Other benefactors also lent a hand. Trustee Charles Crane gave his large residence in Chicago to the school when downtown rents became prohibitive in 1916. But the growing deficit still reached crisis proportions. Sometimes Abbott, Breckinridge, and Taylor had to go without their salaries.[85]

One solution Taylor had actively pursued in 1907 was affiliation with a university. Taylor had approached both the University of Chicago and the University of Illinois. Chicago was as uninterested in 1907 as it had been in 1905. But officials at the University of Illinois felt more favorably inclined, and steps were taken to secure funding for the venture from the state legislature. The bill that would have provided support for the school, however, was vetoed in 1909. In the spring of 1914, the idea of forming ties with a university was brought up again by some of the School of Civics' trustees. A few board members, including Jane Addams, Julia Lathrop, and Taylor, favored continuing the venture as an independent school. They saw no real advantage in a university affiliation.

Harvard law professor Roscoe Pound, a close friend of Edith Abbott and her teacher during the University of Nebraska years, strongly disagreed. He argued that only a university setting could win social work respect as a profession. Indeed, Pound suggested that the creation of a "great school of civics and philanthropy" at Chicago would prove as "epoch-making as . . . the foundation of the Harvard Law School in 1817."[86]

Not surprisingly, Abbott and Breckinridge shared Pound's view. When Felix Frankfurter called for social work schools to join universities at a 1915 meeting of the National Conference of Charities and Corrections, Abbott described his speech as an "eloquent presentation of professional ideals." She saw an analogy to social work in Abraham Flexner's influential report on medical education. Flexner stressed that medical training required both clinical practice and rigorous classroom teaching. Abbott and Breckinridge believed social work education required a similar division of labor.

In 1915, Breckinridge formally requested the School of Civic's trustees to reconsider the case of university affiliation, which she now considered the only lasting solution to the school's troubles. There was influential support for her position on the board, and a subcommittee continued to weigh the affiliation issue along with other strategies for raising money in 1916. The school again made overtures to the presidents of Northwestern University, the University of Illinois, and the University of Chicago. Neither Northwestern nor Illinois expressed much interest. But at a lunch with her former professor Harry Pratt Judson, Breckinridge found that Judson, now president of Chicago, had warmed somewhat to the idea, even though he found reasons why the plan could not then be accomplished.[87]

With no immediate prospects for university affiliation, it became critical to make financial provisions for the survival of the school. Julius Rosenwald and Charles Crane bailed the institution out in 1916 by agreeing to raise significantly their customary contributions and to pay off any deficit the school accrued for the next three years. In a revealing letter of gratitude, Marion Talbot thanked Julius Rosenwald for rescuing her beloved assistant.

> Miss B. has told me of your generous part in assuring the continuance of the School of C. I feel very grateful both because I believe the work of the School to be invaluable and because Miss B. finds in it an opportunity to work for human needs which the Univ. of C. has never afforded her. When I asked for her promotion some years ago, after long and devoted service, I was told that it would not be granted, but she could be allowed part of her time continuing the same rank and salary in the Univ. Two years ago I made the same request and was told she could not be promoted because she did not give all her time to the Univ.! This situation has reconciled me to her finding an outlet for her special ability in the School altho I lament the fact that the University itself does not take up more actively the social needs of the community and use her skills in connection with them. Her happiness has been clouded by the uncertain financial condition of the School. But I have never heard her [complain] that she was working without financial remuneration.

Rosenwald's reply could hardly have allayed Talbot's or Breckinridge's worries. He expressed his pleasure that he could help Breckinridge and the school, but he also stated his hope that the graduate social work program could be "continued indefinitely, although I feel it should be almost, if not entirely, self-supporting."[88]

For Sophonisba Breckinridge and Edith Abbott, no greater success for the school was imaginable than in permanent affiliation with the University of Chicago. Such an arrangement would have likely meant permanent status for them at the university. But there was much more than calculated ambition in their designs. The two women were captives of a set of values they had long ago acquired at the university. Their professional lives had been defined by their efforts to use social knowledge to illuminate social problems. They used their own training as social scientists as a model for the School of Civics.

Breckinridge, in fact, had never really left the University of Chicago. She continued to hold an appointment as an assistant professor in household administration and as assistant dean of women. In 1913, Edith Abbott was hired as a part-time lecturer in sociology, where she taught for another seven years. The two women had become "social workers," in part by necessity, but they never stopped thinking of themselves as professionals or as academics. To return to the University of Chicago and teach where it had all begun would realize long-cherished dreams.[89]

Graham Taylor was increasingly perceived by the women as an obstacle to these plans. Abbott and Breckinridge differed with the school's president on matters such as the relative importance of field work. To Taylor, practice formed the heart of social service: Abbott and Breckinridge believed students had to be rigorously supervised, regularly taught, and systematically exposed to the other social sciences. Breckinridge once complained that Taylor's "educational disqualifications placed and kept" her and Edith Abbott in a "miserable situation."[90]

Several of the school's benefactors saw it differently. Taylor had poured his heart and soul into the institution for over ten years. He considered the school his life work, "the most important thing I have ever undertaken." Taylor's dedication was evident in his tenacious struggle to sustain the venture against formidable odds. However tiring his persistent requests for money, the school president had earned the loyalty of the trustees. Exhausted by the relentless pressure to raise funds, and grief-stricken upon the death of his wife, Taylor tried to resign in 1918. The board insisted that he stay on. Although the minister complied, he began to complain bitterly and regularly about the lonely burdens that he bore.[91]

That complaining incensed Sophonisba Breckinridge, who scolded Taylor for portraying himself as a solitary martyr to the cause. "Of course I know you don't mean it when you tell the Trustees and the students that you 'bear the burden alone,'" she wrote Taylor in 1919. "I know that you don't forget the sums of money that the Research Department has earned, to say nothing of the educational work that has been the basis for the very large tuition receipts." "Some other people" on the staff were also at the end of their rope, Breckinridge reminded Taylor, in obvious reference to herself and Abbott. "They haven't said anything about carrying the burden alone, but they are a little tired of some of the jobs that have been theirs to do." Nonetheless, Taylor was in charge. Abbott and Breckinridge suffered along until the spring of 1920.[92]

When Taylor decided to take a vacation in the spring of that year, the board of the School of Civics appointed Breckinridge acting president. While Taylor was away, Breckinridge again began discussions with University of Chicago president Harry Pratt Judson about the future of the school. She broached the idea of the merger, and Rosenwald, who was also a trustee of the university, backed the plan. Judson now seemed enthusiastic as well. A plan was developed for Chicago to take the institution over, making it a graduate professional school within the university. But affiliation hinged on a guarantee that the School of Civics' benefactors would provide $25,000 a year to the new division during its first five years.[93]

After Taylor learned of this scheme upon returning from his vacation in the summer of 1920, he resisted endorsing it. There was nothing wrong with the School of Civics that a secure financial base could not cure. What would become of "the name and identity of the School" were it to be merged with the University of Chicago? Who and what would hold the institution together? Breckinridge's proposal stressed the advantages of professional graduate training within a university. But what of the pragmatic service the school had long rendered to the city of Chicago? Students of varying educational backgrounds had been permitted to attend the School of Civics. The new institution would cater to the interests and needs of the college graduates enrolled in the Department of Social Investigation. At the heart of Taylor's concerns was a vision of social work that clashed with the academic values of Breckinridge and Abbott.

Whatever the merits of these opposing views, several trustees saw in university affiliation a potential answer to the financial crisis at hand. When the board considered Breckinridge's proposal in July of 1920, most members now leaned toward the merger. The trustees agreed to pursue affiliation even though Jane Addams and Julia Lathrop expressed serious reservations.[94]

Abbott tried to win Lathrop's support by reminding her of the exhausting burdens, and indignities, she and Breckinridge had borne. "We tried very hard to get some money from the Russell Sage Foundation, and twice this spring Mr. Glenn took what seemed to us the very great liberty of sending word to us that what the School needed was 'to reorganize and get a live man at the head of it.'" Glenn "even went so far as to name the 'live man,'" an affront that led Abbott to wonder whether the candidate "would be likely to give up a permanent position with a large and assured departmental budget . . . to come to an institution which paid practically all its faculty the sum of $7,700, and that irregularly."[95]

The necessary money was quickly raised. On August 10, 1920, the University of Chicago's board of trustees agreed to establish a "Graduate School of Social Service Administration." The new school would enjoy the "administrative unity characteristic of professional schools." Breckinridge made certain that the provision of field work, placement services, and fellowship support also received the endorsement of the trustees.

On that very day, Lathrop wrote to Edith Abbott: "about one thing I am certain: the School is yours and S.P.B.'s in a peculiar sense and your judgment as to the best practicable turn is backed by such generous devotion that I accept it and only feel grateful to you for what you have done and will do to uphold the standards of applied social science." Lathrop expressed regrets that Graham Taylor was left behind. But, she continued, "I am sure that the only path is ahead on the university plan. Of course I am sorry, but there is much to be said for the success you have achieved in gaining recognition as a graduate school. That is a genuine triumph which will descend in the history of education." Lathrop was correct. The Chicago School became the first graduate school of social work in the country to be affiliated with a major research university. Abbott and Breckinridge went back to their alma mater as associate professors of social economy.[96]

There they set about building an institution that exemplified truths they had learned twenty years earlier at the same university. The School of Social

Service Administration would offer training to advance effective social policy and deepen social knowledge. Scientific research would be disseminated in a scholarly journal. Students would be asked to balance concern for social problems with a commitment to rigorous research. These goals were largely unprecedented in social work education.

Yet they seemed curiously out of step with new developments in academic social science. As empiricism increasingly defined the social sciences, applied research appeared distinctly old-fashioned. During Abbott's and Breckinridge's years at the School of Civics, a new "Chicago School" had emerged that challenged ideas Edith and Sophonisba considered axiomatic. The once-blurry line that divided social inquiry and social action was now sharply drawn. Clearer definitions of "objectivity" set stricter professional standards. Though the university's social scientists continued to focus on the urban environment, they had developed more sophisticated quantitative and survey techniques. Theory building assumed much greater importance in sociology and economics. In short, social inquiry and social scientific methodology had come of age. The values that inspired Abbott and Breckinridge's remarkable contributions to reform now seemed ill-suited to academe.

So much had changed at the university. Many of the men who knew Sophonisba and Edith as brilliant graduate students were gone. Some Chicago social scientists even warned their students away from the teachings of Miss Breckinridge and Miss Abbott. On one occasion Edith Abbott philosophically reflected on such slights.

> Some of our social science friends are afraid that we cannot be scientific because we really care about what we are doing and we are even charged with being sentimental. . . . This does not frighten me either, for I know that a great physician also cares about the human beings he is taking care of and, like him, we can be kind without being sentimental.

Perhaps the disdain of a few unsympathetic colleagues was not so hard for Breckinridge and Abbott to bear in a school that would forever be remembered as theirs.[97]

In truth, the University of Chicago's School of Social Service Administration was an extraordinary monument to its founders' beliefs. For Breckinridge and Abbott had succeeded in creating an institution committed to social knowledge and social advancement. They believed a modern welfare state would require trained experts skilled in public policy. They hoped their graduate program would meet that need. When the University of Chicago endorsed the School of Social Service Administration, the women's intellectual and progressive ideals seemed finally within reach.

Epilogue

By 1920, the trajectory of Katharine Davis's, Frances Kellor's, Sophonisba Breckinridge's, and Edith Abbott's careers had been well established. Each had arrived at a perspective on social problems and an approach to social change that would shape the remainder of her career. They were now mature women with years of professional experience. The youngest, Edith Abbott, celebrated her forty-fourth birthday in 1920. At sixty Katharine Bement Davis was the oldest; she was entering the final phase of her career. In 1920, Davis had fifteen years to live.

Yet, if there were elements of continuity in their work, the historical setting in which the women activists labored changed dramatically after 1920. Enthusiasm for social reform waned with American intervention in World War I. The Progressive movement never reclaimed national attention after the peace had been won. Economic prosperity soon left social activists preaching to an increasingly inattentive audience. The four women reformers faced these realities in various ways, but none were unaffected by the country's shifting social climate.

II

New sexual mores played an important role in Katharine Davis's postwar career. During the 1920s, she became a pioneer in the field of sex research. Davis's interest in this subject evolved naturally from her studies of prostitution and her persistent preoccupation with the issue of gender. But the war changed the emphasis of her social hygiene work. Davis's long experience in corrections won her a wartime appointment directing a subcommittee on women and girls within the Commission on Training Camp Activities'

(C.T.C.A.) Social Hygiene Division. Appointed by Secretary of War Newton Baker, the C.T.C.A. sought to provide "clean and wholesome influences" for soldiers preparing to fight democracy's war. Setting aside her duties as secretary of the Bureau of Social Hygiene, Davis took an active role in the Social Hygiene Division's campaign to eradicate and prevent venereal disease. The division promoted sex education, emphasizing that high moral standards were a "patriotic duty." Davis helped spread the word to women. She warned in the screenplay of one propaganda film that liaisons with handsome men in uniform could mark the "End of the Road."[1]

Davis also endorsed extremely repressive measures advanced by the C.T.C.A. to control prostitution. With the federal government's support, thousands of prostitutes were rounded up during the war, forcibly detained, and involuntarily subjected to treatment for venereal disease in various institutions. At some facilities, social hygienists studied the interned women in search of the causes of their sexual deviance. It is hardly surprising that Davis supported these programs. They incorporated aspects of the "scientific" approach to prostitution that she had long approved, though never before on such a grand or oppressive scale. Her stance put Davis at odds with some feminists who excoriated the government plan as an indefensible violation of civil liberties. Davis was not at the center of this debate: her position with the C.T.C.A. largely involved "educational work," much of it geared to "normal" women.[2]

When the war came to an end, Davis returned to the Bureau of Social Hygiene as director. With a broad vision of its future, she steered the bureau toward research on human sexuality and narcotics addiction. Old realities, both topics nonetheless seemed thoroughly modern as subjects of scientific research. Davis kept tabs on investigators exploring "the use of narcotics in . . . six communities" under a bureau grant. She made certain that research on women commanded the bureau's support. Under her direction, the organization underwrote the study *Women Police* (1925), Edith Spaulding's *Experimental Study of Psychopathic Delinquent Women* (1923), and a number of similar inquiries. In the fall of 1920, Davis herself began an ambitious study of female sexuality that consumed her attention for another eight years.[3]

The book that resulted from Davis's research, *Factors in the Sex Life of Twenty-two Hundred Women* (1929), was an unusually frank and explicit discussion of female sexual habits. Assisted by psychologist Helen Thompson Wooley and her old friend Jessie Taft, Davis sent out thousands of questionnaires to college graduates and club women. The response rate was gratifyingly high, but only the first 2,200 replies were analyzed. Sex, Davis noted, was "scientifically an unexplored country." A study of "normal" women, she hoped, would suggest remedies for sexual deviance.[4]

Davis's study proved, however, that "normal" was a highly relative term. Both married and unmarried women admitted to a range of sexual behavior and feeling that included premarital intercourse, masturbation, and homosexuality, as well as multiple heterosexual experiences. Homosexuality seemed especially common, Davis observed, among women in the social-service group. Almost all single college graduates confessed to "sex feeling, sex drives, or some form of sex expression." These were, Davis insisted, "sane and sensible" women, "a healthy, well-educated, and happy group." Indeed, the happiest women appeared to be those most sexually active.[5]

Wrapping herself in the social scientist's cloak of objectivity, Davis avoided extensive interpretation of her results. "There has been no attempt to support or disprove any theories . . . nor have we formulated any of our own which we think is desirable or safe to advance." But Davis took pains to address the data on homosexuality, clearly among the most controversial findings in her study. "My own observation in both educational and penological institutions," she explained, "leads me to believe that the phenomena described in this study are much more widespread than is generally suspected, or than most administrators are willing to admit."[6]

These were shocking assertions for a culture that had only recently grown more permissive in its attitudes toward sex. Some attacked the study "because it contained specific information on auto-erotic practices, coupled with the statement that 'the harmful physical and mental effects have been greatly exaggerated.'" Nowhere did the research seem to cause more discomfort than at the Bureau of Social Hygiene. Harper and Brothers "pushed this book slowly and conservatively in order to avoid undesirable publicity," although it predictably sold very well. But the Bureau of Social Hygiene took little pleasure in its success. When one researcher asked for a copy of Davis's questionnaire, his request was declined. "I see no reason whatever," one staff member noted privately, "for the Bureau's lending a certain weight of authority to such half truths by placing them in the hands of a self-appointed adviser in sex matters."[7]

As her controversial study neared publication, Davis herself was increasingly perceived as an obstacle by bureau members impatient with her "female" concerns. Repeated bouts with illness made the aging director vulnerable to such criticism. By the spring of 1927, a consensus had developed among officers of the bureau that Davis would have to go. As her tenth anniversary with the organization approached, John D. Rockefeller, Jr., drafted a letter dismissing her.

It is difficult to believe that with the end of the present year you will have been ten years with the Bureau of Social Hygiene. It seems hardly yesterday that Mr. Mitchel, the Mayer-elect [sic], sent for me to ask what I knew about you and what I thought about you for the position of Commissioner of Corrections. As you know, for some time I have felt that there ought to be a reorganization of the Bureau of Social Hygiene. Just what form of organization would be best . . . will require considerable thought; but that the situation is entirely different than when the Bureau was organized and that its field of usefulness is materially changed . . . would seem to be true. The purpose of this letter is to apprise you of what is in my mind and to point out the fact that while the Bureau may ask you to continue in some relation to it year by year after January 1st, 1928, the probabilities are that may not be possible.

Rockefeller went on to effusively praise his longtime associate. "When I reflect upon what you have done for the Bureau during the ten years of your connection with it and what you have done for the liberation of young women throughout the country from the bondage of vice, my heart swells with pride in you and deep gratitude for you." These warm remarks rankled bureau trustee and Rockefeller adviser Raymond B. Fosdick. His boss's tribute, Fosdick observed, was "just a bit fulsome." "If I were you," he cautioned, "I would omit the last clause of the last paragraph on page one altogether. The probabilities of your wanting to keep Miss Davis in some relationship to the Bureau seem to me to be exceedingly remote and this sentence holds out a hope that would not be justified." Davis, Fosdick insisted, was "fast losing her grip." "There will be little likelihood of our being able to use her even in an advisory position." Rockefeller took Fosdick's recommendation. On April 2, 1927, he wrote a termination letter to Davis, omitting the "fulsome" praise and any reference to future consulting work.[8]

This was painful news for Katharine Davis. "Although it is not unexpected," she replied to Rockefeller, "it *is* hard to see it stated in black and white on paper that my working days are so nearly done." At sixty-eight, Davis had hoped to continue at the bureau for two years more, until her "self appointed age of retirement." "But naturally," she reassured Rockefeller, "I shall submit with I hope good grace to your decision and will not need to be carried off the stage kicking + screaming!" Acknowledging his decisive role in her career, Davis thanked Rockefeller for providing her with the opportunity for service. "It has meant more than I can express. It is hard to say what is in my heart—Perhaps I can before the end of the year."[9]

Though gracious about her impending departure, Davis asked to participate in discussions about the Bureau of Social Hygiene's future. She had, she told Rockefeller, "some ideas which seem to me worthwhile and there is no one who cares more than I to see the vital parts of our work continue under the best possible direction." But Davis's sense of the "vital parts" of the bureau's work put her at odds with her associates.[10]

All agreed that the organization's original focus on prostitution was now outmoded. Davis wanted to pursue a line of inquiry made possible by a new "frankness" in social attitudes. A reorganized Bureau of Social Hygiene, she believed, ought to be one in which "the scientific study of sex is given first place." Sex, she argued, was "the fundamental on which the life of the race depends. It is the most important and the basic fact of human society. Its abuses have led to the social evils the Bureau was organized to combat." Davis's brief for such a plan rested on familiar logic.

> The study of sex in a scientific way has received scant attention until very recently. Opinion and education in this field cannot be sound unless it is based on accurate scientific study of all its aspects and relations. Social teachings will always be tentative and shaky until they are so based.

For Davis, sex research was the new frontier. She wanted to see the Bureau of Social Hygiene "put sex on the scientific map."[11]

Experts consulted by the bureau took issue with Davis's views. "The proposal to lift sex research from its customary setting and to study sex in vacuo, so to speak . . . seems to me unsound," advised Leonard V. Harrison. Most research on sexuality focused on deviance. Investigation of "normal" behavior would not "readily lend itself to research," Harrison believed, for many reasons; including a general reticence to discuss sexuality. Edwin H. Sutherland, a professor of sociology at the University of Chicago, also questioned the wisdom of the bureau's commitment to sex research. "As I figure it, about half of the annual expenditures on projects are concentrated in this sex field. I can see nothing inherent in this particular field that justifies this." W. I. Thomas joined his colleague in advising against "the study of the family," and "the program of maternal health."[12]

After Davis's departure, the reconstituted bureau, now led by Rockefeller associate Lawrence Dunham, committed itself to studies of "delinquency, crime, and criminal justice administration." These would be highly relevant concerns during the Depression decade to come. With its reorganization, the bureau dropped any references to prostitution, the issue that had prompted the organization's creation. Future programs of research would be unencumbered by the restriction of gender.[13]

The repudiation of her leadership and her interests was anguishing for Davis. "Your life," John D. Rockefeller, Jr., reminded her, "has been one of extraordinary usefulness. Few people have been privileged to contribute so largely to the improvement of social conditions as you have; few have been more truly a friend to society at large than yourself." But his expansive praise did little to ease the ache Davis felt. "I appreciate very much what you say of my work," she replied, "all the more since no one knows so well as I how far I have fallen short of my ideals in my achievements." Birth-control activist Margaret Sanger tried to cheer Davis up by recasting recent events in a more positive light. "I was very much surprised at your information regarding the reorganization of the Bureau, perhaps you feel like I should feel, if my work were well launched, that I should welcome an opportunity of leisure, to do the many things I have always wanted to do." If Davis found herself with "more freedom to give other movements some of your experiences and wisdom," Sanger asked that she "reserve a little time for the B. C. movement."[14]

But there would be little time left for such crusades. Davis tidied up her affairs at the Bureau of Social Hygiene late in 1928. Plagued now by her failing health, she at least had the satisfaction of seeing her sex research come to fruition. Not long before *Factors in the Sex Life* appeared, Davis wrote an essay for *Harper's Magazine* exploring a theme that had great relevance to her own life. "Why They Failed to Marry" examined the various forces that kept so many of the early generation of women college graduates single. The data from Davis's sex survey indicated that most "spinsters" felt they had never met the right man. But a range of other factors, including "father fixations," attraction to other women, and sexual conflict, discouraged marriage, as well. ("I have no more interest in sex than in leprosy," reported one woman.)[15]

It was impossible to tell from her tone that Davis herself belonged to the group that had "failed" to marry, though her intense curiosity about the issue was unmistakable. Indeed, Davis's entire foray into sex research betrayed highly personal concerns. Towards the end of her life, the most intimate human relationships emerged as Davis's central intellectual preoccupation. In a rather abrupt about-face, she endorsed pure research on "normal populations," cut free from any campaigns for "education" or "propaganda." What made a woman's life evolve as it did? "Why? Why? Why?" she asked in the *Harper's* essay.[16]

Davis admitted that she regretted not having children and grandchildren. "I miss them. More than I do a husband," she said. Marriage, though, had a good deal less appeal. Although she liked men, Davis never had any "glamorous affairs" or "love stories" in her life. "I was never the sort with whom men were always falling in love," she explained. Although a farmer proposed to her in her girlhood, she spurned his offer, even though her grandmother "lived on a farm until she was eighty-two years old and always seemed happy." Whenever Davis thought about what she might have missed, "I console myself with the reflection that at least I have been spared any desire to go to Reno."[17]

It seems very likely that much more was at work in Davis's "failure" to marry than her breezy comments suggested. For she had plenty of company in her final years. *None* of the Davis girls had married, and when Katharine gave up part-time consulting work in 1930, all three sisters retired to California. "We are three old maids and we have lived together for many years," Davis commented. "Now I feel as if I were going to heaven." After five quiet years in Pacific Grove, Davis died at home of arteriosclerosis in December of 1935. She was seventy-five.

Newspapers had some trouble summing up Katharine Davis's extraordinary career. "A Distinguished American Sociologist," the *New York Herald Tribune* wrote; "Social Worker 56 Years," the *New York Times* headlined. Both papers properly emphasized her unusual achievements in corrections work. They paid tribute to the "Commissioner" who was "the first woman to run the city's jails." Dr. Davis, the journalists agreed, had had a most amazing career.[18]

III

Like Katharine Davis, Frances Kellor made the most of the new culture of the 1920s. Her close association with businessmen during the Americanization campaigns gave her the financial security and political support that made possible the final phase of her career. During the early 'twenties, Kellor used her post at the Inter-Racial Council to press for a national immigration policy that went beyond restrictive measures. The war had greatly heightened Kellor's sense of urgency about American social and economic policy. The United States, she often reminded her readers, was now a "world power" with

international responsibilities. Domestic programs that encouraged fair treatment of the foreign-born and their rapid assimilation were now more imperative than ever.[19]

Along with other moderate Republicans, Kellor came out of the war
firmly committed to internationalism. She supported the League of Nations
idea promoted by her old enemy Woodrow Wilson. And in the early 1920s,
she lobbied very aggressively for American participation in the Court of
International Justice at The Hague. International cooperation and dispute
settlement was, she believed, the best "security against war."[20]

These views put Kellor at odds with prevailing political trends. Harsh legislation restricting immigration was signed into law in 1924. Wilson's grand
vision of an international order collapsed under the weight of unceasing
debate. Isolationism proved far more appealing than internationalism. Once
again, Kellor's idealistic dreams of American state power ran up against the
constraints of the democratic political process. Never again would the
reformer put her hopes so incautiously in the public sphere.

Instead, Kellor turned her attention to conflict resolution in the private
arena. With influential lawyers and businessmen, she helped found the American Arbitration Association (A.A.A.) in 1926. The association sought to
peacefully resolve commercial, and later industrial, disputes outside the formal legal system. By the 1920s many businessmen had become impatient
with the unpredictable, lengthy, and costly process of litigation. Self-regula-
tion seemed preferable to interference from the courts or government agencies. A growing number of modern industrialists began to embrace the alternative of arbitration. After some debate, leading members of the New York
legal profession also endorsed the arbitration movement. The A.A.A. represented the interests of both lawyers and businessmen: it offered a mode of
dispute settlement that was highly legalistic, though formally independent of
the courts.[21]

Arbitration's appeal for businessmen was obvious. It explicitly sought to
protect "a vast amount of property and very substantial rights ... against litigation." The system's attraction for Frances Kellor was more subtle but no
less real. It created a decisive role for disinterested experts, the "arbitrators"
who resolved cases. These officials would be, it was hoped, men and women
of "unquestioned integrity, impartiality, competence and honesty." They
would render fair decisions based on fact, unsullied by legal chicanery, "unassailable on partisan, personal or political grounds." One enthusiast contrasted
the ability of arbitrators with the "ignorance" and "stupidity" of jurors.
Nothing would be left to chance in a process driven by expertise. The entire
scheme was based on principles Kellor had been promoting for nearly thirty
years.[22]

As its first vice-president, Kellor helped chart the American Arbitration
Association's course. The A.A.A. served as a "central planning agency" that
assisted trade associations in devising "arbitration machinery." The American Arbitration Tribunal handled cases in cities across the country under the
association's supervision. Kellor characterized the A.A.A. as an "educational

and research center," committed to promoting "authoritative knowledge in relation to arbitration." The reformer played an especially important part in creating uniform rules and standards for dispute settlement. She wrote the first *Code of Arbitration* (1931), outlining procedures that guided the movement in its early years.[23]

Arbitration, though not without its critics, proved a popular method of conflict resolution throughout the 1920s. The powerful partnership of law, business, and government allowed the system to flourish. This made Kellor's work easy. For once she was in the enviable position of advancing a cause her audience was eager to embrace. Not until the New Deal did the arbitration movement face any real, substantive challenges. With the onset of the Great Depression, confidence in business quickly began to erode. Industrial "self-government" became an object of suspicion rather than confidence. Skeptics questioned the very purpose of arbitration, suggesting that businessmen used the practice to evade public regulation and control.[24]

Kellor worked to bring arbitration into the New Deal alliance. She supported the National Industrial Recovery Act and Roosevelt's federal activism. Fair business codes, she believed, would increase "economic goodwill." An inequitable distribution of wealth, "unfair competition," "destructive" monopolies, and injurious litigation had alienated the people and destroyed economic stability. The "new industrial society" would be built on a foundation of government regulation and business cooperation. The New Deal had created, Kellor argued, a new spirit in industry.

> For competition are being substituted newer ideals concerning cooperation, and for the free operation of economic law a willing assumption of the responsibility by industry to take upon itself a more equitable distribution of wealth . . . and the provision of fairer labor conditions and the prevention of such evils as unemployment. For sole rights are substituted partnership rights. For the privacy of business is substituted full knowledge of its activities.

The reformer was especially gratified to see "the insecurity of unemployment and the dependence on private relief " replaced with "a vision of permanent planning to avoid these evils in the future."[25]

But Kellor's attention was no longer focused on the indigent or the poor. Although she assembled a group of prominent women for relief work during the Depression, her professional interests remained centered on arbitration; her affinities lay with business. The New Deal brought an extraordinary number of women into government service, many of them activists in the old Progressive crusades. But Kellor resisted the lure of political life. At sixty-one she had found professional security at the American Arbitration Association. Why risk what she had worked so hard to achieve? As a veteran of earlier reform battles, Kellor knew how fleeting women's political power could be. Let others enjoy their moment in the sun.[26]

Still, Kellor savored the prospects of federal power. The National Recovery Administration (N.R.A.) would be improved, she insisted, if the President established a "Court of Amity and Arbitration" in New York City. Operating under N.R.A. jurisdiction, this agency would resolve all commercial, industrial, and trade disputes arising under the new statutes and codes. Kellor's plan widened the reach of arbitration while rendering obsolete Senator Robert F. Wagner's proposal for a National Labor Relations Board. Arbitration survived the New Deal, though not in the form Kellor had envisioned. Her monolithic agency never came to pass.[27]

As the American Arbitration Association found an enduring place in modern American society, its vice-president, too, found a lasting place for her talents. From 1926 until her death in 1952, Kellor devoted herself to the association. In the midst of the Depression, she used her contacts with the Rockefeller family to ensure the A.A.A. office space in the new Rockefeller Center. Always "reticent" about her personal affairs, Kellor inspired her staff with her "vision of the future no other eye beheld." One associate lauded his boss's unflinching "integrity." She ruled her organization with a firm hand, demanding a great deal of her colleagues and herself. As a mature woman, she easily won the admiration of powerful men, who were deeply impressed by her "forceful and brilliant" mind.[28]

These rich years brought Kellor intense personal satisfaction. Though tense and often driven in her work, she derived deep pleasure from her enduring relationship with Mary Dreier. The two women created a refuge in Dreier's rambling Brooklyn home. On weekends, they repaired to the Dreier country place in Stonington, Connecticut. As long as her health permitted, Frances took to the outdoors. Dreier's niece loved her for being "such a good sport." By 1951 her health was badly deteriorating, but she would not retire. After a lengthy hospitalization, she died early in January 1952 at seventy-eight. One friend was shocked to find so few of Kellor's compatriots at her funeral. But she had outlived many of them. Indeed, Kellor's death inspired a *New York Times* editorial eulogizing not only the reformer but the age she so exemplified. From across a great historical divide, the *Times* prodded readers to "look back with occasional nostalgia for the reform movements of a generation ago so often led by the pure in heart."[29]

I V

Diminished enthusiasm for reform seemed to have the least effect on Edith Abbott and Sophonisba Breckinridge. They remained devoted to the causes that had inspired them in the Progressive era. Their new profession—social work—legitimized such concerns. The School of Social Service Administration provided an ideal setting for their distinctive talents. From their special outpost at the University of Chicago, Abbott and Breckinridge worked to advance social welfare policy, scientific knowledge of social problems, and the fledgling profession they had adopted as their own.

Grace Abbott's appointment as chief of the United States Children's Bureau in 1921 ensured Edith's and Sophonisba's active participation in social welfare reform throughout the 'twenties. Grace's office put her at the center of two brutal reform battles that her sister and Breckinridge willingly joined. The first involved renewal of the Sheppard-Towner Act, an important bill that provided federal aid to the states for programs to protect maternal and child health. Enacted in 1921, the legislation touched off a major controversy when it came up for review in 1926. Even more controversial was the campaign for a constitutional amendment prohibiting child labor. Edith Abbott and Breckinridge lobbied for both measures, using their social research as a means of persuasion, and providing the Children's Bureau with "expert" advice. "The path between Miss Breckinridge and the Bureau was well traveled in both directions," Grace Abbott's assistant recalled. Edith Abbott and Breckinridge relied on the bureau for help in placing graduates from the School of Social Service Administration.[30]

In calmer moments, the two Chicago professors still found time to support their loyal friends. The intrepid Florence Kelley depended on Edith Abbott's great fund of knowledge, as when she was organizing a National Consumers' League program in 1922. Kelley wrote:

> I have asked Alice Hamilton to speak on poisons, and Felix Frankfurter on the U.S. Supreme Court, - - - - (Greatest of All Poisons), - and I mean to take ten minutes on the proposed federal child labor amendment. I am counting on you for ten minutes and nobly leaving you free to select your own subject. . . . R.S.V.P. as to subject. I am counting on you, of course, to be present since your definite promise to come.

Abbott's assurance that she would indeed attend had left Kelley, she reported, "grinning broadly ever since." Felix Frankfurter directed a "colleague. . . pursuing research into our immigration laws and policy" to Abbott in 1925. "I told him that were I interested in his problems, I should make Chicago my center and count on your help more than any I would be likely to find elsewhere."[31]

These warm associations sustained the social activists during several discouraging political defeats. The Sheppard-Towner Act won reappropriation in 1927 for just two years; after 1929 funding was repealed. The child labor amendment languished, as well. The 'twenties, Grace Abbott once commented, were "uphill all the way." Nonetheless, Edith and Sophonisba spent the decade of prosperity pressing the case of those in poverty. Abbott published widely on immigration, especially during the quota debates of the early 1920s. Her scholarly research, as always, invoked the lessons of history; while Breckinridge made ample use of her legal training in essays on public welfare concerns. Both women continued to stress the advantages of British social insurance, including widows' pensions and a national health plan.[32]

The Depression revived national interest in these issues. Abbott had supported Herbert Hoover in 1928 because he endorsed key items on the Children's Bureau agenda. But she quickly realized her terrible mistake. Contact with Chicago charity organizations, and Edith's statistical studies of local relief, convinced Abbott and Breckinridge that this economic downturn would be a disaster. In October of 1932 Abbott ridiculed Hoover's secretary of the interior in a *New Republic* essay. After a six-week tour of the country, Secretary Wilbur had announced that "no abject poverty" existed in the nation's cities. Abbott knew otherwise. In one Chicago tenement alone, she reported, two hundred people huddled around "charcoal bucket-stoves" in total darkness. "In Chicago, in the twentieth century!" Abbott exclaimed.[33]

Early in November of 1932, a month that ushered in the "fourth bread-line winter" of the Great Depression, Abbott leveled a blistering attack against local relief in *The New Republic*. The essay targeted Hoover's recently enlarged Reconstruction Finance Corporation. Although Congress had given the R.F.C. $300 million in state relief loans to distribute, in ten weeks just a fraction of the money had been spent. Intense resistance to a federal "dole" led members of the R.F.C. to award loans grudgingly, and then only after state governors offered ample proof that local funds had been exhausted. This miserly approach to public welfare offended Abbott. The Hoover administration's tenacious commitment to local relief evolved from no modern theories, she wrote. Rather, it relied on a tradition that reached back to Elizabethan poor laws.

> The principle of local relief belongs to the parochial England of the sixteenth century and not to modern America. It is the doctrine of a day and age when a man's parish was his world—not the accepted doctrine of any modern theory of local government, central government or any other kind of government. Local relief is not like parental love. There is nothing immutable and sacred about it. It belongs to the days when national funds went to the king . . . when no one in London knew or cared about local highways or village destitution. The world has changed since that day.[34]

Breckinridge delivered a similar message elsewhere in 1932. Before the National Conference of Social Work, she described the "heart-breaking" conditions endured by the unemployed and their children. Like Abbott, Breckinridge invoked the lessons of history. "We already knew what a depression meant to children," she reminded her audience. A 1922 report issued by the Children's Bureau offered decisive proof that sudden joblessness could thrust even a comfortably situated American family into devastating poverty. "A new depression was not necessary to teach us what its effects would be," Breckinridge argued. But now the nation had to accept reality. A massive program of federal relief, financed through steep taxes on the income of the wealthy, was imperative. "If we come out of the depression," Breckinridge wrote, "with a truly national program of adequate relief . . . a true national insurance of child care and child welfare . . . we shall have wrung something infinitely precious from the experience."[35]

Their sweeping commitment to *federal* relief at a relatively early stage of the Depression distinguished Abbott and Breckinridge from many witnesses to the nation's social and economic crisis. Resistance to permanent social welfare measures remained strong throughout the Depression; the New Deal itself was but a tentative step toward a welfare state. In the fall of 1932, presidential candidate Franklin Delano Roosevelt carefully avoided open commitment to broad-based federal relief programs. He also side-stepped any talk of decisive new income taxes for the very rich. Abbott's and Breckinridge's insistence on federal responsibility for social welfare was not new—either to them or to the Depression. Their forward-looking ideas about the nature of poverty and their activist vision of government had been embraced long ago.[36]

Both women supported Roosevelt and the New Deal, though Edith Abbott constantly called relief administrator Harry Hopkins on the carpet for not committing himself to permanent social welfare measures. When Hopkins visited one of Abbott's classes and graciously praised his friendly critic with references to the future realization of her visionary goals, Abbott interrupted: "When, Harry? When!" Although Abbott's pacifism had tempered her enthusiasm for Roosevelt by 1940, she put her loyalty to the New Deal first.

> I support President Roosevelt for re-election because of the magnificent gains that have been made on the home front under his leadership—the great reforms like social security, federal aid for relief, the farm security administration, and the great public power program, all of which will be sacrificed if Mr. Wilkie is elected.[37]

In spite of their support for New Deal reforms, neither Abbott nor Breckinridge pursued active government service. Breckinridge happily accepted when F.D.R. asked her to represent the United States at the first Pan-American Conference in 1933. She also took part in several White House conferences on children. Abbott agreed to serve on the Wickersham Commission on Law Observance and Enforcement in 1929. But these activities were never allowed to interfere with the women's primary interests in teaching and research. After all, they had academic work to do and a professional school to run.[38]

Through the School of Social Service Administration, Abbott and Breckinridge left an indelible impression on an emerging profession, a new generation, and the institution they so revered—the University of Chicago. The two women set standards at the school they would hold for the social work profession. Rigorous training for social service, they believed, required immersion in the social sciences and hands-on experience with social problems. Abbott and Breckinridge rejected both the purely "vocational" approach to social work education and complete reliance on the "casework" method. They emphasized the importance of scientific analysis and scholarly research. But they insisted that such inquiry be directed to practical social problems. In short, a social work professional took on responsibility for advancing knowledge and social progress.[39]

This emphasis differed substantially from that of most schools of social work. After World War I, psychiatry exerted a profound influence on social work education, and casework increasingly focused on the treatment of individuals. Abbott not only opposed this approach, she was quite hostile to it.

When the leading school of psychiatric social work was being reviewed by its sponsor, Smith College, in the early 1940s, Abbott expressed her doubts to Katherine Lenroot.

> About the so-called Smith School of Social Work which has never really been a professional School but a series of Summer Institutes, I think the sooner it comes to an end the better. It has been a stumbling block for nearly 25 years that has "got by" on the name of Smith College.

Abbott believed it was "impossible to run a good School in an out-of-the-way place like Northampton," since students could not be placed in "good social agencies." A tour of duty in a state insane asylum was no substitute for training in a well-run public welfare agency. "These college towns are not good places for Schools of Social Work any more than medical schools," Abbott insisted. Bryn Mawr also ran a "very poor" school for this reason, she said, though it was "200 per cent better than Smith." Of the Smith School, Abbott dismissively wrote: "Therefore, since it can never be made into anything good, I would say the sooner it is given up the better . . . it is not for me to 'attack' another School, but I do want you to know that many of us think this School does more harm than good."[40]

At the School of Social Service Administration, the emphasis was on social welfare policy. To broaden their perspective on social problems, students were expected to study law, economics, history, and the other social sciences. "I think we have succeeded in putting our Social Service work very closely in relation to the Departments of Political Economy and Political Science," Abbott wrote to her former professor J. Laurence Laughlin, "instead of letting it drift along as a sort of appendage to the Sociology department. This, I think, is our real contribution to the educational field."

The curriculum reflected its architects' concern that social workers take the broadest possible view of their mission. "Rehabilitating Mr. and Mrs. Jones and their children," Abbott once instructed, "is a very important and necessary occupation, but while we are at work on this piece of social reconstruction let us get rid of the ditches that have been responsible for the downfall of the Jones." Hence, though casework and field assignments had an important place in the training offered at Chicago, students were also expected to conduct serious social research.[41]

In 1927 Abbott and Breckinridge founded a professional journal, the *Social Service Review*, which permitted students and faculty to publish their investigative findings. It fulfilled the same purpose for their graduate students that the *Journal of Political Economy* once served for Edith and Sophonisba. The *Review* instantly established itself as the first really scholarly journal in the field of social work. By the 1930s the women had also launched a series, published by the University of Chicago Press, that enabled graduate students to turn their dissertations into scholarly books. These monographs reflected Depression-era concerns; many focused on public assistance and the legal treatment of the poor.[42]

Indeed, the Depression appeared to offer decisive proof of the value of

Abbott's and Breckinridge's school. Expanding social welfare programs created a new bureaucracy that required well-trained administrators. The two women easily placed many of their graduates in public welfare agencies. Enrollments at the School of Social Service Administration skyrocketed: by 1935 over thirteen hundred students attended.[43]

Both women used their formidable intellectual abilities, their long experience in reform, and their ample wit in classroom teaching. Some students feared them. Driven in their work, Abbott and Breckinridge expected young faculty and students to be equally committed. To one Chicagoan, Breckinridge seemed "a valiant figure, hurrying past our house to her office each morning—whatever Chicago's weather might be doing." Those mornings often included Sundays. Abbott considered the marriage of a gifted student an occasion fit for mourning rather than celebration. But this seriousness of purpose instilled in some young social workers a sense of self-respect. "Edith Abbott gave status to social work; students saw her almost as a master of their profession. If she saw you as a person to assume a certain responsibility, then you must be that person, and you rose to it," one remembered.[44]

The success of the School of Social Service Administration enhanced Abbott's and Breckinridge's standing at the University of Chicago. But their elevated status was hard-won. A male dean ran the school from 1920 until 1924, when Edith Abbott was finally put in charge. Once again, Breckinridge was passed over by the university, probably because of her age this time. (She was fifty-eight.) Chicago did not firmly commit itself to the school until 1924, when the president told Abbott "he did not want us to be worrying about any possibility that the School might be discontinued ... whether we got any more money or whether we did not ... the University would find a way to help us go on." The school, President Burton assured Abbott, would have "bread and butter before anybody else had jam." A gift of $725,000 from the Laura Spelman Rockefeller Memorial, stipulating matching funds of $1,000,000 from the university, gave the school a permanent endowment in 1926.[45]

Promotion to full professorships came in 1925, but only after a full-scale revolt by women faculty. In a final rebellion before retirement, Dean of Women Marion Talbot publicly complained about Chicago's treatment of women to the president and board of trustees. Talbot and the other two women holding full professorships charged the university with violating the terms of its charter by failing to provide women with equal "opportunities." The offenses ranged from failing to seat women on the board of trustees to discrimination in hiring, salaries, and promotion. "There are three women faculty members," they noted, "who received their Doctor's degree in 1907 or earlier and who are still only associate professors; whereas twenty-one men who received their Doctor's degree in 1907 or later hold full professorships."

The accusations were accurate and embarrassing. When the trustees next met to vote upon promotions, they advanced Abbott, Breckinridge, and another distinguished woman faculty member to the rank of full professor. Edith and Sophonisba would never be quite so vulnerable again. Indeed, they were greatly cheered by the sensitive leadership of President Robert Hutchins. Though terribly suspicious of his youth, the two women adopted a wait-and-see attitude when Hutchins took office in 1929. Hutchins came to respect deeply the social work leaders. "They were never obliging at any stage of their lives, certainly not for the purpose of advancing their careers," he later remembered. His affection was returned in kind. "You have always been entirely fair about the position of women on your faculties," Abbott once told Hutchins. "I wanted you to know that some of us have deeply appreciated the rare freedom from prejudice in this respect which has characterized your administration."[46]

Her experience in academic life made Sophonisba Breckinridge more reflective than embittered. Late in her professional life, she decided to write a book exploring the changing status of American women. When *Women in the Twentieth Century* was published in 1933, its author introduced her subject with this wry observation: "It should be recalled that until some one is persuaded or persuades himself to walk through prejudice, it is an impenetrable as well as an immovable obstacle." Breckinridge surveyed women's organizations, employment, and "their relationship to government." In all three areas, she found a record of extraordinary progress against "formidable" and persistent odds.[47]

Breckinridge appraised with some detachment historical changes that had profoundly shaped her own life. She carefully described the reality of sex discrimination in the academy. Men who earned doctoral degrees "went in considerable numbers on to the faculties of the colleges and universities. The women could, it is true, only in relatively small numbers avail themselves of these opportunities." And she puzzled over the troubling problem of marriage. Did "the access of women to the satisfactions of life . . . require celibacy?" she asked. "Many professional women" needed meaningful work to be happy. "The question of continuing employment after marriage," Breckinridge mused, was a matter of grave importance. Like Katharine Davis, Breckinridge seemed preoccupied with the choices she had made, though intellectual inquiry again served as a tonic for any doubts.[48]

Research, teaching, and participation in the lively academic community at Chicago proved intensely rewarding for both Edith Abbott and Sophonisba Breckinridge. By 1940 they made an extraordinary picture on the campus—two "Victorian ladies" in large hats, and long, dark dresses. The death of her sister Grace in 1939 greatly affected Edith, who had lived with her sister for many years. When Sophonisba retired from the university in 1942, she moved out of her apartment in Green Hall and into the home the Abbott sisters had shared on Woodlawn Avenue. Edith relinquished her duties as dean the same year, though she continued to teach.[49]

Breckinridge spent her final years attempting to write an autobiography, as well as a family history. She struggled with what were clearly painful tasks, remembering those she had loved and reexperiencing traumatic losses. She could not complete the work, though she made certain the Breckinridge family papers found a place in the Library of Congress. As Sophonisba became increasingly infirm, Edith took care of her until Breckinridge died in July 1948 at eighty-two. This was, Alice Hamilton told Edith, "the saddest part of old age. One sees friend after friend die, and one is lonelier as the years pass. This loss of yours is very great, for your friendship lasted so long."[50]

Life without her sister and Sophonisba became very hard for Edith, alone now in her old age. She moved back to Hull House in 1949, giving up her various duties at the university only slowly and usually under duress. She never abandoned her principles. When the National Conference of Social Work honored the seventy-five-year-old Abbott in 1951, she used the occasion to lecture her audience about inadequacies in the social welfare system. "Social security is not social security when it reaches only the destitute," she said. Abbott endorsed "allowances" for *all* children instead of Aid to Dependent Children, and she looked forward to the day when the nation would give "old age pensions to everyone at a certain age without any question as to need." With that, she accepted her plaque, adding that it was "completely undeserved."[51]

When Abbott's health began to fail in the early 1950s, her brother Arthur took Edith home to Grand Island, Nebraska. In July of 1957 she died at the age of eighty-one in the home where she was born. Her brother sadly described these last years in a letter to one of Edith's friends in Chicago.

> Edith always thought so much of you and always enjoyed your letters altho she could not write legibly. She kept speaking of you and Anne Davis the past two years. In fact all her thoughts and interests were of the school and the friends in Chicago. Her old friends here were dead or had left and Chicago was all she could talk about.[52]

Abbott's death marked the passing of a generation. "You are the only survivor at U. of C. of that original force which broadened opportunity for women in U.S.A. (and for that matter the rest of the world)," one of Abbott's admirers had written when Breckinridge died. "Have you some promising stalwarts in your department coming on to meet the challenge of tomorrow?"[53]

The question had no simple answer. Of course, the students of Breckinridge and Abbott took up their professors' charge, much as Edith and Sophonisba had done so many years ago. A younger generation advanced the new social welfare profession. Widening access to higher education swelled the academic ranks with women with Ph.D.s. Colleges and universities gradually made places on their faculty for a growing number of women scholars. Professional women more often struggled to combine marriage, children, and a career.

But many felt less compelled to direct their talents to social uplift and reform. As institutional barriers began to fall, it required less creativity to find a profession. Also gone was the extraordinary climate of upheaval and reform that accompanied the emergence of a modern industrial society. Ironically, the four women activists had uncovered remarkable opportunities in a highly uncertain age.

V

Breckinridge's, Davis's, Kellor's, and Abbott's quest to place social science in the service of reform invigorated the Progressive cause, but it did not produce a method that ensured effective social change. The intellectual principles they revered could not, by their very nature, provide clear and unassailable guidelines for social policy. Empirical research and social knowledge did not lead to a unified explanation of social problems: the slow process of intellectual understanding that academics savored was ill-suited to the hurried demands of political reform.

In truth, the academic approach to social change seemed most at home in the universities. There social knowledge could be valued as an end unto itself, a goal to strive for regardless of what was ever realized or achieved. Ironically, Abbott's and Breckinridge's School of Social Service Administration became the most lasting expression of the women social scientists' distinctive approach to reform. The road to intellectual understanding led back to where it had all begun.

Still, the values that had shaped the women's early careers proved remarkably resilient as the twentieth century unfolded. Social research became a natural component of social policy. Social scientists played increasingly important roles in government affairs, a phenomenon that gained public recognition when Roosevelt's "Brain Trust" came together during the New Deal. As the century wore on, environmental interpretations of social and economic problems that had once seemed revolutionary assumed the characteristics of an orthodoxy. Eventually even the women reformers' political ideals were realized in legislation that created the outlines of a welfare state. The ideas that had inspired Breckinridge, Davis, Kellor, and Abbott endured.

Notes

Introduction

1. John Allen Gable, *The Bull Moose Years* (Port Washington, N.Y.: Kennikat Press, 1978), 42, 76, 81–85; Lela B. Costin, *Two Sisters for Social Justice* (Urbana, Ill.: Univ. of Illinois Press, 1983), 48–49.

2. Historians disagree about the nature, and even the existence, of a "Progressive Movement" at the turn of the century. In this book, the phrase is meant to describe the various individuals and organizations who came together to advance social and political reform during the late nineteenth and early twentieth century. The women discussed in this book were "Progressives" in two senses. First, they participated in various reform organizations that developed out of the growth of industrial society, and in response to the multiple problems that accompanied rapid social and economic change. Second, they joined the Progressive Party in 1912, thereby aligning themselves with other reformers who struggled to advance the social and political agenda embodied in the new party's platform. Though historians have been rightly skeptical of interpretations that invoke a singular, unified Progressive movement, many Bull Moosers at least considered themselves members of a coherent reform group. Frances Kellor, for instance, once solicited an article from Jane Addams by reminding her, "we want to have some enduring literature on the Progressive movement." Frances A. Kellor to Jane Addams, 4 September 1912, Jane Addams Papers, Swarthmore College Peace Collection, Swarthmore, Pennsylvania (hereafter, Addams Papers, SC).

3. There is a wide literature on Progressivism. See, for example, Richard Hofstadter, *The Age of Reform* (New York: Vintage Books, 1955); Robert Wiebe, *The Search for Order* (New York: Hill & Wang, 1967); Samuel P. Hays, *The Response to Industrialism* (Chicago: Univ. of Chicago Press, 1957); John D. Buenker, John C. Burnham, and Robert M. Crunden, *Progressivism* (Cambridge, Mass.: Schenkman, 1977); Arthur S. Link and Richard L. McCormick, *Progressivism* (Arlington Heights, Ill.: Harlan Davidson, 1983); George Mowry, *The Era of Theodore Roosevelt and the Rise of Modern America* (New York: Harper and Brothers, 1958); Robert M. Crunden, *Ministers of Reform* (New York: Basic Books, 1982); David Thelen, *The New Citizen-*

ship (Columbia: Univ. of Missouri Press, 1972); James T. Kloppenberg, *Uncertain Victory: Social Democracy and Progressivism in European and American Thought, 1870–1920* (New York: Oxford Univ. Press, 1986); Nell Irvin Painter, *Standing at Armageddon* (New York: W. W. Norton, 1987). For a critique of the concept of the "Progressive Movement," see Peter Filene, "An Obituary for the 'Progressive Movement,'" *American Quarterly* 22 (1970). For an assessment of women, education, and reform, see Ellen Condliffe Lagemann, *A Generation of Women: Education in the Lives of Women Progressive Reformers* (Cambridge, Mass.: Harvard Univ. Press, 1979).

4. The most important recent study of intellectuals and Progressivism is Kloppenberg, *Uncertain Victory*. Older studies include Charles Forcey, *The Crossroads of Liberalism: Croly, Weyl, Lippman, and the Progressive Era, 1900–1925* (New York: Oxford Univ. Press, 1961); Benjamin G. Rader, *The Academic Mind and Reform* (Lexington, Ky.: Univ. Press of Kentucky, 1966); R. Jackson Wilson, *In Quest of Community* (New York: John Wiley, 1968); Jean Quandt, *From the Small Town to the Great Community* (New Brunswick, N.J.: Rutgers Univ. Press, 1970); David Noble, *The Paradox of Progressive Thought* (Minneapolis: Univ. of Minnesota Press, 1958); Morton White, *Social Thought in America: The Revolt Against Formalism*, 3rd ed. (New York: Oxford Univ. Press, 1979); and Christopher Lasch, *The New Radicalism in America* (New York: Vintage Books, 1965).

5. By "social sciences," I mean here the policy sciences of sociology, political economy, and political science. See Walter Crosby Eells, "Earned Doctorates for Women in the Nineteenth Century," American Association of University Professors Bulletin, vol. 42 (1956), 648; Margaret W. Rossiter, *Women Scientists in America* (Baltimore, Md.: Johns Hopkins Univ. Press, 1982), 36.

Chapter 1: Pathways to Chicago

1. Sophonisba Breckinridge, "Autobiography," Sophonisba Breckinridge Papers, University of Chicago Library, Chicago, Illinois (hereafter S. P. Breckinridge Papers, UCL). Breckinridge's "Autobiography" is an incomplete, unpublished draft, which she began in 1947. The work is short and very fragmented, but informative nonetheless. There are no consistent page numbers.

2. *Notable American Women*, s.v. "Breckinridge, Sophonisba Preston," 233; *National Cyclopedia of American Biography*, s.v. "Breckinridge, William Campbell Preston," 42; William C. P. Breckinridge to Sophonisba Breckinridge, 30 March 1885, Sophonisba P. Breckinridge Papers, Library of Congress, Washington, D.C. (hereafter S. P. Breckinridge Papers, LC). A wonderfully evocative account of Breckinridge's early years may be found in James C. Klotter, "Family Influences on a Progressive: The Early Years of Sophonisba P. Breckinridge," in James C. Klotter and Peter J. Sehlinger, eds., *Kentucky Profiles: Biographical Essays in Honor of Holman Hamilton* (Frankfort, Ky.: Kentucky Historical Society, 1982).

3. *National Cyclopedia of American Biography*, s.v. "Breckinridge, William Campbell Preston," 42; S. Breckinridge, "Autobiography"; *New York Times*, 30 March 1894, p. 3; *New York Times*, 8 May 1894, p. 3.

4. William Breckinridge to Sophonisba Breckinridge, 30 March 1885, S. P. Breckinridge Papers, LC. For a fine selection of the letters written by Sophonisba's father to her at Wellesley, see Helen Lefkowitz Horowitz, "With More Love Than I Can Write: A Nineteenth Century Father to His Daughter," *Wellesley* 65, no. 1 (Fall 1980): 16–20.

5. S. Breckinridge, "Autobiography"; *National Cyclopedia of American Biography*, s.v. "Breckinridge, William Campbell Preston," 42.

6. S. Breckinridge, "Autobiography"; Issa Breckinridge to S. Breckinridge, 12 October 1884, S. P. Breckinridge Papers, LC.

7. S. Breckinridge, "Autobiography".

8. Issa Breckinridge to Sophonisba Breckinridge, 6 April 1885, S. P. Breckinridge Papers, LC; S. Breckinridge, "Autobiography"; James C. Klotter, *The Breckinridges of Kentucky, 1760–1981* (Lexington, Ky.: Univ. Press of Kentucky, 1986), 195.

9. S. Breckinridge, "Autobiography"; Tom Morgan to S. Breckinridge, 15 November 1884, S. P. Breckinridge Papers, LC; Klotter, "Family Influences," 1335.

10. S. Breckinridge, "Autobiography"; Issa Breckinridge to S. Breckinridge, 20 September 1884, Issa Breckinridge to S. Breckinridge, 19 September 1884, O. S. Sumner to S. Breckinridge, 29 September 1884, all S. P. Breckinridge Papers, LC.

11. Barbara Miller Solomon, *In the Company of Educated Women* (New Haven: Yale Univ. Press, 1985), 64. For the best summaries of the early generations, see chaps. 5 and 6: Jill Ker Conway, "The First Generation of American Women Graduates," (Ph.D. diss., Harvard Univ., 1969); Patricia A. Graham, "Expansion and Exclusion: A History of Women in Higher Education," *Signs* 3 (Summer, 1978).

12. On Breckinridge's finances, see William Breckinridge to S. Breckinridge, 30 March 1885, and William Breckinridge to S. Breckinridge, 10 May 1885, both S. P. Breckinridge Papers, LC; Solomon, *Company of Educated Women*, 66; Lynn D. Gordon, "Women on Campus in the Progressive Era," (Ph.D. diss., Univ. of Chicago, 1981), 183.

13. William Breckinridge to S. Breckinridge, 8 Oct. 1884, and William Breckinridge to S. Breckinridge, 30 March 1884, both S. P. Breckinridge Papers, LC.

14. Issa Breckinridge to S. Breckinridge, 20 Sept. 1884, S. P. Breckinridge Papers, LC.

15. Solomon, *Company of Educated Women*, chap. 7; Helen Lefkowitz Horowitz, *Alma Mater* (New York: Alfred A. Knopf, 1984).

16. Breckinridge, "Autobiography"; William Breckinridge to S. Breckinridge, 17 Dec. 1884, William Breckinridge to S. Breckinridge, 11 Feb. 1885, Issa Breckinridge to S. Breckinridge, 27 May 1885, Issa Breckinridge to S. Breckinridge, 17 May 1885, all S. P. Breckinridge Papers, LC. On Palmer, see Gordon, "Women on Campus," 180–82; *Notable American Women*, s.v. "Palmer, Alice Freeman"; Alice Freeman to S. Breckinridge, 12 July 1887, and Alice Freeman Palmer to S. Breckinridge, 30 December 1887, both S. P. Breckinridge Papers, LC. For a discussion of the special environment at Wellesley College at the turn of the century, see Patricia Palmieri, "In Adamless Eden: A Social Portrait of the Academic Community at Wellesley College, 1875–1920," (Ph.D. diss., Harvard Univ. School of Education, 1981). Palmieri notes that Palmer began an acting presidency at Wellesley in 1881: 87.

17. Breckinridge, "Autobiography."

18. Issa Breckinridge to S. Breckinridge, 19 September 1884, S. P. Breckinridge Papers, LC.

19. Breckinridge, "Autobiography"; William Breckinridge to S. Breckinridge, 3 October 1884, S. P. Breckinridge Papers, LC.

20. Breckinridge, "Autobiography."

21. Ibid.

22. William Breckinridge to S. Breckinridge, 3 Oct. 1884, William Breckinridge to S. Breckinridge, 22 Oct. 1884, William Breckinridge to S. Breckinridge, 7 March 1885, all S. P. Breckinridge Papers, LC; Solomon, *Company of Educated Women*, 90–91.

23. Solomon, *Company of Educated Women*, chap. 8; Joyce Antler, "The Educated Woman and Professionalization: The Search for a New Feminine Identity, 1890–1920," (Ph.D. diss., State Univ. of New York at Stony Brook, 1977); Charles F. Thwing, *The College Woman* (New York: Baker and Taylor, 1894); Jane Addams, *Twenty Years at Hull House* (New York: New American Library, 1961), 65.

24. Breckinridge, "Autobiography."

25. Breckinridge, "Autobiography"; Marion Talbot to S. Breckinridge, 3 Jan. 1892, Frederick B. Hawley to S. Breckinridge, 11 April 1891, both S. P. Breckinridge Papers, LC.

26. Breckinridge, "Autobiography"; *New York Times*, 29 November 1892, p. 1.

27. Breckinridge, "Autobiography."

28. Gerald S. Lee to S. Breckinridge, 1 June 1891, Issa Breckinridge to S. Breckinridge, 11 May 1892, both S. P. Breckinridge Papers, LC; Breckinridge, "Autobiography."

29. Breckinridge, "Autobiography"; Vida Scudder to S. Breckinridge, 9 August 1892, S. P. Breckinridge Papers, LC; C. R. Henderson, *Social Settlements* (New York: Lentilhon, 1899), 52–54; Solomon, *Company of Educated Women*, 109–10; Allen F. Davis, *Spearheads for Reform: The Social Settlements and the Progressive Movement, 1890–1914* (New York: Oxford Univ. Press, 1967); John Rousmaniere, "Cultural Hybrid in the Slums: The College Woman and the Settlement House, 1889–1894," *American Quarterly* 22, no. 1 (Spring 1970).

30. Breckinridge, "Autobiography"; Addams, *Twenty Years*, 94; Desha Breckinridge to S. Breckinridge, 16 August 1892, S. P. Breckinridge Papers, LC.

31. Breckinridge, "Autobiography."

32. *New York Times*, 29 November 1892, p. 1; Breckinridge, "Autobiography."

33. *National Cyclopedia of American Biography*, s.v. "Breckinridge, William Campbell Preston," 42; *New York Times*, 5 April 1894, 6; *New York Times*, 13 August 1893, p. 2.

34. *New York Times*, 22 March 1894, p. 3; *New York Times*, 15 April 1894, p. 2; *New York Times*, 29 April 1894, p. 9.

35. Breckinridge, "Autobiography"; *New York Times*, 25 March 1894, p. 3; *New York Times*, 27 March 1894, p. 3; *New York Times*, 6 April 1894, p. 8; *New York Times*, 3 May 1894, p. 1.

36. *New York Times*, 6 May 1894, p. 2; *New York Times*, 12 June 1894, p. 5; *New York Times*, 15 May 1894, p. 5; *New York Times*, 3 May 1894, p. 1; *New York Times*, 8 May 1894, p. 3.

37. *New York Times*, 15 September 1894, p. 1; *New York Times*, 10 June 1894, p. 1; *New York Times*, 16 September 1894, p. 1; *New York Times*, 6 May 1894, p. 2; *New York Times*, 16 September 1894, p. 1; Breckinridge, "Autobiography."

38. Breckinridge, "Autobiography"; University of Chicago, *Annual Register, 1895–1896* (Chicago: Univ. of Chicago Press).

39. Breckinridge, "Autobiography"; Marion Talbot, *More Than Lore* (Chicago: Univ. of Chicago Press, 1936), chap. 1.

40. Breckinridge, "Autobiography"; Elizabeth Wallace, *Unending Journey* (Minneapolis: Univ. of Minnesota Press, 1952), 75; "Annals of the Class of 1886," (January 1899) and (January 1894), 24, Wellesley College Archives, box 6/Class of 1886; Eells, "Earned Doctorates for Women"; Association of Collegiate Alumnae, *Preliminary Statistical Study of Certain Women College Graduates* (Bryn Mawr, Pa.: A.C.A. Publishing, 1917), 29–30.

41. Madeleine Wallin, "First Impressions of the University of Chicago," 1893,

Madeleine Wallin Papers, University of Chicago Library, Chicago, Ill. (hereafter, Wallin Papers, UCL).

42. Fellowships awarded to men and women were computed from the University of Chicago, *Annual Registers* for various years cited.

43. Breckinridge, "Autobiography."

44. Ibid.

45. University of Chicago, *Annual Register, 1892–1898.* For more on Davis's later career, see Estelle Freedman, *Their Sisters' Keepers* (Ann Arbor: Univ. of Michigan Press, 1981).

46. *Notable American Women,* s.v. "Davis, Katharine Bement," 439; Lynn D. Gordon, "Katharine Bement Davis," in *Biographical Dictionary of Social Welfare in America,* ed. Walter Trattner, (Westport, Conn.: Greenwood Press, 1986) [referred to hereafter as Gordon, "KBD"]; *Dictionary of American Biography,* s.v. "Davis, Katharine Bement," 227.

47. Katharine Bement Davis, "Three Score Years and Ten," *University of Chicago Magazine,* vol. 26, no. 2 (December 1933), 58.

48. *Notable American Women,* s.v. "Davis, Katharine Bement," 439; Gordon, "KBD."

49. *Notable American Women,* s.v. "Davis, Katharine Bement," 439; *Dictionary of American Biography,* s.v. "Davis, Katharine Bement"; Gordon, "KBD."

50. Rossiter, *Women Scientists in America,* 12–15.

51. Ibid., 67–69; Dolores Hayden, *The Grand Domestic Revolution* (Cambridge, Mass.: M.I.T. Press, 1981), 151–59.

52. Rossiter, *Women Scientists in America,* 52–53, 67–69; Vassar College, *Catalogue, 1891–1892; Dictionary of American Biography,* s.v. "Davis, Katharine Bement"; Gordon, "KBD."

53. Gordon, "KBD"; *Notable American Women,* s.v. "Davis, Katharine Bement," 439; *Dictionary of American Biography,* s.v. "Davis, Katharine Bement"; Katharine Bement Davis, *Report on the Exhibit of the Workingman's Model Home as Exhibited by the State of New York at the World's Columbian Exposition* (Albany: James B. Lyon, 1895), 395.

54. Davis, *Report on the Exhibit,* 395–97, 442–43, and passim; *Dictionary of American Biography,* s.v. "Davis Katharine Bement"; *Notable American Women,* s.v. "Davis, Katharine Bement"; Hayden, *Grand Domestic Revolution,* 151, 159; Rossiter, *Women Scientists,* 68–69; Gordon, "KBD."

55. Gordon, "KBD"; *Notable American Women,* s.v. "Davis, Katharine Bement"; Henderson, *Social Settlements,* 55–58.

56. Davis, "Three Score Years," 60.

57. Dorothy Ross, "The Development of the Social Sciences," in *The Organization of Knowledge in Modern American 1860–1920,* ed. Alexandra Oleson and John Voss (Baltimore, Md.: Johns Hopkins Univ. Press, 1979); Davis, "Three Score Years," 60.

58. University of Chicago, *Annual Register, 1898–1899.*

59. *Dictionary of American Biography,* s.v. "Kellor, Frances (Alice)"; *Notable American Women,* s.v. "Kellor, Frances"; Phyllis M. Palmer, "Two Friends of the Immigrant," (M.A. thesis, Ohio State University, 1967), 13; Phyllis Holbrook to the author, 17 August 1986. It seems at least possible that Kellor's "older sister" was actually her mother. Mrs. Kellor had her first daughter, Elizabeth, at the age of fifteen. She was forty-two when Frances was born, and there were no intervening children. Elizabeth, however, had a son at the age of sixteen, and she was twenty-seven when Frances was born. It appears that Kellor's sister left Coldwater when she married for the second

time in 1875. Frances was not even two years old at that time. See Branch County, Michigan, Record of Marriages, vol. E, p. 147, #84; Green Lawn Cemetary Records; Elizabeth Pontius death certificate, and other miscellaneous family records in Holbrook Collection.

60. Palmer, "Two Friends," 13; *Notable American Women*, s.v. "Kellor, Frances"; *Coldwater Courier*, 4 October 1911, p. 2; Grace Kitchel to William J. Maxwell, 4 August 1965. (Photocopy privately held by Phyllis Holbrook, Coldwater, Michigan. Ms. Holbrook's materials on Kellor are hereafter referred to as the Holbrook Collection.) *Coldwater Courier*, 4 October 1911, p. 2.

61. Georgia Starr to Phyllis Holbrook, 30 June 1960, Holbrook Collection; Palmer, "Two Friends," 13; *Notable American Women*, s.v. "Kellor, Frances."

62. *Coldwater Courier*, 4 October 1911, p. 2.

63. Ibid.; *Coldwater Daily Republican*, 23 June 1962, p. 7; Mary Dreier to Phyllis Holbrook, 16 December 1961, Holbrook Collection; Palmer, "Two Friends," 13–14; *Notable American Women*, s.v. "Kellor, Frances"; *Dictionary of American Biography*, s.v. "Kellor, Frances."

64. *Notable American Women*, s.v. "Kellor, Frances"; *Dictionary of American Biography*, s.v. "Kellor, Frances"; *Coldwater Republican*, 29 July 1892, n.p. (photocopy in Holbrook Collection); *Coldwater Republican*, 24 October 1892, p. 2; *Coldwater Republican*, 31 October 1893, p. 3; *Coldwater Republican*, 7 August 1894, n.p.; *Coldwater Republican*, 2 November 1894, n.p.

65. Phyllis Holbrook to the author, 17 August 1986; *Coldwater Republican*, 28 April 1893, p. 2; *Coldwater Republican*, 29 December 1893, n.p.; *Coldwater Republican*, 25 May 1894, p. 4; *Coldwater Republican*, 27 July 1894, p. 3.

66. *Coldwater Republican*, 23 August 1895, p. 2; *Coldwater Republican*, 10 September 1895, p. 2; *Coldwater Republican*, 14 September 1895, p. 5; *Coldwater Republican*, 29 October 1895, n.p.; Phyllis Holbrook to the author, 17 August 1986. Kellor took an *undergraduate* course in law at Cornell. She earned a Bachelor of Law degree.

67. Palmer, "Two Friends," 14; Charlotte Conable, *Women at Cornell* (Ithaca, N.Y.: Cornell Univ. Press, 1977), 117–18.

68. Conable, *Women at Cornell*, 115–18.

69. Mary Dreier to Phyllis Holbrook, 23 November 1960, Holbrook Collection; *Coldwater Republican*, 28 January 1896, p. 1; *Coldwater Courier and Republican*, 25 June 1897, p. 1.

70. Florence Kelley to Marion Talbot, 12 October 1896, Marion Talbot Papers, University of Chicago Library, Chicago, Illinois (hereafter, Talbot Papers, UCL); Celsa Parker Wooley, *The Western Slope*, (Evanston, Ill.: William S. Lord, 1903), 84–89.

71. Wooley, *Western Slope*, 84–85; Thomas Haskell, *The Emergence of Professional Social Science* (Urbana: Univ. of Illinois Press, 1977), 197–200.

72. Wooley, *Western Slope*, 85; *Dictionary of American Biography*, 380; Frances A. Kellor, *Experimental Sociology* (New York: Macmillan, 1901); Charles Richmond Henderson, *Modern Prison Systems* (Washington, D.C.: U.S. Government Printing Office, 1903), 191.

73. *Notable American Women*, s.v. "Abbott, Edith," 1; Costin, *Two Sisters*, 13.

74. Costin, *Two Sisters*, chap. 1; Othman A. Abbott, *Recollections of a Pioneer Lawyer* (Lincoln: Nebraska State Historical Society, 1929), 5, 27, 141–43.

75. Abbott, *Recollections*, 82–113.

76. Costin, *Two Sisters*, chap. 1; Abbott, *Recollections*, 141; Palmer, "Two Friends," 9.

77. Abbott, *Recollections*, 144–45; Costin, *Two Sisters*, 4.

78. Abbott, *Recollections*, 141–42, 145, 150.

79. Costin, *Two Sisters*, 5, and chap. 1, passim; Edith Abbott, "Grace Abbott: A Sister's Memories," *Social Service Review* vol. 13, no. 3 (September 1939), 351–52, 354; Abbott, *Recollections*, 148.

80. Abbott, "Grace Abbott," 352–53.

81. Ibid.; Costin, *Two Sisters*, chap. 1.

82. Abbott, *Recollections*, 145, 148; Abbott, "Grace Abbott," 354; Costin, *Two Sisters*, 8, 9–10.

83. Palmer, "Two Friends," 9; Abbott, "Grace Abbott," 353–54.

84. Abbott, *Recollections*, 148–51.

85. Quoted in Costin, *Two Sisters*, 11–12.

86. Ibid., 12–13.

87. Ibid., 13.

88. Ibid., 13–14; Abbott, *Recollections*, 175–76.

89. Othman Abbott to J. W. Dewers, 18 June 1897, Edith and Grace Abbott Papers, addenda, University of Chicago Library (hereafter, Abbott Papers, addenda, UCL); Elizabeth Abbott to Edith Abbott, 20 January 1897, Abbott Papers addenda, UCL; Elizabeth Abbott to Edith Abbott, 2 July 1897, Abbott Papers addenda, UCL; Costin, *Two Sisters*, 14, 16.

90. Costin, *Two Sisters*, 18–19.

91. Ibid., 19; Edith Abbott, "Sophonisba Preston Breckinridge: Over the Years," *Social Service Review*, vol. 22, no. 4 (December 1948), 417.

92. Costin, *Two Sisters*, 19; University of Chicago, *Annual Register, 1903–4.*

93. The cult of domesticity is explained by Barbara Welter in "The Cult of True Womanhood," *American Quarterly* 18 (Summer 1966): 131–175.

94. The special factors influencing opportunities for education are analyzed fully in Solomon, *Company of Educated Women*, esp. chaps. 4, 5.

Chapter 2: White City, Gray City

1. Madeleine Wallin, "First Impressions of the University of Chicago," 1893, Wallin Papers, UCL, 1, 3, 4.

2. Wallin, "First Impressions," 1; Lawrence Veysey, *Emergence of the American University* (Chicago: Univ. of Chicago Press, 1965); Haskell, *Emergence of Professional Social Science*; Solomon, *Company of Educated Women*, 133–38; Richard J. Storr, *Harper's University* (Chicago: Univ. of Chicago Press, 1966), 3; David F. Burg, *Chicago's White City of 1893* (Lexington: Univ. Press of Kentucky, 1976), 45.

3. Wallin, "First Impressions," 5; Veysey, *Emergence of the American University*, especially 158–75; Storr, *Harper's University.*

4. Thomas Wakefield Goodspeed, *A History of the University of Chicago, 1891–1916* (Chicago: Univ. of Chicago Press, 1916), 137–38; Rossiter, *Women Scientists in America*, chaps. 1 and 2; Solomon, *Company of Educated Women*, chap. 4 and pp. 133–38.

5. These enrollment figures are based on the University of Chicago's *Annual Register* for the years 1893–1894 through 1903–1904. Students who had political economy, sociology, political science, or social science listed under their names as a major field of study were counted. These figures may overestimate the number of male and

female students concentrating in social science because some students listed two fields. See also registration figures for women in graduate departments in Marion Talbot, "The Women of the University," in *The President's Report, 1897–1898* (Chicago: Univ. of Chicago Press), 120–23. Talbot's figures show a relatively small number of graduate women in the social sciences compared with other fields. The largest concentration of women graduate students were in the departments of English, history, and Latin.

6. "Annals of the Class of 1886," (January 1899), Wellesley College Archives, box 6/Class of 1886; Davis,"Three Score Years and Ten," 60. For an extensive discussion of the female academic community at Chicago, see Lynn D. Gordon, "Women on Campus in the Progressive Era," chap. 6. I am most grateful to Professor Gordon for permitting me to read her work.

7. Wallin, "First Impressions," 6.

8. Davis, "Three Score Years and Ten," 60; Wallin,"First Impressions," 6. See also Talbot, "Women of the University," *President's Report, 1897–1898*, table 14: "Academic Age of Graduate Women," 119.

9. For Talbot's role at Chicago, see Gordon, "Women on Campus"; Rosalind Rosenberg, *Beyond Separate Spheres* (New Haven: Yale Univ. Press, 1982), especially chap. 1 and 2; and Talbot's own account, *More Than Lore*.

10. *Notable American Women*, s.v. "Talbot, Marion" 423–24; *Dictionary of American Biography*, s.v. "Talbot, Israel Tisdale," and "Talbot, Emily;" Rosenberg, *Beyond Separate Spheres*, 2–4; Marion Talbot and Lois Rosenberry, *The History of the American Association of University Women* (Boston: Houghton Mifflin, 1931), 3–4.

11. Talbot and Rosenberry, *History of the A.A.U.W.*, 6–9; *Notable American Women*, s.v. "Marion Talbot."

12. Gordon, "Women on Campus," chap. 5; Wallin, "First Impressions," 7.

13. Marion Talbot to William Rainey Harper, 22 August 1892, Talbot Papers, UCL.

14. Marion Talbot to William Rainey Harper, 13 August 1892, William Rainey Harper to Marion Talbot, 22 August 1892, both Talbot Papers, UCL.

15. William Rainey Harper to Marion Talbot, 11 August 1892, Talbot Papers, UCL; Gordon, "Women on Campus," 195; Talbot,"Women of the University," *President's Report, 1898–1899*, 72.

16. Talbot, *More Than Lore*, 64; Rosenberg, *Beyond Separate Spheres*, 47–48; statements by Marion Talbot, "Women of the University," in the *President's Report* for various years.

17. William Rainey Harper to Marion Talbot, 24 October 1904, Talbot Papers, UCL.

18. Goodspeed, *History of the University*, 183; Kathleen McCarthy, *Noblesse Oblige* (Chicago: Univ. of Chicago Press, 1982), preface and pp. 27–30.

19. Goodspeed, *History of the University*, 229.

20. Ibid., 103, 136–37, 369.

21. Storr, *Harper's University*, 17, chap. 1.

22. Ibid., chap. 4.

23. Ibid., 194.

24. Veysey, *Emergence of the American University*; Haskell, *Emergence of Professional Social Science*; Steven J. Diner, *A City and Its Universities* (Chapel Hill: Univ. of North Carolina Press, 1980), 5–10.

25. Ross, "Development of the Social Sciences," 109–12; Richard Hofstadter,

Social Darwinism in American Thought (New York: George Braziller, 1944), 3–6 and passim; Sidney Fine, *Laissez Faire and the General Welfare State* (Ann Arbor: Univ. of Michigan Press, 1967), 23–30 and passim.

26. Louise C. Wade, *Graham Taylor: Pioneer for Social Justice* (Chicago: Univ. of Chicago Press, 1964), 51–55, 60; Ray Ginger, *Altgeld's America* (New York: Funk and Wagnalls, 1958), 23–26; Allan H. Spear, *Black Chicago* (Chicago: Univ. of Chicago Press, 1967), 12.

27. Ginger, *Altgeld's America*, 24; Wade, *Graham Taylor*, 56.

28. Wade, *Graham Taylor*, 54–55; Bessie L. Pierce, *A History of Chicago*, vol. 3, *The Rise of a Modern City, 1871–1893* (New York: Alfred A. Knopf, 1957), chaps. 4 and 5.

29. Paul Avrich, *The Haymarket Tragedy* (Princeton, N.J.: Princeton Univ. Press, 1984), 423–27; Ginger, *Altgeld's America*, 85–88, chap. 6; Wade, *Graham Taylor*, 76–77.

30. Pierce, *A History of Chicago*, 3:465–66.

31. University of Chicago, *The World's Columbian Exposition and the University of Chicago* (n.d., n.p.), p. 7; Stanley Appelbaum, *The Chicago World's Fair of 1893* (New York: Dover Publications, 1980).

32. Goodspeed, *History of the University*, 219–21; Appelbaum, *Chicago World's Fair*, 72, 97; Talbot, *More Than Lore*, 116; Goodspeed, *History of the University*, 308.

33. Thomas Wakefield Goodspeed, *Story of the University of Chicago, 1890–1925* (Chicago: Univ. of Chicago Press, 1925), 112; Talbot, *More Than Lore*, 111–12.

34. Burg, *Chicago's White City*, chap. 5.

35. Ibid., 106; Smith College, *Commencement Poems* (North Brookfield, Mass.: H. J. Lawrence, 1888), 3, 16; Jeanne Weimann, *The Fair Women* (Chicago: Academy Chicago, 1981); Hayden, *Grand Domestic Revolution*.

36. Burg, *Chicago's White City*, 236.

37. Ibid., chap. 6; Appelbaum, *Chicago World's Fair*, 103; Pierce, *History of Chicago*, 3:508–10.

38. Pierce, *History of Chicago*, 3:509; Appelbaum, *Chicago World's Fair*, 106; Ginger, *Altgeld's America*, 21.

39. Pierce, *History of Chicago*, 3:509; Burg, *Chicago's White City*, 274.

40. Burg, *Chicago's White City*, 284; Ginger, *Altgeld's America*, 216; Pierce, *History of Chicago*, 3:378.

Chapter 3: Scientists of Society

1. On the growth of social science in this period, see especially Ross, "Development of the Social Sciences"; Mary Furner, *Advocacy and Objectivity* (Lexington: Univ. Press of Kentucky, 1975); Haskell, *Emergence of Professional Social Science*; Dorothy Ross, "Socialism and American Liberalism" in *Perspectives in American History*, ed. Donald Fleming, vol. 11 (Cambridge, Mass.: Charles Warren Center for Studies in American History, 1977–78). James T. Kloppenberg discusses related developments in turn-of-the-century political and social philosophy in *Uncertain Victory*.

2. University of Chicago, *Programme of the Departments of Political Economy, Political Science, History, Sociology and Anthropology, 1899–1900* (Chicago: Univ. of Chicago Press, 1899), 7–8; University of Chicago, *Programme of Courses in Political Economy 1892–93* (Chicago: Univ. of Chicago Press, 1892), 13; Diner, *A City and Its*

Universities, 47–48. For a full and enlightening discussion of the Bemis case, see Furner, *Advocacy and Objectivity.*

3. University of Chicago, *Programme of the Departments,* 7–8.

4. University of Chicago, *Annual Register, 1893–94,* 48; Madeleine Wallin to Alfred Wallin, 23 October 1892, Wallin Papers, UCL.

5. University of Chicago, *Annual Register, 1893–94,* 59.

6. On the professionalization of academic life, see Ross, "Development of the Social Sciences"; and Haskell, *Emergence of Professional Social Science.*

7. University of Chicago, *Annual Register, 1893–94,* 46, 48, 59; University of Chicago, *Programme of Courses in Political Economy,* 9.

8. J. Laurence Laughlin, "The Study of Political Economy in the United States," *Journal of Political Economy* 1 (1893): 1, 17; University of Chicago, *Programme of Courses in Political Economy,* 18; Albion Small, "The Era of Sociology," *American Journal of Sociology* 1 (July 1895): 15.

9. Laughlin, "Study of Political Economy," 2, 17; Small, "Era of Sociology," 3.

10. Laughlin, "Study of Political Economy," 14; Small, "Era of Sociology," 7; Laughlin, "Study of Political Economy," 2.

11. Small, "Era of Sociology," 3; Laughlin, "Study of Political Economy," 14.

12. Ross, "Development of the Social Sciences," 109, 113; Haskell, *Emergence of Professional Social Science.* William Leach analyzes the role of women in pre-professional social science in *True Love and Perfect Union: The Feminist Reform of Sex and Society* (N.Y.: Basic Books, 1980).

13. For a discussion of these issues, see Ross, "Development of the Social Sciences"; Haskell, *Emergence of Professional Social Science*; Robert L. Church, "Economists as Experts: The Rise of an Academic Profession in the United States, 1870–1920," in *The University in Society,* vol. 2, ed. Lawrence Stone, (Princeton, N.J.: Princeton Univ. Press, 1974); Furner, *Advocacy and Objectivity.*

14. Laughlin, "Study of Political Economy," 3, 2; Albion Small, "Scholarship and Social Agitation," *American Journal of Sociology* 1 (March 1896): 564, 567; Small, "Era of Sociology," 13, 15. See Kloppenberg, *Uncertain Victory,* for changing ideas about intellectuals and political action during the Progressive period.

15. Ross, "Development of the Social Sciences," 113–21.

16. Breckinridge, "Autobiography"; University of Chicago, Office of the University Registrar, official transcript of the scholastic work of Sophonisba Preston Breckinridge, number 3239 (hereafter referred to as Breckinridge—Official University Transcript).

17. Oscar Kraines, *The World and Ideas of Ernst Freund* (University, Ala.: Univ. of Alabama Press, 1974), 1–14; Barry D. Karl, *Charles E. Merriam and the Study of Politics* (Chicago: Univ. of Chicago Press, 1974), 44–45.

18. Kraines, *World and Ideas of Freund,* 2; *Dictionary of American Biography,* s.v. "Freund, Ernst," 323; Jurgen Herbst, *The German Historical School in American Scholarship* (Ithaca, N.Y.: Cornell Univ. Press, 1965), 6–7, 16–19, 111, 132; Albert Somit and Joseph Tanenhaus, *Development of Political Science* (Boston: Allyn and Bacon, 1967), 18–19, 28; Kraines, *World and Ideas of Freund,* 1.

19. *Dictionary of American Biography,* s.v. "Freund, Ernst" 323; Karl, *Charles Merriam,* 44; Kraines, *World and Ideas of Freund,* 8–14 and passim.

20. Ernst Freund, *The Police Power* (Chicago: Callaghan and Co., 1904); Breckinridge, "Autobiography."

21. Freund, *Police Power,* iii, 3, 5.

22. Ibid., iii, iv, 7, 8, 11. See Kraines, *World and Ideas of Freund,* for a more extensive discussion of Freund's views, especially pp. 15–63.

23. Freund, *Police Power*, 16–17, 296–99, 303, 312–31.

24. Breckinridge, "Autobiography"; Madeleine Wallin to Alfred Wallin, 23 October 1892, Wallin Papers, UCL; Breckinridge—Official University Transcript.

25. *Dictionary of American Biography*, s.v. "Veblen, Thorstein Bunde," 242; Joseph Dorfman, *Thorstein Veblen and His America* (New York: Viking Press, 1934), chap. 2, 38–43, 79–80.

26. Dorfman, *Thorstein Veblen*, chap. 6 and passim; University of Chicago, *Programme of Courses in Political Economy*; *Dictionary of American Biography*, s.v. "Veblen"; Thorstein Veblen, *Theory of the Leisure Class* (New York: Modern Library, 1934).

27. Breckinridge, "Autobiography"; Dorfman, *Thorstein Veblen*, 119, 248, 251. Herbert Hoover considered Adolph Miller to be the only exception to the rule of "mediocrities" serving on the Federal Reserve Board in the late 1920s. John Kenneth Galbraith, *The Great Crash* (Boston: Houghton Mifflin, 1972), 33.

28. Ross, "Development of the Social Sciences," 113; Church, "Economists as Experts," 581; Alfred Bornemann, *J. Laurence Laughlin* (Washington, D.C.: American Council on Public Affairs, 1940), 1–5 and passim.

29. Church, "Economists as Experts," 578; Bornemann, *J. Laurence Laughlin*, chap. 5; Ross, "Development of the Social Sciences," 109–13.

30. Richard Hofstadter, "Free Silver and the Mind of 'Coin' Harvey" in *The Paranoid Style in American Politics* (New York: Alfred A. Knopf, 1965), 243, 264, and passim.

31. Bornemann, *J. Laurence Laughlin*, 8, 40; Hofstadter, "Free Silver," 243–44, 264; Richard Hofstadter, ed., *Coin's Financial School* (Cambridge, Mass.: Harvard Univ. Press, 1963), 174–75; Hofstadter, "Free Silver," 243–44; Bornemann, *J. Laurence Laughlin*, 41.

32. Hofstadter, "Free Silver," 279–80, 286–88; Bornemann, *J. Laurence Laughlin*, 41–43; Lawrence Goodwyn, *The Populist Moment*, (New York: Oxford Univ. Press, 1978), 265–67.

33. Students' views quoted in Bornemann, *J. Laurence Laughlin*, 18, 20.

34. Margaret Farrand Thorp, *Smith Grants Radcliffe's First Ph.D.* (Northampton, Mass.: Smith College, April 1965); Bornemann, *J. Laurence Laughlin*, 23–24.

35. Breckinridge, "Autobiography"; Breckinridge—Official University Transcript.

36. Breckinridge, "Autobiography."

37. Ibid.; Breckinridge—Official University Transcript; Sophonisba P. Breckinridge to William C. P. Breckinridge, 10 December 1897, William C. P. Breckinridge Papers, Library of Congress (hereafter, W. C. P. Brekinridge Papers, LC).

38. Breckinridge, "Autobiography"; S. P. Breckinridge, *Legal Tender: A Study in English and American Monetary History*, The Decennial Publications of the University of Chicago, second series, vol. 7 (Chicago: Univ. of Chicago Press, 1903), xi, 1.

39. Hofstadter, "Free Silver," 238–40, 250–64; Walter T. K. Nugent, *Money and American Society, 1865–1880* (New York: The Free Press, 1968), esp. chaps. 2, 11, 22; Morton Keller, *Affairs of State* (Cambridge, Mass.: Harvard Univ. Press, 1977).

40. Breckinridge, *Legal Tender*, xi, 2.

41. Ibid., 9, 47, 87, 114–18, 119, 131; Nugent, *Money and American Society*, 9–10.

42. Breckinridge, *Legal Tender*, 155.

43. Ibid., 132.

44. Katharine Bement Davis, "Three Score Years and Ten," 60; University of Chi-

cago, Office of the University Registrar, official transcript of the scholastic work of Katharine Bement Davis, number 5406 (hereafter referred to as Davis—Official University Transcript).

45. Davis, "Three Score Years," 60; Davis—Official University Transcript.

46. Davis, "Three Score Years," 60; Dorfman, *Thorstein Veblen*, 252–54; Edith Abbott quoted in Costin, *Two Sisters*, 246, note 25.

47. Davis, "Three Score Years," 60; Dorfman, *Thorstein Veblen*, 295.

48. Davis, "Three Score Years," 60–61; Davis—Official University Transcript.

49. Dorfman, *Thorstein Veblen*, 96; Thorstein Veblen, "The Price of Wheat Since 1867," *Journal of Political Economy*, vol. 1 (December 1892), 68–103; Thorstein Veblen, "The Food Supply and the Price of Wheat," *Journal of Political Economy*, vol. 1 (June 1892), 365–79; Katharine Bement Davis, "Tables Relating to the Price of Wheat and Other Farm Products Since 1890," *Journal of Political Economy*, vol. 6, (June 1898), 404–10.

50. Dorfman, *Thorstein Veblen*, 96; Davis, "Price of Wheat,"407, 408.

51. Dorfman, *Thorstein Veblen*, 132, 133; Davis, "Three Score Years," 61; Davis—Official University Transcript; Robert E. L. Faris, *Chicago Sociology, 1920–1932* (San Francisco: Chandler Publishing, 1967), 12; Darnell Rucker, *The Chicago Pragmatists* (Minneapolis: Univ. of Minnesota Press, 1969), 133–34.

52. Ross, "Development of the Social Sciences," 113; Steven J. Diner, "Department and Discipline: The Department of Sociology at the University of Chicago, 1892–1920," *Minerva* vol. 13, no. 4 (Winter 1975); Ross, "Socialism and American Liberalism," 17–20; George Christakes, *Albion W. Small* (Boston: Twayne Pub., 1978), chap. 1; Faris, *Chicago Sociology*, chap. 1; Herbst, *German Historical School*, 154–59; Vernon K. Dibble, *The Legacy of Albion Small* (Chicago: Univ. of Chicago Press, 1975), 2–4.

53. *Dictionary of American Biography*, s.v. "Small, Albion Woodbury"; Dibble, *Legacy of Albion Small*, 2–4, chap. 5; Herbst, *German Historical School*, chap. 1 and passim.

54. Christakes, *Albion W. Small*, 17–18, 97–99; Ross, "Development of the Social Sciences," 113–16, 125–26.

55. Christakes, *Albion W. Small*, 17, 97–99; Herbst, *German Historical School*, 144–47, 156–58; Dibble, *Legacy of Albion Small*, 17–19; Ross, "Development of the Social Sciences," 114–15.

56. Rucker, *Chicago Pragmatists*, 134; Faris, *Chicago Sociology*, 13–14; Dorfman, *Thorstein Veblen*, 101, 126; Martin Bulmer, *The Chicago School of Sociology* (Chicago: Univ. of Chicago Press, 1984), 35–36.

57. University of Chicago, *Announcements*, 31:19, May 15, 1931, "Doctors of Philosophy, June 1893–April 1931," (Chicago: Univ. of Chicago Press); Gordon, "KBD"; Davis, "Three Score Years," 59; Katharine Bement Davis, "The Modern Condition of Agricultural Labor in Bohemia," *Journal of Political Economy*, vol. 8 (September 1900), 491–523.

58. Davis, "Agricultural Labor in Bohemia," 492–97.

59. Bulmer, *Chicago School of Sociology*, 45 and passim; Lewis A. Coser, *Masters of Sociological Thought* (New York: Harcourt Brace Jovanovich, 1971), 380–81.

60. Davis, "Agricultural Labor in Bohemia," 516–17.

61. Ibid., 511–19.

62. Ibid., 498, 503, 523; W. I. Thomas and Florian Znaniecki, *The Polish Peasant in Europe and America*, 5 vols. (Boston: Richard Badger, 1918–20).

63. Thomas and Znaniecki, *Polish Peasant;* Faris, *Chicago Sociology*, 14–15, 16–

17. Ross is quoted in John Higham, *Strangers in the Land* (New York: Athaeneum, 1955), 109. Thomas's progressive views of race evolved later in his career. In the 1890s, he was still emphasizing the importance of instincts.

64. Davis, "The Condition of the Negro," 248–49, 253, 260.

65. Ibid., 249–52, 258.

66. Ibid., 252–53.

67. Bulmer, *Chicago School of Sociology*, 35.

68. Frances A. Kellor, *Experimental Sociology* (New York: Macmillan, 1901), viii; University of Chicago, Office of the University Registrar, official transcript of the scholastic work of Frances Alice Kellor, Number 6991 (hereafter referred to as Kellor—Official University Transcript); Rosenberg, *Beyond Separate Spheres*, 58–59, 64, 68; Bulmer, *Chicago School of Sociology*, 40; Rucker, *Chicago Pragmatists*, 62–63. Kellor's intellectual debts are expressed in her preface to *Experimental Sociology*.

69. *Dictionary of American Biography*, s.v. "Henderson, Charles Richmond"; Ross, "Development of the Social Sciences," 113; Church, "Economists as Experts," 581; Faris, *Chicago Sociology*, 12–13; Kellor—Official University Transcript.

70. *Dictionary of American Biography*, s.v. "Henderson, Charles Richmond," 524.

71. Ibid.; Haskell, *Emergence of Professional Social Science*, v–vi and passim; Ross, "Development of the Social Sciences," 109–12; Charles Richmond Henderson, "Practical Sociology in the Service of Social Ethics," *Decennial Publications*, ed. Univ. of Chicago (Chicago: Univ. of Chicago Press, 1902).

72. Charles Richmond Henderson, *An Introduction to the Study of Dependent, Defective, and Delinquent Classes* (Boston: D.C. Heath, 1893), 13; Freedman, *Their Sisters' Keepers*, 112.

73. Henderson, *Dependent, Defective, and Delinquent Classes*, 111–12, 118–19; Freedman, *Their Sisters' Keepers*, 112–13.

74. Charles Henderson, "Introduction," in Kellor, *Experimental Sociology*.

75. Wooley, *Western Slope*, 85–86.

76. Kellor had already published a piece on women and athletics, "The Physiological Basis for Physical Culture," in *Education*, vol. 19 (1898), 100–104. Frances Alice Kellor, "Criminal Anthropology in Its Relation to Criminal Jurisprudence," Part I, *American Journal of Sociology*, vol. 4, no. 4 (January 1899); ibid., Part II, *American Journal of Sociology*, vol. 4, no. 5 (March 1899).

77. Kellor, "Criminal Anthropology," 516–18.

78. Ibid., 518–19.

79. Ibid., 515–16, 519, 522–24, 645.

80. Ibid., 630–31.

81. Ibid., 630–31, 635–36.

82. Ibid., 642–44.

83. Ibid., 642, 643, 644.

84. See David J. Rothman, *Conscience and Convenience* (Boston: Little, Brown, 1980); Freedman, *Their Sisters' Keepers*, 110–15.

85. Frances A. Kellor, "Psychological and Environmental Study of Women Criminals I," *American Journal of Sociology*, vol. 5, no. 4, (January 1900), 527. For a thorough discussion of Kellor's importance to the women's prison reform movement, see Freedman, *Their Sisters' Keepers*.

86. Kellor, "Psychological and Environmental Study, I," 528, 532; Freedman, *Their Sisters' Keepers*, 113.

87. Kellor, "Psychological and Environmental Study, I," 530, 531.

88. Ibid., 534, 538. Kellor did consider prostitutes to be constitutionally inferior

to other female offenders. Comparing the results of tests given to streetwalkers and women imprisoned for felonies, she concluded: "The prostitute mentally and physically is more defective than the criminal." Kellor, "Psychological and Environmental Study, I," 543.

89. Frances A. Kellor, "Psychological and Environmental Study of Women Criminals II," *American Journal of Sociology*, vol. 5, no. 5 (March 1900), 674, 676, 680, 681.

90. Ibid., 679.

91. Frances A. Kellor, "Criminal Sociology," *Arena* (January and March 1900); Frances A. Kellor, "My Experiments with the Kymograph," *Harper's Bazar*, vol. 33 (November 10, 1900), 1755–60; *Notable American Women*, s.v. "Kellor, Frances," 393.

92. *Notable American Women*, s.v. "Kellor, Frances," 393; Kellor, *Experimental Sociology*, viii.

93. Kellor, *Experimental Sociology*, viii–ix.

94. Ibid., 20–21, 23.

95. Ibid., 18, 34, 154.

96. Ibid., 109, 207–211, 212.

97. Ibid., 257, 280.

98. University of Chicago, Office of the University Registrar, official transcript of the scholastic work of Edith Abbott, number 14481 (hereafter referred to as Abbott—Official University Transcript); Church, "Economists as Experts,"595; Dorfman, *Thorstein Veblen*, 155; Ross, "Development of the Social Sciences," 126.

99. University of Chicago, "Doctors of Philosophy"; Abbott—Official University Transcript; Dorfman, *Thorstein Veblen*, 120.

100. Edith Abbott, "Wage Statistics in the Twelfth Census," *Journal of Political Economy*, vol. 12 (June 1904), 339–61.

101. Abbott, "Wage Statistics," 342, 343, 344; Robert H. Bremner, *From the Depths* (New York: New York Univ. Press, 1956), 216–19.

102. Abbott, "Wage Statistics," 345, 347.

103. Ibid., 352–53, 357–58. Abbott's views here reflect the influence of Laughlin. Mitchell's early work also supported Laughlin's opinion, especially regarding the detrimental economic effects of inflated currency. See Bornemann, *J. Laurence Laughlin*, 31.

104. Abbott, "Wage Statistics," 358, 359.

105. Edith Abbott, "The Wages of Unskilled Labor in the United States, 1850–1900," *Journal of Political Economy*, vol. 13 (June 1905), 321, 322; Edith Abbott, *The Wages of Unskilled Labor in the United States, 1850–1900* (1905; reprint, Chicago: Univ. of Chicago Press).

106. Abbott, "The Wages of Unskilled Labor," 322, 323.

107. Ibid., 323–25.

108. Ibid., 326, 339, 342, 359–60.

109. Ibid., 360, 369. See, for example, David Montgomery, *The Fall of the House of Labor* (New York: Cambridge Univ. Press, 1987), 69–70.

110. Abbott, "Wages of Unskilled Labor," 369; Abbott—Official University Transcript.

111. University of Chicago, "Doctors of Philosophy"; Faris, *Chicago Sociology*, 135–50.

112. Thorstein Veblen, "The Barbarian Status of Women," *American Journal of Sociology* vol. 4, no. 4 (January 1899), 503–14; Rosenberg, *Beyond Separate Spheres*,

120–31, and passim. Rosenberg points out that Chicago became the very center of the intellectual challenge to theories of sex differences, as women graduate students in psychology and related fields conducted ground-breaking research.

Chapter 4: "The Thing for Which You Are Well Fitted"

1. See University of Chicago, *Announcements*, vol. 31 (May 15, 1931), no. 19 "Doctors of Philosophy, June 1893–April 1931" (Chicago: Univ. of Chicago Press, 1931).

2. Harper is quoted in Thomas Woody, *History of Women's Education in the United States* (New York: Science Press, 1929), 328; Bureau of Education, Department of the Interior, *Biennial Survey of Education, 1916–1918*, vol. 3, (Washington, D.C.: U.S. Government Printing Office, 1921), 688–89.

3. Jo Freeman, "Women on the Social Science Faculties Since 1892," (speech delivered at Political Science Association, Winter 1969), Sophia Smith Collection, Smith College; Harry Pratt Judson to Madeleine Wallin, 22 May 1896, Wallin Papers, UCL.

4. See University of Chicago, *Announcement*; Freeman, "Women on the Social Science Faculties," 6.

5. Woody, *History of Women's Education*, 329, 330.

6. Rosenberg, *Beyond Separate Spheres*, 214; Emilie J. Hutchinson, *Women and the Ph.D.* (n.p.: North Carolina College for Women, 1929), 15–16, 56.

7. Hutchinson, *Women and the Ph.D.*, 52, 61.

8. Woody, *History of Women's Education*, 327, 329.

9. Woody, *History of Women's Education*, 160; Rossiter, *Women Scientists in America*, 17, 23.

10. Woody, *History of Women's Education*, 156; Eells, "Earned Doctorates for Women," 648.

11. Rossiter, *Women Scientists in America*, 35; Eells, "Earned Doctorates for Women," 648.

12. Davis, "Three Score Years and Ten," 61. Notable for their absence are any complaints about treatment by male students in reminiscences such as Sophonisba Breckinridge's, "Autobiography," S. P. Breckinridge Papers, UCL; Wallin Papers, UCL. Wesley Mitchell married a very "modern woman," as Joyce Antler makes plain in *Lucy Sprague Mitchell: The Making of a Modern Women* (New Haven: Yale Univ. Press, 1987).

13. Davis, "Three Score Years and Ten," 61.

14. Ibid.; R. H. Jesse to Marion Talbot, 19 February 1900, Talbot Papers, UCL; Jesse to Talbot, 18 April 1900, Talbot Papers, UCL.

15. R. H. Jesse to Marion Talbot, 18 April 1900, Talbot Papers, UCL; Jesse to Talbot, 21 April 1900, Talbot Papers, UCL.

16. Josephine Shaw Lowell to Marion Talbot, 7 March 1900, Talbot Papers, UCL; Rosenberg, *Beyond Separate Spheres*, 34; Freedman, *Their Sisters' Keepers*, 56–57.

17. Lowell to Talbot, 7 March 1900, Talbot Papers, UCL; *Notable American Women*, s.v. "Davis, Katharine Bement"; Freedman, *Their Sisters' Keepers*, 117; Rosenberg, *Beyond Separate Spheres*, 34.

18. Davis' comment that J. Laurence Laughlin "was suspicious of me ever afterward" when she told him her reasons for pursuing graduate studies suggests that she

did not have a traditional academic career in mind. See Davis, "Three Score Years and Ten," 60.

19. Freedman, *Their Sisters' Keepers*, esp. parts 1 and 2.

20. There is an extensive literature on the "Progressive Movement." Among the classics are Richard Hofstadter, *The Age of Reform*; George Mowry, *The Era of Theodore Roosevelt*; Samuel Hays, *The Response to Industrialism*; and Robert Wiebe, *The Search for Order*.

21. The most active period of reform involvement for the Chicago professors did not commence until early in the twentieth century, when most of the women discussed herein had completed their studies. For more on their activities see Diner, "Department and Discipline." Diner, *A City and Its Universities*, 31, 69; Christakes, *Albion W. Small*, 108; Stanley Buder, *Pullman* (New York: Oxford Univ. Press, 1967), 176; Diner, "Department and Discipline," 524; Diner, *A City and Its Universities*, 124. See this last for a thorough and illuminating discussion of Chicago professors and reform.

22. University of Chicago, *Programme of the Departments of Political Economy, Sociology and Anthropology, 1899–1900*, 4, 14. For research by Chicago students that included a strong reform component, see, especially, Annie Marion MacLean, "Factory Legislation for Women in the United States," *American Journal of Sociology* 3 (September 1897); Annie Marion MacLean, "Two Weeks in Department Stores," *American Journal of Sociology* 4 (May 1899); Nellie Mason Auten, "Some Phases of the Sweating System in the Garment Trades of Chicago," *American Journal of Sociology* 6 (March 1901).

23. It seems clear that Bemis was drummed out of the university. The Bemis case is discussed in Furner, *Advocacy and Objectivity*; and Church, "Economists as Experts."

24. Helen R. Wright, "Three Against Time," *Social Service Review*, vol. 28 (1954), 42.

25. Jane Addams is the best source for a description of Hull House. See Addams, *Twenty Years at Hull House*. Also profitable in understanding her settlement activities are Allen F. Davis, *American Heroine: The Life and Legend of Jane Addams* (New York: Oxford Univ. Press, 1973); Davis, *Spearheads for Reform*;, and Lasch, *New Radicalism in America*.

26. Madeleine Wallin to her mother, 12 December 1892, Wallin Papers, UCL; Madeleine Wallin to her mother, 15 January 1893, Wallin Papers, UCL.

27. Madeleine Wallin to her mother, 15 January 1893, Wallin Papers, UCL.

28. William Joseph Maxwell, "Frances Kellor in the Progressive Era," (Ph.D. diss., Teacher's College, Columbia Univ., 1968), 136.

29. Information on fellowship awards is available in the University of Chicago's *Annual Registers* for various years cited. For the sociology department, see chart in Marion Talbot, "The Women of the University," *The President's Report, 1897–1898*, 123. Kellor articles appear in the *American Journal of Sociology*, volumes 4 (1899–1900) and 5 (1900). Maxwell, "Frances Kellor," 114; Kellor—Official University Transcript.

30. Mary Dreier to Phyllis Holbrook, 16 December 1961, Holbrook Collection.

31. *Notable American Women*, s.v. "Kellor, Frances"; *Dictionary of American Biography*, s.v. "Kellor, Frances (Alice)."

32. J. Laurence Laughlin to Sophonisba P. Breckinridge, 25 May 1901, S. P. Breckinridge Papers, LC.

33. Abbott, "Sophonisba Preston Breckinridge," 418–19, 420; Charles E. Merriam,

"A Member of the University Community," *Social Service Review*, vol. 22, no. 4 (December 1948), 424, 426.

34. Breckinridge, "Autobiography"; University of Chicago, *Announcements.*

35. Breckinridge, "Autobiography"; Marion Talbot to William Rainey Harper, 1 December 1900, President's Papers, 1889–1925, University of Chicago Library (hereafter, President's Papers, UCL); William Rainey Harper to Marion Talbot, 16 February 1901, President's Papers, 1889–1925, UCL.

36. Breckinridge, "Autobiography"; Breckinridge—Official University Transcript; Ernst Freund to Sophonisba Breckinridge, various postcards, S. P. Breckinridge Papers, 740, Folder 8, LC.

37. Breckinridge, "Autobiography"; Abbott, "Sophonisba Preston Breckinridge," 418; Breckinridge—Official University Transcript. Abbott points out that Breckinridge had already been admitted to Coif before her second "honorary membership" was conferred.

38. Talbot to Harper, 23 January 1902, President's Papers, 1889–1925, UCL.

39. Harper to Talbot, 28 January 1902, President's Papers, 1889–1925, UCL.

40. Talbot to Harper, 16 November 1903, President's Papers, 1889–1925, UCL.

41. "The Department of Household Administration," *The President's Report, 1904–1905*, 118; Marion Talbot to William Rainey Harper, 19 April 1901, President's Papers, 1889–1925, UCL; Harper to Talbot, 17 January 1902, President's Papers, 1889–1925, UCL; Talbot to Harper, 23 January 1902, President's Papers, 1889–1925, UCL.

42. Marion Talbot to William Rainey Harper, 19 April 1901, President's Papers, 1889–1925, UCL; Ellen Clements, "The University's First and Only Civil War," *The Chicago Maroon*, 11 January 1977, p. 6; Gordon, "Women on Campus," 215–25; Rosenberg, *Beyond Separate Spheres*, 43–53; Talbot to ?Clough, 18 December 1919, Talbot Papers, UCL.

43. Talbot to Harper, 23 January 1902, President's Papers, 1889–1925, UCL.

44. "The Department of Household Administration," *The President's Report, 1904–1905*, 118.

45. Ibid.

46. William Rainey Harper to Marion Talbot, 28 March 1904, Talbot Papers, UCL.

47. Ibid.; Harper to Talbot, 23 April 1904, Talbot Papers, UCL.

48. Talbot, "The Department of Household Administration," *The President's Report, 1905–1906*, 118.

49. Breckinridge, "Autobiography."

50. Chicago Committee of the Association of Collegiate Alumnae, *Public and Social Service as Vocations for College Women* (Chicago: A.C.A., June 1904), 1, 8; Talbot, "Women of the University," *The President's Report, 1905–1906*, 52.

51. J. Laurence Laughlin to Edith Abbott, 13 June 1905, Edith and Grace Abbott Papers, University of Chicago Library, Chicago, Illinois (hereafter, Abbott Papers, UCL); Abbott—Official University Transcript; *Notable American Women*, s.v. "Abbott, Edith."

52. J. Laurence Laughlin, "Report of the Department of Political Economy," *President's Report, 1904–1905*, 115; J. Laurence Laughlin to Edith Abbott, 13 June 1905, Abbott Papers, UCL; Costin, *Two Sisters*, 28.

53. Costin, *Two Sisters*, 28–29; Wright, "Three Against Time," 43; Carroll D. Wright to Sophonisba P. Breckinridge, 20 August 1905, S. P. Breckinridge Papers, LC.

54. Quoted in Costin, *Two Sisters*, 29.

55. Costin, *Two Sisters*, 29; J. Laurence Laughlin to Edith Abbott, 9 January 1906, Abbott Papers, UCL.

56. Costin, *Two Sisters*, 31; J. Laurence Laughlin to Edith Abbott, 7 April 1906, Abbott Papers, UCL.

57. Costin, *Two Sisters*, 31–34. For an excellent discussion of Webb's political and philosophical stance, see Kloppenberg, *Uncertain Victory*, esp. chap. 7.

58. Costin, *Two Sisters*, 34–35, 37; Edith Abbott, "Woman Suffrage Militant," *Independent* 61 (November 29, 1906), 1276–78.

59. Edith Abbott to Othman Abbott, 6 June 1907, Abbott Papers, addenda, UCL; Edith Abbott to family, various undated postcards, circa spring 1907, Abbott Papers, addenda, UCL; Costin, *Two Sisters*, 32–36.

60. Costin, *Two Sisters*, 37.

61. J. Laurence Laughlin to Edith Abbott, 19 April 1907, Abbott Papers, UCL; Carroll D. Wright to Edith Abbott, 16 September 1907, Abbott Papers, UCL.

62. Quoted in Costin, *Two Sisters*, 39. For a fascinating discussion of the atmosphere at Wellesley, see Palmieri, "In Adamless Eden."

63. Edith Abbott to Marion Talbot, 15 October 1907, Talbot Papers, UCL.

64. Ibid.

65. Sophonisba Breckinridge to Edith Abbott, 15 July 1907, S. P. Breckinridge Papers, LC; Steven J. Diner, "Scholarship in Quest of Social Welfare: A Fifty-Year History of the Social Service Review," *Social Service Review* vol. 51 (March 1977), 5–6; *Notable American Women*, s.v. "Abbott, Edith."

66. Breckinridge to Abbott, 13 April 1908, S. P. Breckinridge Papers, LC; Wright, "Three Against Time," 44; Breckinridge to Abbott, 6 May 1908, S. P. Breckinridge Papers, LC.

67. *Chicago News*, September/October, 1946, clipping located in Class of 1888 materials, Wellesley College Archives, Wellesley College.

Chapter 5: "A Most Scientific Institution"

1. *Prison Progress*, 69th Annual Report of the Prison Association of New York, 1913, p. 208; Rothman, *Conscience and Convenience;* Nicole Hahn Rafter, *Partial Justice: Women in State Prisons, 1800–1935* (Boston: Northeastern Univ. Press, 1985), 60.

2. "Investigation into the Charges Made Against the New York State Reformatory for Women at Bedford Hills, N.Y.," New York State Board of Charities, *Annual Report*, 1915, vol. 1, pp. 31–34, 847–74.

3. Rafter, *Partial Justice*, 23–24, 28–29; Freedman, *Their Sisters' Keepers*, 49; Blake McKelvey, *American Prisons* (Chicago: Univ. of Chicago Press, 1936), 65–68; Freedman, *Their Sisters Keepers*, 46.

4. Freedman, *Their Sisters' Keepers*, 31, 131–32; New York Commission of Prisons, *Seventh Annual Report*, 1901, 102; New York State Commission of Prisons, *Ninth Annual Report*, 1903, 87; Isabel C. Barrows, "Reformatory Treatment of Women in the United States," in *Penal and Reformatory Institutions*, ed. Charles Richmond Henderson (New York: Charities Publication Committee, 1910), 157.

5. New York State Commission of Prisons, *Ninth Annual Report*, 1903, 87; Katharine Bement Davis, "Introduction," in Jean Weidensall, *The Mentality of Criminal Women* (Baltimore: Warwick and York, 1916), ix; New York State Board of Charities,

Annual Report, 1915, 850; Eugenia C. Lekkerkerker, *Reformatories for Women in the United States* (The Hague: J. B. Wolters, 1931), 102; Rafter, *Partial Justice*, 36, 38.

6. McKelvey, *American Prisons*, 214; New York State Commission of Prisons, *Ninth Annual Report*, 1903, 87.

7. Freedman, *Their Sisters' Keepers*, 132, 133; Rafter, *Partial Justice*, 65–66. Eventually women convicted of felonies were taken to Bedford Hills. See *Proceedings of the American Prison Association*, Annual Congress, 1913, 285. Lekkerkerker, *Reformatories for Women*, 105; Barrows, "Reformatory Treatment," 156.

8. Lekkerkerker, *Reformatories for Women*, 105; New York State Commission of Prisons, *Ninth Annual Report*, 1903, p. 88.

9. Lekkerkerker, *Reformatories for Women*, 105; Katharine Bement Davis, "The Fresh Air Treatment for Moral Disease," *Proceedings of the Annual Congress of the National Prison Association of the U.S., 1905,* 209–11; Barrows, "Reformatory Treatment," 157; New York State Commission of Prisons, *Eleventh Annual Report*, 1905, p. 55.

10. Barrows, "Reformatory Treatment," 156, 159; Freedman, *Their Sisters' Keepers*, 132–33; Lekkerkerker, *Reformatories for Women*, 482, 492–93.

11. Davis, "Fresh Air Treatment," 205–6.

12. Ibid., 206–7.

13. Ibid., 208–12.

14. Ibid., 205, 210–212.

15. Ibid., 205; Davis, "Moral Imbeciles," *Proceedings of the Annual Congress of the National Prison Association of the U.S., 1906,* p. 345.

16. Freedman, *Their Sisters' Keepers*, 116, 120; Katharine Bement Davis, "The Reformatory Method," *Proceedings of the National Conference of Charities and Corrections*, 1916, 27–28.

17. Davis, "Reformatory Method," 27–28.

18. Higham, *Strangers in the Land*, 150–53, 313–15; Donald K. Pickens, *Eugenics and the Progressives* (Nashville, Tenn.: Vanderbilt Univ. Press, 1968), 195–96, and passim.

19. Davis, "Moral Imbeciles," 346.

20. Ibid.; Freedman, *Their Sisters' Keepers*, 139; Rafter, *Partial Justice*, 152–53.

21. Davis, "Moral Imbeciles," 346.

22. Ibid., 346–47.

23. Ibid., 347; Freedman, *Their Sisters' Keepers*, 116, 120; Davis, "Reformatory Method," 27–28.

24. Davis, "Moral Imbeciles," 347, 349, 350.

25. New York State Commission of Prisons, *Eleventh Annual Report*, 1905, 55; Rafter, *Partial Justice*, 66; Freedman, *Their Sisters' Keepers*, 138–42.

26. Davis, "Reformatory Method," 27. See Rothman, *Conscience and Convenience*, for more on the Progressive approach.

27. Davis, "Reformatory Method," 27; Katharine Bement Davis, "Outdoor Work for Women Prisoners," *Proceedings of the National Conference of Charities and Corrections*, 1909, p. 10; Davis, "Fresh Air Treatment," 205; Rafter, *Partial Justice*, 60.

28. See, for example, Davis, "Reformatory Method," 30, 37.

29. New York State Commission of Prisons, *Fourteenth Annual Report*, 1908, 106; Freedman, *Their Sisters' Keepers*, 138; New York State Commission of Prisons, *Fifteenth Annual Report*, 1909, 88.

30. Weidensall, *Mentality of Criminal Women*, x; Freedman, *Their Sisters' Keepers*, 138; Lekkerkerker, *Reformatories for Women*, 106.

31. New York State Commission of Prisons, *Fifteenth Annual Report*, 1909, p. 88; Lekkerkerker, *Reformatories for Women*, 106. See statistics on Albion in New York State Commission of Prisons, *Fifteenth Annual Report*, 87–88; New York State Commission of Prisons, *Thirteenth Annual Report*, 1907, p. 12; Freedman, *Their Sisters' Keepers*, 138. By 1905, a third institution, the House of Refuge for Women at Hudson, was turned into a state training school for girls between the ages of 12 and 15. See New York State Commission of Prisons, *Fifteenth Annual Report*, 87; *Eleventh Annual Report*, 53.

32. Weidensall, *Mentality of Criminal Women*, ix–x.

33. Ibid., xi.

34. Ibid.

35. Katharine Bement Davis, "A Plan of Rational Treatment for Women Offenders," *Journal of Criminal Law and Criminology*, 4:3 (1913–14), 405.

36. Weidensall, *Mentality of Criminal Women*, x, 68; Lekkerkerker, *Reformatories for Women*, 106; Freedman, *Their Sisters' Keepers*, 117; Rafter, *Partial Justice*, 69; Katharine Bement Davis, "Feeble Minded Women in Reformatory Institutions," *The Survey* 27 (March 1912), 1850; Katharine Bement Davis to John D. Rockefeller, Jr., 13 September 1911, box 6, Office of the Messrs. Rockefeller, Rockefeller Boards, Rockefeller Archive Center, North Tarrytown, New York, (hereafter abbreviated OMR, Brds.)

37. Weidensall, *Mentality of Criminal Women*, x; Freedman, *Their Sisters' Keepers*, 118. See Rosenberg, *Beyond Separate Spheres*, for a discussion of women social scientists who pioneered in the study of sex differences.

38. Freedman, *Their Sisters' Keepers*, 118; Rosenberg, *Beyond Separate Spheres*, 109; Ellen Ryerson, *The Best Laid Plans* (New York: Hill and Wang, 1978), 83; Rothman, *Conscience and Convenience*, 54–55.

39. Weidensall, *Mentality of Criminal Women*, 1, 3.

40. Davis, "Feeble Minded Women," 1851; Weidensall, *Mentality of Criminal Women*, 4–5.

41. Lekkerkerker, *Reformatories for Women*, 107; John D. Rockefeller, Jr., "The Origin, Work and Plans of the Bureau of Social Hygiene," press release, 1913, January 27, box 2, Bureau of Social Hygiene Collection, Rockefeller Archive Center; Mark Connelly, *The Response to Prostitution in the Progressive Era* (Chapel Hill: Univ. of North Carolina Press, 1980), 16; John D. Rockefeller, Jr., "Introduction," in George J. Kneeland, *Commercialized Prostitution in New York City* (New York: The Century Co., 1913), vii.

42. Rockefeller, "Origin, Work and Plans"; John D. Rockefeller, Jr., to Paul Warburg, 24 November 1911, box 6, OMR, Brds.; Katharine B. Davis to John D. Rockefeller, Jr., 13 September 1911, box 6, OMR, Brds.

43. Katharine B. Davis to John D. Rockefeller, Jr., 13 September 1911, box 6, OMR, Brds.

44. Raymond B. Fosdick, *The Story of the Rockefeller Foundation* (New York: Harper and Brothers, 1952), 11, 14–20.

45. Fosdick, *Story of the Rockefeller Foundation*, 192. The Laura Spelman Rockefeller Memorial began in 1923 to enlarge the Foundation's support of social science research. See Fosdick, p. 194; and Martin Bulmer, "Support for Sociology in the 1920s: The Laura Spelman Rockefeller Memorial and the Beginnings of Modern,

Large-Scale Sociological Research in the University," *American Sociologist* 17 (November 1982), 185–92.

46. John D. Rockefeller, Jr., to Katharine B. Davis, 17 October 1911, Starr Murphy to John D. Rockefeller, Jr., 18 October 1911, both box 6, OMR, Brds.

47. Katharine B. Davis to John D. Rockefeller, Jr., 9 November 1911, box 6, OMR, Brds.; Davis, "Plan of Rational Treatment," 405–6; James Bronson Reynolds to John D. Rockefeller, Jr., 9 November 1911, box 6, OMR, Brds.

48. John D. Rockefeller, Jr., to Katharine B. Davis, 13 November 1911, Katharine B. Davis to John D. Rockefeller, Jr., 15 November 1911, Katharine B. Davis to John D. Rockefeller, Jr., 9 November 1911, all box 6, OMR, Brds.

49. Katharine B. Davis to John D. Rockefeller, Jr., 15 November 1911, box 6, OMR, Brds.

50. John D. Rockefeller, Jr., to Paul Warburg, 24 November 1911, box 6, OMR, Brds.

51. Ibid. Rockefeller's perspective on prostitution was typical of that of many in the Progressive generation. See Ruth Rosen, *The Lost Sisterhood* (Baltimore: Johns Hopkins Univ. Press, 1982), 23 and passim.

52. John D. Rockefeller, Jr., to Katharine B. Davis, 29 December 1911, John D. Rockefeller, Jr., to Nicholas Murray Butler, 27 January 1912; Katharine B. Davis to John D. Rockefeller, Jr., 26 January 1912, all box 6, OMR, Brds.

53. John D. Rockefeller, Jr., to Nicholas Murray Butler, 29 December 1912, box 6, OMR, Brds.; "Meeting of April 3, 1912," 5, Minutes of the Bureau of Social Hygiene 1912, box 2, Bureau of Social Hygiene Collection, Rockefeller Archive Center, North Tarrytown, N.Y.

54. John D. Rockefeller, Jr., to Katharine B. Davis, 29 December 1911, Katharine B. Davis to John D. Rockefeller, Jr., 13 January 1912, Katharine B. Davis to John D. Rockefeller, Jr., 26 January 1912, all box 6, OMR, Brds.; Rosenberg, *Beyond Separate Spheres*, 115–17, 139–46; John D. Rockefeller, Jr., to Katharine B. Davis, 27 January 1912, Katharine B. Davis to John D. Rockefeller, Jr., 7 February 1912, both box 6, OMR, Brds.

55. Katharine B. Davis to John D. Rockefeller, Jr., 30 January 1912, box 6, OMR, Brds. On the Woman's Prison Association, see Freedman, *Their Sisters' Keepers*, 33–35, 53–57.

56. Katharine B. Davis to John D. Rockefeller, Jr., 30 January 1912, box 6, OMR, Brds. Davis especially objected to the W.P.A.'s "fight against Clause 79 of the Page Bill" and to their support for the then-unopened Women's Farm Colony, which was to be under the supervision of the State Prison Commission rather than a Board of Managers. The State Farm and the Woman's Prison Association are discussed in Rafter, *Partial Justice*, 93–96.

57. Bureau of Social Hygiene, "Meeting of April 3, 1912."

58. Ibid; Weidensall, *Mentality of Criminal Women*, xii.

59. John D. Rockefeller, Jr., to Katharine B. Davis, 2 May 1912, box 6, OMR, Brds.

60. Ibid.; John D. Rockefeller, Jr., to Paul M. Warburg, 3 May 1912, box 7, OMR, Brds.

61. Kneeland, *Commercialized Prostitution*, x, 163; Katharine B. Davis to John D. Rockefeller, Jr., 7 February 1912, box 6, OMR, Brds. Robinson is quoted in Rosenberg, *Beyond Separate Spheres*, 117.

62. Rosen, *Lost Sisterhood*, 15; Connelly, *Response to Prostitution*, 16; Kneeland, *Commercialized Prostitution*, 51.

63. Kneeland, *Commercialized Prostitution*, 182.

64. Ibid., 164, 168, 170–173, 175, 177, 178.

65. Ibid., 173.

66. Ibid., 186–90.

67. Charles O. Heydt, "Memorandum Regarding Bedford Hills Property," January 6, 1926, Box 6, OMR, Brds.; Prison Association of New York, *Seventieth Annual Report*, 1914, p. 241; Lekkerkerker, *Reformatories for Women*, 107.

68. Heydt, "Memorandum"; Lekkerkerker, *Reformatories for Women*, 107; James Angell to John D. Rockefeller, Jr., 6 January 1914, box 6, OMR, Brds.

69. Lekkerkerker, *Reformatories for Women*, 107–8; Weidensall, *Mentality of Criminal Women*, 19; Prison Association of New York, *Seventieth Annual Report*, 1914, p. 241.

70. Weidensall, *Mentality of Criminal Women*, 6–8, 20, 21; "Recommendations of the Laboratory of Social Hygiene for the Disposition of First One Hundred Cases Studied," 1914, box 6, OMR, Brds.; Rosenberg, *Beyond Separate Spheres*, 68–81 and passim.

71. Jean Large, "A Man's Job," *University of Chicago Magazine* 27 (January 1934), 105; John D. Rockefeller, Jr., to Katharine B. Davis, 2 April 1927, OMR, Brds.; Obituary of Katharine B. Davis, *New York Herald Tribune*, 11 December 1935.

72. *Notable American Women*, s.v. "Davis, Katharine Bement"; Eleanor Flexner, *Century of Struggle* (Cambridge, Mass.: Harvard Univ. Press, 1977), 266–68.

73. *Dictionary of American Biography*, s.v. "Davis, Katharine Bement"; Large, "A Man's Job," 105.

74. Large, "A Man's Job," 106; *Notable American Women*, s.v. "Davis, Katharine Bement."

75. Large, "A Man's Job," 106; *Notable American Women*, s.v. "Davis, Katharine Bement"; Lynn D. Gordon, "Katharine Bement Davis," in *Biographical Dictionary of Social Welfare in America*, ed. Walter Trattner (Westport, Conn.: Greenwood Press, 1986).

76. Large, "A Man's Job," 105.

77. Ibid., 106.

78. *Dictionary of American Biography*, s.v. "Davis, Katharine Bement"; *Notable American Women*, s.v. "Davis, Katharine Bement"; Clifford M. Young, *Women's Prisons Past and Present* (New York: Summary Press, 1932), 21–22; "Pennsylvania Penal Commission's Report," *Journal of Criminal Law and Criminology* 6 (1915–16), 50–51.

79. *Notable American Women*, s.v. "Davis, Katharine Bement"; Freedman, *Their Sisters' Keepers*, 170–71; Lekkerkerker, *Reformatories for Women*, 126–28; Davis, "Three Score Years and Ten," 60; Mary Belle Harris, *I Knew Them in Prison* (New York: Viking Press, 1936).

80. Large, "A Man's Job," 107–8; Gordon, "Katharine Bement Davis."

81. Large, "A Man's Job," 107–8; *Dictionary of American Biography*, s.v. "Davis, Katharine Bement"; *Notable American Women*, s.v. "Davis, Katharine Bement"; obituary of Davis in *New York Herald Tribune*, 11 December, 1935.

82. "Minutes of the Bureau of Social Hygiene, 1919," series 1, box 3, folio 31, Bureau of Social Hygiene Collection, Rockefeller Archive Center.

83. *Notable American Women*, s.v. "Davis, Katharine Bement"; *Dictionary of American Biography*, s.v. "Davis, Katharine Bement."

84. Katharine Bement Davis, "Report of Committee on Probation and Parole," *Proceedings of the Annual Congress of the American Prison Association*, 1915.

85. Ibid., 389–91.

86. Ibid., 394–97 and passim.

87. *Dictionary of American Biography*, s.v. "Davis, Katharine Bement"; *Notable American Women*, s.v. "Davis, Katharine Bement"; Gordon, "Katharine Bement Davis"; Davis, "Probation and Parole," 393; Davis obituary, *New York Herald Tribune*, 11 December 1935.

88. On Davis's suffrage activities, see various articles in the *New York Times*, including 9 April, 1914, p. 11; 17 April, 1914, p. 6; 3 May, 1914, p. 12; and Ida Husted Harper, ed., *The History of Woman Suffrage* 5 (New York: J. J. Little and Ives, 1922), 195, 227. On Davis and the Progressive cause, see Frances Kellor to Theodore Roosevelt, 13 October 19[14?], Theodore Roosevelt Papers, Library of Congress (hereafter, T. Roosevelt Papers, LC). On her participation in the Hughes campaign, see *New York Times*, 12 September, 1916, p. 12; *New York Times*, 10 October, 1916, p. 11; Katharine B. Davis to Abraham Flexner, 6 November 1916, Bureau of Social Hygiene Collection, series 3, box 9, Rockefeller Archive Center; *Notable American Women*, s.v. "Davis, Katharine Bement."

89. New York State Commission of Prisons, *Eighteenth Annual Report*, 1912, 170–71.

90. New York State Board of Charities, *Forty-ninth Annual Report*, 1913, 851.

91. Ibid., 851–53.

92. Ibid., 853–57; Prison Association of New York, *Seventeenth Annual Report*, 1914, 242–43.

93. New York State Commission of Prisons, *Twentieth Annual Report*, 1914, pp. 116–19.

94. James Angell to Starr Murphy, 3 December 1915, box 6, OMR, Brds.

95. New York State Board of Charities, *Forty-ninth Annual Report*, 849, 857, 871–74.

96. New York State Commission of Prisons, *Twentieth Annual Report*, 1914, p. 118; New York State Board of Charities, *Forty-ninth Annual Report*, 874.

97. Katharine B. Davis to John D. Rockefeller, Jr., 13 January 1915, box 6, OMR, Brds. Additional money for salaries to hire nurses and a housekeeper would have added another $2,200 a year to the hospital's budget. The new building was to be part of the property offered to the state when the laboratory's lease expired at the end of five years.

98. Ibid.

99. See various papers of John D. Rockefeller, Jr., box 6, OMR, Brds., for 1915–1917; Freedman, *Their Sisters' Keepers*, 119; Lekkerkerker, *Reformatories for Women*, 108.

100. Rafter, *Partial Justice*, 72–74; Weidensall, *Mentality of Criminal Women*, xiii–xiv.

101. James Angell to Starr Murphy, 31 December 1915, OMR, Brds.

102. Angell to Murphy, 31 December 1915. See also Mabel Fernald to John D. Rockefeller, Jr., 18 February 1916, box 6, OMR, Brds.

103. "Notes on a Conference . . . Held at the Offices of the Rockefeller Foundation on the Proposed Expansion of the Work of the Bureau of Social Hygiene, Dec. 7, 1915," box 2, folio 18, Bureau of Social Hygiene Collection, Rockefeller Archive Center.

104. Waldemar Nielsen, *The Big Foundations* (New York: Columbia Univ. Press, 1972), 53–54; James R. Green, *The World of the Worker* (New York: Hill and Wang, 1980), 89; Fosdick, *Story of the Rockefeller Foundation*, 26–28.

105. "Notes on a Conference."

106. Ibid., 9–10.

107. "Memoranda on the Proposed Expansion of the Work of the Bureau of Social Hygiene," box 6, OMR, Brds.

108. "Memoranda on the Proposed Expansion"; L. B. Dunham to Raymond Fosdick, 24 November 1930, series 1, box 2, folio 15, Bureau of Social Hygiene Collection.

109. "Plan for the Conversion of the Laboratory of Social Hygiene," 1916; Starr Murphy memorandum on meeting with Katharine B. Davis and Mabel Fernald, 4 April 1916, box 6, OMR, Brds.

110. Murphy, "Memorandum."

111. Katharine B. Davis to John D. Rockefeller, Jr., 6 December 1916, John D. Rockefeller, Jr., to Governor Charles L. Whitman, 27 December 1916, and Senate Bill no. 571, 15 February 1917, "An Act to Amend the State Charities Law," all box 6, OMR, Brds.; "Minutes of the Bureau of Social Hygiene, 1917," series 1, box 3, folio 29, Bureau of Social Hygiene Collection, Rockefeller Archive Center.

112. "Minutes of the Bureau, 1917," 4.

113. Ibid., 2; John D. Rockefeller, Jr., to John S. Kennedy, 6 December 1919, box 6, OMR, Brds.; Lekkerkerker, *Reformatories for Women*, 108.

114. John S. Kennedy to John D. Rockefeller, Jr., 24 November 1919, box 6, OMR, Brds.; Lekkerkerker, *Reformatories for Women*, 109–11; Freedman, *Their Sisters' Keepers*, 141–42; *New York Herald Tribune* clipping, 14 December 1919, Katharine B. Davis to John D. Rockefeller, Jr., 3 December 1919; John D. Rockefeller, Jr., to John S. Kennedy, 6 December 1919, box 6, OMR, Brds.

115. Lekkerkerker, *Reformatories for Women*, 110–11; Katharine B. Davis to Starr Murphy, 26 May 1920, John D. Rockefeller, Jr., to Starr Murphy, 27 May 1920, Charles O. Heydt, "Memorandum Regarding Bedford Hills Property," 8 January 1926, all box 6, OMR, Brds.; Freedman, *Their Sisters' Keepers*, 141.

Chapter 6: "If Sex Could Be Eliminated"

1. Frances A. Kellor, *Out of Work* (New York: G. P. Putnam's Sons, 1904), pp. v–vi; Maxwell, "Frances Kellor in the Progressive Era," 1, 136–37; *Notable American Women*, s.v. "Kellor, Frances"; *Dictionary of American Biography*, s.v. "Kellor, Frances (Alice)"; Mary E. Dreier, *Margaret Dreier Robins: Her Life, Letters, and Work* (New York: Island Press Cooperative, 1950), 18; Kellor—Official University Transcript.

2. Dreier, *Margaret Dreier Robins*, 18; William R. Stewart, *The Philanthropic Work of Josephine Shaw Lowell* (New York: The Macmillan Co., 1911), 416–18; Kellor, *Out of Work*, v–vi.

3. Daniel T. Rodgers, *The Work Ethic in Industrial America* (Chicago: Univ. of Chicago Press, 1978); Bremner, *From the Depths*, 161; John A. Garraty, *Unemployment in History* (New York: Harper and Row, 1978), 114; Alexander Keyssar, *Out of Work: The First Century of Unemployment in Massachusetts* (Cambridge, U.K.: Cambridge Univ. Press, 1986). Garraty cites William Leiserson's (1911) and William Beveridge's (1909) studies of unemployment as groundbreaking, but Kellor's study preceded, and in some respects anticipated, them.

4. Kellor, *Out of Work*, v–vi, 1–16.

5. Ibid., 17–23, 29, 30, 32, 35.

6. Ibid., chap. 3, pp. 80–83, 91, 103, 157. For examples of Kellor's bigotry and racism, see pp. 37–38, 97.

7. Ibid., chap. 3, pp. vii, 80–83, 179–80, 184–96, 204–10.

8. Ibid., 105, 132–34, 215, 216, 222.

9. Ibid., 105, 132–34; 138, 139–44.

10. Ibid., 138, 139–44, 146–47, 148, 151, 155–56, 210–11.

11. Ibid., 152–54.

12. Ibid., 165, 166–67, 170; "To the Women Voters of the United States from the Women in Political Bondage," political handout, Progressive Party Papers, Houghton Library, Harvard University, Cambridge, Mass. (hereafter, Progressive Party Papers, HL).

13. Kellor, Out of Work, 47, 251.

14. Ibid., 256, 281. The idea of "labor exchanges" was also promoted by Beatrice Webb in England: see Kloppenberg, Uncertain Victory, 273–75.

15. Dreier, Margaret Dreier Robins, 18–20; Kellor, Out of Work, 267–77.

16. Dreier, Margaret Dreier Robins, 18–30; Kellor, Out of Work, 275–76.

17. Kellor, Out of Work, 165–67, 277; Maxwell, "Frances Kellor in the Progressive Era," 140–42, 144.

18. Frances A. Kellor to Mary E. Dreier, 10 October 1904, Mary E. Dreier Papers, Schlesinger Library, Radcliffe College, Cambridge, Mass.; Mary E. Dreier to Phyllis Holbrook, 23 November 1960, Holbrook Collection. The rich emotional ties between Kellor and Dreier are apparent in the Mary E. Dreier Papers (hereafter, Mary E. Dreier Papers, RC). For an assessment of the Dreier-Kellor relationship, see Nancy Costello, "The Personal Relationship of Frances Kellor and Mary Dreier" (Graduate research paper, Harvard University, 1985).

19. Dreier, Margaret Dreier Robins, 20; Kellor, Out of Work, 165; Maxwell, "Frances Kellor," 143–45.

20. William S. Bennet to American Arbitration Association, 7 January 1952, Mary E. Dreier Papers, box 6, folder 84, RC; Theodore Roosevelt to Frances Kellor, 4 July 1906, T. Roosevelt Papers, vol. 65, p. 149, LC.

21. Maxwell, "Frances Kellor," 156; Connelly, Response to Prostitution, 13; "Portrait," The Survey 25 (1910), 172.

22. Maxwell, "Frances Kellor," 154.

23. Ibid., 154–56; Gilbert Osofsky, Harlem: The Making of a Ghetto (New York: Harper and Row, 1966), 57–58, 667; E. M. Rhodes, "The Protection of Girls Who Travel: A National Movement," Colored American Magazine, 13 (August 1907), 113–19; Notable American Women, s.v. "Kellor, Frances."

24. Maxwell, "Frances Kellor," 164–66; Frances A. Kellor, "The Protection of Immigrant Women," Atlantic, vol. 101 (Feb. 1908), 251; Elting G. Morison, ed., The Letters of Theodore Roosevelt, vol. 5 (Cambridge, Mass.: Harvard Univ. Press, 1954), 523–24; Higham, Strangers in the Land, 190.

25. Maxwell, "Frances Kellor," 166; Kellor, "Protection of Immigrant Women," 401–3, 405–6.

26. Kellor, "Protection of Immigrant Women," 250–51, 253–54; Higham, Strangers in the Land, 158–82. Higham points out that nativism in this period had important regional variations. Many progressives in the Northeast continued to be sympathetic to the foreign-born.

27. Kellor, "Protection of Immigrant Women," 254–55. In 1907, a Federal Division of Information was established in the Bureau of Immigration. See Higham, Strangers in the Land, 129–30.

28. Kellor, "Protection of Immigrant Women," 254.

29. Maxwell, "Frances Kellor," 170; Higham, *Strangers in the Land*, 240; Robert F. Wesser, *Charles Evans Hughes: Politics and Reform in New York* (Ithaca, N.Y.: Cornell Univ. Press, 1967), 322–23; Edward George Hartmann, *The Movement to Americanize the Immigrant* (New York: Columbia Univ. Press, 1948), 53–54.

30. Maxwell, "Frances Kellor," 172; Higham, *Strangers in the Land*, 240; Hartmann, *Movement to Americanize*, 53–55; Wesser, *Charles Evans Hughes*, 323.

31. Maxwell, "Frances Kellor," 177; Higham, *Strangers in the Land*, 240; Hartmann, *Movement to Americanize*, 53–55; Wesser, *Charles Evans Hughes*, 323; "Portrait," 172.

32. Wesser, *Charles Evans Hughes*, 323; Richard L. McCormick, *From Realignment to Reform: Political Change in New York State, 1893–1910* (Ithaca, N.Y.: Cornell Univ. Press, 1981), 230–32; Hartmann, *Movement to Americanize*, 55–57; Maxwell, "Frances Kellor," 177–79; Higham, *Strangers in the Land*, 240.

33. James Weinstein, *The Corporate Ideal in the Liberal State, 1900–1918* (Boston: Beacon Press, 1968), 10 and passim; Maxwell, "Frances Kellor," 170; Hartmann, *Movement to Americanize*, 56; Higham, *Strangers in the Land*, 241; Nancy Woloch, *Women and the American Experience* (New York: Alfred A. Knopf, 1984), 210.

34. Hartmann, *Movement to Americanize*, 56, 59–60, 70; Wesser, *Charles Evans Hughes*, 323; "Portrait," 171; Maxwell, "Frances Kellor," 184.

35. Hartmann, *Movement to Americanize*, 59, 68–70; Maxwell, "Frances Kellor," 191–95; Edward Corsi, "Frances A. Kellor Sponsored New State Policy Toward Immigrant," *New York State Department of Labor Industrial Bulletin*, 51 (March, 1952); Higham, *Strangers in the Land*, 240.

36. See Gerd Korman, *Industrialization, Immigrants, and Americanizers* (Madison: Univ. of Wisconsin Press, 1967), for a detailed discussion of labor and immigration reform.

37. Corsi, "Frances A. Kellor," 16–17 and passim; Hartmann, *Movement to Americanize*, 69–70; Higham, *Strangers in the Land*, 240; Maxwell, "Frances Kellor," 192, 195, 196; *Dictionary of American Biography*, s.v. "Kellor, Frances (Alice)."

38. Higham, *Strangers in the Land*, 189; Frances Kellor, "Needed—A Domestic Immigration Policy," *North American Review* 193 (April 1911), 561–62.

39. Higham, *Strangers in the Land*, 186–93; Kellor, "Needed," 564, 573.

40. Kellor, "Needed," 564, 567, 570, 573. Kellor opposed rural settlement plans, noting that "no system can be a good one which sends men away from cities with their advantages to communities . . . where they live like animals, with no opportunity for education, religion or culture" (p. 573).

41. Frances A. Kellor to Theodore Roosevelt, 1 August 1911, T. Roosevelt Papers, LC; Kellor to Roosevelt, 13 September 1911, T. Roosevelt Papers, LC; Roosevelt to Kellor, 5 August 1911, T. Roosevelt Papers, LC.

42. Davis, *Spearheads for Reform* 194, 200; Gable, *Bull Moose Years*, 10, 17, 26.

43. Theodore Roosevelt, *An Autobiography* (New York: Macmillan Co., 1919), 180; Theodore Roosevelt to Mary Dreier, 4 February 1913, Mary E. Dreier Papers, box 9, folder 143, RC.

44. William Menkel, "The Progressives at Chicago," *Review of Reviews*, September 1912, p. 311; *Roll of Delegates to the First National Progressive Convention, The Coliseum, Chicago, Illinois: August 5, 6, 7, 1912*, Theodore Roosevelt Collection, Widener Library, Harvard University; *Chicago Daily Tribune*, 7 August 1912, p. 1; *Chicago Daily Tribune*, 6 August 1912, p. 5; *Chicago Daily Tribune*, 14 August 1912, in Mary Lake Kilgour scrapbook, Progressive Party Papers, HL.

45. John Gable, "The Bull Moose Years," (Ph.D. diss., Brown Univ., 1972), 254; *Chicago Daily Tribune*, 7 August 1912, p. 1; Morison, *Letters of Theodore Roosevelt*, vol. 7, pp. 594–95; minutes of the National Committee of the Progressive Party, August 8, 1912, p. 4, Progressive Party Papers, HL. Only once before Jane Addams had a woman seconded the nomination of a presidential candidate at a national convention: Mary Lease performed this duty for the People's Party in 1892. Painter, *Standing at Armageddon*, 268. Elisabeth I. Perry's *Belle Moskowitz* (New York: Oxford Univ. Press, 1987) describes a female political power broker in "the age of Al Smith."

46. "A Comparison of the Platforms of the Progressive Party and of the Social Scientists—as to Social and Industrial Justice," Progressive Party political handout, Progressive Party Papers, HL; Gable, "Bull Moose Years," 135–37 and passim; Davis, *Spearheads for Reform*, 195–97, 207; Maxwell, "Frances Kellor," 200; Higham, *Strangers in the Land*, 238; Gable, *Bull Moose Years*, 40; *Coldwater Daily Courier*, 10 August 1912, Holbrook Collection.

47. Gable, "Bull Moose Years," 92; Davis, *Spearheads for Reform*, 201, 204–6; Frances Kellor to anonymous woman correspondent, 1912, S. P. Breckinridge Papers, LC; Aileen Kraditor, *Ideas of the Woman Suffrage Movement* (New York: Anchor Books, 1971), 203–4, note 13.

48. Kraditor, *Ideas of the Woman Suffrage Movement*, 204, note 13; Frances A. Kellor to Jane Addams, 1912, S. P. Breckinridge Papers, LC.

49. Frances A. Kellor to Jane Addams, 1913, S. P. Breckinridge Papers, LC.

50. Frances A. Kellor to anonymous correspondent, 6 September 1912, S. P. Breckinridge Papers, LC; Flexner, *Century of Struggle*, 259–60; Davis, *Spearheads for Reform*, 201; *Coldwater Courier*, 12 October 1910, p. 1, Holbrook Collection.

51. Frances A. Kellor to Theodore Roosevelt, 1912 (no month or day), T. Roosevelt Papers, LC; Frances A. Kellor to Theodore Roosevelt, circa ?1913, T. Roosevelt Papers, LC; "To the Women Voters of the United States from the Women in Political Bondage," political handout, Progressive Party Papers, HL.

52. Frances A. Kellor, "What Women Can Do for the Progressive Cause—Why They Should Do It," *The Progressive Bulletin*, vols. 1–2, 1912, Progressive Party Papers, HL.

53. Theodore Roosevelt to Jane Addams, 5 November 1912, Microfilm Reel #7, Addams Papers, SC.

54. Davis, *Spearheads for Reform*, 205–6; Morison, *Letters of Theodore Roosevelt*, vol. 7, pp. 658, 675; Gable, *Bull Moose Years*, 154–55; Frances Kellor, "A New Spirit in Party Organization," *North American Review*, vol. 199 (June 1914).

55. Davis, *Spearheads for Reform*, 206. Morison, *Letters of Theodore Roosevelt*, vol. 7, p. 658; Gable, *Bull Moose Years*, 162–65; Kellor, "New Spirit," 896. Belle Moskowitz exerted similar leadership in the campaigns of Al Smith: see Perry, *Belle Moskowitz*.

56. Gable, *Bull Moose Years*, 4, 38, 165–66; Davis, *Spearheads for Reform*, 206–7.

57. Davis, *Spearheads for Reform*, 207; Gable, *Bull Moose Years*, 166–67.

58. Kellor, "New Spirit," 879–80.

59. Ibid., 879–83.

60. Ibid., 883.

61. Ibid., 884–85.

62. Morison, *Letters of Theodore Roosevelt*, vol. 7, p. 748; "Progressive Service Documents," *Progressive National Service Bulletin* no. 3, political handouts, Progres-

sive Party Papers, HL. For more on changing political styles during this period, see Michael E. McGerr, *The Decline of Popular Politics* (New York: Oxford Univ. Press, 1986).

63. Gable, *Bull Moose Years*, 169; Progressive National Service, "Do You Know What Progressive Service Is?" political handout, Progressive Party Papers, HL; staff member quoted in *Bull Moose Years*, 169; "Minutes of Progressive Service Committee," Progressive National Service—Original Arrangements folder, National Committee Correspondence, Progressive Party Papers, HL.

64. Gable, *Bull Moose Years*, 169–75; Frances A. Kellor to Theodore Roosevelt, 1912 (no month or day), T. Roosevelt Papers, LC; Davis, *Spearheads for Reform*, 214; Kellor, "New Spirit," 887.

65. Gable, *Bull Moose Years*, 184–89; Thomas E. Vadney, *The Wayward Liberal: A Political Biography of Donald Richberg* (Lexington: Univ. Press of Kentucky, 1970), 24–25; J. M. Stricker to Frances A. Kellor, 6 June 1913, National Committee Correspondence, Progressive Party Papers, HL; Frances A. Kellor to E. H. Hooker, 2 August 1913, National Committee Correspondence, Progressive Party Papers, HL; Frances A. Kellor to E. H. Hooker, 7 October 1913, National Committee Correspondence, Progressive Party Papers, HL; General Secretary to J. M. Stricker, National Committee Correspondence, Progressive Party Papers, HL; Mary Dreier to Phyllis Holbrook, 11 January 1960, Holbrook Collection.

66. Official Navy Day program, souvenirs box, Progressive Party Papers, HL; Donald Richberg, *Tents of the Mighty* (New York: Willett, Clark and Colby, 1930), 44–47.

67. Everett L. Walling to National Progressive Service, 23 July 1913; Frances A. Kellor to Paxton Hibbens, no date (circa July 1913); E. H. Hooker to Frances A. Kellor, 29 August 1913; National Committee Correspondence, Progressive Party Papers, HL.

68. Gable, "Bull Moose Years," 417–18; Frances A. Kellor to Theodore Roosevelt, 22 September 1913, Kellor to Roosevelt, 27 September 1913, Kellor to Roosevelt circa 1913, George Perkins to Frances Kellor, 17 December 1914 [the index to the Roosevelt collection lists the author of this unsigned letter as Roosevelt; but Perkins clearly wrote the letter], Theodore Roosevelt to George Perkins, 19 December 1914, all T. Roosevelt Papers, LC; Frances A. Kellor to E. H. Hooker, 6 February 1914, National Committee Correspondence, Progressive Party Papers, HL.

69. Gable, *Bull Moose Years*, 184–89 and passim; Gable, "Bull Moose Years," 481–83. Frances A. Kellor to Theodore Roosevelt, 20 May 1913, T. Roosevelt Papers, LC; George Perkins to Charles Warner, 29 May 1913, National Committee Correspondence, Progressive Party Papers, HL.

70. Gable, "Bull Moose Years," 482–88.

71. For the deteriorating relationship between Perkins and Kellor, see Perkins to Kellor, 14 December 1914, Kellor to Perkins, no date [circa 1914], both National Committee Correspondence, Progressive Party Papers, HL; Kellor to Perkins, 15 December 1914, Perkins to Roosevelt, 21 December 1914, both T. Roosevelt Papers, LC. Letter to Roosevelt quoted in Gable, *Bull Moose Years*, 184–89.

72. Frances A. Kellor to Members of the Office, 25 November 1913, National Committee Correspondence, Progressive Party Papers, HL; Vadney, *Wayward Liberal*, 24.

73. Gable, *Bull Moose Years*, 184–89; minutes of meeting of Executive Committee, 14 January 1914, Progressive Party Papers, HL; Davis, *Spearheads for Reform*, 215.

74. Gable, "Bull Moose Years," 485–86; George Perkins to Frances A. Kellor, 17 December 1914, T. Roosevelt Papers, LC.

75. Jane Addams to Frances A. Kellor, 18 December [1914], T. Roosevelt Papers, LC; Frances Kellor to Theodore Roosevelt, circa 1914, T. Roosevelt Papers, LC; meeting of the Executive Committee of the Progressive National Committee, 2 December 1914, Progressive Party Papers, HL.

76. George Perkins to Frances A. Kellor, 14 December 1914, National Committee Correspondence, Progressive Party Papers, HL; Kellor to Perkins, 15 December 1914, T. Roosevelt Papers, LC; Theodore Roosevelt to George Perkins, 19 December 1914, T. Roosevelt Papers, LC; Perkins to Roosevelt, 21 December 1914, T. Roosevelt Papers, LC.

77. Gable, *Bull Moose Years*, 184–89; Gable, "Bull Moose Years," 485–88. Participant (Donald Richberg) quoted in *Bull Moose Years*, 187. See also Richberg, *Tents of the Mighty*, 50–51.

78. Maxwell, "Frances Kellor, " 203, 209; Bremner, *From the Depths*, 160–61; Frances A. Kellor, "The Crying Need for Connecting Up the Man and the Job," *Survey*, vol. 31 (7 February 1914), 341.

79. Frances Kellor, "The Way Out of the Unemployment Situation," *Survey*, vol. 31 (21 February 1914), 638–39; Frances A. Kellor, "Unemployment in Our Cities," *National Municipal Review* 4 (January 1915), 69; Frances A. Kellor, "Three Bills to Distribute Labor and Reduce Unemployment," *Survey*, vol. 31 (7 March, 1914), 694.

80. Bremner, *From the Depths*, 160–61; Kellor, "Crying Need," 541–42; Frances A. Kellor, "Organizing to Fight Unemployment Effectively," *Survey*, vol. 31, (14 February 1914), 611.

81. Kellor, "Unemployment in Our Cities," 69; Kellor, "Three Bills to Distribute Labor," 694. By 1914 many Progressive reformers endorsed similar measures: see Keyssar, *Out of Work*, 262–78 and passim.

82. Higham, *Strangers in the Land*, 241; Hartmann, *Movement to Americanize*, 96–97.

83. Higham, *Strangers in the Land*, 241; Hartmann, *Movement to Americanize*, 97; Maxwell, "Frances Kellor," 224. See also Frances A. Kellor, "The Education of the Immigrant," *Educational Review* 48 (June, 1914).

84. Higham, *Strangers in the Land*, 241–42; Maxwell, "Frances Kellor," 224; Hartmann, *Movement to Americanize*, 98, 100; John F. McClymer, "The Federal Government and the Americanization Movement, 1915–24," *Prologue* 10 (Spring 1978), 30–31 and passim. For a detailed discussion of Americanization crusades during the war, see John F. McClymer, *War and Welfare* (Westport, Conn.: Greenwood Press, 1980).

85. Hartmann, *Movement to Americanize*, 98–101; Maxwell, "Frances Kellor," 225.

86. Hartmann, *Movement to Americanize*, 101.

87. See Higham, *Strangers in the Land*, 243, chaps. 7 and 8; Hartmann, *Movement to Americanize*, 108–112; McClymer, "Federal Government and the Americanization Movement."

88. Frances A. Kellor, "Immigrants in America," *Immigrants in America Review* vol. 1, no. 1 (March 1915), 9–10.

89. Ibid.

90. Kellor quoted in Hartmann, *Movement to Americanize*, 116–22; Higham, *Strangers in the Land*, 243.

91. Frances A. Kellor, "Unemployment and Immigration," *Annals of the American Academy of Political and Social Science*, vol. 61 (Sept. 1915), 40; Hartmann, *Movement to Americanize*, 124–33; Higham, *Strangers in the Land*, 243.

92. Frances A. Kellor, "Lo, the Poor Immigrant," *Atlantic*, vol. 17 (January 1916),

60; Higham, *Strangers in the Land*, 199, 244; Hartmann, *Movement to Americanize*, 131–32, 140–53.

93. Frances A. Kellor, *Straight America* (New York: Macmillan Co., 1916), 4–5.

94. Ibid., 7–8, 142, 153.

95. Frances A. Kellor, "Women in the Campaign," *Yale Review* 6 (January 1917), 234–35.

96. Ibid., 237–38, 243.

97. Higham, *Strangers in the Land*, 257–60; Robert E. Park, *The Immigrant Press and Its Control* (New York: Harper and Brothers, 1922), 449–58.

Chapter 7: "The School Is Yours"

1. Edith Abbott, *Women in Industry* (New York: D. Appleton and Co., 1910), xiii–xiv; Edith Abbott and Sophonisba P. Breckinridge, "Employment of Women in Industries—Twelfth Census Statistics," *Journal of Political Economy* 14 (January 1906).

2. Abbott and Breckinridge, "Employment of Women," 14–16.

3. Ibid., 16.

4. Ibid., 26, 28–29, 34–36, 37–38, 40.

5. Ibid., 40.

6. Davis, *Spearheads for Reform*, 133–35; Flexner, *Century of Struggle*, 213; Costin, *Two Sisters*, 101–2.

7. Davis, *Spearheads for Reform*, 134–35; Mary McDowell to S. P. Breckinridge, 27 December 1906, S. P. Breckinridge Papers, LC.

8. Davis, *Spearheads for Reform*, 135; Flexner, *Century of Struggle*, 213; Sophonisba P. Breckinridge, "Beginnings of Child Labor Legislation," *The Survey*, vol. 27 (21 October 1911), 1045.

9. S. P. Breckinridge, "Two Decisions Relating to Organized Labor," *Journal of Political Economy* 13 (September 1905); S. P. Breckinridge, "Legislative Control of Women's Work," *Journal of Political Economy* 14 (February 1906), 108–9.

10. S. P. Breckinridge, "The Illinois Ten-Hour Law," *Journal of Political Economy* 18 (June 1910), 465, 467–68.

11. Abbott, *Women in Industry*, preface; Charles R. Nuttes to Sophonisba P. Breckinridge, 14 July 1909, 2 August 1909, both S. P. Breckinridge Papers, LC.

12. Abbott, *Women in Industry*, 8–9.

13. Ibid., 1, 2, 6–7, 8.

14. Ibid., 34, 42, 61–62.

15. Ibid., 66–67, 76, 84–86.

16. Ibid., 110–111, 119, 125–26, 136; Caroline F. Ware, *The Early New England Cotton Manufacture* (Boston: Houghton Mifflin, 1931); Hannah Josephson, *The Golden Threads: New England's Mill Girls and Magnates* (New York: Duell, Sloan, and Pearce, 1949); Thomas Dublin, *Women at Work* (New York: Columbia Univ. Press, 1979).

17. Abbott, *Women in Industry*, 152, 155–57, 166–67, 174–80, 183, 186, 190, 193–204, 230–251, and passim.

18. Ibid., 319–21.

19. Ibid., 227–29, 297, 302–4, 306–11, 313, 315–16, 331–32, 343–47, 349.

20. *Notable American Women*, s.v. "Breckinridge, Sophonisba Preston"; Costin, *Two Sisters*, 40; Wade, *Graham Taylor*, 163–68; Graham Taylor, *Pioneering on Social*

Frontiers (Chicago: Univ. of Chicago Press, 1930), 305–9; Rayman L. Solomon, "Practical Training Versus Pure Research," (M.A. thesis, Univ. of Chicago, 1972), 2–4.

21. Taylor, *Pioneering*, 308; Wade, *Graham Taylor*, 166–68.

22. Taylor, *Pioneering*, 308–9; Wade, *Graham Taylor*, 168; *Notable American Women*, s.v. "Breckinridge, Sophonisba Preston"; Edith Abbott, "Sophonisba Preston Breckinridge over the Years," *Social Service Review*, vol. 22, no. 4 (December 1948), 419; Russell W. Ballard, "The Years at Hull House," *Social Service Review*, vol. 22, no. 4 (December 1948), 432; Werner Paul Harder, *The Emergence of a Profession: Social Work Education in Chicago, 1903–1920* (Chicago: Univ. of Chicago School of Social Service Administration, 1976), 10.

23. Wade, *Graham Taylor*, 169; Graham Taylor, *Chicago Commons Through Forty Years* (Chicago: Chicago Commons Association, 1936), 158.

24. Taylor quoted in Rayman L. Solomon, "The Founding and Development of the Graduate School of Social Service Administration at the University of Chicago: A Study of Foundations and Public Policy Research," (seminar paper, University of Chicago, 1976), 4; Taylor, *Pioneering*, 305–7; Wade, *Graham Taylor*, 163, 169–70; Solomon, "Practical Training," 6; Barbara Elizabeth Brand, "Influence of Higher Education on Sex-Typing in Three Professions, 1870–1920: Librarianship, Social Work, and Public Health," (Ph.D. diss., Univ. of Washington, 1978), 261–62.

25. Wade, *Graham Taylor*, 169–71; Harder, *Emergence of a Profession*, 12–13; Solomon, "Practical Training," 18.

26. "Report to the Director of the Russell Sage Foundation Concerning the Work of the Department of Social Investigation in the Chicago School of Civics and Philanthropy," 13 January 1913, Julius Rosenwald Papers, University of Chicago Library, Chicago, Illinois (hereafter referred to as Rosenwald Papers, UCL); Wade, *Graham Taylor*, 172, 180; Wright, "Three Against Time," 49; Harder, *Emergence of a Profession*, 12; Solomon, "Practical Training," 18–19; Taylor, *Pioneering*, 309–10. The history of social work is discussed in Roy Lubove, *The Professional Altruist* (Cambridge, Mass.: Harvard Univ. Press, 1965); Frank J. Bruno, *Trends in Social Work, 1874–1956* (New York: Columbia Univ. Press, 1957); John H. Ehrenreich, *The Altruistic Imagination* (Ithaca, N.Y.: Cornell Univ. Press, 1985); Penina Migdal Glazer and Miriam Slater, *Unequal Colleagues* (New Brunswick, N.J.: Rutgers Univ. Press, 1987); Costin, *Two Sisters*; James Lieby, *A History of Social Welfare and Social Work in the U.S.* (New York: Columbia Univ. Press, 1978); Walter I. Trattner, *From Poor Law to Welfare State: A History of Social Welfare in America*, 2nd ed. (New York: Free Press, 1979).

27. S. Breckinridge, "Autobiography"; Diner, *A City and Its Universities*; Ballard, "The Years at Hull House," 432 and passim; Costin, *Two Sisters*, 41 and passim.

28. S. P. Breckinridge and Edith Abbott, "Introductory Note" in Milton B. Hunt, "The Housing of Non-Family Groups of Men in Chicago," *American Journal of Sociology*, vol. 16, no. 2, (September, 1910); David Ross to Sophonisba P. Breckinridge, 26 February 1906; and 11 April 1906, both S. P. Breckinridge Papers, LC.

29. *Notable American Women*, s.v. "Breckinridge, Sophonisba Preston"; Hartmann, *Movement to Americanize*, 50–52; Diner, *A City and Its Universities*, 129–31; Costin, *Two Sisters*, 69–70.

30. Edith Abbott, "Grace Abbott," 355.

31. See Hunt, "Housing of Non-Family Groups"; Sophonisba P. Breckinridge and Edith Abbott, "Chicago's Housing Problem: Families in Furnished Rooms," *American Journal of Sociology*, vol. 16, no. 3 (November 1910); Sophonisba P. Breckinridge and Edith Abbott, "Housing Conditions in Chicago, III: Back of the Yards," *American*

Journal of Sociology, vol. 16, no. 4 (January 1911); Sophonisba P. Breckinridge and Edith Abbott, "Chicago Housing Conditions, IV: The West Side Revisited," *American Journal of Sociology*, vol. 17, no. 1 (July 1911); Charles Ball to Sophonisba P. Breckinridge, 6 October 1909, Breckinridge to Ball, 1 November 1909, Breckinridge to Ball, 2 November 1909, all S. P. Breckinridge Papers, LC.

32. Breckinridge and Abbott, "Chicago's Housing Problem," 290, 301, 303. For an excellent analysis of the complicated world view of middle-class female reformers, see Eileen Boris and Peter Bardaglio, "Reconstructing the 'Family': Women, Progressive Reform, and the Problem of Social Control," (paper presented at the Conference on Women in the Progressive Era, National Museum of American History, Washington, D.C., March 1988).

33. Hunt, "Housing of Non-Family Groups," 146, 170, and passim; Breckinridge and Abbott, "Chicago's Housing Problem," 306, 307, 308.

34. Breckinridge and Abbott, "Back of the Yards," 436–39.

35. Ibid., 435, 450, 468; Breckinridge and Abbott, "West Side Revisited," 34.

36. Charles Ball to Edith Abbott, 4 October 1909, Sophonisba P. Breckinridge to Ball, 1 November 1909, Ball to Breckinridge, 4 November 1909, all S. P. Breckinridge Papers, LC.

37. Caroline L. Bedford to Sophonisba P. Breckinridge, 17 May 1910, Edgar T. Davies to Sophonisba P. Breckinridge, 24 October 1909, William L. Chenery to Charles Merriam, 25 October 1909, all S. P. Breckinridge Papers, LC.

38. Sophonisba P. Breckinridge to Charles Ball, 2 November 1909, Ball to Breckinridge, 8 November 1909, both S. P. Breckinridge Papers, LC; Sophonisba P. Breckinridge, "The Color Line in the Housing Problem," *The Survey*, vol. 29 (February 1, 1913), 575. Edith Abbott displayed a similar attitude toward racial discrimination. In a 1914 letter to her mother reporting on a trip to the South, Abbott wrote: "It is so dreadful to see the colored people without schools—ignorant and knocked about—made to sit in separate departments of the churches street cars etc.—" Edith Abbott to Elizabeth Abbott, 17 May 1914, Abbott Papers, addenda, UCL.

39. Breckinridge, "Color Line," 575–76; Spear, *Black Chicago*, 1–36, 169, 202, and passim.

40. Breckinridge, "Color Line," 575–76; Spear, *Black Chicago*.

41. Sophonisba P. Breckinridge to Julius Rosenwald, 5 March 1912, Rosenwald Papers, UCL; Julius Rosenwald to Sophonisba P. Breckinridge, 16 July 1913, Rosenwald Papers, UCL; Walter T. Sumner to Julius Rosenwald, 28 November 1913, Rosenwald Papers, UCL; Julius Rosenwald to Sophonisba Breckinridge, 16 December 1911, Rosenwald Papers, UCL; Julius Rosenwald to Sophonisba Breckinridge, 27 January 1912, Rosenwald Papers, UCL; Sophonisba P. Breckinridge to Julius Rosenwald, 1 June 1912, Rosenwald Papers, UCL; Abbott, "Breckinridge Over the Years," 420; *Notable American Women*, s.v. "Breckinridge, Sophonisba Preston"; Klotter, *Breckinridges of Kentucky*, 203; Diner, *A City and Its Universities*, 131–32; Spear, *Black Chicago*, 105.

42. S. Breckinridge, "Autobiography"; Sophonisba Breckinridge to Edith Abbott, 28 June 1907, Sophonisba Breckinridge to W. E. B. DuBois, 19 August 1914, W. E. B. DuBois to Sophonisba Breckinridge, 14 August 1914, Sophonisba Breckinridge to W. E. B. DuBois, 6 August 1914, all S. P. Breckinridge Papers, LC.

43. Sophonisba P. Breckinridge and Edith Abbott, *The Delinquent Child and the Home* (New York: Charities Publication Committee, 1912), 14; Rothman, *Conscience and Convenience*, 51–54. For more on Progressive views of child protection, see Elizabeth Pleck, *Domestic Tyranny* (New York: Oxford Univ. Press, 1987). Linda Gordon

explores the impact on families in *Heroes of Their Own Lives* (New York: Viking Press, 1988). There is an extensive literature on child welfare reform and the juvenile court during the Progressive era: see, for example, Ryerson, *The Best Laid Plans*; Anthony Platt, *The Child Savers* (Chicago: Univ. of Chicago Press, 1969); Steven L. Schlossman, *Love and the American Delinquent* (Chicago: Univ. of Chicago Press, 1977); Robert M. Mennel, *Thorns and Thistles: Juvenile Delinquents in the United States, 1825-1940* (Hanover, N.H.: Univ. Press of New England, 1973); Susan Tiffin, *In Whose Best Interest? Child Welfare Reform in the Progressive Era* (Westport, Conn.: Greenwood Press, 1982).

44. Julia C. Lathrop, "Introduction," in Breckinridge and Abbott, *Delinquent Child*, 1–5, also p. 11; Rothman, *Conscience and Convenience*, 215.

45. Breckinridge and Abbott, *Delinquent Child*, 13–17; 38, 105, 114, 150–51.

46. Ibid., 70, 75–76, 84–85, 89, 105, 131.

47. Ibid., 59–62, 65, 69.

48. Ibid., 29–33.

49. Ibid., 35–38, 40–41.

50. See Freedman, *Their Sisters' Keepers,* for a discussion of women reformers and the double standard.

58. Breckinridge and Abbott, *Delinquent Child*, 13, 19.

59. Ibid., 173–75.

60. Ibid., 173–75, 177.

61. Grace Abbott is quoted in Costin, *Two Sisters*, 40, see also 39–40; Diner, *A City and Its Universities*, 104–6; Edith Abbott and Sophonisba Breckinridge, *Truancy and Non-Attendance in the Chicago Schools* (Chicago: Univ. of Chicago Press, 1917), 232–35; Addams, *Twenty Years at Hull House*, 228–29.

62. Rothman, *Conscience and Convenience*, 251 and passim; Gordon, *Heroes of Their Own Lives*, chaps. 2 and 3.

63. Abbott and Breckinridge, *Truancy and Non-Attendance*, vii.

64. Ibid., 148 and chap. 9, passim.

65. Ibid., 130, 134, 136.

66. Ibid., 135, 139, 140, 201, 330.

67. Ibid., 72–73.

68. Ibid., 226–27, 342, 348–49, 353.

69. Ibid., 1–2, 8–9, 16, 346–47.

70. Ibid., 139, 145, 241.

71. Ibid., 455–57; Diner, *A City and Its Universities*, 98–99.

72. Abbott and Breckinridge, *Truancy and Non-Attendance*, 458–60.

73. Kathryn Kish Sklar, "Hull House in the 1890s," *Signs* 10 (Summer 1985); Melissa Hield, "The Shelter We Together Build Is All That Keeps Us Warm," (paper delivered at the Berkshire Conference of Women Historians, Smith College, Northampton, Mass., June 1984); Costin, *Two Sisters*, 35–36, 41–50; Klotter, *The Breckinridges*, 202; Ballard, "Years at Hull House"; Wright, "Three Against Time," 44; Addams, *Twenty Years at Hull House*, 214–15; Barbara Sicherman, *Alice Hamilton: A Life in Letters* (Cambridge, Mass.: Harvard Univ. Press, 1984); Sophonisba P. Breckinridge to Jane Addams, "Memorandum for Miss Addams, suggesting a plan to be proposed by the Relief Committee for the Care of Tramps Who Ask for Food at Hull House," March 1911, S. P. Breckinridge Papers, LC.

74. See especially correspondence for the years 1910–1912 in S. P. Breckinridge Papers, LC; Jane Addams to Sophonisba P. Breckinridge, 1 October 1912, Addams to

Breckinridge, 10 June 1912, Jane Addams to Sophonisba P. Breckinridge, 5 September 1912, all S. P. Breckinridge Papers, LC.

75. Lucius Wilson to Breckinridge, 21 November 1913, Fannie A. Bivans to Breckinridge, 11 November 1913, both S. P. Breckinridge Papers, LC; *Notable American Women*, s.v. "Breckinridge, Sophonisba Preston"; Costin, *Two Sisters*, 54; Martha Branscombe, "A Friend of International Welfare," *Social Service Review*, vol. 22, no. 4 (December 1948); Jane Addams et al., *Women at The Hague* (New York: Macmillan Co., 1915).

76. Abbott, quoted in Diner, *A City and Its Universities*, 114, 115, 130–31, 138–39. Diner's book is an excellent portrait of the relationship between academics and reform movements in Chicago.

77. Commission, quoted in Diner, *A City and Its Universities*, 148–51.

78. *Notable American Women*, s.v. "Breckinridge, Sophonisba Preston"; Merriam, "Member of the University Community," 425; Costin, *Two Sisters*, 47–49; Davis, *Spearheads for Reform*, 195–97, 207; Jane Addams, *Second Twenty Years at Hull House* (New York: Macmillan, 1930); Jane Addams to Sophonisba P. Breckinridge, 12 March 1912, Jane Addams to Sophonisba P. Breckinridge, 7 May 1912, Jane Addams to Sophonisba P. Breckinridge, 20 October 1912, Jane Addams to Sophonisba P. Breckinridge, 7 September 1912, Addams to Miss Ashley, 19 October 1912, Jessie Ashley to Addams, 17 October 1912, Clara Landsberg to Breckinridge, 19 October 1912, all S. P. Breckinridge Papers, LC.

79. "A Comparison of the Platforms of the Progressive Party and of the Social Scientists—as to Social and Industrial Justice," political handouts, Progressive Party Papers, HL. Edith Abbott's support for the Progressive Party in 1912 reflected the evolution of her political sensibilities from her cautious days in London in 1907. That year she reassured her father, in a discussion of Nebraska politics: "If I had a vote I would vote with you against the Progressives. I don't like experimenting with the public money when the poor people pay so much of the taxes—and I don't like mad experiments out of any body's money." This was not, of course, a reference to the yet-to-be-created national Progressive party. Edith Abbott to Othman Abbott, 6 June 1907, Abbott Papers, addenda, UCL.

80. Klotter, *The Breckinridges*, 203; Flexner, *Century of Struggle*, 257–58 and passim; Kraditor, *Ideas of the Woman Suffrage Movement*, 121; S. P. Breckinridge, "Political Equality for Women and Women's Wages," *Annals of the American Academy of Political and Social Science* 56 (November 1914), 123, 129, 133.

81. Edith Abbott, "Are Women a Force for Good Government?" *National Municipal Review* 4 (1915), 437–39; Edith Abbott, "Statistics in Chicago Suffrage—Letter to the Editor," *New Republic* 3 (June 12, 1915), 151; Edith Abbott, "The Woman Voter and the Spoils System in Chicago," *National Municipal Review* 5 (1916), 460, 465. In the summer of 1914, Abbott apparently spent some of her vacation time in Grand Island, Nebraska, canvassing local farmers for suffrage. Edith Abbott to Elizabeth Abbott, 17 May 1914, Abbott Papers, addenda, UCL.

82. Costin, *Two Sisters*, 49–50.

83. Sophonisba P. Breckinridge, "The Family in the Community, But Not Yet of the Community," *Proceedings of the National Conference of Charities and Corrections*, 1914, pp. 73–74; Edith Abbott, "Progress of the Minimum Wage in England," *Journal of Political Economy* 23 (March 1915), 268, 277.

84. Edith Abbott, *Democracy and Social Progress in England* (Chicago: Univ. of Chicago Press, 1918), 3–8, 10, 15, and passim.

85. Minutes of the Annual Meeting of the Board of Trustees, School of Civics and Philanthropy, 12 November 1913, Rosenwald Papers, UCL; Minutes of the Board of Trustees of the Chicago School of Civics and Philanthropy, 27 April 1917, Graham Taylor Papers, Newberry Library, Chicago, Illinois (hereafter referred to as Taylor Papers, NL); Graham Taylor to Julius Rosenwald, 11 April 1914, Rosenwald Papers, UCL; Graham Taylor to Julius Rosenwald, 17 June 1914, Rosenwald Papers, UCL; Graham Taylor to Julius Rosenwald, 7 July 1914, Rosenwald Papers, UCL; Graham Taylor to Julius Rosenwald, 15 February 1916, Rosenwald Papers, UCL; Graham Taylor to Julius Rosenwald, 4 March 1916, Rosenwald Papers, UCL; Julius Rosenwald to Graham Taylor, 6 March 1916, Rosenwald Papers, UCL; Solomon, "Practical Training," 14; Wade, *Graham Taylor*, 133, 172–4; Costin, *Two Sisters*, 62–63.

86. Wade, *Graham Taylor*, 174; Solomon, "Practical Training," 15; W. C. Graves to Julius Rosenwald, 15 April 1914, Rosenwald Papers, UCL; Roscoe Pound to Sophonisba Breckinridge, 22 November 1915, Rosenwald Papers, UCL.

87. Edith Abbott, "Field Work and the Training of the Social Worker," *Proceedings of the National Conference of Charities and Corrections*, 1915, pp. 619, 621; Costin, *Two Sisters*, 63; Wade, *Graham Taylor*, 174; Solomon, "Founding and Development," 6; Brand, "Influence of Higher Education," 267; Sophonisba P. Breckinridge to William C. Graves, 17 December 1915 [two letters, same date], Rosenwald Papers, UCL; Richard C. Cabot to Sophonisba Breckinridge, no date [circa December 1915], Rosenwald Papers, UCL; Jane Addams et al. to Julius Rosenwald, 5 February 1916, Rosenwald Papers, UCL; Julius Rosenwald to Victor Elting, 19 June 1916, Rosenwald Papers, UCL; Victor Elting to William C. Graves, 5 July 1916, Rosenwald Papers, UCL. Ironically, Flexner was deeply skeptical of social work's professional ambitions. Diner, "Scholarship in the Quest for Social Welfare," 3–4.

88. Graham Taylor and Julian Mack to Julius Rosenwald, 22 August 1916, Rosenwald Papers, UCL; Graham Taylor and Julian Mack to Charles R. Crane, 22 August 1916, Rosenwald Papers, UCL; William C. Graves "Memo," 11 September 1916, Rosenwald Papers, UCL; Julius Rosenwald to Julian Mack, 18 September 1916, Rosenwald Papers, UCL; Graham Taylor to William C. Graves, 2 October 1916, Rosenwald Papers, UCL; Costin, *Two Sisters*, 63; Solomon, "Founding and Development," 7; Marion Talbot to Julius Rosenwald, 16 September 1916, Talbot Papers, UCL; Rosenwald to Talbot, 22 September 1916, Talbot Papers, UCL. The school staff's dependence on private benefactors put tremendous pressure on them. See Breckinridge's obsequious letter to Julius Rosenwald; written out of concern that her decisions regarding scholarship recipients had alienated a friend of the businessman: Sophonisba P. Breckinridge to Julius Rosenwald, 30 September 1914, Rosenwald Papers, UCL.

89. Bulmer, *Chicago School of Sociology*, 39; *Dictionary of American Biography*, s.v. "Abbott, Edith."

90. Costin, *Two Sisters*, 63–64; Breckinridge quoted in Brand, "Influence of Higher Education," 271; Wade, *Graham Taylor*, 176, 180–185; Solomon, "Practical Training," 20.

91. Graham Taylor to Mrs. William F. Dummer, 7 June 1912, Rosenwald Papers, UCL; Graham Taylor to Julius Rosenwald, 4 March 1916, Rosenwald Papers, UCL; Julia Lathrop to Graham Taylor, 4 April 1918, Taylor Papers, NL; Graham Taylor to Board of Trustees of the Chicago School of Civics and Philanthropy, 1 April 1918, Taylor Papers, NL; "President's Statement," 8 May 1918, Taylor Papers, NL; Graham Taylor to Julius Rosenwald, 17 October 1918, Rosenwald Papers, UCL; "Resolution

on the President's Resignation," 17 October 1918, Taylor Papers, NL; "President's Report for the Year 1917–18," Taylor Papers, NL; William C. Graves to Julius Rosenwald, 1 August 1918, Rosenwald Papers, UCL; Annual Meeting of the Board of Trustees, 17 October 1918, Taylor Papers, NL; Graham Taylor to Julius Rosenwald, 8 November 1919, Rosenwald Papers, UCL.

92. Sophonisba P. Breckinridge to Graham Taylor, 25 November 1919, Taylor Papers, NL.

93. Minutes of Meeting of Executive Committee of Board of Trustees, 14 April 1920, Taylor Papers, NL; Sophonisba Breckinridge to Charles Crane, 8 December 1920, Rosenwald Papers, UCL; Sophonisba Breckinridge to Ernest Burton, 18 July 1923, President's Papers, 1889—1925, UCL; Sophonisba Breckinridge to Graham Taylor, 3 July 1920, Taylor Papers, NL; Minutes of the Board of Trustees of the Chicago School of Civics and Philanthropy, 9 July 1920, Taylor Papers, NL; Sophonisba Breckinridge to Julius Rosenwald, 16 August 1920, Rosenwald Papers, UCL; Louis M. Cahn to Julius Rosenwald, 21 July 1920, Rosenwald Papers, UCL; Costin, *Two Sisters,* 63–64; Wade, *Graham Taylor,* 176, 180–85; Solomon, "Practical Training," 20.

94. Sophonisba P. Breckinridge to Graham Taylor, 3 July 1920, Taylor Papers, NL; Sophonisba P. Breckinridge to Julius Rosenwald, 5 August 1920, Rosenwald Papers, UCL; Sophonisba Breckinridge to Graham Taylor, 7 July 1920, Taylor Papers, NL; "Extract from the Minutes of School of Civics Trustees' Meeting," 9 July 1920, Taylor Papers, NL; Solomon, "Practical Training," 21–22; Wade, *Graham Taylor,* 176–78; Minutes of the Meeting of the Board of Trustees of the Chicago School of Civics and Philanthropy, 9 July 1920, Taylor Papers, NL; Statement of Special Committee to University of Chicago's Board of Trustees, 4 August 1920, Rosenwald Papers, UCL.

95. Edith Abbott to Julia Lathrop, 7 August 1920, Abbott Papers, UCL.

96. Statement of Special Committee to the University of Chicago's Board of Trustees, 4 August 1920, Rosenwald Papers, UCL; Minutes of the Board of Trustees of the Chicago School of Civics and Philanthropy, 9 July 1920, Taylor Papers, NL; Julius Rosenwald to the Trustees of the University of Chicago, 30 July 1920, Taylor Papers, NL; Resolution adopted by the Board of Trustees of the University of Chicago, 10 August 1920, Rosenwald Papers, UCL; Julia Lathrop to Edith Abbott, 10 August 1920, Edith and Grace Abbott Papers, UCL; Solomon, "Practical Training," 20–21; Wade, *Graham Taylor,* 176–78.

97. Edith Abbott quoted in Diner, "Scholarship in the Quest," 11, also 4, 8–13; Bulmer, *Chicago School of Sociology,* passim.

Epilogue

1. Minutes of the Bureau of Social Hygiene, April 1, 1918, Rockefeller Archive Center. The mission of the C.T.C.A. is quoted in Allan M. Brandt, *No Magic Bullet* (New York: Oxford Univ. Press, 1987), 60, 83; David J. Pivar, "Cleansing the Nation: The War on Prostitution, 1917–1921," *Prologue* 12 (Spring 1980) no. 1, 30–33.

2. Brandt, *No Magic Bullet,* 84–92; Pivar, "Cleansing the Nation," 40 and passim; Minutes of the Bureau of Social Hygiene, 1 April, 1918.

3. Bureau of Social Hygiene, Annual Report, 1929, Records of the Bureau of Social Hygiene, series 1, box 1, folio 2, Rockefeller Archive Center; Minutes of the Bureau of Social Hygiene, October 26, 1920, box 3, folio 33, 1921, Rockefeller Archive Center.

4. Katharine Bement Davis, *Factors in the Sex Life of Twenty-two Hundred Women* (New York: Harper and Brothers, 1929), ix–xiv; Rosenberg, *Beyond Separate Spheres*, 197–200.

5. Davis, *Factors in the Sex Life*, xiv, 11, 76–153, 215, 263, and passim.

6. Ibid., xvii, 245.

7. Ruth Topping to Lawrence B. Dunham, 15 February 1930, Records of the Bureau of Social Hygiene, series 3, box 8, folio 179, Rockefeller Archive Center; "File Memo Ruth Topping," 19 October 1932, Records of the Bureau of Social Hygiene, series 3, box 8, folio 179, Rockefeller Archive Center.

8. Miss Addams to Raymond B. Fosdick, 16 March 1927, OMR, Brds., box 7; John D. Rockefeller, Jr., to Katharine Bement Davis, no date, OMR, Brds., box 7; Raymond B. Fosdick to John D. Rockefeller, Jr., 23 March 1927, OMR, Brds,. box 7; John D. Rockefeller, Jr., to Katharine Bement Davis, 2 April 1927, OMR, Brds., box 7.

9. Katharine Bement Davis to John D. Rockefeller, Jr., 5 April 1927, OMR, Brds., box 7.

10. Ibid.

11. Katharine Bement Davis to John D. Rockefeller, Jr., 27 April 1927, OMR, Brds., box 7.

12. Leonard V. Harrison, "Comment on Proposals Made by Miss Katherine Bement Davis for the Reorganization of the Bureau of Social Hygiene," 6 December 1927, Records of the Bureau of Social Hygiene, K. B. Davis Correspondence, 1925–32, box 1, folio 7, Rockefeller Archive Center; Edwin H. Sutherland to Lawrence B. Dunham, 15 February 1932, Records of the Bureau of Social Hygiene, box 1, folio 3, Rockefeller Archive Center; W. I. Thomas to Lawrence B. Dunham, 3 March 1932, Records of the Bureau of Social Hygiene, box 1, folio 3, Rockefeller Archive Center.

13. Annual Report of the Bureau of Social Hygiene 1929, box 1, folio 2, p. 4, Rockefeller Archive Center.

14. John D. Rockefeller, Jr., to Katharine Bement Davis, 2 April 1927, OMR, Brds., box 7; Katharine Bement Davis to John D. Rockefeller, Jr., 5 April 1927, OMR, Brds., box 7; Margaret Sanger to Katharine Bement Davis, ?no date, Records of the Bureau of Social Hygiene, series 3, box 10, Folio 213, Rockefeller Archive Center.

15. Katharine Bement Davis, "Why They Failed to Marry," *Harper's Magazine* 156 (March 1928), 466 and passim.

16. Katharine Bement Davis to John D. Rockefeller, Jr., 27 April 1927, OMR, Brds., box 7; Davis, "Why They Failed to Marry," 463.

17. Davis, "Three Score Years and Ten," 58.

18. Obituary of Katharine Bement Davis, *New York Herald Tribune*, 11 December 1935; Obituary of Katharine Bement Davis, *New York Times*, 11 December 1935; Records of the Bureau of Social Hygiene, miscellaneous, 1935, Rockefeller Archive Center; Gordon, "Katharine Bement Davis."

19. Frances A. Kellor, "Immigration in Reconstruction," *North American Review* 209 (February 1919), 206; Frances Kellor, "Future Immigration," *North American Review* 214 (July 1921); Frances Kellor, "Immigration and the Future," *Annals of the American Academy of Political and Social Science* 93 (January 1921); Frances A. Kellor, *Immigration and the Future* (New York: George H. Doran, 1920).

20. Frances A. Kellor, *Security Against War* (New York: Macmillan, 1924); Frances Kellor and Antonia Hatvany, *The United States Senate and the International Court* (New York: Thomas Seltzer, 1925).

21. Jerold S. Auerbach, *Justice Without Law?* (New York: Oxford Univ. Press, 1983), 100–109; Frances Kellor, *Code of Arbitration* (New York: Commerce Clearing

House, 1931), 1–4; Frances Kellor, *Arbitration and the Legal Profession* (New York: American Arbitration Association, 1952), 19–21; Sylvan Gotshal, "Unforgettable Character . . . Frances Kellor," *Arbitration Journal* clipping in Holbrook Collection.

22. Frances Kellor, *Arbitration in the New Industrial Society* (New York: McGraw Hill, 1934), 19, 31, 71. Critic of the jury system quoted in Auerbach, *Justice Without Law?* 107.

23. Kellor, *Arbitration in the New Industrial Society*, 70–71 and passim; Kellor, *Code of Arbitration*; Kellor, *Arbitration and the Legal Profession*, 54; *Notable American Women: The Modern Period*, s.v. "Kellor, Frances."

24. Auerbach, *Justice Without Law*, 111–13.

25. Kellor, *Arbitration in the New Industrial Society*, 10–11, 76, 99–100, and passim.

26. For women in the New Deal, see, especially, Susan Ware, *Beyond Suffrage* (Cambridge, Mass.: Harvard Univ. Press, 1981); Susan Ware, *Partner and I: Molly Dewson, Feminism, and New Deal Politics* (New Haven: Yale Univ. Press, 1987).

27. Mary E. Dreier to Phyllis Holbrook, 30 November 1960, Holbrook Collection; Kellor, *Arbitration in the New Industrial Society*, 200–205.

28. Gotshal, "Unforgettable Character," 7–8; A. Hatvany to Phyllis Holbrook, 20 September 1960, Mary Dreier to Phyllis Holbrook, 23 November 1960, both Holbrook Collection.

29. *New York Times* editorial, Mary E. Dreier Papers, box 6, folder 88; Mary E. Dreier to Phyllis Holbrook, 23 November 1960, Holbrook Collection. For Kellor's final years, see correspondence in the Mary E. Dreier Papers, RC, especially the letters written to Dreier upon Kellor's death.

30. Katharine F. Lenroot, "Friend of the Children's Bureau," *Social Service Review* 22 (1948), 428; Costin, *Two Sisters*, 130–58, 180–81, and passim.

31. Florence Kelley to Edith Abbott, 9 June 1922, Abbott Papers, UCL; Florence Kelley to Edith Abbott, 4 June 1922, Abbott Papers, UCL; Felix Frankfurter to Edith Abbott, 1 December 1925, Abbott Papers, UCL.

32. Grace Abbott quoted in Costin, *Two Sisters*, 179, also 148, 154–57; Edith Abbott, "Tragedy of the Excess Quota," *New Republic* 30 (March 9, 1922); Edith Abbott, *Historical Aspects of the Immigration Problem* (Chicago: Univ. of Chicago Press, 1926); Edith Abbott, *Immigration: Select Documents and Case Records* (Chicago: Univ. of Chicago Press, 1924); Sophonisba Breckinridge, "Summary of the Present State Systems for the Organization and Administration of Public Welfare," *Annals of the American Academy of Political and Social Science* 105 (January 1923); "The Family and the Law," *National Conference of Social Work Proceedings* 52 (1925); Edith Abbott, "Health Insurance in Great Britain," Report of the Health Insurance Commission of the State of Illinois, 1 May 1919; Sophonisba Breckinridge, "Widows' and Orphans' Pensions in Great Britain," *Social Service Review* 1 (June 1927).

33. Edith Abbott, "Poor People in Chicago," *The New Republic* 72 (October 5, 1932), 209; Costin, *Two Sisters*, 204–5.

34. Edith Abbott, "The Fallacy of Local Relief," *The New Republic* 72 (November 9, 1932), 349–50.

35. Sophonisba P. Breckinridge, "Children and the Depression," *Proceedings of the National Conference of Social Work*, 1932, pp. 126, 134–35.

36. William E. Leuchtenburg, *Franklin D. Roosevelt and the New Deal* (New York: Harper and Row, 1963), 12; Robert H. Bremner, "The New Deal and Social Welfare," in *Fifty Years Later: The New Deal Evaluated*, ed. Harvard Sitkoff (New York: Alfred A. Knopf, 1985), 70–73.

37. Abbott's comment to Hopkins quoted in Costin, *Two Sisters*, 221; Statement of Support for Roosevelt, no date, Abbott Papers, UCL.

38. Diner, "Scholarship in Quest for Social Welfare," 5; Lenroot, "Friend of Children," 428; *Notable American Women—The Modern Period*, s.v. "Abbott, Edith."

39. Diner, "Scholarship in Quest for Social Welfare," 8–13 and passim; Edith Abbott, *Social Welfare and Professional Education* (Chicago: Univ. of Chicago Press, 1931); Edith Abbott, "Social Case Worker and the Enforcement of Industrial Legislation," *Proceedings of the National Conference of Social Work*, 1918; Edith Abbott and Sophonisba Breckinridge, "The Graduate School of Social Service Administration—Material Submitted to Dean Tufts, " November 1924, President's Papers, 1900–1925, UCL; William C. Graves to Sophonisba P. Breckinridge, 25 January 1924, President's Papers, 1900–1925, UCL; Sophonisba P. Breckinridge to William C. Graves, 21 January 1924, President's Papers 1900–1925, UCL; Edith Abbott to J. H. Tufts, 10 June 1924, President's Papers 1900–1925, UCL.

40. Edith Abbott to Katherine Lenroot, 7 November 1941, Abbott Papers, UCL; Diner, "Scholarship in Quest of Social Welfare," 4 and passim. Charlotte Towle influenced Abbott in softening her views on psychiatric social work in the 1930s, but Abbott remained suspicious of this approach. See Costin, *Two Sisters*, 200–203.

41. Edith Abbott to J. Laurence Laughlin, 18 March 1924, Abbott Papers, UCL; Abbott, "The Social Case Worker," 318; Rayman Solomon, "Graduate School of Social Service Administration," 16–17, 24–25, and passim.

42. Diner, "Scholarship in Quest for Social Welfare"; Fredric Veeder, *Development of the Montana Poor Law* (Chicago: Univ. of Chicago Press, 1938); Aileen Kennedy, *Ohio Poor Law* (Chicago; Univ. of Chicago Press, 1934); Grace Browning, *Development of Poor Relief Legislation in Kansas* (Chicago: Univ. of Chicago Press, 1935); Isabel Bruce, *Michigan Poor Law* (Chicago: Univ. of Chicago Press, 1936); Elizabeth Milchrist, *State Administration of Child Welfare in Illinois* (Chicago: Univ. of Chicago Press, 1937); Dorothy Puttee, *Illegitimate Child in Illinois* (Chicago: Univ. of Chicago Press, 1937).

43. Costin, *Two Sisters*, 228–30; *Notable American Women*, s.v. "Breckinridge, Sophonisba Preston."

44. Mary Jane Gilkey to Edith Abbott, 1 August 1948, S. P. Breckinridge Papers, LC; Costin, *Two Sisters*, 181; social worker quoted on p. 230.

45. Edith Abbott to Julia Lathrop, 14 June 1924, Abbott Papers, UCL; Sophonisba Breckinridge to Ernest Burton, 12 December 1923, President's Papers, 1900–1925, UCL; Solomon, "Founding and Development," 22–26. The school's first dean, L. C. Marshall, asked Chicago's president to fund a faculty appointment in 1921 designed to "bring in a man who will emphasize community organization and structure and theories of social progress as a means of giving balance to a curriculum too strongly devoted to pathological interests." "Budget Recommendations for the Year 1921–22—School of Social Service Administration," President's Papers, 1889–1925, UCL. For correspondence regarding the university's growing commitment to the school, see President's Papers 1900–1925, box 61, UCL.

46. Talbot, *More Than Lore*, 127–43; *Notable American Women*, s.v. "Breckinridge, Sophonisba Preston"; Hutchins, quoted in Costin, *Two Sisters*, 196; Edith Abbott to Robert Hutchins, 13 January 1951, Abbott Papers, UCL.

47. Sophonisba P. Breckinridge, *Women in the Twentieth Century* (New York: McGraw Hill, 1933), vii, ix, 32, and passim.

48. Ibid., 107–120, 190–200.

49. Costin, *Two Sisters*, 199, 230, 236; *Notable American Women*, s.v. "Breckinridge, Sophonisba Preston."

50. Breckinridge, "Autobiography"; see final years of the S. P. Breckinridge Papers, LC, for her negotiations with the Library of Congress; Alice Hamilton to Edith Abbott, 5 August 1948, S. P. Breckinridge Papers, LC; Costin, *Two Sisters*, 236.

51. Edith Abbott, "Acceptance Speech at Presentation of the Survey Award," *Proceedings of the National Conference of Social Work* 1951, ix–x; Costin, *Two Sisters*, 237.

52. Arthur Abbott to Wilma [Walker?], 4 August 1957, Abbott Papers, UCL; Costin, *Two Sisters*, 238.

53. Bernice E. C. to Edith Abbott, 25 August 1948, S. P. Breckinridge Papers, LC.

Index

Abbott, Breckinridge, Davis, and Kellor: commonalities among, xii–xiii, 25–27, 69–72, 78–79, 91; differences among, xii; family encouragement for, 25; interest in social issues of families of, 26; and the internalization of scientific methods/values, 71–72

Abbott, Edith: accomplishments of, xii, xiii, xv, 91, 166–67, 200, 212, 214, 216; Breckinridge's relationship with, 81, 87–88, 90–91, 167, 170, 215–16; childhood of, 20–23; commitment of, 177; courses taught by, 175; death of, 216; English influence on, 189; European studies of, 88–89; father of, 20–21, 22, 24, 25, 88, 89; graduate studies of, 24–25, 66–70, 87, 167; mother of, 21–22, 23, 24, 26, 90; personal characteristics of, 26–27; and religion, 22; reputation of, 87, 183, 190, 191, 200, 214; retirement of, 215–16; as a role model, 176; siblings of, 21, 24; as a teacher, 24, 25, 214; at the University of Nebraska, 24. See also Abbott, Breckinridge, Davis, and Kellor; name of specific person or topic

Abbott, Edith—positions of: and Breckinridge's help getting jobs, 87–88, 90–91; and the Chicago School of Civics and Philanthropy, 90–91, 173–90, 196–200; and the difficulty of finding first-rate positions after graduate school, 71–72; as a part-time lecturer in sociology at the University of Chicago, 197; and the Social Service Administration School, xiii, 199–200, 209, 212–14; at Wellesley,

87, 89–91; and the Women's Trade Union League, 87–88

Abbott, Edith—speeches/writings of: about delinquency, 183–87; and the dissertation, 68–69, 87; about the history of women's industrial work, 170–73; about housing, 178; about immigration, 210; about labor issues, 167, 195; about poverty in the United States, 210–11; purpose of, 190; about relief efforts, 211; about the social welfare system, 216; about suffrage, 89, 194; about truancy, 187–90; about wages, 66–69, 87

Abbott, Grace: and Breckinridge, xv, 177; childhood of, 22; and the Children's Bureau, 209–10; death of, 215; and Edith Abbott, xv, 24, 88, 177–78, 215; graduate studies of, xv, 90; and Hull House, 177–78; and the Immigrant's Protective League, 177; and the International Congress of Women, 192; and the Juvenile Protective Association, 187; and the Progressive party, 150–51, 193; reputation of, xv; and suffrage, 194–95

Academia: careers for women in, 71–75, 76, 81–82; isolation in, 81; male dominance of, 72; and politics, 152; promotions in, 214–15; and reform, xiv, 71–72, 200, 217; segregation in, 182; sex discrimination in, 76–77; and social work, 196

Adams, Henry, 48

Adams, Herbert Baxter, 46

Addams, Jane: and Abbott, 169, 191; and
    Breckinridge, 10, 169, 177, 191, 192; as
    a central figure at Hull House, 35, 36,
    191; and the Chicago School of Civics
    and Philanthropy, 196, 199; education
    of, 21; and a federal study of female
    employment, 169; and the Immigrant's
    Protective League, 177; and Kellor, 156;
    and knowledge and social service, 8; and
    the Laboratory for Social Hygiene, 109;
    and the Progressive party, 146–48, 149,
    150, 156, 192, 193; and the Progressive
    Service, 149, 150, 156; and reform in
    Chicago, 35, 36, 79; and Roosevelt,
    146–48, 149; and the Social Science
    Center, 174
Albion [New York] prison, 93, 102
"Aldrich Report" [U.S. Senate], 69
Altgeld, John Peter, 35
American Arbitration Association
    [A.A.A.], 207–9
American Association of Foreign Language
    Newspapers, 164
American Association of University
    Professors, 73, 74
American Association of University
    Women, 31
American Economic Association, 9
American Federation of Labor, 169
Americanization, 160, 161, 162–63, 164,
    206–7
American Journal of Sociology, 42, 58, 60,
    62–63, 80, 178, 179–80
American Prison Association, 96–97
American Social Science Association, 20,
    59
Angell, James, 58, 65, 104, 113, 123–24
Anthony, Susan B., 9, 23, 37
Anthropology, 53–54, 60, 61, 62
Arbitration, 207–9
Assimilation, 140, 142, 145
Association of Collegiate Alumnae
    [A.C.A.], 9, 31, 86, 137, 190
Association of Colored Women, 182
Association of Household Research [New
    York City], 137

Balch, Emily Greene, 90, 150
Ball, Charles, 177, 178, 180
"The Barbarian Status of Women"
    [Veblen], 70
Bedford Hills [New York State
    Reformatory for Women]: as a center for
    prison reform, 92, 93, 120, 129, 186;
    characteristics of prisoners at, 93, 102;
    clearing house plan for, 127, 128; Davis
    as superintendent of, xii, 76–77, 92–114,
    120–29; and the Dieckmann report,
    120–21; educational programs at, 94–95,
    120; Honor Cottage at, 95;
    investigations of, 92, 120–21, 128; and

the Laboratory of Social Hygiene, 93,
    101–14, 120, 122–29, 152; mentally
    defective inmates at, 102–14, 122, 128–
    29; opening of, 93; overcrowding at,
    102, 120, 121–22, 128; philanthropic
    support for, 93, 105–11, 127–29;
    physical facilities at, 93, 102, 113, 121;
    psychopathic hospital at, 122–23, 124,
    128; punishments at, 121; segregation at,
    98–99, 120–21; work at, 94–96, 115,
    121
Beecher, Mary, 32–33
Bemis, Edward, 40
Bennet, William S., 138
Biennial Survey of Education [U.S.
    Government], 72, 74
Binet intelligence test, 104–5, 112–13
Biology, 58–61, 63, 104. See also Heredity
Black community: Breckinridge's views/
    studies about the, 180–82; in Chicago,
    180–82; and crime, 62, 65–66, 98–99,
    112; Davis's views about the, 57–58,
    139; DuBois's work about the, 57;
    Eaton's work about the, 57; and
    employment, 133; and the environment/
    heredity debate, 98–99; and housing,
    180–81; Kellor's views/work on the, 62,
    65–66, 133, 139; organizations founded
    to help the, 139; and prostitution, 112;
    and segregation in prison, 120–21
Blackwell's Island [New York City prison],
    63, 115, 117–18, 121
Blaine, Mrs. Emmons, 175
Bohemia, 55–56, 92, 98
Bonney, Charles, 38
Boston, Massachusetts, 88, 131, 132, 140–
    45
Boston University, 31
Breckinridge, Sophonisba: Abbott's
    relationship with, 81, 87–88, 90–91,
    167, 170, 215–16; accomplishments of,
    xii, xiii, xv, 91, 166–67, 170, 200, 212;
    admitted to the bar, 11; careers and
    college comment by, 9; childhood of, 3–
    11; commitment of, 176–77, 214;
    conservatism of, 51–52; courses taught
    by, 87, 175; death of, 216; European trip
    of, 9–10, 13; father of, 4, 5, 6, 9, 10, 11–
    12, 13, 50; graduate studies of, 13–14,
    25, 49–52, 69–70, 81; health of, 9–10,
    12, 13, 215–16; as a high school teacher,
    9, 13; legal practice of, 11; legal studies
    of, 9, 10–11, 45–46, 82–83, 169, 210;
    mother of, 4–5, 6–7, 9, 10, 13, 26;
    personal characteristics of, 26–27; and
    religion, 8, 10; reputation of, 81, 176,
    183, 190, 191, 192, 200, 214; retirement
    of, 215–16; reveres the University of
    Chicago, 13, 212; as a role model, 176;
    salary of, 82–84; siblings of, 4, 5, 10, 50;
    as a social activist, 87; student reaction

to, 214; teaching style of, 214; values of, 81; and Wellesley, 5–8, 9, 13. *See also* Abbott, Breckinridge, Davis, and Kellor; *name of specific person or topic*

Breckinridge, Sophonisba—positions of: and the Chicago Institute of Social Science, 174–75; and the Chicago School of Civics and Philanthropy, 173–90, 196–200; and the difficulty of finding first-rate positions after graduate school, 71–72; as a full professor at the University of Chicago, 82; and the Household Administration Department of the University of Chicago, 85–86, 197; and the Immigrant's Protective League, 177; and the Social Service Administration School, xiii, 199–200, 209, 212–14; as Talbot's assistant, 50, 81, 82–84, 197; Talbot's help in getting, 81–86; as Tenement Inspector for Chicago, 180

Breckinridge, Sophonisba—speeches/ writings of: and an autobiography, 215; about the changing status of American women, 215; about children, 211; and the dissertation, 50–52; about employment, 194, 211; about government, 170; about housing, 178, 180–81; about immigration, 195; about juvenile delinquency, 183–87; about labor issues, 167; and the master's thesis, 49; about packing-house workers, 86; about public welfare, 210; purpose of, 181–82, 190; about race issues, 180–81; about relief efforts, 211; about suffrage, 194; about truancy, 187–90

Breckinridge and Abbott, 81, 87–88, 90–91, 167, 170, 215–16

Brown, Walter, 155

Bryn Mawr College, 13, 213

Bureaus of Information [Kellor proposal], 135–36

Bureau of Social Hygiene [Rockefeller organization], 105, 110–11, 113, 118, 122, 124, 125–26, 127–29, 202–5

Bureau of Vocational Supervision [Chicago Board of Education], 190

Burgess, John, 44

Business community, 78, 139, 143–44, 158, 162, 163, 164, 193, 206–7

Careers: in academia, 71–75, 76, 81–82; and college, 9, 13; factors shaping, 77–78; and marriage, 73, 76. *See also name of specific person*

Carnegie Institution, 87, 88

Case study approach, 56

Casework methods, 212–13

Catt, Carrie Chapman, 115

Census Bureau, 67–68

Centre College [Danville, Kentucky], 4

Charities: as sources of funding for social reform, 77

Charity organizations, 188, 189, 190

Charity Organization Society, 103

Chauncy School, 31

Chautauqua, 33

Chenery, William 180

Chicago, Illinois: in the 1890s, 34–36; Abbott's views/studies about, 90, 167, 170–90, 194; as an attraction for the four women, 27; black community in, 180–82; Breckinridge's views/studies about, 167–70, 173–90; corruption in, 167; education in, 187–90; employment in, 131, 132; housing in, 177–79; immigrants in, 140–45, 177–78; and industrialization, 34–35; influence on the four women, 78–79; influence on students of, 78–79; juvenile delinquency in, 183–87; Kellor's studies of, 131; as a laboratory, xiii, 41, 46, 70, 78–79, 175, 178, 182; labor issues in, 192–93; political machines in, 194; race issues in, 180–82; relief efforts in, 191–92; segregation in, 181; social problems of, 34–36; social reform in, 35–36; and the Stock Yards, 179–80; study of crime in, 192; truancy in, 187–90; University of Chicago's relationship with, 29, 32–34; women's role in the reform of, 78–79

Chicago Commons [settlement house], 173, 174

Chicago Institute of Social Science, 174–75

Chicago School of Civics and Philanthropy: financing of the, 90–91, 196–99; founding of the, 173–76; housing study sponsored by the, 177–81; juvenile delinquency study of the, 183–87; reputation of the, 190; and research, 190; truancy study of the, 187–90; and the University of Chicago, 196–200

Chicago Stock Yards, 179–80

Chicago Urban League, 182

Chicago Women's Club, 20, 65, 80

Chicago World's Fair [1893], 15–16, 18, 23, 36–38

Child labor, 67–68, 97, 138, 147, 169, 186–87, 188–89, 195, 210

Children: Abbott's views/studies about, 183–90, 209–10, 216; Breckinridge's views/studies about, 180, 183–90, 209–10, 211, 212; and delinquency, 183–87; prisoners as, 118; research about, 210; and truancy, 187–90; White House Conferences about, 212

Children's Bureau, 209–10, 211

Civic Club [Philadelphia, Pennsylvania], 137

Class distinctions, 42–43, 57–58, 161, 170, 173

Classification of prisoners, 102–3, 122

Claxton, P. P., 159
Clay, Laura, 9
Clearing houses: Bedford Hills prison plan for, 127, 128; for immigration issues, 159–60; for information needed by political parties, 152; and labor issues, 135–36, 137
Clothes, prison, 115–16
Club of Women Fellows [University of Chicago], 32
Cobb, Henry Ives, 36
College Settlement Association [C.S.A.], 10, 80, 131, 137
College Settlement House, 80
College Settlement in Philadelphia, 16, 92
Colorado Fuel and Iron, 125
Columbia University, 15, 44–45
Coman, Katharine, 89–91
Commercialized Prostitution in New York City [Kneeland], 111–13
Commissioner of Corrections [New York City], 114–19, 203
Commission on Training Camp Activities, 201–2
Committee on Immigrants in America, 159–60, 161–62
Committee on Industrial Relations, 158
Communist Manifesto [Marx], 68
Conflict resolution, 207–9
Congress of Labor, 38
Cook, May Estelle, 12, 13
Cooley, Charles, 175
Cornell University, 18–20
Corporal punishment, 66
Corruption, 141, 167
Court of International Justice at The Hague, 207
Crane, Charles, 175, 196, 197
Crime: Abbott's views/studies about, 183–87, 192, 212; and biology, 59–61; and the black community, 62, 65–66, 98–99, 112; Breckinridge's views/studies about, 183–87; and the Bureau of Social Hygiene, 205; causes of, 64, 92, 94, 97–100, 108, 123; Chicago study about, 192; Davis's views/studies about, 184; and economic inequality, 94, 95–96; and education, 64, 66, 94–95, 100, 119, 120, 127, 186–87; and employment, 92, 94–95, 97, 131; and the environment, 59–61, 62, 92, 97–100, 104, 114; and expertise, 103–5, 107, 108, 118–19, 124, 126, 129, 186; and the government, 99–100, 186; and heredity, 62, 63, 97–100, 104, 112–13, 114; and housing, 97; and immigration/immigrants, 98, 99, 184; and individual rights, 61–62; and insanity, 61–62; and juvenile delinquency, 183–87; Kellor's views/studies about, 58–66, 131, 184; and knowledge, 97, 107, 124; and mental

defectives, 102–14, 122, 127, 128–29; as a mental illness, 123; and moral imbeciles, 99–100; and morality, 95, 96, 97, 185; and native-born Americans, 99; and the New York legislature, 107–8, 119, 120, 122, 126–27, 128; and philanthropy, 65, 93, 104–11, 118, 127–29; and political support, 107–8; and the psychology of clothes, 115–16; and public health, 97; and punishment, 99–100, 121, 185; and research, 102–14, 122, 123–24, 127, 129, 135, 186; and sex-role stereotypes, 64; suggestions for prevention of, 66; and testing, 63–64, 102–5, 112–13, 114, 123; and the treatment of prisoners, 66, 94–96, 118–19, 128, 129; and voluntary societies, 65; and work, 94–95, 96, 115, 120, 121
Czechoslovakia, 55–56, 98

Darrow, Clarence, 38
Darwin, Charles, 8, 34
Davenport, Herbert, 75, 82
Davis, Anna S., 190
Davis, Anne, 216
Davis, Katharine: University of Chicago comment of, 30
Davis, Katharine Bement: accomplishments of, xii, xiii, xv, 91, 119, 129, 205, 206; childhood of, 14–15; death of, 206; European study of, 55–56; father of, 14; graduate studies of, xii, 15, 16, 52–58, 69–70; grandmother of, 14, 26; as a high school teacher, 15; illness of, 203; personal characteristics of, 16, 26–27; and the Philadelphia settlement house, 16, 92; receives her doctorate, 75–76; and religion, 117, 120; reputation of, 75, 92, 97, 101, 108–9, 115, 118, 119, 120, 124, 126, 133, 201–2, 205, 206; siblings of, 14, 206; at Vassar, 15. See also Abbott, Breckinridge, Davis, and Kellor; name of specific person or topic
Davis, Katharine Bement—positions of: after graduation, 75–77; as Bedford Hills superintendent, xii, 76–77, 92–114, 120–29; and the Bureau of Social Hygiene, 128, 129, 202–5; and the Commission on Training Camp Activities, 201–2; and the difficulty of finding first-rate positions after graduate school, 71–72; as New York City commissioner of corrections, 92, 114–19, 203; and the New York City Parole Commission, 119, 128
Davis, Katharine Bement—speeches/ writings of: about the black community, 57; about crime, 96–98, 103, 105–6; and the dissertation, 55–56, 98; about the environment/heredity debate, 97, 98;

about farm prices, 53; about labor issues, 55–56, 98; about marriage, 205–6; about morality, 96; about a plan for treatment of women prisoners, 103, 105–6; about prostitution, 111; about sex education, 202–3; about social service, 86–87; and the Vassar commencement speech, 15
Delinquency, 183–87, 205
The Delinquent Child and the Home [Breckinridge and Abbott], 183–87
Democratic party, 164
Denison House [Boston settlement], 88
Depression, 210–11, 213–14
Devine, Edward, 109, 138
Dewey, John, 47, 150
Dieckmann Report, 120–21
Blaine, Mrs. Emmons, 175

Division of Immigrant Education [United States Bureau of Education], 159–60, 163
Doctorates, 72, 73–75, 77, 82, 126, 214, 215. See also name of specific person
Dodge, Grace, 138
Domestic Reform League, 135
Domestic service, 95–96, 112, 132–35, 140
Douglass, Frederick, 4
Dreier, Margaret, 132, 136–37, 138, 193
Dreier, Mary, 137–38, 142–43, 146, 209
Dresser, Daniel Leroy, 154–55
DuBois, W. E. B., 57, 182
Dudley, Gertrude, 80
Dummer, Mrs. William F., 175
Dunham, Lawrence, 205
Durant, Henry Fowle, 5

Eaton, Isabel, 57
Economic inequality, 94, 95–96
Eddy, Frances, 18–19, 20
Eddy, Mary, 18–19
Education: Abbott's views about, 184, 186–87; and arbitration, 207–8; Breckinridge's views about, 182, 184, 186–87; and crime, 64, 66, 94–95, 100, 119, 120, 127, 186–87; and delinquency, 184; and the government, 189; and immigration, 141, 142, 145, 159, 163; importance to families of the four women of, 25–26; Kellor's views about, 141, 164, 207–8; as a means for mobility, 25; and reform, 182; and social problems, 101; and truancy, 187–90; and women's higher education, 4, 5, 6, 8–9
Ellis, Havelock, 107
Elmira [New York] prison, 93
Ely, Richard, 18, 46, 175
Employment: Abbott's views/studies about, 89, 189–90, 193; and the black community, 133; Breckinridge's views/studies about, 189–90, 194, 211, 215;

causes of, 68, 135; and crime, 92, 94–95, 97, 131; Davis's views about, 133; and the government, 135, 157–59; and immigrants, 133–34, 145; investigations about, 169; Kellor's views/studies about, 80, 131–39, 157–59, 162, 164–65, 208; and marriage, 215; and prostitution, 112; and research, 158–59; and segregation, 168; as a social problem, 132–46; and truancy, 189–90
Employment agencies, 131, 132–36
England, 88–89, 189, 195, 211
Environment: Abbott's views about the, 179, 184, 187, 188; and the black community, 98–99; Breckinridge's views about the, 179, 184, 187, 188; and criminal behavior, 59–61, 62, 92, 97–99, 104, 114; Davis's views about the, 56, 57–58, 92, 97–99, 139; Henderson's views about the, 59–60; and immigrants, 98, 99; Kellor's views about the, 60–61, 64, 131, 139, 164–65; as an orthodox interpretation of social problems, 217; and prostitution, 112; Thomas's views about the, 56; and truancy, 188
Ethnicity. See Immigration/immigrants
Eugenics, 98
Experimental Sociology: Descriptive and Analytical. Delinquents [Kellor], 58, 65–66
Experimental Study of Psychopathic Delinquent Women [Spaulding], 202
Expertise: Abbott's views about, 186, 200; and arbitration, 207; Breckinridge's views about, 186, 200; and crime, 103–5, 107, 108, 118–19, 124, 126, 129, 186; as critical to society, 71–72; Davis's reputation for, 101; and immigration, 140; Kellor's views about, 138, 163, 165, 207; and labor issues, 135–36; medical, 126; and politics, 155–56, 157; and the Progressive party, 155–56, 157, 193; and reform, xiii–xiv, 54–55, 91, 192; scientific methods/values as basis of, 43–44; and the solving of social problems, 101

Fabianism, 89
Factors in the Sex Life of Twenty-two Hundred Women [Davis], 202–3, 205
Federal Immigration Commission, 144
Federal Trade Commission, 153
Fellowships, 50, 80, 85
Fernald, Mabel, 124, 127
Flexner, Abraham, 123, 126, 196
Forsyth, R. K., 154–55
Fosdick, Raymond, 204
Foster, Nancy S., 32–33
Frankfurter, Felix, 196, 210
Freund, Ernst: and Breckinridge, 13, 44–46, 49, 50, 82–83, 86, 169, 170, 177,

Freund, Ernst (*continued*)
    186; educational background of, 44–45;
    government views of, 45–46, 52; and
    immigration, 177; influences on, 44;
    interest in social issues of, 45–46; joins
    the faculty of the University of Chicago,
    45; police power views of, 45–46, 170,
    186; political science emphasis of, 41; as
    a social activist, 192
Fry, Elizabeth, 113

General Federation of Women's Clubs, 169
George, Henry, 38
German influence, 44, 47, 54–55, 136, 195
Glenn, John, 109, 199
Glover, Ethel, 12
Gompers, Samuel, 38
Goodnow, Frank, 45
Government: Abbott's views about the,
    186, 187, 188, 195, 212; and arbitration,
    207–9; Breckinridge's views about the,
    52, 170, 186, 187, 188, 212, 215; and
    crime, 99–100, 186, 187; Davis's views
    about the, 202; and education, 189; and
    employment, 135, 157–59; Freund's
    views about the, 45–46, 52; and
    immigration, 140, 141, 144–45, 147;
    Kellor's views about the, 62, 131, 135,
    136, 140, 144, 145, 147, 157–64, 165,
    207–9; and labor issues, 135, 136, 195;
    as malleable, 52; private financing of
    agencies of, 110–11, 113, 118, 127–29,
    159–60, 190; and the Progressive party,
    146, 153; regulation by, 157–64; and
    relief efforts, 212; as responsible for
    social cripples, 100; and truancy, 188;
    women in, 208
Graduate education: and the difficulty of
    finding a first-rate position after
    graduation, 71–72; financial support for,
    13, 50; need for, 41; number of women
    undertaking, 13; and student
    relationships, 75–76. *See also name of
    specific educational institution*
Greene, Jerome, 125–26

Hamilton, Alice, 191, 192, 210, 216
Hammond, John Hayes, 143
Harper, Ida Husted, 147
Harper, Samuel, 177
Harper, William Rainey: and the academic
    appointments of women, 72, 83; and
    Breckinridge, 82–85; death of, 174; as an
    educational leader, 28, 33–34; graduate
    education commitment of, 29; hires
    Palmer, 12, 13; and the Household
    Administration Department, 85; and a
    Public Health/Sanitary Science
    Department, 84; and religion, 33; and
    social work offerings, 174; as a supporter

of women, 30–32; and Talbot, 31–32,
    82–85; and town–gown relations, 32–34
Harriman, Mrs. E. H., 143
Harris, Mary Belle, 117
Harrison, Carter, 38
Harrison, Leonard V., 205
Hart's Island [New York City], 115
Harvey, William, 48
Healy, William, 104
Henderson, Charles, 20, 44, 58–60, 62, 65,
    77, 78, 86, 131, 174, 192–93
Hepburn vs. *Griswold* [1870], 51
Heredity: and the black community, 98–
    99; and crime, 60–61, 62, 63, 97–100,
    104, 112–13, 114; Davis's views about,
    97–100, 112–13; and immigrants, 99;
    Kellor's views about, 60–61, 63; and
    prostitution, 112–13. *See also* Biology
Hibbens, Paxton, 154–55, 156
Home economics, 84–85
Homosexuality, 202–3
Hoover, Herbert, 210–11
Hopkins, Harry, 212
Household Administration Department
    [University of Chicago], 84–86
Housing, 57–58, 97, 177–79, 180–81
Hudson [New York] prison, 93
Hughes, Charles Evans, 119–20, 140, 141,
    142, 163, 164
Hughes Commission, 141–42, 143
Hull House, 35, 79, 80, 131, 174–78, 188,
    191–92, 216
Hunter, Robert, 174
Hutchins, Robert, 214–15
Hutchinson, Emilie, 73–74
Hydrotherapy, 123

Illinois Charitable Eye and Ear Infirmary,
    180
Immigrant's Protective League, 177
Immigration/immigrants: Abbott's views/
    studies about, 177–78, 179, 187, 210;
    from Bohemia, 56, 92, 98;
    Breckinridge's views/studies about, 177–
    78, 179, 187, 195; in Chicago, 177–78,
    179; and crime, 98, 99, 184; from
    Czechoslovakia, 98; Davis's views/
    studies about, 56, 92, 98, 99, 184; as
    degenerate, 98; and delinquency, 184,
    187; and education, 141, 142, 145, 159,
    163; and employment, 133–34, 145; and
    the environment, 99; and expertise, 140;
    Freund's views/studies about, 177; and
    the government, 140, 141, 144–45, 147;
    and heredity, 99; housing of, 177–78,
    179; investigations about, 141–42;
    Kellor's views/studies about, 133–34,
    140–45, 147, 159–60, 162–63, 164, 165,
    184, 206–7; and knowledge, 145; and
    labor issues, 159, 162; and the New

York State Legislature, 142, 143, 144;
and philanthropy, 141, 142–43, 159; and
the Progressive party, 147; and
prostitution, 112; and research, 131,
143; and suffrage, 195; and wages, 140,
145
Indeterminate sentencing, 118, 119
Individual rights, 61–62
Industrialism, 59, 100–101, 132, 152, 167,
179
Industrial Workers of the World, 117, 161
Insanity, 61–62
Institute of Social Science and Arts
[University of Chicago], 174
Intellectuals. See Expertise
Inter-Municipal Committee on Household
Research, 137, 138, 139, 140–45
International Congress of Women, 192
Internationalism, 207
International Ladies Garment Workers
Union, 153
Inter-Racial Council, 164, 206–7
Investigations: of Bedford Hills, 92, 120–
21, 128; about female employment, 169;
of immigration, 141–42; of labor, 125;
in the Progressive era, 77; purpose of,
166–67. See also name of specific
investigation

Jesse, R. H., 76
Johns Hopkins University, 29
Joliet [Illinois] State Prison, 63
Journal of Political Economy, 42, 53, 55,
56, 57, 67–68, 167, 170, 195, 213
Journals, 42, 85, 200, 213. See also name
of specific journal
Judges, 185–86
The Judicial System of Kentucky
[Breckinridge], 49
Judson, Harry Pratt, 41, 46, 73, 82, 197, 198
The Jungle [Sinclair], 179
Jury system, 61
Juvenile delinquency, 183–87
Juvenile Protective Association, 187

Kehew, Mary, 88
Kelley, Florence, 19, 36, 78, 79, 138, 188–
89, 191, 210
Kellogg, Paul, 151
Kellor, Frances: accomplishments of, xii,
xiii, xv, 80, 91, 164–65, 209; as an
administrator, 154; Chicago's influence
on, 80; childhood of, 17–18;
commitment of, 138; conservatism of,
163; at Cornell, 18–20; death of, 209;
father of, 17; graduate study of, 20, 58–
66, 69–70, 80, 131; has difficulties doing
research, 65; legal studies of, 18, 20;
mother of, 17, 26; personal
characteristics of, 17–18, 26–27, 80,

137, 148, 154, 209; and religion, 18, 60;
reputation of, 138, 140, 146, 161, 209.
See also Abbott, Breckinridge, Davis,
and Kellor; name of specific person or
topic
Kellor, Frances—positions of: and the
American Association of Foreign
Language Newspapers, 164; and the
Committee for Immigrants in America,
159–60, 161–62; and the difficulty of
finding first-rate positions after graduate
school, 71–72; and the Hughes
Commission, 141–42, 143; and the
Inter-Municipal Committee, 137–39,
140–45; and the Inter-Racial Council,
206–7; and the New York City
Committee of Fourteen, 139; and the
New York School of Philanthropy and
Civics, 80; and the New York State
Bureau of Industries and Immigration,
131, 143–44, 150; and the North
American Civic League, 142–43; and the
Progressive Service, 131, 149–57; with
Trumbull, 162; and the Women's
Municipal League, 131–32, 136–37, 138,
140–43. See also Americanization
Kellor, Frances—speeches/writings of:
about crime, 60, 62–63, 64; about
employment, 132–36, 138, 157–59; as a
graduate student, 58, 60, 62–63, 64–65,
80; about immigration, 140, 160–61;
about the preparedness campaign, 162–
63; purpose of, 64–65, 130–31, 136–37;
about social service, 87; about suffrage,
149, 163
Kelly, Elizabeth G., 32–33
Kennedy, John S., 128
King, W. L. MacKenzie, 125
Kirchwey, George, 151
Kneeland [George] study, 111–13
Knowledge: Abbott's views about, 91, 166–
67, 169–70, 173, 190, 212;
Breckinridge's views about, 91, 166–67,
169–70, 173, 181–82, 190, 212; and
class distinctions, 42–43; and crime, 97,
107, 124, 186; as a cure for the nation's
ills, 37, 91; Davis's views about, 57, 91;
as an end in itself, 217; and
immigration, 145; Kellor's views about,
91, 164, 207–8; and labor issues, 135,
158–59; as a means of illuminating
social and economic problems, 48, 101;
and power, 71; and reform, xiii–xiv, 56,
58, 59, 60, 61, 66, 137, 141; as a remedy
for social unrest, 42; and social work, 212

Labor, U.S. Department of, 135–36
Laboratory of Social Hygiene [Bedford
Hills, N.Y.], 93, 101–14, 118, 120, 122–
29, 152

Labor issues: Abbott's views/studies about, 66–69, 87–88, 167, 170–73, 188–89, 195; in Bohemia, 55–56; Breckinridge's views/studies about, 167–70, 188–89, 192–93; in Chicago, 192–93; clearing houses for information about, 135–36, 137; in Czechoslovakia, 55–56; Davis's views/studies about, 15–16, 55–56; and expertise, 135–36; German influences on, 136, 195; and the government, 135, 136, 195; and immigration, 159, 162; investigations of, 125; Kellor's views/ studies about, 131–39, 147, 208–9; and knowledge, 135, 158–59; in New York City, 131–39; and the New York State Legislature, 137; philanthropy for, 131–39; in Poland, 56; and the Progressive party, 147, 153; and research, 135, 167–73; and segregation, 134–35, 168; and social control, 69; and truancy, 189. See also Employment; Immigration/ immigrants; Wages
Labor strikes, 125, 153
Labor unions, 35, 89, 135, 153, 162, 170, 173
Lane, Franklin, 159
Lathrop, Julia, 86, 174–76, 196, 199
Laughlin, J. Laurence: and Abbott, 49, 66, 67, 87, 88, 89–90, 91, 170, 213; as an activist, 78; applied research interest of, 48; and Breckinridge, 47–49, 50, 81, 86; conservatism of, 48–49; courses taught by, 40; and Davis, 16, 52, 54, 56; educational background of, 47; emphasis on knowledge of, 48; ideology of, 47–48; influences on, 44, 47; and the *Journal of Political Economy*, 42; and monetary policy, 48, 50, 52; and the role of research in reform, 43; and scientific objectivity, 43; students of, 66; as sympathetic to women, 49; and Veblen, 46
Laura Spelman Rockefeller Memorial, 106
Law as an instrument of social welfare, 46
League of Nations, 207
Legal reform, 60. See also Crime
Lenroot, Katherine, 213
Lewis, Burdette, 115
Lewis, William Draper, 150, 154
Lindsay, Samuel, 150
Linsey, Ben, 151
Lombroso, Cesare, 59–61, 63
London School of Economics, 88–89
Lovejoy, Owen, 147, 193
Low, Seth, 136
Lowell, Josephine Shaw, 76–77, 131–32
Lowell mill girls, 172
Ludlow massacre, 125

McAdoo, Russell, 103
McDowell, Mary, 150, 169, 193

Mack, Julian, 174
MacLean, Annie Marion, 73
Marriage, 73, 76, 205–6, 214, 215
Marx, Karl, 68
Massachusetts Institute of Technology, 15, 31
Matthews, Victoria Earle, 139
Mead, George Herbert, 177, 192–93
Medical expertise, 126
Mental defectives, 102–14, 122, 127, 128–29
Mental illness: criminality as a, 123
Mentors. See name of specific person
Merriam, Charles, 81, 150, 151, 180, 192
Meyer, Adolph, 123, 126
Miller, Adolph, 46, 52, 82, 115
Millis, Harry, 82
Mitchel, John P., 114–15, 118, 119, 203
Mitchell, Maria, 15
Mitchell, S. J., 82
Mitchell, Wesley Clair, 66, 67, 75, 82
"The Modern Condition of Agricultural Labor in Bohemia" [Davis], 55–56
Monetary policy, 48, 50–52
Moore, Superintendent, 121, 123–25
Moral imbeciles, 99–100
Morality, 95, 96, 97, 99–100, 101, 185
Morgan, Ann, 143, 149
Morgan, Tom, 5
Moskowitz, Henry, 147
Mott, Lucretia, 14
Muckrakers, 77
Murphy, Starr, 105, 106, 108, 111, 123, 124, 127, 128–29

NAACP [National Association for the Advancement of Colored People], 8, 182
Nathan, Mrs., 149
National Americanization Committee, 161, 162
National American Woman Suffrage Association, 115, 119, 147
National Conference of Charities and Corrections, 97, 147, 195, 196
National Conference of Social Work, 211, 216
National Consumers' League, 210
National Hughes Alliance, 164
National Industrial Recovery Act, 208
Nationalism, 163
National Labor Relations Board, 209
National League for the Protection of Colored Women, 139
National Prison Association, 96, 97, 99
National Progressive Service, 149–57
National Recovery Administration [N.R.A.], 208–9
National Urban League, 139
National Woman's Suffrage Association, 194–95
Nativism, 144–45, 184

Naturalization, 160, 161, 163
Navy Day debacle [July 1913], 154–55
New Deal, 208, 209, 211–12, 217
New England Women's Educational
    Association, 55
Newport Progressive Club, 154–55
New York [City]: Committee of Fourteen
    in, 139; Davis as commissioner of
    corrections in, 114–19, 203;
    employment agencies in, 132–35;
    immigrants in, 140–45; Kellor's studies
    in, 132–45; labor issues in, 132–39;
    Parole Commission of, 119, 128
New York Foundation, 104
New York Public Education Association,
    102–3
New York School of Philanthropy and
    Civics, 80, 131, 132
New York State Board of Charities and
    Corrections, 92, 120, 121–22
New York State Bureau of Industries and
    Immigration, 131, 143–44, 150
New York State Legislature: and crime
    issues, 107–8, 119, 120, 122, 126–27,
    128; and immigration, 142, 143, 144;
    and labor issues, 137
New York State Prison Commission, 118,
    120, 128
North American Civic League for
    Immigrants, 142–43, 159
Northwestern University, 197

Objectivity, 43–44, 54, 69, 71–72, 132,
    168, 173, 200, 203
Olson, Harry, 194
Orange County [N.Y.] farm school, 115
Outdoor work, 94–95, 96, 115, 121
Out of Work [Kellor], 132–36, 138, 157–
    58
Overcrowding, prison, 100, 102, 120, 121–
    22, 128

Packing-house workers, 86
Palmer, Alice Freeman, 7, 8, 12, 13, 30, 31
Palmer, Mrs. Potter, 37
Pan-American Conference: [1933], 212
Parole, 118, 119
Patronage, 151
Peabody, Susan Wade, 12
Peirce, Charles, 46
Perkins, George, 155, 156–57
Philadelphia, Pennsylvania, 16, 92, 131,
    132, 140–45
Philanthropy: and Bedford Hills, 93, 104,
    105–11, 127–29; and crime issues, 93,
    104, 105–11, 118, 127–29; Davis's
    dependence on, 93, 104–11, 118;
    financing of government agencies by,
    110–11, 113, 118, 127–29, 159–60, 190;
    and immigration issues, 141, 142–43,
    159; for labor issues, 131–39; and race

issues, 182; as a source of funding for
    social reform, 77; and women as
    philanthropists, 32–33. See also name of
    specific person or granting agency
Pinchot, Gifford, 150
Pinchot, Mrs. Gifford, 156
Poland, 56
Police power, 45–46, 169–70, 186
The Polish Peasant in Europe and America
    [Thomas and Znaniecki], 56
Political Economy, Department of
    [University of Chicago], 13, 29–30, 40–
    44, 213
Political economy [discipline], 43. See also
    name of specific person
Political Equality Association, 117
Political machines, 136, 141, 192, 193, 194
Political parties, 151–53, 157, 163–64. See
    also name of specific party
Political Science, Department of
    [University of Chicago], 13, 29–30, 40–
    44, 213
Political science [discipline], 43. See also
    name of specific person
Porter, Noah, 46
Pound, Roscoe, 196
Preparedness campaign, 162–63
Prison Association of New York, 92, 98,
    121
Prisoners: characteristics of, 93, 102; as
    children, 118; classification of, 102–3,
    122; clothes of, 115–16; segregation of,
    98–99, 120–21; testing of, 63–64, 102–5,
    112–13, 114, 123; treatment of, 94–96,
    118–19, 128, 129
Prisons: as educational institutions, 102;
    Henderson's work on, 59; Kellor's work
    on, 62–64, 65–66, 139; overcrowding in,
    100, 102, 120, 121–22, 128; procedures
    in, 115; riots in, 117–18; segregation in,
    98–99, 120–21
Privacy, invasions of, 114
Probation, 118–19
Professors, 40–44, 69–70, 78, 192. See also
    name of specific person
Progressive movement, xii, 78, 201, 218
    note 2. See also Progressive party
Progressive party: Abbott's role in the, xi,
    167, 193; Breckinridge's role in the, xi,
    167, 192, 193; conventions of the, xi,
    146, 193; Davis's role in the, xi, 119–20;
    death of the, 163; and the election of
    1914, 155, 156; and expertise, 155–56,
    157, 193; financing of the, 155; and the
    government, 146, 153; and immigration,
    147; Kellor's role in the, xi, xii, 131,
    146–57, 165, 193; and labor issues, 147;
    and research, 149–57; and suffrage, 146–
    49, 193; tensions within the, 154–57;
    women's role in the, 146–48. See also
    name of specific person

Progressive Service, 131, 149–57, 163, 193
Prostitution, 105, 108, 109, 111–13, 133, 139, 181, 185, 202, 205
Psychiatry, 212–13
Psychopathic hospital [Bedford Hills prison], 122–23, 124, 128
Public health, 15, 84–85, 97, 170, 180
Public Health/Sanitary Science Department [Talbot proposal], 84. *See also* Household Administration Department
Pullman Strike, 40, 78
Punishments, 99–100, 121, 185

Quantitative techniques, 66–69, 200

Race issues: Breckinridge's views about, 180–82; in Chicago, 180–82; Davis's views about, 139; and employment, 134–35; Kellor's views about, 139, 161; and philanthropy, 182; and the University of Chicago, 182; at Wellesley, 7–8
Radcliffe College, 49
Recidivism, 100
Reconstruction Finance Corporation, 211
Record, George, 150
Reform: and academia, xiv, 71–72; 200, 217; and education, 182; and expertise, 54–55, 91; intellectual dimension of, xiii–xiv; and knowledge, xiii–xiv, 56, 58, 59, 61, 66, 137, 141; national movement for, 77–78; philanthropy as source of funding for, 77; and religion, 59; and research, xiii, 42–43, 69, 70, 88, 93, 135, 137, 141; scientific methods/values as basis of, xiv, 43–44, 70, 88, 93
Regulation, 157–64
Relief efforts, 191–92, 208, 211–12
Religion, 33, 38, 54, 59, 60, 90, 117, 120. *See also name of specific person*
The Report on the Conditions of Women and Child Wage Earners in the United States, 169
Republican party, 119–20, 141, 146, 163–64, 194–95
Research: Abbott's views about, 166–67, 168–69, 178–79, 180, 183, 187, 190, 210, 212, 213, 215; and arbitration, 207–8; Breckinridge's views about, 166–67, 168–69, 176, 178–79, 180, 181, 183, 187, 190, 210, 212, 213, 215; as a central task of a social scientist, 71; and the Chicago School of Civics and Philanthropy, 176, 190; about children, 187, 210; about crime, 102–14, 122, 123–24, 127, 129, 135, 186, 187; Davis's views about, 135, 206; and employment, 158–59; and immigration, 131, 143; institutionalization of, 93; Kellor's views about, 131, 135, 137, 141,

152, 207–8; and labor issues, 135, 167–73; and politics, 152, 157; and reform, xiii, 42–43, 69, 70, 88, 93, 135, 137, 141; and social problems, 125–26; and social work, 212
Reynolds, Myra, 30
Richards, Ellen Swallow, 15, 31
Richberg, Donald, 150, 154, 156
Riis, Jacob, 150
Riker's Island [New York City], 118
Robins, Margaret Dreier, 87
Robins, Raymond, 156
Robinson, Virginia, 109, 111, 124
Rockefeller, John D., Jr.: Davis's relationship with, 120, 126, 203–4, 205; and the Laboratory of Social Hygiene, 105–11, 122–23, 127–29; and the psychopathic hospital at Bedford Hills, 122–23, 124; recommends Davis as commissioner of corrections, 114, 203; and the Riker's Island project, 118
Rockefeller, John D., Sr., 28, 106
Rockefeller family, 209
Rockefeller Foundation, 106, 125–26, 129
Rockford [Illinois] Female Seminary, 21
Roosevelt, Franklin Delano, 211–12, 217
Roosevelt, Theodore: and the 1912 campaign, xi, xii, 146–49; and Addams, 146–48, 149; and Davis, 119–20; and a federal study of female employment, 169; and immigration, 161; Kellor's relationship with, 131, 138, 140, 145, 146–49, 155–56; and labor issues, 153; and the Navy Day debacle [July 1913], 154; and party politics, 152–53; and the Progressive Service, 150, 156–57; and suffrage, 193; as a symbol of reform, 141
Rosenwald, Julius, 182, 197, 198
Ross, Edward A., 56
Rowland, Emily, 103
Ryerson, Edward L., 175

Sage College, 19–20
Sage [Russell] Foundation, 90–91, 109, 174, 196, 199
St. Hilda's [settlement house], 88–89
Salmon, Lucy, 16
Saloons, 135, 158
Sanborn, Francis, 20
Sanger, Margaret, 205
Sanitary [domestic] science, 15, 31
Schmoller, Gustav, 54
School of Civics. *See* Chicago School of Civics and Philanthropy
Scientific methodology/values. *See* Knowledge; Research; *name of specific person or study*
Scudder, Vida, 10, 90
Segregation: in academia, 182; at the University of Chicago, 84; by gender, 96, 134–35; in Chicago, 181; and

employment, 168; and labor issues, 134–35, 168; of prisoners, 96, 98–99, 120–21
Seneca Falls [N.Y.] convention, 14
Settlement houses/workers, xiii, 10, 56, 80, 175, 190. See also name of specific house or person
Sex research, 201–6
Sex-role stereotypes, 64
Sheppard-Towner Act, 210
Simkhovitch, Mary, 138, 149
Simpson, Georgiana, 182
Sinclair, Upton, 179
Small, Albion, 38, 41–42, 43, 44, 54–55, 58, 65, 77, 78, 173
Smith, Herbert Knox, 151
Smith College, 213
Social control, 60, 69, 100, 140, 161
The Social Evil in New York City: A Study in Law Enforcement [Committee of Fourteen, Kellor], 139
Social gospel, 18, 33, 38
Socialism, 47, 53, 88, 89
Social policy: progressive approach to, 100–101
Social problems: of Chicago, 34–36; and the Chicago World's Fair, 37–38; and education, 101; environment as an orthodox interpretation of, 217; expertise as a method for solving, 101; and knowledge, 101; and morality, 101; and research, 125–26. See also name of specific problem
Social science, xiii, xiv–xv, 59, 69. See also name of specific person or topic
Social Science Center for Practical Training in Philanthropic and Social Work [University of Chicago], 174
Social Security, 216
Social Service Administration, School of [University of Chicago], 167, 196–200, 212–14, 217
Social Service Review [journal], 213
Social welfare, xiv, 46, 77. See also name of specific person or topic
Social work [discipline], 167, 174, 196–200, 212
Sociology, Department of [University of Chicago], 13, 29–30, 40–44, 54, 78, 80, 213
Sociology [discipline], 43, 54–55, 62, 63, 77. See also name of specific person
Southard, E. E., 126
Spaulding, Edith, 123, 202
Speranza, Gino C., 134
Stanton, Elizabeth Cady, 14, 37
"The State and the Immigrant" [Kellor], 140
Statistical studies, 66–69
A Statistical Study of the Wages of Unskilled Labor, 1830–1900 [Abbott], 66–67

Stone, Lucy, 23, 37
Straight America [Kellor], 162–63
Strikes, labor, 125, 153, 192–93. See also Pullman Strike
Suffrage: Abbott family attitudes toward, 22; Abbott's [Grace] views about, 194–95; Abbott's views about, 89, 167, 194–95; Breckinridge family attitudes toward, 9; Breckinridge's views about, 167, 194–95; and contributions to reform of the suffragists, xiii; Davis's views about, 119–20; in England, 89; and Hughes, 163, 164; and immigration/immigrants, 195; Kellor's views about, 146–49, 163–64, 165; Mitchel's views about, 115; and the Progressive party, 146–49, 193; and the Progressive Service, 153; Roosevelt's views about, 193. See also name of specific person
Sumner, William Graham, 46
Sutherland, Edwin H., 205

"Tables Relating to the Price of Wheat and Other Farm Products Since 1890" [Davis], 53
Taft, Jessie, 109, 111, 202
Taft, William Howard, 146
Talbot, Marion: and Abbott, 90; accomplishments of, 86; annual reports of, 32; as an assistant professor at the University of Chicago, 31; and Breckinridge, 12, 13, 50, 81, 82–84, 85–86, 197; career of, 30; and the Chicago School of Civics and Philanthropy, 197; and the Chicago World's Fair, 36–37; and Davis, 75–77; father of, 30; graduates from Boston University, 31; and Harper, 31–32, 82–85; and the Household Administration Department, 84–85; mother of, 30–31; as woman faculty appointment at Chicago in the 1890s, 73; and promotions for women at the University of Chicago, 214; proposes the creation of a Public Health Department at the University of Chicago, 31; and race issues, 182; responsibilities at the University of Chicago of, 32; as a role model, 13, 30–32; and sanitary science, 31; at Wellesley, 31
Tannenbaum, Frank, 118
Tarkington, Booth, 150
Taylor, Graham, 109, 173–76, 193, 196–99
Technology, 172
Temperance, 135
Testing, 63–64, 102–5, 112–13, 114, 123
Thomas, Martha Carey, 74
Thomas, W. I., 54, 55, 56, 58, 70, 205
Thompson, William Hale, 194
Tiffany and Company, 161

Titchener, Edward B., 58, 65
Tombs, the [New York City prison], 115,
117
Tramps, 191–92
Treatment of prisoners, 66, 94–96, 118–
19, 128, 129
Truancy, 187–90
Truancy and Non-Attendance in the
Chicago Public Schools [Breckinridge
and Abbott], 187–90
Trumbull, Frank, 142–43, 159, 162
Turner, Frederick Jackson, 38

Unemployment. See Employment; Labor
United Charities of Chicago, 180
United States Bureau of Education, 159–60
United States Bureau of Naturalization,
160
United States Commission on Industrial
Relations, 125
Universities. See Academia; name of
specific university
University of Chicago: and the academic
appointments of women, 72–73;
activism of professors at the, 40–44, 69–
70, 78, 192; as a Baptist university, 33;
Chicago as a laboratory for the, 41, 46,
70, 78–79; and the Chicago School of
Civics and Philanthropy, 196–200;
Chicago's relationship with the, 29–34;
coeducation at the, 84; dissertation titles
at the, 70; doctorates conferred by the,
72, 75; financial support at the, 32, 50;
graduate education commitment of the,
29–34; graduate enrollment in the 1890s
at, 74; graduate student relationships at
the, 75–76; as a haven for women, xiv–
xv, 13, 27, 29–34, 71, 75, 84, 214;
journals established by the, 42; Junior
College at the, 84; as a leader in
developing social science, xiv–xv; as a
leader in social reform, 91; living
arrangements at the, 30, 79;
philanthropy for the, 32–33; professors
at the, 70; promotions for women at the,
214–15; Public Health Department at
the, 31; racism at the, 182; as a revered
symbol, 212; segregation at the, 84;
social responsibility emphasis of the, 40–
44; as a tie between Abbott,
Breckinridge, Kellor, and Davis, xiii, 91;
uniqueness in 1890s of the, xiv–xv, 28;
"Wellesley presence" at the, 12–13, 30.
See also name of specific person or
department/school
University of Chicago Law School, 44, 82–
83
University of Chicago Press, 33, 213
University of Illinois, 196, 197
University of Michigan, 9
University of Minnesota, 82

University of Missouri, 76
University of Nebraska, 24
University of Pennsylvania, 29
Uplift, 57–58, 59, 216
U.S. Chamber of Commerce, 162

Valentine, Robert G., 150
Vanderbilt, Mrs. Cornelius, 161
Vanderbilt, Mrs. William, 118
Vanderlip, Frank, 143
Vassar College, 15
Veblen, Thorstein: and Abbott, 25, 53, 67;
and anthropology, 53–54; and
Breckinridge, 46–47; criticisms of
traditions in political economy by, 66;
and Davis, xii, 16, 52–54, 67;
educational background of, 46–47;
influences on, 44; and Kellor, 80; and
Laughlin, 46; and Mitchell, 67; as a
professor/fellow at the University of
Chicago, 47; and scientific methodology,
47; as shy with women, 53; and
socialism, 47; as source of names for
filling jobs, 77; as sympathetic to
women, 70; as a teacher, 40, 47, 49; and
Thomas, 55; writings of, 53, 66, 70
Victims, 101, 139, 179
Vincent, George, 54, 55, 77
Voluntary associations, 65, 77, 130, 131–
39. See also name of specific association

Wages: Abbott's views/studies about, 66–
69, 87, 168, 169, 172–73, 184, 189, 195;
Breckinridge's views/studies about, 168,
169, 184, 189, 194; Davis's work on, 56;
and delinquency, 184; and domestic
service, 132–35; in England, 195; and
immigration, 140, 145; Kellor's views/
studies about, 132–35, 145, 147; and
prostitution, 139; and truancy, 189. See
also Labor issues
"Wage Statistics in the Twelfth Census"
[Abbott], 67–68
"The Wages of Unskilled Labor in the
United States, 1850–1900" [Abbott],
68–69
Wagner, Adolph, 54
Wagner, Robert F., 209
Wald, Lillian, 138, 141, 142–43, 149, 151
Wallace, Elizabeth, 30, 73
Wallin, Madeleine, 73, 79
Warburg, Felix, 142–43, 159
Warburg, Paul, 105, 108–9, 111
Ware, Franklin B., 118
Wassermann tests, 112–13
Webb, Beatrice, 88, 89
Webb, Sidney, 88
Weidensall, Jean, 104–5, 109, 113, 114
Welfare state: Abbott's views about, 166,
185–91, 195, 200, 210–12;
Breckinridge's views about, 52, 166,

170, 185–91, 193, 200, 210–12; creation
of, 217; Davis's views about, 100–101,
106–7; Kellor's views about, 130–31,
135–36, 140–41, 144, 160; New Deal
and, 211–12, 217; Progressives and,
100–101, 193. *See also* Government,
Social policy, Social welfare
Wellesley College, 5–8, 9, 12–13, 30, 31,
74, 87, 89–91
Wendell Phillips Settlement, 182
White House Conferences on Children, 212
White Rose Working Girls' Home, 139
White slavery, 139
Whitman, Charles L., 127
*Wholesale Wages, Prices and
Transportation* [Aldrich Report of the
U.S. Senate], 69
"Why Is Economics Not an Evolutionary
Science?" [Veblen], 66
"Why They Failed to Marry" [Davis],
205–6
Wickersham Commission on Law
Observance and Enforcement, 212
Willis, Parker, 75, 82
Wilson, James, 140
Wilson, Woodrow, 146, 149, 160, 161,
163, 207
Woman's Party, 163
Woman's Peace Party, 192
Woman's Prison Association, 109–10
Women in Industry [Abbott], 170–73
Women Police [Bureau of Social Hygiene],
202

Women's Christian Temperance Union,
37–38
Women's City Club, 190
Women's Clubs, 190
Women's colleges, 74. *See also name of
specific college*
Women's Educational and Industrial
Union [Boston, Massachusetts], 135,
137
Women's higher education, 4, 5, 6, 8–9
Women's International League for Peace
and Freedom, 192
Women's Municipal League, 131–32, 136–
37, 138, 140–43
Women's Trade Union League, 87–88,
169, 176
Women's Union [University of Chicago],
87
Women in the Twentieth Century
[Breckinridge], 215
Wooley, Celia Parker, 18, 20, 60, 80
Wooley, Helen Thompson, 202
Workingmen, 15–16, 35, 38, 168
Work. *See* Employment; Outdoor work
World War I, 160, 162, 192
Wright, Carroll D., 87–88, 90

Yale University, 29, 74, 82
Young, Ella Flagg, 190
Youngman, Anna, 91

Zeublein, Charles, 58, 77, 174
Znaniecki, Florian, 56